GenBench 2023: The First Workshop on Generalisation (Bencharking) in NLP

Held at ACL 2016

Singapore
6 December 2023

ISBN: 978-1-7138-8600-6

Printed from e-media with permission by:

Curran Associates, Inc.
57 Morehouse Lane
Red Hook, NY 12571

Some format issues inherent in the e-media version may also appear in this print version.

Printed with permission by Curran Associates, Inc. (2024)

Association for Computational Linguistics
209 N. Eighth Street
Stroudsburg, Pennsylvania 18360

Phone: 1-570-476-8006
Fax: 1-570-476-0860

acl@aclweb.org

Additional copies of this publication are available from:

Curran Associates, Inc.
57 Morehouse Lane
Red Hook, NY 12571 USA
Phone: 845-758-0400
Fax: 845-758-2633
Email: curran@proceedings.com
Web: www.proceedings.com

GenBench 2023

GenBench: The first workshop on generalisation (benchmarking) in NLP

Proceedings of the Workshop

December 6, 2023

The GenBench organizers gratefully acknowledge the support from the following sponsors.

Supported by

amazon

Message from the Organisers

The ability to generalise well is often mentioned as one of the primary desiderata for models of natural language processing (NLP). However, how generalisation should be defined and evaluated, or when it is particularly important, is a far from trivial question. The GenBench workshop on generalisation (benchmarking) in NLP aims to provide a platform to discuss challenging questions related to generalisation in NLP and establish a shared platform for state-of-the-art generalisation testing. We invited submitters to contribute work discussing generalisation in NLP and also held a collaborative benchmarking task, for which we called for submissions of challenging generalisation tests.

The first edition of the workshop was held at EMNLP 2023 in Singapore. For this edition, we accepted 11 archival papers in our main track, 7 archival papers for our collaborative benchmarking track, and 6 extended abstracts. The workshop also provided a platform for the authors of 29 EMNLP findings papers related to the workshop's topic to present their work as a poster at the workshop.

The workshop would not have been possible without the dedication of the programme committee, whom we would like to thank for their contributions. We would also like to thank Amazon for their sponsorship of 5000 dollars, which we used to fund one of our invited speakers, to grant travel awards to allow participants that could otherwise not have attended to participate in the workshop, and to grant two awards, to the best submitted paper and best submitted benchmark. Lastly, we are grateful to our invited speakers, Adina Williams, Anna Rogers, and Tatsunori Hashimoto, for contributing to our programme.

Organizing Committee

Workshop Organizers

Dieuwke Hupkes, Meta
Verna Dankers, University of Edinburgh
Khuyagbaatar Batsuren, National University of Mongolia
Koustuv Sinha, Meta
Amirhossein Kazemnejad, McGill University and Mila
Christos Christodoulopoulos, Amazon Research
Ryan Cotterell, ETH Zürich
Elia Bruni, University of Osnabrück

Program Committee

Reviewers

Lisa Beinborn, Vrije Universiteit Amsterdam
Jonathan Brophy, University of Oregon
Lisa Bylinina, University of Groningen
Benoit Crabbé, Université de Paris
Ghazi Felhi, University Paris 13
Robert Frank, Yale University
Mario Giulianelli, University of Amsterdam
Yangfeng Ji, University of Virginia
Robin Jia, University of Southern California
Richard Johansson, Chalmers University
Jenny Kunz, Linköping University
Carolin Lawrence, NEC Laboratories Europe
Alessandro Lenci, University of Pisa
Sheng Liang, Ludwig-Maximilians-Universität München
Tomasz Limisiewicz, Charles University Prague
Matthias Lindemann, University of Edinburgh
R. Thomas McCoy, Princeton University
William Merrill, New York University
Anmol Nayak, Bosch
Joakim Nivre, Uppsala University
Maria Ryskina, Massachusetts Institute of Technology
Niladri S. Chatterji, Stanford University
Hendrik Schuff, Technische Universität Darmstadt
Rico Sennrich, University of Zurich
Mattia Setzu, University of Pisa
Sanchit Sinha, University of Virginia, Charlottesville
Shane Steinert-Threlkeld, University of Washington, Seattle
Aarne Talman, Basement AI
Oskar van der Wal, University of Amsterdam
Alex Warstadt, New York University
Hao Yang, Beijing University of Post and Telecommunication
Naoki Yoshinaga, Institute of Industrial Science, the University of Tokyo
Dylan Z Slack, University of California, Irvine
Sheng Zhang, Amazon
Yichu Zhou, Yahoo

Keynote Talk: Invited Talk 1

Anna Rogers
IT University of Copenhagen

2023-12-06 – Time: **555** –

Abstract: One of the frequent points in the mainstream narrative about large language models is that they have "emergent properties" (sometimes even dangerous enough to be considered existential risk to mankind). However, there is much disagreement about even the very definition of such properties. If they are understood as a kind of generalization beyond training data - as something that a model does without being explicitly trained for it - I argue that we have not in fact established the existence of any such properties, and at the moment we do not even have the methodology for doing so.

Bio: Dr. Anna Rogers is an assistant professor at IT University of Copenhagen working on analysis, interpretability, and evaluation of NLP models, their societal impact, and NLP research methodology.

Keynote Talk: Invited Talk 2

Adina Williams
Meta AI

2023-12-06 – Time: **675** –

Bio: Adina is a Research Scientist at Meta on the Fundamental AI Research (FAIR) team in NYC. Her research spans several topics in NLP and computational linguistics, with a focus on dataset creation and model evaluation for humanlikeness, fairness, generalization and robustness.

Keynote Talk: Invited Talk 3

Tatsunori Hashimoto
Stanford University

2023-12-06 – Time: **840** –

Abstract: Instruction following language models have shown a remarkable ability to perform a wide range of tasks with little to no additional training data. Do these abilities come from a revolution in pre-training and instruction-following, or are there other more mundane explanations for how these models work? In this talk, I will discuss our efforts to answer these questions by replicating instruction-following models that generalize across tasks, studying the consistency of these models across different task formats, and building tests for benchmark contamination in pretraining.

Bio: Tatsunori Hashimoto is an Assistant Professor in the Computer Science Department at Stanford University. He is a member of the statistical machine learning and natural language processing groups at Stanford, and his research uses tools from statistics to make machine learning systems more robust and trustworthy — especially in complex systems such as large language models. He is a Kavli fellow, a Sony and Amazon research award winner, and his work has been recognized with best paper awards at ICML and CHI. Before becoming an Assistant Professor, he was a postdoctoral researcher at Stanford with Percy Liang and John Duchi and received his Ph.D. from MIT under the supervision of Tommi Jaakkola and David Gifford.

Table of Contents

Program

Wednesday, December 6, 2023

09:00 - 09:15 *Opening Remarks*

09:15 - 10:00 *Keynote 1 by Anna Rogers: A sanity check on emergent properties*

10:00 - 11:15 *Poster Session 1*

Cross-Lingual Consistency of Factual Knowledge in Multilingual Language Models
Jirui Qi, Raquel Fernández and Arianna Bisazza

Temporal Generalizability in Multimodal Misinformation Detection
Nataliya Stepanova and Björn Ross

Robust Generalization Strategies for Morpheme Glossing in an Endangered Language Documentation Context
Michael Ginn and Alexis Palmer

Walking a Tightrope – Evaluating Large Language Models in High-Risk Domains
Chia-Chien Hung, Wiem Ben Rim, Lindsay Frost, Lars Bruckner and Carolin Lawrence

The ICL Consistency Test
Lucas Weber, Elia Bruni and Dieuwke Hupkes

Generalizability and Robustness of Large Language Models Detecting Alzheimer's Disease from Speech
Jekaterina Novikova

Syntax-Guided Transformers: Elevating Compositional Generalization and Grounding in Multimodal Environments
Danial Kamali and Parisa Kordjamshidi

Inductive Bias Is in the Eye of the Beholder
Michael Wilson and Robert Frank

On using distribution-based compositionality assessment to evaluate compositional generalisation in machine translation
Anssi Moisio, Mathias Creutz and Mikko Kurimo

Wednesday, December 6, 2023 (continued)

10:30 - 11:00 *Morning Coffee Break*

11:15 - 12:00 *Keynote 2 by Adina Williams: Evaluation after the LLM boom: frustrations, fallacies, and the future*

12:00 - 12:30 *CBT Spotlights*

GenCodeSearchNet: A Benchmark Test Suite for Evaluating Generalization in Programming Language Understanding
Andor Diera, Abdelhalim Dahou, Lukas Galke, Fabian Karl, Florian Sihler and Ansgar Scherp

Latent Feature-based Data Splits to Improve Generalisation Evaluation: A Hate Speech Detection Case Study
Maike Züfle, Verna Dankers and Ivan Titov

On using distribution-based compositionality assessment to evaluate compositional generalisation in machine translation
Anssi Moisio, Mathias Creutz and Mikko Kurimo

Cross-Lingual Consistency of Factual Knowledge in Multilingual Language Models
Jirui Qi, Raquel Fernández and Arianna Bisazza

12:30 - 14:00 *Lunch break*

14:00 - 14:45 *Keynote 3 by Tatsunori Hashimoto: Understanding generalization for instruction following and black-box language models*

14:45 - 15:30 *Oral presentations*

Evaluating Neural Language Models as Cognitive Models of Language Acquisition
Hector Javier Vazquez Martinez, Annika Lea Heuser, Charles Yang and Jordan Kodner

Robust Code Summarization
Debanjan Mondal, Abhilasha Lodha, Ankita Sahoo and Beena Kumari

Cross-Lingual Data Augmentation For Thai Question-Answering
Parinthapat Pengpun, Can Udomcharoenchaikit, Weerayut Buaphet and Peerat Limkonchotiwat

Wednesday, December 6, 2023 (continued)

15:30 - 16:00 *Afternoon Coffee Break*

16:00 - 17:00 *Poster session 2 (hybrid)*

90% F1 Score in Relation Triple Extraction: Is it Real?
Pratik Saini, Samiran Pal, Tapas Nayak and Indrajit Bhattacharya

mSCAN: A Dataset for Multilingual Compositional Generalisation Evaluation
Amélie Reymond and Shane Steinert-Threlkeld

GQG: Generalized Quantifier Generalization - A Dataset for Evaluating Quantifier Semantics Understanding in Language Models
Leroy Zhifei Wang and Shane Steinert-Threlkeld

Fighting Bias with Bias: Promoting Model Robustness by Amplifying Dataset Biases
Yuval Reif and Roy Schwartz

GenCodeSearchNet: A Benchmark Test Suite for Evaluating Generalization in Programming Language Understanding
Andor Diera, Abdelhalim Dahou, Lukas Galke, Fabian Karl, Florian Sihler and Ansgar Scherp

Latent Feature-based Data Splits to Improve Generalisation Evaluation: A Hate Speech Detection Case Study
Maike Züfle, Verna Dankers and Ivan Titov

Blackbird Language Matrices Tasks for Generalization
Paola Merlo, Chunyang Jiang, Giuseppe Samo and Vivi Nastase

In-Context Learning for Text Classification with Many Labels
Aristides Milios, Siva Reddy and Dzmitry Bahdanau

Shifted PAUQ: Distribution shift in text-to-SQL
Oleg Somov and Elena Tutubalina

17:00 - 17:30 *Pannel*

Wednesday, December 6, 2023 (continued)

17:30 - 17:45 *Closing Remarks and Best Paper Award*

90% F1 Score in Relational Triple Extraction: Is it Real ?

Pratik Saini and **Samiran Pal** and **Tapas Nayak** and **Indrajit Bhattacharya**
TCS Research, India
{pratik.saini,samiran.pal,nayak.tapas,b.indrajit}@tcs.com

Abstract

Extracting relational triples from text is a crucial task for constructing knowledge bases. Recent advancements in joint entity and relation extraction models have demonstrated remarkable F1 scores ($\geq 90\%$) in accurately extracting relational triples from free text. However, these models have been evaluated under restrictive experimental settings and unrealistic datasets. They overlook sentences with zero triples (zero-cardinality), thereby simplifying the task. In this paper, we present a benchmark study of state-of-the-art joint entity and relation extraction models under a more realistic setting. We include sentences that lack any triples in our experiments, providing a comprehensive evaluation. Our findings reveal a significant decline (approximately 10-15% in one dataset and 6-14% in another dataset) in the models' F1 scores within this realistic experimental setup. Furthermore, we propose a two-step modeling approach that utilizes a simple BERT-based classifier. This approach leads to overall performance improvement in these models within the realistic experimental setting.

1 Introduction

A crucial aspect of the relation extraction task involves the identification of sentences that lack any relational triples. This aspect naturally arises in real-world relation extraction scenarios. For instance, when extracting knowledge graph triples from online text, the majority of sentences may not mention any such triples. Although this aspect has been explored in other NLP tasks, such as machine reading comprehension, where models should correctly identify when a given passage lacks an answer rather than providing an incorrect one (Rajpurkar et al., 2018; Kundu and Ng, 2018; Sulem et al., 2021), it has not received sufficient attention in recent relation extraction research.

There are two distinct approaches for entity and relation extraction: Classification approach and joint approach. In the classification approach (Hoffmann et al., 2011; Zeng et al., 2014, 2015; Nayak and Ng, 2019; Jat et al., 2017), entities are already given and models focus on classifying the relations among pairs of entities. This approach includes sentences with zero triples in the experiments, where the relation among all entity pairs in such sentences is labeled as a 'None' relation. On the other hand, the joint extraction approach (Zeng et al., 2018; Takanobu et al., 2019; Nayak and Ng, 2020; Wei et al., 2020; Wang et al., 2020; Zheng et al., 2021; Li et al., 2021; Wei et al., 2020; Yan et al., 2021; Shang et al., 2022) involves models extracting both entities and relations simultaneously. However, in this approach, sentences with zero triples are not considered in the experiments, which makes the task significantly easier. Consequently, recent joint extraction models achieve exceptionally high F1 scores on benchmark datasets.

In this study, our objective is to assess the performance of state-of-the-art relational triples extraction models when sentences with zero triples are included. To achieve this, we conduct comprehensive experiments using the widely used New York Times (NYT) datasets. We evaluate a total of 9 recent state-of-the-art models in an end-to-end fashion. The results of our experiments reveal a significant decline in the performance of these models under this experimental setting. Across all of the evaluated models, we observe an approximate drop of 10-15% in the F1 score in one dataset, and a drop of around 6-14% in another dataset. These findings highlight the challenges posed by sentences without triples and emphasize the need for improved approaches to handle such cases effectively.

Additionally, we have identified that sentences often contain clue tokens that can be leveraged to detect the presence of relations, even without identifying the corresponding entities. We include such examples in Table 1 for illustrations. Building upon this observation, we introduce a BERT-based

Proceedings of the 1st GenBench Workshop on (Benchmarking) Generalisation in NLP, pages 1–11
December 6, 2023 ©2023 Association for Computational Linguistics

Sentence	Triples
Paul Allen , a co-founder of Microsoft , paid the bills for aircraft designer Burt Rutan to develop SpaceShipOne , the craft that won the $ 10 million Ansari X Prize last year for reaching suborbital space .	Microsoft ; Paul Allen ; /business/company/founders Paul Allen ; Microsoft ; /business/person/company
But Schaap seems as comfortable in that role as Joe Buck , the Fox baseball and football sportscaster who so clearly benefited from learning beside his father , Jack Buck , the late voice of the St. Louis Cardinals .	Jack Buck ; Joe Buck ; /people/person/children

Table 1: Examples of relation clue tokens (in Pink) for determining the presence of a relation in the sentences.

zero-cardinality classifier (ZCC) model that effectively filters out sentences with zero triples. We explore both binary classification and multi-class multi-label (MCML) classification approaches for this purpose. To tackle the task at hand, we propose a two-step modeling approach. In the first step, we employ the ZCC model to classify the sentences, determining whether they contain zero triples or not. In the second step, we utilize the outputs of the ZCC model to guide the 9 state-of-the-art triples extraction models, effectively solving the task. Notably, our experimental results demonstrate that this two-step approach outperforms or achieves competitive performance compared to end-to-end modeling in this novel setting of the task. Furthermore, it offers advantages in terms of training time for the models[1].

2 End-to-End Modeling of Relation Extraction with Zero-Cardinality

For our experiments, we select nine state-of-the-art joint entity and relation extraction models: PtrNet (Nayak and Ng, 2020), TPLinker (Wang et al., 2020), CasRel (Wei et al., 2020), TDEER (Li et al., 2021), PRGC (Zheng et al., 2021), PFN (Yan et al., 2021), GRTE (Ren et al., 2021), OneRel (Shang et al., 2022), and BiRTE (Ren et al., 2022). All of these models utilize BERT (Devlin et al., 2019) as an encoder. For our experiments with the NYT24* dataset, where sentences are cased, we utilize the BERT_base_cased model. On the other hand, for the NYT29* dataset, where sentences are uncased, we use the BERT_base_uncased model.

PtrNet (Nayak and Ng, 2020) adopts a sequence-to-sequence (seq2seq) approach, extracting triples uniformly regardless of the relations involved. The remaining models employ relation-specific sequence or matrix labeling methods to extract triples.

[1]Any code or data related to this paper will be made available at `https://github.com/pratiksaini4/ZeroCardinalityImpactOnRE`.

Originally, these models are trained solely on sentences containing one or more triples, excluding sentences with zero triples from their training and test datasets. However, we adapt these models to handle sentences with zero triples as well. In the case of sequence labeling or matrix labeling approaches, all tokens in the zero-cardinality sentences are labeled with the 'O' tag (representing the "other" tag). For sequence generation approaches (such as seq2seq), the decoder generates the "end of sequence" (EOS) tag as the first token, indicating the absence of any relational triple in the sentence.

Below is a brief description of each of these models. We employ the same hyper-parameters as specified in their respective papers.

2.1 PtrNet (Nayak and Ng, 2020)

This model utilizes a seq2seq framework with pointer network-based decoding for joint entity and relation extraction. Each triple is represented by the start and end indices of the subject and object entities in the sentence, along with the corresponding relation class label. To generate the complete triple, their decoding framework extracts four indexes at each time step, capturing the subject and object entities as well as the relation between them. This enables the model to incrementally construct the entire triple. For a fair comparison with other state-of-the-art (SOTA) models, the original BiLSTM encoder is replaced with BERT, a powerful language representation model. This integration of BERT into the model ensures compatibility and consistency with the advancements in the field, allowing for more accurate and robust results.

2.2 CasRel (Wei et al., 2020)

CasRel employs a two-stage extraction process for relation extraction. In the first stage, it utilizes a 0/1 tagging scheme to identify all subject entities present in the text. This initial stage focuses on accurately identifying and labeling the subject entities involved in the relations. In the subsequent stage, for each subject entity and for each relation, CasRel applies another round of 0/1 tagging to identify the corresponding object entities. This object tagging process is iterative and carried out sequentially for each subject entity. By performing this iterative tagging approach, CasRel ensures comprehensive identification of the object entities associated with each subject entity, enabling a more precise extraction of relational triples.

2.3 TPLinker (Wang et al., 2020)

TPLinker also adopts a sequence labeling approach for the relation extraction task. However, to effectively address the challenges posed by overlapping triples, it employs a separate sequence labeling process for each relation. To link the tokens within the sentence, TPLinker utilizes a handshaking tagging scheme. It constructs a matrix representing the tokens in the sentence, where the rows and columns correspond to the tokens. The handshaking tags are employed to establish connections between tokens. Initially, TPLinker identifies all entities in the sentence using the 'EH-ET' (entity head to entity tail) tag. In the matrix, a cell with a value of 1 indicates that the token in the corresponding row represents the start of an entity, while the token in the column represents the end of the entity. Additionally, TPLinker employs two other handshaking tags, namely SH-OH' (subject head to object head) and ST-OT' (subject tail to object tail). These tags are used to link the subject and object entities for each specific relation. Separate matrices are tagged for each relation using these handshaking tags. By applying this approach, TPLinker effectively links the subject and object entities for each relation, enabling accurate extraction of relational triples. The initial set of entities obtained from the 'EH-ET' tagging stage serves to filter out unwanted triples extracted during the relation-specific tagging stage.

2.4 TDEER (Li et al., 2021)

This task employs a multi-stage sequence labeling approach. In the initial stage, a 0/1 tagging scheme is utilized to extract subject and object entities. Additionally, a multi-label classification technique is employed to identify all possible relations present in the sentence. In the subsequent stage, for each subject entity and relation pair, the start position of the corresponding object entity is identified. If this start position aligns with any of the object entities extracted in the first stage, the triple is considered valid and retained. Conversely, if no match is found, the triple is deemed invalid and discarded. This rigorous validation process ensures the accuracy and reliability of the extracted triples.

2.5 PRGC (Zheng et al., 2021)

In this model, the first step involves identifying a set of potential relations within the sentence, as well as establishing a global correspondence matrix between the subject and object entities. In the subsequent stage, relation-specific sequence taggers are employed to label the subject and object entities accordingly. These taggers provide fine-grained annotations, enabling precise identification of the entities involved. Finally, the global correspondence matrix is utilized to make informed decisions regarding which triples to accept or discard. By considering the interplay between the subject and object entities and their respective relations, the model ensures the selection of valid and meaningful triples while discarding any irrelevant or incorrect ones.

2.6 GRTE (Ren et al., 2021)

This approach utilizes a table filling method where separate tables are maintained for each relation. Each cell in the table represents whether a token pair is associated with the corresponding relation or not. These tables are populated using local features or the historical information of a limited number of token pairs. GRTE enhances the table-filling by incorporating two types of global features. The first type pertains to the global association of entity pairs, while the second type focuses on relations. GRTE initially generates a table feature for each relation. Subsequently, these table features for all relations are combined, resulting in the creation of a subject-related global feature and an object-related global feature. These global features are then utilized iteratively to refine the individual table features. By employing this refined table-filling approach, all triples can be extracted based on the information stored in the populated tables. This method enables the accurate and comprehensive extraction of relational triples.

2.7 PFN (Yan et al., 2021)

The model consists of two main modules: the Named Entity Recognition (NER) module and the Relation Extraction (RE) module. In the NER module, all named entities in the sentences are extracted, capturing their complete spans. This module focuses on identifying and delineating entities present in the text. The RE module operates separately for each relation. It employs matrix labeling techniques to identify the starting tokens of subject and object entity pairs. The full span of these entities is obtained from the entities previously identified by the NER module. By leveraging the information provided by the NER module, the RE module can accurately determine the boundaries and positions of the subject and object entities for each relation.

2.8 OneRel (Shang et al., 2022)

The approach utilized in this task is a relation-specific horns-tagging method. For each relation in the set of relations, a matrix is maintained, consisting of four types of tags: 'HB-TB', 'HB-TE', 'HE-TE', and 'O'. Here, 'H/T' represents the head or tail entity, while 'B/E' denotes the beginning and ending of an entity. The rows of this matrix correspond to the head entity tokens, while the columns correspond to the tail entity tokens derived from the source text. Following the tagging of these matrices, a scoring-based classifier is employed to iterate through all possible combinations and discard triples with low confidence scores. This process enables the identification and retention of high-quality triples based on their associated confidence scores.

2.9 BiRTE (Ren et al., 2022)

This model employs a multi-stage bidirectional tagging-based mechanism. In the initial stage, the model focuses on identifying subject and object entities. Subsequently, in the second stage, it further refines the identification of object entities based on the previously identified subject entities, and vice versa. Finally, in the last stage, subject-object pairs are classified based on their respective relations. All these stages are trained together as a single model, ensuring a comprehensive and integrated approach to relation extraction.

3 Two-step Modeling of Relation Extraction with Zero-Cardinality

We have observed that most relational triples in sentences are associated with specific clue tokens. While this may not always hold true due to the distant supervision used in creating the NYT datasets, it is applicable to many cases. We have included relevant examples in Table 1. Based on this observation, we aim to investigate whether a BERT-based classification model can learn to identify the

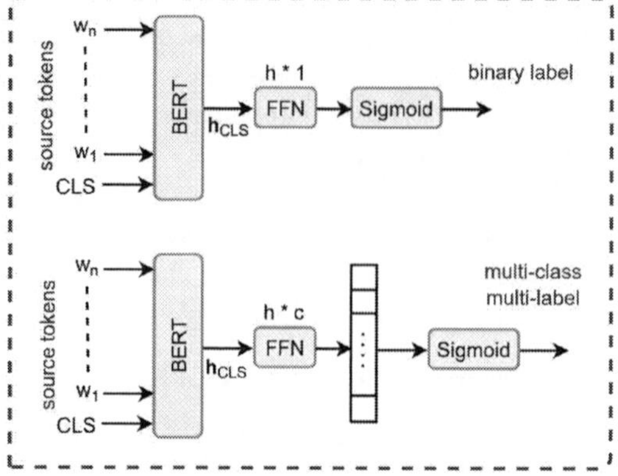

Figure 1: Architecture of our zero-cardinality classifier. c is the number of relations.

presence of relational triples in these sentences using the clue tokens, without requiring knowledge of the specific entities involved in the triples.

To accomplish this, we feed the sentences with a 'CLS' prefix token (CLS w_1 w_2 ..... w_n) into a pre-trained BERT_base model with a hidden dimension of h. We utilize the vector representation of the 'CLS' token to determine whether the sentence contains any relational triples or not. We refer to this classifier as the zero-cardinality classifier (ZCC).

We explore two distinct approaches for this classifier:

(i) The first approach involves binary classification to determine whether a sentence contains any triples or not. However, in this approach, we do not explicitly utilize the set of relations.

(ii) The second approach employs a multi-class multi-label (MCML) classification, which focuses on identifying the specific relations within the relation set. Sentences without any triples are assigned no positive labels.

To begin, we train the classifier on the 'WZ' training dataset, while training the joint extraction models on the 'NZ' training set. During the inference phase, if the classifier model indicates the presence of triples in a test instance, we subsequently pass it to the joint extraction models to extract the exact triples. This two-step process enables us to effectively filter out sentences that do not contain any triples.

We include the architecture of our proposed zero-cardinality classifier in Fig 1. We use binary cross-entropy loss and AdamW (Loshchilov and Hutter, 2019) optimizer to update the model parameters. We use mini-batch size of 16 and an early stop

	NYT24*			NYT29*		
	Train	Validation	Test	Train	Validation	Test
#sentences with >=1 triples	56,196	5,000	5,000	63,306	7,033	4,006
#triples in above sentences	88,366	8,489	8,120	78,973	8,766	5,859
#sentences with zero triples	145,767	4,969	4,969	177,861	4,940	4,601

Table 2: The statistics of the NYT24* and NYT29* datasets.

criterion during training. Our experiments have demonstrated that this two-step approach significantly enhances the overall performance of the joint models on the test set, encompassing sentences both with and without triples.

4 Datasets Preparation & Evaluation Metric

The New York Times (NYT) dataset holds significant importance as a benchmark for relation extraction. Several studies (Zeng et al., 2018; Takanobu et al., 2019; Nayak and Ng, 2020) utilize the derived NYT29 and NYT24 datasets, which originate from the original NYT10 (Riedel et al., 2010) and NYT11 (Hoffmann et al., 2011) training corpus, respectively. Zeng et al. (2018); Takanobu et al. (2019); Nayak and Ng (2020) exclude sentences without triples and partition the dataset into training, validation, and test sets. Subsequent research papers (Wei et al., 2020; Wang et al., 2020; Zheng et al., 2021; Li et al., 2021; Wei et al., 2020; Yan et al., 2021; Shang et al., 2022) build upon this modified version of the datasets, which is comparatively easier, and achieve exceptionally high F1 scores on these datasets. This trend reflects the prevalence of simplified datasets in recent works, potentially overestimating the performance of relation extraction models when faced with more realistic scenarios.

In order to enhance the realism of the joint extraction task, we augment the NYT29 and NYT24 datasets by incorporating sentences with zero triples from the original NYT10 and NYT11 training corpus, respectively. These augmented datasets are referred to as NYT29* and NYT24* hereafter. The specifics regarding the training, validation, and test splits of the NYT24* and NYT29* datasets can be found in Table 2.

To evaluate the state-of-the-art (SOTA) models, we conduct experiments using two distinct training and test settings. These settings are as follows:

(i) **NoZero (NZ)**: In this setting, only sentences containing one or more triples are included for training and testing purposes.

(ii) **WithZero (WZ)**: This setting encompasses the sentences from the NZ set, along with additional sentences with zero triples from the corresponding original NYT datasets.

By employing these two different experimental designs, we aim to gain insights into the robustness of the joint extraction models and their ability to handle different scenarios.

4.1 Evaluation Metric

For evaluating the performance of the state-of-the-art (SOTA) models, we employ triple-level precision, recall, and F1 score as the evaluation metrics. In order to determine the correctness of an extracted triple, we compare it with the ground truth triple. A triple is considered correct if both the corresponding entities and the relation match accurately. In the case of an 'Exact' match, we require the full span of the entities to match precisely, as specified in the respective papers. However, in the case of a 'Partial' match, we only compare the first or last token of the entities with the ground truth.

5 Results & Discussion

To begin our analysis, we assess the performance of state-of-the-art (SOTA) end-to-end models under the new experiment settings, which now include sentences with zero cardinality. The results of these experiments are presented in Table 3. Initially, we train these models solely on the 'NZ' sentences and evaluate their performance on both the 'NZ' and 'WZ' sentences. Upon evaluation, we observe a significant decline in the F1 score on the WZ' sentences compared to the NZ' sentences. Across the NYT24* and NYT29* datasets, the F1 score experiences a decrease of approximately 14-24%. Furthermore, the precision score for all these models exhibits a sharp drop, as they extract triples from sentences that do not contain any triples. This outcome is expected since the models have not been exposed to any examples featuring zero triples during the training phase.

Next, we proceed to train these models using the

		Test setting →	NZ			WZ				
	Training setting ↓	Model	Prec.	Rec.	F1	Prec.	Rec.	F1	% point ↓	
NYT24*	NZ	OneRel	0.926	0.918	0.922	0.678	0.918	0.780	14.2	
		BiRTE	0.914	0.920	0.917	0.628	0.920	0.747	17.0	
		TDEER	0.922	0.908	0.915	0.644	0.908	0.754	16.1	
		PRGC	0.918	0.884	0.901	0.670	0.884	0.762	13.9	
		GRTE	0.929	0.924	0.926	0.645	0.924	0.760	16.6	
		PtrNet	0.898	0.894	0.896	0.538	0.894	0.671	22.5	
		CasRel	0.894	0.890	0.892	0.612	0.890	0.725	16.7	
		TPLinker	0.913	0.917	0.915	0.643	0.917	0.756	15.9	
		PFN*	0.892	0.919	0.905	0.557	0.919	0.694	21.1	
	WZ	OneRel	0.926	0.773	0.843	0.828	0.773	0.800	4.3	**12.2**
		BiRTE	0.898	0.858	0.878	0.786	0.858	0.820	5.8	**9.7**
		TDEER	0.914	0.905	0.909	0.637	0.905	0.748	16.1	**16.7**
		PRGC	0.905	0.777	0.836	0.791	0.777	0.784	5.2	**11.7**
		GRTE	0.920	0.769	0.838	0.824	0.769	0.796	4.2	**13.0**
		PtrNet	0.932	0.697	0.798	0.838	0.697	0.761	3.7	**13.5**
		CasRel	0.915	0.878	0.896	0.643	0.878	0.742	15.4	**15.0**
		TPLinker	0.923	0.808	0.861	0.823	0.807	0.815	4.6	**10.0**
		PFN*	0.910	0.732	0.812	0.804	0.732	0.766	4.6	**13.9**
NYT29*	NZ	OneRel	0.805	0.726	0.763	0.528	0.726	0.611	15.2	
		BiRTE	0.794	0.724	0.757	0.484	0.724	0.580	17.7	
		TDEER	0.813	0.707	0.756	0.530	0.707	0.606	15.0	
		PRGC	0.807	0.701	0.750	0.509	0.701	0.590	16.0	
		GRTE	0.804	0.726	0.763	0.492	0.726	0.587	17.6	
		PtrNet	0.790	0.710	0.748	0.394	0.710	0.507	24.1	
		CasRel	0.795	0.712	0.751	0.488	0.712	0.579	17.2	
		TPLinker	0.805	0.718	0.759	0.456	0.718	0.558	20.1	
		PFN*	0.777	0.720	0.748	0.474	0.720	0.572	17.6	
	WZ	OneRel	0.841	0.657	0.738	0.755	0.657	0.703	3.5	**6.0**
		BiRTE	0.833	0.663	0.738	0.698	0.663	0.680	5.8	**7.7**
		TDEER	0.788	0.708	0.746	0.536	0.708	0.611	13.5	**14.5**
		PRGC	0.842	0.639	0.727	0.755	0.639	0.692	3.5	**5.8**
		GRTE	0.840	0.624	0.716	0.759	0.623	0.684	3.2	**7.9**
		PtrNet	0.876	0.620	0.726	0.720	0.620	0.666	6.0	**8.2**
		CasRel	0.807	0.708	0.754	0.541	0.708	0.613	14.1	**13.8**
		TPLinker	0.775	0.636	0.698	0.686	0.636	0.660	3.8	**9.9**
		PFN*	0.833	0.600	0.697	0.748	0.600	0.666	3.1	**8.2**

Table 3: Performance of the joint extraction models in the end-to-end approach on the NYT24* and NYT29* datasets with different train/test settings. * marked models are evaluated using partial entity matching as per their paper. F1 score in green color are the results obtained without zero-cardinality sentences. F1 score in red color are the results obtained with zero-cardinality sentences. The % point ↓ numbers in **bold** are the difference between the F1 scores in green and red.

'WZ' sentences. Upon analysis, we note that their performance on the 'NZ' sentences experiences a decline of 4-8%, with the exception of the TDEER and CasRel models. Interestingly, the TDEER and CasRel models exhibit comparable performance on the 'NZ' test set, regardless of whether they were trained on 'NZ' or 'WZ' training data. However, the introduction of sentences with zero triples during the training process tends to confuse these models, leading to a negative impact on their recall. Consequently, the models struggle to accurately extract valid triples due to the presence of such adversarial examples. Furthermore, in this training setting, we observe an improvement of 2-8% in the models' performance on 'WZ' sentences. Nevertheless, the best F1 score reported on the stringent 'NZ' test set for NYT24* is 0.926 (achieved by the GRTE model). In contrast, the best F1 score attained on the 'WZ' test set for NYT24* is 0.82 (achieved by the BiRTE model). This signifies a 10% drop in the best F1 score when transitioning to the experiment's more diverse setting. Similarly, we observe a 6% decrease in the best achieved F1 scores on the 'WZ' test set for NYT29* compared to the 'NZ' test set.

Next, we delve into the analysis of the impact of our proposed two-step approach for this task. The first step involves utilizing the zero-cardinality classifier to predict sentences with zero cardinality, i.e., sentences that either contain triples or do not. The performance of the classification model using both binary and multi-class multi-label (MCML)

	NYT24*			NYT29*		
	Prec.	Rec.	F1	Prec.	Rec.	F1
ZCC_{binary}	0.887	0.867	0.877	0.801	0.888	0.842
ZCC_{MCML}	0.881	0.884	0.883	0.823	0.824	0.823

Table 4: Performance of the zero cardinality classifier (ZCC) model on NYT24* and NYT29* datasets in the binary classification and multi-class multi-label classification (MCML) settings.

	NYT24*				NYT29*			
	multi-class multi-label				binary			
Model	Prec.	Rec.	F1	% ↑	Prec.	Rec.	F1	% ↑
OneRel	0.832	0.836	0.834	3.43	0.740	0.664	0.700	-0.27
BiRTE	0.819	0.839	0.829	0.85	0.679	0.663	0.671	-0.95
TDEER	0.830	0.830	0.830	8.23	0.749	0.649	0.696	8.52
PRGC	0.822	0.811	0.816	3.26	0.744	0.645	0.691	-0.14
GRTE	0.835	0.842	0.839	4.30	0.740	0.661	0.699	1.41
PtrNet	0.806	0.815	0.811	4.95	0.677	0.650	0.663	-0.33
CasRel	0.807	0.812	0.810	6.73	0.676	0.653	0.665	5.13
TPLinker	0.816	0.839	0.828	1.23	0.681	0.656	0.668	0.81
PFN*	0.805	0.833	0.818	5.20	0.726	0.658	0.690	2.42

Table 5: Performance of the SOTA models in the two-step modeling on the relational triple extraction task with zero-cardinalty sentences. At the first-step, we use multi-class multi-label classification for NYT24* dataset and binary classification for NYT29* dataset.

classification is provided in Table 4. The classification model was trained on 'WZ' sentences for both the NYT24* and NYT29* datasets. Both binary classification and multi-class multi-label classification demonstrate competitive performance on both datasets. Multi-class multi-label classification exhibits slightly higher performance on the NYT24* dataset, while binary classification yields marginally better results on the NYT29* dataset.

In the second step of our two-step approach, only the sentences predicted by the classification model to have existing triples are passed on to the triple extraction model. For this step, we train the state-of-the-art (SOTA) models exclusively on the 'NZ' sentences to facilitate triple extraction. In Table 5, we present the comprehensive performance evaluation of the state-of-the-art (SOTA) model using the two-step approach for the triple extraction task. For the NYT24* dataset, we utilize the multi-class multi-label classifier, while for the NYT29* dataset, we employ the binary classification approach for zero-cardinality prediction.

Our observations reveal an improvement of approximately $\sim 8\%$ in the 'WZ' sentences for both the NYT24* and NYT29* datasets when employing the two-step approach compared to the end-to-end approach. Specifically, for the NYT24* dataset, all SOTA models exhibit enhanced performance with the two-step approach over the end-to-end approach. However, for the NYT29* dataset, the performance is not consistently improved. In the case of four models (OneRel, BiRTE, PRGC, and PtrNet), we observed a minor drop of up to $\sim 1\%$ with the two-step approach.

Overall, we conclude that the two-step approach either improves the performance of these models or achieves competitive performance when compared to the end-to-end approach in this new experimental setting for relation extraction.

5.1 Training Time of the Models

Table 6 presents the training time of various models used in our experiments. All training was conducted on an NVIDIA A100 GPU with 20 GB GPU memory. Our two-step approach for the relation extraction task in this new setting offers advantages over the end-to-end approach.

The training time for the SOTA models solely using 'NZ' data is considerable, primarily due to their utilization of BERT as the sentence encoder. However, when we incorporate sentences with zero triples in the training process (which account for almost three times the number of sentences with triples, as shown in Table 2), the training time sig-

	NYT24*		NYT29*	
	NZ	WZ	NZ	WZ
Onrel	18.33	68.35	21.05	83.06
BiRTE	6.67	25.49	6.24	32.74
TDEER	43.51	50.85	45.11	63.68
PRGC	20.25	56.70	18.96	62.87
GRTE	20.70	65.08	21.87	80.51
PtrNet	17.17	41.03	12.24	24.30
CasRel	18.23	65.20	20.54	75.95
TPLinker	26.19	122.65	43.40	168.91
PFN*	22.40	317.18	188.68	393.35
ZCC_{binary}	-	14.67	-	25.55
ZCC_{MCML}	-	14.49	-	25.65

Table 6: Training time of the models. First 9 rows are avg. training epoch time (in minutes) of five SOTA models on the 'NZ' and 'WZ' training data. Last two rows are avg. training time of the zero cardinality classification (ZCC) models with WZ training data.

nificantly increases for all models (refer to Table 6).

On the contrary, the zero-cardinality classifier only needs to be trained once for all models, resulting in substantial time savings. Additionally, training the zero-cardinality classifier itself is relatively quick due to its simple architecture.

6 Related Work

Extracting relational triples from text is a crucial task for constructing new knowledge bases or enhancing existing ones. In their efforts to address this task, Mintz et al. (2009); Riedel et al. (2010); Hoffmann et al. (2011) employed feature-based classification models. More recently, Zeng et al. (2014, 2015) utilized CNN models, which automatically extract features, for this purpose. Shen and Huang (2016); Jat et al. (2017); Nayak and Ng (2019) incorporated attention mechanisms into their models to enhance performance. Approaches such as Surdeanu et al. (2012); Lin et al. (2016); Vashishth et al. (2018) adopted a multi-instance relation extraction setting, where multiple sentences are used to capture features associated with a pair of entities. These approaches assume that entities have already been identified and focus solely on classifying relations between entity pairs.

Katiyar and Cardie (2016); Miwa and Bansal (2016); Bekoulis et al. (2018); Nguyen and Verspoor (2019); Nayak and Ng (2020) tried to bring the named entity recognition task and relation classification task together. Zheng et al. (2017) used a sequence tagging scheme to jointly extract the entities and relations. Zeng et al. (2018); Nayak and Ng (2020) proposed an encoder-decoder model to extract relational triples with overlapping entities. Takanobu et al. (2019) proposed a joint extraction model based on hierarchical reinforcement learning (HRL).

With the introduction of pre-trained models such as BERT (Devlin et al., 2019), many models used such models as sentence encoder to improve their performance. Models such as TPLinker (Wang et al., 2020), CasRel (Wei et al., 2020), TDEER (Li et al., 2021), PRGC (Zheng et al., 2021), PFN (Yan et al., 2021), GRTE (Ren et al., 2021), OneRel (Shang et al., 2022), and BiRTE (Ren et al., 2022) use BERT_base (Devlin et al., 2019) as an encoder and proposed table-filling method or relation specific tagging mechanism for joint entity and relation extraction. These models show remarkable performance on the NYT datasets in the restrictive experimental setting without considering the zero-cardinal sentences.

7 Conclusion

In this work, we present an innovative and challenging experiment design for relation extraction, which incorporates sentences containing zero triples (referred to as zero-cardinal sentences) in the dataset. We conduct comprehensive experiments involving 9 state-of-the-art (SOTA) models using the widely-used New York Times datasets. To tackle this task, we devise both an end-to-end modeling approach and a two-step modeling approach.

During our investigations, we make a significant observation in the end-to-end modeling, where we notice a drop in the F1 score by approximately 10-15% and 6-14% in two versions of the NYT dataset. To address this issue, we propose the integration of a BERT-based classifier as an additional step for this task. Remarkably, this approach either achieves performance comparable to the end-to-end approach or even surpasses it.

We believe that our benchmark, focusing on relational triple extraction with zero-cardinality, will prove immensely valuable for future research in this domain. By introducing this unique experiment design, we aim to stimulate further advancements and foster progress in this field.

8 Limitations

One limitation of this work is that we benchmark this task using 9 SOTA joint models. There are many other SOTA models published in this area but it is difficult to benchmark all of them. We chose the 9 models in such as way that different kind of design choices in these models are represented in our study. We chose Seq2Seq model (Nayak and Ng, 2020), horn tagging-based models (Wang et al., 2020; Shang et al., 2022), 0/1 tagging-based models (Wei et al., 2020; Li et al., 2021), table-filling models (Ren et al., 2021) for rigorous study of this area.

9 Ethics Statements

Our work does not have any ethical concerns.

References

Giannis Bekoulis, Johannes Deleu, Thomas Demeester, and Chris Develder. 2018. Joint entity recognition and relation extraction as a multi-head selection problem. *Expert Systems with Applications.*

Jacob Devlin, Ming-Wei Chang, Kenton Lee, and Kristina Toutanova. 2019. BERT: Pre-training of deep bidirectional transformers for language understanding. In *NAACL.*

Raphael Hoffmann, Congle Zhang, Xiao Ling, Luke Zettlemoyer, and Daniel S Weld. 2011. Knowledge-based weak supervision for information extraction of overlapping relations. In *ACL.*

Sharmistha Jat, Siddhesh Khandelwal, and Partha Talukdar. 2017. Improving distantly supervised relation extraction using word and entity based attention. In *AKBC.*

Arzoo Katiyar and Claire Cardie. 2016. Investigating LSTMs for joint extraction of opinion entities and relations. In *ACL.*

Souvik Kundu and Hwee Tou Ng. 2018. A nil-aware answer extraction framework for question answering. In *EMNLP.*

Xianming Li, Xiaotian Luo, Cheng Jie Dong, Daichuan Yang, Beidi Luan, and Zhen He. 2021. TDEER: An efficient translating decoding schema for joint extraction of entities and relations. In *EMNLP.*

Yankai Lin, Shiqi Shen, Zhiyuan Liu, Huanbo Luan, and Maosong Sun. 2016. Neural relation extraction with selective attention over instances. In *ACL.*

Ilya Loshchilov and Frank Hutter. 2019. Decoupled weight decay regularization. In *ICLR.*

Mike Mintz, Steven Bills, Rion Snow, and Dan Jurafsky. 2009. Distant supervision for relation extraction without labeled data. In *ACL.*

Makoto Miwa and Mohit Bansal. 2016. End-to-end relation extraction using LSTMs on sequences and tree structures. In *ACL.*

Tapas Nayak and Hwee Tou Ng. 2019. Effective attention modeling for neural relation extraction. In *CoNLL.*

Tapas Nayak and Hwee Tou Ng. 2020. Effective modeling of encoder-decoder architecture for joint entity and relation extraction. In *AAAI.*

Dat Quoc Nguyen and Karin Verspoor. 2019. End-to-end neural relation extraction using deep biaffine attention. In *ECIR.*

Pranav Rajpurkar, Robin Jia, and Percy Liang. 2018. Know what you don't know: Unanswerable questions for SQuAD. In *ACL.*

Feiliang Ren, Longhui Zhang, Shujuan Yin, Xiaofeng Zhao, Shilei Liu, Bochao Li, and Yaduo Liu. 2021. A novel global feature-oriented relational triple extraction model based on table filling. In *EMNLP.*

Feiliang Ren, Longhui Zhang, Xiaofeng Zhao, Shujuan Yin, Shilei Liu, and Bochao Li. 2022. A simple but effective bidirectional framework for relational triple extraction. *Proceedings of the Fifteenth ACM International Conference on Web Search and Data Mining.*

Sebastian Riedel, Limin Yao, and Andrew McCallum. 2010. Modeling relations and their mentions without labeled text. In *ECML and KDD.*

Y. Shang, Heyan Huang, and Xian-Ling Mao. 2022. OneRel: Joint entity and relation extraction with one module in one step. In *AAAI.*

Yatian Shen and Xuanjing Huang. 2016. Attention-based convolutional neural network for semantic relation extraction. In *COLING.*

Elior Sulem, Jamaal Hay, and Dan Roth. 2021. Do we know what we don't know? studying unanswerable questions beyond SQuAD 2.0. In *EMNLP.*

Mihai Surdeanu, Julie Tibshirani, Ramesh Nallapati, and Christopher D. Manning. 2012. Multi-instance multi-label learning for relation extraction. In *EMNLP and CoNLL.*

Ryuichi Takanobu, Tianyang Zhang, Jiexi Liu, and Minlie Huang. 2019. A hierarchical framework for relation extraction with reinforcement learning. In *AAAI.*

Shikhar Vashishth, Rishabh Joshi, Sai Suman Prayaga, Chiranjib Bhattacharyya, and Partha Talukdar. 2018. Reside: Improving distantly-supervised neural relation extraction using side information. In *EMNLP.*

Yucheng Wang, Bowen Yu, Yueyang Zhang, Tingwen Liu, Hongsong Zhu, and Limin Sun. 2020. TPLinker: Single-stage joint extraction of entities and relations through token pair linking. In *COLING.*

Zhepei Wei, Jianlin Su, Yue Wang, Yuan Tian, and Yi Chang. 2020. A novel cascade binary tagging framework for relational triple extraction. In *ACL.*

Zhiheng Yan, Chong Zhang, Jinlan Fu, Qi Zhang, and Zhongyu Wei. 2021. A partition filter network for joint entity and relation extraction. In *EMNLP*.

Daojian Zeng, Kang Liu, Yubo Chen, and Jun Zhao. 2015. Distant supervision for relation extraction via piecewise convolutional neural networks. In *EMNLP*.

Daojian Zeng, Kang Liu, Siwei Lai, Guangyou Zhou, and Jun Zhao. 2014. Relation classification via convolutional deep neural network. In *COLING*.

Xiangrong Zeng, Daojian Zeng, Shizhu He, Kang Liu, and Jun Zhao. 2018. Extracting relational facts by an end-to-end neural model with copy mechanism. In *ACL*.

Heng Zheng, Rui Wen, Xi Chen, Yifan Yang, Yunyan Zhang, Ziheng Zhang, Ningyu Zhang, Bin Qin, Ming Xu, and Yefeng Zheng. 2021. PRGC: Potential relation and global correspondence based joint relational triple extraction. In *ACL*.

Suncong Zheng, Feng Wang, Hongyun Bao, Yuexing Hao, Peng Zhou, and Bo Xu. 2017. Joint extraction of entities and relations based on a novel tagging scheme. In *ACL*.

A Appendix

A.1 GenBench Evaluation Cards

Motivation			
Practical	*Cognitive*	*Intrinsic*	*Fairness*
○			

Generalisation type					
Compositional	*Structural*	*Cross Task*	*Cross Language*	*Cross Domain*	*Robustness*
				○	

Shift type			
Covariate	*Label*	*Full*	*Assumed*
	○		

Shift source			
Naturally occuring	*Partitioned natural*	*Generated shift*	*Fully generated*
○			

Shift locus			
Train–test	*Finetune train–test*	*Pretrain–train*	*Pretrain–test*
○			

Table 7: We characterise all our experiments of Section 5 (○) in this datacard.

GenCodeSearchNet: A Benchmark Test Suite for Evaluating Generalization in Programming Language Understanding

Andor Diera
Ulm University,
Germany
andor.diera@uni-ulm.de

Abdelhalim Dahou
GESIS - Institute for Social Sciences,
Germany
abdelhalim.dahou@gesis.org

Lukas Galke
Max Planck Institute for Psycholinguistics,
Netherlands
lukas.galke@mpi.nl

Fabian Karl
Ulm University,
Germany
fabian.karl@uni-ulm.de

Florian Sihler
Ulm University,
Germany
florian.sihler@uni-ulm.de

Ansgar Scherp
Ulm University,
Germany
ansgar.scherp@uni-ulm.de

Abstract

Language models can serve as a valuable tool for software developers to increase productivity. Large generative models can be used for code generation and code completion, while smaller encoder-only models are capable of performing code search tasks using natural language queries. These capabilities are heavily influenced by the quality and diversity of the available training data. Source code datasets used for training usually focus on the most popular languages and testing is mostly conducted on the same distributions, often overlooking low-resource programming languages. Motivated by the NLP generalization taxonomy proposed by Hupkes et. al., we propose a new benchmark dataset called GenCodeSearchNet (GeCS) which builds upon existing natural language code search datasets to systemically evaluate the programming language understanding generalization capabilities of language models. As part of the full dataset, we introduce a new, manually curated subset StatCodeSearch that focuses on R, a popular but so far underrepresented programming language that is often used by researchers outside the field of computer science. For evaluation and comparison, we collect several baseline results using fine-tuned BERT-style models and GPT-style large language models in a zero-shot setting.

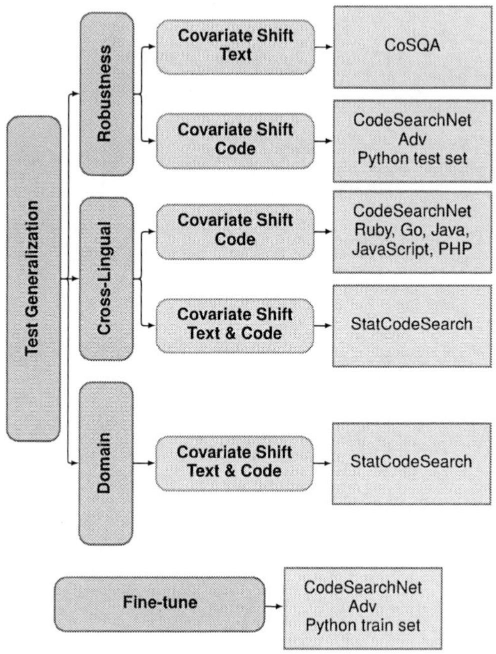

Figure 1: Overview of the benchmark composition w.r.t. the generalization taxonomy of Hupkes et al. (2023)

1 Introduction

Language models have found their use in various tasks dealing with source code, ranging from code search to code summarization, code completion, and code translation (Lu et al., 2021). With the release of Codex (Chen et al., 2021) and ChatGPT (Ouyang et al., 2022) large language models (LLMs) became popular and widely used for AI-assisted coding. Still, as of August 2023, code completion and code-related question answering with LLMs is far from reliable (Kabir et al., 2023). An alternative to using general purpose LLMs for code completion is code search (i.e., finding relevant source code based on a natural language query) in curated datasets (Cambronero et al., 2019; Husain et al., 2019) which provides a more transparent aid for AI-assisted coding. However, so far it is unclear how well code search models generalize across different programming languages, different domains, and how robust they are against distribution shifts.

Although both natural language queries and source code are represented as text, one cannot safely assume to have an overlap in the words/characters used, since function and variable

Proceedings of the 1st GenBench Workshop on (Benchmarking) Generalisation in NLP, pages 12–24
December 6, 2023 ©2023 Association for Computational Linguistics

names do not necessarily consist of words. Still, classical string-based matching between a query and documents (Manning, 2009) is used in many information retrieval systems and practical applications (Lin et al., 2022). When documents consist of code, natural language queries will have little to no matching words, resulting in a lexical gap. Due to this lexical gap, the task of finding code snippets based on natural language queries is difficult and requires specific bimodal language models capable of processing both natural and programming languages (Feng et al., 2020; Guo et al., 2020; Wang et al., 2021, 2023).

However, this bimodal training approach is likely limited to the programming languages on which the models were trained. It is unknown how such models would generalize to programming languages that were not part of the training data or have only little representation in the dataset, i. e., a low-resource programming language. Evaluating the models on programming languages that were not part of the training data (i. e., a distribution shift occurs) would shed new light on the generalization capabilities of hybrid models for code and text – which is the aim of this work.

Moreover, there are low-resource programming languages such as R that in terms of quantity are underrepresented on popular code-sharing platforms like GitHub. However, it is the de facto programming language in many research fields relying on statistical analysis, such as economics, statistics, social sciences, and psychology. Thus, the coding conventions and style in these fields also differ from the code corpora used in existing benchmark datasets (Husain et al., 2019; Lu et al., 2021). This produces a blind spot on the current methods for code search as they are usually only tested on datasets of well-curated source code in the most popular programming languages.

We propose a new benchmark dataset called GenCodeSearchNet (GeCS) which combines a new, manually curated dataset StatCodeSearch with existing code search datasets. StatCodeSearch consists of code-comment pairs extracted from R scripts written for statistical analysis. We further propose an evaluation protocol for the benchmark that allows future researchers to systemically test the language models' generalization capabilities for programming language understanding. The evaluation setup for our dataset is illustrated in Figure 1 and consists of three generalization tests for robustness, cross-lingual, and domain generalization. We provide a detailed description of this benchmark in Section 3. In summary, the contributions of this work are three-fold:

- We create a benchmark for *programming language understanding* named GenCodeSearchNet that tests text-code matching and ranking, organized along different types of out-of-distribution generalization. The composition of the benchmark is described in Section 3 and its evaluation protocol in Section 4.
- To facilitate the new benchmark, we introduce a new, manually-curated dataset named StatCodeSearch, consisting of 1,070 text-code pairs from statistical research code written in R, which is described in Section 3.2.
- Initial baselines for this new benchmark are introduced in Section 5. We provide results for RoBERTA, CodeBERT, CodeT5+, and GPT-based LLMs in Section 5.2.

2 Related Work

Code Search Code search is an established research field with various tools and solutions available. Below, we briefly summarize existing classical works on source code search, followed by works on semantic code search based on neural networks, particularly pre-trained language models.

An established classical tool for source code search is Oracle OpenGrok[1] based on the popular full-text index Lucene. As a result, OpenGrok enables textual searching of code for strings based on Google-like search queries. Similar systems for textual searching on code are searchcode[2] and Sourcegraph[3]. The ANNE (Vinayakarao et al., 2017) system extends the purely textual search to source code by mapping natural language queries to syntactic keywords of programming languages. Search engines supporting structured queries include Aroma (Luan et al., 2019), which takes an incomplete code fragment as a query (called a snippet) and suggests concise code snippets from the code database. A similar approach is also taken by Mukherjee et al. (Mukherjee et al., 2020).

Neural networks have also been successfully applied for code search allowing semantics-based natural language code search. Just as in most fields

[1]https://github.com/oracle/opengrok
[2]https://searchcode.com/
[3]https://about.sourcegraph.com/

of NLP, the best-performing models for semantic code search are transformer-based language models. These models are pretrained on both natural language and programming language corpora and often use a contrastive loss to better align text and code representations (Li et al., 2022b; Wang et al., 2023; Neelakantan et al., 2022). Prominent examples of encoder-only bimodal language models include CodeBERT (Feng et al., 2020), GraphCodeBERT (Guo et al., 2020), and CodeRetriever (Li et al., 2022a). Encoder-decoder models designed to handle a wide range of programming language tasks such as CodeT5 (Wang et al., 2021) and CodeT5+ (Wang et al., 2023) also perform strongly on the task of semantic code search. Lastly, decoder-only models (Brown et al., 2020) can be also employed for code search, albeit they either require careful prompting (Ouyang et al., 2022) or extensive fine-tuning (Neelakantan et al., 2022).

Generalization in Programming Language Understanding Generalization, or the ability of a model to perform well on data not seen during training, is sought after in all domains of machine learning (Goodfellow et al., 2016). However, generalization can refer to a wide range of different scenarios in NLP. To tackle this lack of agreement and systematic testing, Hupkes et al. (2023) proposed a taxonomy for characterizing generalization research in NLP. Their taxonomy consists of five axes to classify the motivation, generalization type, data shift type, source, and locus of the shift.

Even though neural networks capable of handling both natural and programming languages are usually called bimodal models (Allamanis et al., 2015; Feng et al., 2020; Wang et al., 2023), the representations of these two input modalities share a lot of commonalities, including predictable statistical properties (Hindle et al., 2012). Therefore, we argue that the NLP generalization taxonomy proposed by Hupkes et al. (2023) also offers valuable insights for research in programming language understanding.

Generalization research on code-related tasks is still in short supply. The HumanEval dataset (Chen et al., 2021) used for benchmarking generative models only contains Python source code, while CodeXGLUE (Lu et al., 2021), the comprehensive programming language understanding benchmark suite is designed to evaluate on in-distribution test data. CodeS (Hu et al., 2023) offers an extensive dataset for evaluating against different types of out-of-distribution samples, but only uses two languages (Python and Java) with the singular downstream task of code classification. To the best of our knowledge, the only large-scale benchmarks for evaluating generalization of code-related tasks are CrossCodeBench (Niu et al., 2023) and XLCoST (Zhu et al., 2022). While XLCoST focuses solely on cross-lingual generalization, CrossCodeBench only includes tasks that are formulated in a text-to-text form, leaving out retrieval tasks, such as code search. In contrast to the aforementioned works, our proposed benchmark focuses on the task of natural language code search and offers evaluations against multiple types of distribution shifts.

3 Composition of GenCodeSearchNet

In this section, we describe the datasets used in our benchmark suite. The datasets are chosen and created based on the criterion to evaluate different types of generalization in programming language processing to foster further research in the field.

The GeCS dataset includes one fine-tuning set and eight test sets. It contains three previously proposed datasets, namely CodeSearchNet (Husain et al., 2019), CodeSearchNet AdvTest (Lu et al., 2021), and CoSQA (Huang et al., 2021). We add a novel set that focuses on statistical tests in the programming language R, named StatCodeSearch. Each dataset contains a natural language description (either a code comment or a search engine query) and a source code snippet. The test suite is designed to study generalization from a practical perspective, i. e., to assess programming language understanding in various evaluation scenarios. The source of datashifts between the different test sets is considered to be naturally occurring, with the locus of the shift appearing between the pretraining/finetuning data and test data. The types of generalization covered by the test suite include robustness to covariate shifts and generalization across programming languages and programming domains.

A detailed breakdown of the experimental design in the generalization framework proposed by Hupkes et al. (2023) can be seen in Figure 1. The main characteristics of the different subsets can be found in Table 1. The average number of tokens have been calculated using the pretrained RoBERTa tokenizer sourced from HuggingFace (Wolf et al., 2019). Furthermore, we also measure the covariate shift in texts and codes using the total variation dis-

Table 1: Statistics of the different subsets used in the GenCodeSearchNet test suite. The numbers shown include only the positive (matching) examples

Subset	# text-code pairs	avg # text tokens	avg # code tokens	total variation distance text	total variation distance code
Fine-tuning set					
CodeSearchNet AdvTest train	251 820	15.97	166.94	0.0	0.0
Test sets					
CodeSearchNet AdvTest test	19 210	16.08	177.64	0.1268	0.5372
CodeSearchNet Go	14 291	27.46	159.08	0.3281	0.6110
CodeSearchNet Java	26 909	29.07	179.63	0.3126	0.5972
CodeSearchNet JavaScript	6 483	21.93	240.21	0.2892	0.5479
CodeSearchNet Ruby	2 279	23.88	138.09	0.2962	0.5610
CodeSearchNet PHP	29 391	14.73	189.00	0.2858	0.5819
CoSQA	10 293	10.42	55.93	0.5322	0.4453
StatCodeSearch	1 070	24.55	134.02	0.5386	0.8032
Combined Test set	109 926	21.01	159.20	0.3386	0.5855

tance (Goldenberg and Webb, 2019). We calculate the total variation distance to the CodeSearchNet Adv train set (used for fine-tuning) on the tokenized samples.

3.1 Existing Datasets

The **CodeSearchNet** dataset (Husain et al., 2019) was introduced as a semantic code search evaluation tool. Since then it has been a staple benchmark dataset for studying the code search capabilities of machine learning models. It encompasses code-comment pairs from six different programming languages: Python, Go, Java, JavaScript, Ruby, and PHP. The full corpus includes 6 million functions scraped from GitHub, with 2 million of those including associated function documentation. Functions less than three lines and documentation shorter than three tokens were removed from the scraped corpus. Duplicate or near duplicate functions were also discarded to control for auto-generated code snippets and copy & paste between GitHub users. For the GeCS test suite, we collected the test sets from the HuggingFace Hub (Lhoest et al., 2021) and discarded the Python subset (since it is included later in the CodeSearchNet AdvTest dataset). We employed no further preprocessing and formatted the data into JSONL files. For each sample, we defined three fields: the *input* field contains the code comment and code snippet separated by a '[CODESPLIT]' token, the *target* field contains the index of the binary labels ('no_match','match'), which are found in the *target_options* field. This dataset is used to measure cross-lingual generalization.

The **CodeSearchNet AdvTest** dataset was developed for the CodeXGLUE benchmark dataset (Lu et al., 2021) by applying further preprocessing steps on the Python subset of the CodeSearchNet dataset. First, all code snippets that could not be parsed into an abstract syntax tree were removed, then documentations with more than 256 tokens were removed alongside samples that contained special tokens such as *"http://"* or *"<img... >"*. Finally, the functions and variables in the code snippets of the test set have been normalized by renaming them to *func* and arg_i, respectively. This normalization of the test set makes it a good fit to test robustness against a covariate shift in the source code. For the inclusion in the GeCS test suite, we sourced both the train and test set from the official CodeXGLUE repository[4]. We employed no further preprocessing and applied the same formatting as described above.

The Code Search And Question Answering (**CoSQA**) corpus (Huang et al., 2021) uses the Python subset of the CodeSearchNet dataset and matches the code snippets with real-world search queries from the Microsoft Bing search engine. The search logs were carefully filtered to only include queries that incorporate the keyword *python* and have none of the predefined keywords that relate to search intents other than code search (e. g., debugging, conceptual queries, tool usage). After this initial rule-based filtering, a fine-tuned CodeBERT encoder (Feng et al., 2020) was used to measure cosine similarity between candidate queries and code snippets. Each code snippet was then matched with the query of the highest similarity. Pairs with a similarity value of less than 0.5 were discarded. Finally, a number of human annotators were instructed to label each code-query pair whether the code snippet answers the query or not. For the GeCS dataset, we use the training set re-

[4]https://github.com/microsoft/CodeXGLUE

trieved from the official CodeXGLUE repository and discard query-code pairs that are labeled as non-matching (we create our own negative samples as described in Section 4). We apply no further preprocessing and use the same formatting as described before.

3.2 New Dataset: StatCodeSearch

The StatCodeSearch dataset is a benchmark test set consisting of code comment pairs extracted from R programming language scripts authored mostly by researchers. The dataset is sourced from the Open Science Framework (OSF)[5]. It includes text and code samples from R projects that pertain to the fields of social science and psychology with a focus on the statistical analysis of research data. These projects are often linked with research articles published in journals such as *Political Communication*, *Behavior Research Methods*, and *Cognitive Science*. R scripts in these domains seldom use branching or explicit looping constructs, as most logic is handled by higher-order functions and R's implicit vectorization. Furthermore, they heavily rely on functions of loaded libraries (Sihler, 2023).

The initial scraping of the OSF website resulted in 11,775 R projects. After discarding projects that did not have any specific permissive software license, the dataset was narrowed down to 2,832 projects, from which the code-comment pairs of the final dataset were extracted. The creation of code-comment pairs involved a three-step procedure. First, we implemented a rule-based extraction, which included the following steps. We removed empty lines and leading spaces from each line. We discarded lines identified as library loading. We detected lines commencing with "#" that include more than one word. If multiple subsequent comment lines were found, we concatenated them into one text item. We categorized lines without the leading "#" symbol as associated code blocks to the preceding text item.

After the extraction of code-comment pairs through these rules, an additional post-processing step was applied where we discarded common comment trailing symbols from the text items such as "#", "-", and "=". This first step resulted in 40,041 pairs of code and comments. In order to filter out irrelevant comments, in the second step we employed GPT 3.5 Turbo to classify the comments into four predefined classes (the prompts used for this subtask can be found in Appendix A.3.2). These classes were defined as statistical tests, statistical modeling, visualization, and data variables. On a small subset of 400 pairs, we experimented with three prompting methods for this task: zero-shot, one-shot, and few-shot. Our pre-experiments showed zero-shot to be the most suitable approach for this filtering, as it produced fewer false-negatives than the other two approaches. This automated filtering resulted in a total of 10,137 code comment pairs. The third step involved the review and evaluation of the remaining selection by the authors. We manually filtered the remaining 10,137 code pairs and removed those with irrelevant comments, or code blocks that did not correspond to the comment. This step served as a critical quality control measure and yielded a total of 1,070 pairs of code and comments. We applied the same formatting as described in Section 3.1.

[5]https://osf.io/

4 Evaluation Protocol

4.1 Fine-tuning

Fine-tuning is an optional step for evaluating smaller models that did not have a text-code matching objective during their pretraining phase. For a fair comparison, we suggest only using the training set of the CodeSearchNet AdvTest dataset for fine-tuning, which is based on Python, a widely-used general-purpose programming language.

4.2 Measures

We apply two measures for assessing the performance of the models.

Matching We test whether a given text-code pair is a matching pair (positive) or not (negative). We evaluate the accuracy on balanced test sets with an equal number of positive and negative examples. The non-matching examples are sampled uniformly within the respective dataset.

Ranking To evaluate the ranking in the code search task, we employ Mean Reciprocal Rank (MRR). For each query, we consider 99 distractors sampled uniformly at random. For each query, the reciprocal of the best-ranked correct answer is considered. Formally, for a set of queries Q, the reciprocal of the best-ranked correct answer at rank r_i is aggregated and averaged as $\text{MRR} = \frac{1}{|Q|} \sum_{i=1,\ldots,|Q|} \frac{1}{r_i}$.

The rationale for the choice of MRR over alternative ranking metrics, such as mean average precision (MAP) or normalized discounted cumulative gain (nDCG) (Manning, 2009; Lin et al., 2022), is that we have only a single relevant code snippet for each query and the ratings are binary. When there is only a single relevant document, as in CodeSearchNet, MRR and MAP coincide to the same formula. Furthermore, nDCG can reflect different degrees of relevance, but in our case, since we only have a binary assessment of the code-comment pairs, there is no benefit of using this metric.

4.3 Evaluation by Generalization Type

Our proposed benchmark groups the evaluations by the generalization types proposed by Hupkes et al. (2023). For this, we take the unweighted average of the classification and ranking scores across different datasets (see Figure 1). To evaluate **robustness**, we aggregate scores on test sets that exhibit a covariate shift in either text or code. For this, we employ CoSQA and CodeSearchNet AdvTest (as described in Section 3.1). For **cross-lingual generalization** (cross-lingual referring to "across programming languages"), we average the scores across datasets CodeSearchNet and StatCodeSearch. In this generalization type, the locus of the covariate shift is mainly in the code snippets due to the differing syntax. For **domain generalization**, the sole test set is StatCodeSearch from the domain of statistical analysis, which entails a different coding/commenting style (cf. Section 3.2).

5 Baselines

5.1 Baseline Methods

We provide the results for three main types of baseline models using two evaluation strategies. We employ the encoder-only models RoBERTa and CodeBERT, the encoder-decoder model CodeT5+, and GPT-based models GPT 3.5 Turbo and Text-embedding-ada-002. For RoBERTa and CodeBERT we employ an additional fine-tuning step on the CodeSearchNet AdvTest train set. The GPT-based models are evaluated in a zero-shot setup, while CodeT5+ is tested both in the fine-tuning and zero-shot setup.

For fine-tuning, we follow the same sampling procedure that is also in the evaluation of the matching task, i. e., single negative example for matching. To tackle the matching task, we concatenate the query and code to a singular input and train an output layer on binary classification. To tackle the ranking task with fine-tuned models, we concatenate the query with each of the 100 candidate code snippets. Then, we rank all 100 candidate pairs according to the matching score emitted by the model. In the zero-shot ranking setups we create the ranking based on the cosine similarity between text and code inputs. The choice of hyperparameters for fine-tuning can be found in Appendix A.1. Below we briefly describe the existing models that we use as initial baselines for the proposed benchmark.

RoBERTa is an encoder-only transformer model that builds upon the foundations of the BERT model (Devlin et al., 2019). RoBERTa is designed to improve upon some limitations of BERT by optimizing the pretraining process. These improvements include dynamic masking in masked language modeling, larger batch sizes, increased training data size, and a more thorough hyperparameter optimization (Liu et al., 2019). RoBERTa is a commonly used baseline model for numerous NLP tasks, including semantic code search (Feng et al., 2020). Our experiments are based on the pretrained HuggingFace implementation of the *RoBERTa-base* model (Wolf et al., 2019).

CodeBERT is a pretrained transformer model designed for both natural language and programming language tasks (Feng et al., 2020). It uses the RoBERTa-base architecture with a masked language modeling objective for bimodal (natural language and programming language input pairs) training data and replaced token detection for unimodal (only programming language input) training data. Similarly to other BERT-based models, CodeBERT performs best with task-specific fine-tuning, and is a common baseline in programming language understanding tasks such as semantic code search, code summarization, and code-clone detection (Lu et al., 2021). We use the pre-trained CodeBERT model from HuggingFace (Wolf et al., 2019) and follow the original paper's fine-tuning procedure.

CodeT5+ is an encoder-decoder transformer model suited to solve a wide range of code tasks (Wang et al., 2023). This is made possible by employing a mixture of pretraining objectives, including span denoising, contrastive learning, text-code matching, and causal language modeling on both unimodal and bimodal training data. The CodeT5+ model can be be successfully deployed in multiple settings (zero-shot, fine-tuning, and instruction-tuning) and performs very well on over 20 code-related benchmark tasks. We run our experiments with the *codet5p-110m-embedding* model variant sourced from HuggingFace. This version, denoted as *CodeT5+ (encoder only)* in our experiments, includes only the encoder layers of the bimodal model. This makes it suitable to create high quality embeddings with lower computational costs. For the matching evaluation, we extend this model with a binary classifier head (similar to the RoBERTa and CodeBERT setups) and apply fine-tuning. In the ranking evaluation, we use both the fine-tuned version and the base model in a zero-shot setup.

GPT-3.5 Turbo developed by OpenAI as a member of the GPT family (Brown et al., 2020) is specifically designed to understand and generate both natural language and code. GPT-3.5 Turbo is optimized primarily for chat applications but also excels in traditional understanding and completion tasks. The model is also a successor to the OpenAI Codex model (Chen et al., 2021) and has exhibited significant enhancements in code generation, error detection, debugging, and analysis. Like other LLMs, it is built on the transformer architecture, is pre-trained on vast amounts of text and code, and is heavily fine-tuned through human feedback (Ouyang et al., 2022). We employ GPT-3.5 for the binary classification evaluation in a zero shot setup (prompts can be found in Appendix A.3.2).

Text-embedding-ada-002 denoted as Ada 2 in our experiments, is an embedding model released by OpenAI in late 2022. Embedding models are designed to generate vectors of floating point numbers that capture the semantic meaning of the input (Neelakantan et al., 2022). The second generation of the OpenAI Ada model has been created by merging the functionalities of five distinct embedding models related to text search, text similarity, and code search into one unified interface. We employ Text-embedding-ada-002 to calculate the cosine similarity between the embeddings of the input pairs in the ranking evaluation setup.

5.2 Baseline Results

The evaluation results for the GeCS dataset are shown in Table 2. The aggregated results for each generalization type (as described in Section 4.3) are displayed in Table 3. A breakdown of results by programming language within CodeSearchNet can be found in Appendix A.2.

Matching The fine-tuned models achieve on average around 90% accuracy on the matching task, with RoBERTa producing both the lowest (84.41% on CodeSearchNet AdvTest) and highest (99.18% on CodeSearchNet Go) results. The matching results of GPT 3.5 Turbo range from 32.82% (CoSQA) to 62.71% (StatCodeSearch). The highest results across the fine-tuned models were achieved on the CoSQA and CodeSearchNet Go datasets, while the lowest values were seen in the PHP subset of CodeSearchNet. Aggregating by generalization type, we find that CodeT5+ yields the highest scores on Robustness, while CodeBERT yields the highest scores on Cross-Lingual and Domain.

Ranking In the ranking evaluation, the highest MRR ratings are achieved by the Ada 2 model, which consistently places the correct code snippet in the first two ranks on average. The zero-shot CodeT5+ models also attain similarly strong performance. Compared to the zero-shot models, fine-tuned models performed poorly on ranking, achieving the highest MRR scores on the robustness tests (CodeSearchNet AdvTest and CoSQA), while scoring below 0.1 on the cross-lingual and domain tests. The highest results across all models were obtained on the CodeSearchNet Ruby datasets, while the lowest values are seen in the StatCodeSearch dataset. Aggregating by generalization type, we find that all models yield higher scores for Robustness than for Cross-Lingual and Domain.

6 Discussion

Our newly introduced benchmark dataset provides several new insights on the generalization capabilities of pre-trained language models. Compared to existing benchmarks, such as CodeSearchNet and CodexGLUE, it focuses on evaluating different types of out-of-distribution generalization, leading to new insights about existing models.

First, we observe that encoder-only models completely fail at ranking when tested out of distribution (on datasets for which they were not specifically fine-tuned). In general, we find that ranking performance suffers substantially from fine-tuning, suggesting that the models are overfitting to the fine-tuning set, resulting in limited generalization capabilities in all three investigated generalization types.

Table 2: Baseline Results on GenCodeSearchNet

Model	CodeSearchNet Avg		CodeSearchNet AdvTest		CoSQA		StatCodeSearch	
	Acc	MRR	Acc	MRR	Acc	MRR	Acc	MRR
Fine-tuned Models								
RoBERTa	0.9263	0.1054	0.8441	0.3853	0.9596	0.0441	0.8958	0.0557
CodeBERT	0.9056	0.0907	0.8862	0.4191	0.9758	0.1087	0.9607	0.0251
CodeT5+ (encoder only)	0.8734	0.0616	0.9002	0.2767	0.9773	0.0482	0.9056	0.0582
Zero-shot Models								
CodeT5+ (encoder only)	-	0.8198	-	0.8547	-	0.7972	-	0.6311
GPT 3.5 Turbo	0.5882	-	0.5687	-	0.3282	-	0.6271	-
Ada 2	-	0.8852	-	0.8264	-	0.9439	-	0.7945

Table 3: Aggregated Performance for Each Generalization Type

Model	Robustness		Cross-Lingual		Domain		Combined	
	Acc	MRR	Acc	MRR	Acc	MRR	Acc	MRR
RoBERTa	0.9018	0.2147	0.9110	0.0322	0.8958	0.0557	0.9028	0.1008
CodeBERT	0.9310	0.2639	0.9170	0.0579	0.9607	0.0251	0.9362	0.1236
CodeT5+ (encoder only) FT	0.9387	0.1156	0.8895	0.0599	0.9056	0.0582	0.9112	0.0779
CodeT5+ (encoder only) ZS	-	0.8259	-	0.7254	-	0.6311	-	0.7274
GPT 3.5 Turbo	0.4485	-	0.6076	-	0.6271	-	0.5610	-
Ada 2	-	0.8851	-	0.8398		0.7945	-	0.8398

On the other hand, large-scale pre-trained models, especially Ada 2, excel at ranking on all datasets. The dataset on which such zero-shot models yield the lowest performance is the newly introduced StatCodeSearch. A possible explanation is that the other datasets originate from GitHub and likely suffer from contamination, i.e., their test data could be part of the training data of the large language models (Golchin and Surdeanu, 2023).

The low performance (hardly better than chance) of GPT-3.5 Turbo in zero-shot matching is surprising. We cannot exclude that the performance could be increased by providing a few examples in the prompt. We opted for testing its zero-shot capabilities for a fair comparison with the other LLMs, leaving room for future work with more refined prompting strategies.

Reflecting Hupkes et al. (2023)'s generalization framework for code-related tasks has allowed us to better understand how the generalization type affects language model performance on tasks involving both natural and programming language understanding: Overall our results suggest that fine-tuned encoder-only models are strong at matching even in out-of-distribution test sets, while large-scale embedding models are strong at zero-shot ranking. Bimodal language models have been shown to achieve high performances on in-distribution natural language code search (Feng et al., 2020; Wang et al., 2023). Their results on our benchmark indicate shortcomings of existing models when tested against out-of-distribution data. We hope our newly introduced benchmark can facilitate the development of bimodal language models that generalize well beyond the training or fine-tuning distribution.

7 Conclusion

We have introduced a new benchmark called GenCodeSearchNet (GeCS) for testing the generalization capabilities of language models. The benchmark specifically aims at scrutinizing different types of generalization (robustness, cross-lingual, and domain), and evaluates matching and ranking for each type. To test generalization with covariate shifts in both textual descriptions and code snippets, we provide a new, manually curated dataset StatCodeSearch with R code comment pairs harvested from OSF. As initial baselines, we have evaluated RoBERTa, CodeBERT, CodeT5+, GPT 3.5 Turbo, and Ada 2. The baseline results of our benchmark reveal that models that are good at matching are not necessarily good at ranking and vice-versa. Hence, we hope that the new benchmark spurs the development of programming language-agnostic models that are good at both ranking and matching. Moving forward, one could extend GeCS with other low-resource programming languages to further facilitate the systematic evaluation of pre-trained language models against different aspects of generalization. We make our experiments and baseline models available on GitHub[6]. The final dataset is available on Zenodo[7].

[6] https://github.com/drndr/gencodesearchnet
[7] https://doi.org/10.5281/zenodo.8310891

Acknowledgements

This research is co-funded by the CodeInspector project (No. 504226141) of the DFG, German Research Foundation. The authors also acknowledge support by the state of Baden-Württemberg through bwHPC computing infrastructure. We would also like to thank Saurav Karmakar, Marcel Hoffmann, and Nicolas Lell for their insightful comments and reviews on our work.

Limitations

As with most benchmark collections, there is a risk that part of the test data has been present in the pre-training data of a large language model. As the new dataset StatCodeSeach is not based on code harvested from GitHub but from OSF, we assume that current language models did not have access to it in their pre-training data. However, due to the intransparency of the training set of corporate language models, we cannot fully exclude it.

We did not apply Ada 2 to the matching task. Although such embedding models can be also adapted for matching tasks, doing so in a zero-shot fashion is not straightforward as it would require determining a threshold on the (cosine) similarity. We also did not apply GPT-3.5 Turbo to the ranking task because of context size limitations and incurred costs for, e.g., running pair-wise ranking.

Our newly created dataset StatCodeSearch consists only of a single programming language, which is R. There are other tools and programming languages that are used by researchers for statistical analysis. For a more extensive dataset in the domain of statistical research code, StatCodeSearch could be extended with code snippets from SPSS, STATA, SAS, and Python.

Finally, it may seem counterintuitive that we have consulted GPT-3.5 Turbo for filtering, given its performance as a baseline for the matching is subpar. However, in the filtering step, the assessment of the pre-experiments showed that it was useful for discarding comments that were not suitable for the dataset, i.e., producing low numbers of false negatives. After this semi-automated pre-filtering, we manually filtered out the remaining code-comment pairs that were not suited for the dataset.

Ethical Considerations

Large language models come with ethical concerns regarding ethical bias, fairness, and transparency. The purpose of the paper is to introduce a benchmark that aims at increasing our understanding of large language models' capabilities in the application of code search. Therefore, we do not see any new risks introduced by our paper.

Our dataset is derived solely from source code files released under public licenses enabling re-distribution. As described in Husain et al. (2019) the CodeSearchNet dataset was filtered to include GitHub projects only with licenses explicitly permitting re-distribution. The CoSQA and CodeSearchNet AdvTest sets are released under the Computational Use of Data Agreement (C-UDA) on the official CodeXGLUE repository[8]. The newly created dataset StatCodeSearch consists of public content scraped from the Open Science Framework (OSF). All OSF content marked "Public" is available for commercial and non-commercial use according to the terms of use[9]. Additionally we filtered out projects that did not include public licenses explicitly permitting modification and re-distribution. The source code files in the StatCodeSearch dataset include the public licenses *Apache License, MIT License, CC-By Attribution 4.0, BSD 3-Clause, CC0 1.0 Universal, GNU General Public License, GNU Lesser General Public License*, and *Mozilla Public License*.

[8] https://github.com/microsoft/Computational-Use-of-Data-Agreement

[9] https://github.com/CenterForOpenScience/cos.io/blob/master/TERMS_OF_USE.md

References

Miltos Allamanis, Daniel Tarlow, Andrew Gordon, and Yi Wei. 2015. Bimodal modelling of source code and natural language. In *International conference on machine learning*, pages 2123–2132. PMLR.

Tom Brown, Benjamin Mann, Nick Ryder, Melanie Subbiah, Jared D Kaplan, Prafulla Dhariwal, Arvind Neelakantan, Pranav Shyam, Girish Sastry, Amanda Askell, et al. 2020. Language models are few-shot learners. *Advances in neural information processing systems*, 33:1877–1901.

José Cambronero, Hongyu Li, Seohyun Kim, Koushik Sen, and Satish Chandra. 2019. When deep learning met code search. In *Proceedings of the ACM Joint Meeting on European Software Engineering Conference and Symposium on the Foundations of Software Engineering, ESEC/SIGSOFT FSE 2019, Tallinn, Estonia, August 26-30, 2019*, pages 964–974. ACM.

Mark Chen, Jerry Tworek, Heewoo Jun, Qiming Yuan, Henrique Ponde de Oliveira Pinto, Jared Kaplan, Harri Edwards, Yuri Burda, Nicholas Joseph, Greg Brockman, et al. 2021. Evaluating large language models trained on code. *arXiv preprint arXiv:2107.03374*.

Jacob Devlin, Chang Ming-Wei, Lee Kenton, and Kristina Toutanova. 2019. BERT: Pre-training of deep bidirectional transformers for language understanding. In *Proceedings of NAACL-HLT*, pages 4171–4186.

Zhangyin Feng, Daya Guo, Duyu Tang, Nan Duan, Xiaocheng Feng, Ming Gong, Linjun Shou, Bing Qin, Ting Liu, Daxin Jiang, et al. 2020. CodeBERT: A pre-trained model for programming and natural languages. *arXiv preprint arXiv:2002.08155*.

Shahriar Golchin and Mihai Surdeanu. 2023. Time travel in llms: Tracing data contamination in large language models. *arXiv preprint arXiv:2308.08493*.

Igor Goldenberg and Geoffrey I Webb. 2019. Survey of distance measures for quantifying concept drift and shift in numeric data. *Knowledge and Information Systems*, 60(2):591–615.

Ian J. Goodfellow, Yoshua Bengio, and Aaron C. Courville. 2016. *Deep Learning*. Adaptive Computation and Machine Learning. MIT Press.

Daya Guo, Shuo Ren, Shuai Lu, Zhangyin Feng, Duyu Tang, Shujie Liu, Long Zhou, Nan Duan, Alexey Svyatkovskiy, Shengyu Fu, et al. 2020. Graphcodebert: Pre-training code representations with data flow. *arXiv preprint arXiv:2009.08366*.

Abram Hindle, Earl T. Barr, Zhendong Su, Mark Gabel, and Premkumar Devanbu. 2012. On the naturalness of software. In *Proceedings of the 34th International Conference on Software Engineering*, ICSE '12, page 837–847. IEEE Press.

Qiang Hu, Yuejun Guo, Xiaofei Xie, Maxime Cordy, Mike Papadakis, Lei Ma, and Yves Le Traon. 2023. Codes: towards code model generalization under distribution shift. In *International Conference on Software Engineering (ICSE): New Ideas and Emerging Results (NIER)*.

Junjie Huang, Duyu Tang, Linjun Shou, Ming Gong, Ke Xu, Daxin Jiang, Ming Zhou, and Nan Duan. 2021. Cosqa: 20,000+ web queries for code search and question answering. In *Proceedings of the 59th Annual Meeting of the Association for Computational Linguistics and the 11th International Joint Conference on Natural Language Processing (Volume 1: Long Papers)*, pages 5690–5700.

Dieuwke Hupkes, Mario Giulianelli, Verna Dankers, Mikel Artetxe, Yanai Elazar, Tiago Pimentel, Christos Christodoulopoulos, Karim Lasri, Naomi Saphra, Arabella Sinclair, et al. 2023. A taxonomy and review of generalization research in NLP. *Nature Machine Intelligence*, 5(10):1161–1174.

Hamel Husain, Ho-Hsiang Wu, Tiferet Gazit, Miltiadis Allamanis, and Marc Brockschmidt. 2019. Codesearchnet challenge: Evaluating the state of semantic code search. *arXiv preprint arXiv:1909.09436*.

Samia Kabir, David N Udo-Imeh, Bonan Kou, and Tianyi Zhang. 2023. Who answers it better? an in-depth analysis of chatgpt and stack overflow answers to software engineering questions. *arXiv preprint arXiv:2308.02312*.

Quentin Lhoest, Albert Villanova del Moral, Yacine Jernite, Abhishek Thakur, Patrick von Platen, Suraj Patil, Julien Chaumond, Mariama Drame, Julien Plu, Lewis Tunstall, et al. 2021. Datasets: A community library for natural language processing. In *Proceedings of the 2021 Conference on Empirical Methods in Natural Language Processing: System Demonstrations*, pages 175–184.

Xiaonan Li, Yeyun Gong, Yelong Shen, Xipeng Qiu, Hang Zhang, Bolun Yao, Weizhen Qi, Daxin Jiang, Weizhu Chen, and Nan Duan. 2022a. CodeRetriever: A large scale contrastive pre-training method for code search. In *Proceedings of the 2022 Conference on Empirical Methods in Natural Language Processing*, pages 2898–2910, Abu Dhabi, United Arab Emirates. Association for Computational Linguistics.

Xiaonan Li, Yeyun Gong, Yelong Shen, Xipeng Qiu, Hang Zhang, Bolun Yao, Weizhen Qi, Daxin Jiang, Weizhu Chen, and Nan Duan. 2022b. Coderetriever: Unimodal and bimodal contrastive learning. *arXiv preprint arXiv:2201.10866*.

Jimmy Lin, Rodrigo Nogueira, and Andrew Yates. 2022. *Pretrained transformers for text ranking: Bert and beyond*. Springer Nature.

Yinhan Liu, Myle Ott, Naman Goyal, Jingfei Du, Mandar Joshi, Danqi Chen, Omer Levy, Mike Lewis, Luke Zettlemoyer, and Veselin Stoyanov. 2019.

RoBERTa: A robustly optimized BERT pretraining approach. *arXiv preprint arXiv:1907.11692*.

Shuai Lu, Daya Guo, Shuo Ren, Junjie Huang, Alexey Svyatkovskiy, Ambrosio Blanco, Colin Clement, Dawn Drain, Daxin Jiang, Duyu Tang, et al. 2021. Codexglue: A machine learning benchmark dataset for code understanding and generation. In *Thirty-fifth Conference on Neural Information Processing Systems Datasets and Benchmarks Track (Round 1)*.

Sifei Luan, Di Yang, Celeste Barnaby, Koushik Sen, and Satish Chandra. 2019. Aroma: code recommendation via structural code search. *Proc. ACM Program. Lang.*, 3(OOPSLA):152:1–152:28.

Christopher D Manning. 2009. *An introduction to information retrieval*. Cambridge university press.

Rohan Mukherjee, Chris Jermaine, and Swarat Chaudhuri. 2020. Searching a database of source codes using contextualized code search. *Proc. VLDB Endow.*, 13(10):1765–1778.

Arvind Neelakantan, Tao Xu, Raul Puri, Alec Radford, Jesse Michael Han, Jerry Tworek, Qiming Yuan, Nikolas Tezak, Jong Wook Kim, Chris Hallacy, et al. 2022. Text and code embeddings by contrastive pretraining. *arXiv preprint arXiv:2201.10005*.

Changan Niu, Chuanyi Li, Vincent Ng, and Bin Luo. 2023. Crosscodebench: Benchmarking cross-task generalization of source code models. *arXiv preprint arXiv:2302.04030*.

Long Ouyang, Jeffrey Wu, Xu Jiang, Diogo Almeida, Carroll Wainwright, Pamela Mishkin, Chong Zhang, Sandhini Agarwal, Katarina Slama, Alex Ray, et al. 2022. Training language models to follow instructions with human feedback. *Advances in Neural Information Processing Systems*, 35:27730–27744.

Florian Sihler. 2023. Constructing a static program slicer for R programs. Master's thesis, Ulm University.

Venkatesh Vinayakarao, Anita Sarma, Rahul Purandare, Shuktika Jain, and Saumya Jain. 2017. ANNE: improving source code search using entity retrieval approach. In *Proceedings of the Tenth ACM International Conference on Web Search and Data Mining, WSDM 2017, Cambridge, United Kingdom, February 6-10, 2017*, pages 211–220. ACM.

Yue Wang, Hung Le, Akhilesh Deepak Gotmare, Nghi DQ Bui, Junnan Li, and Steven CH Hoi. 2023. Codet5+: Open code large language models for code understanding and generation. *arXiv preprint arXiv:2305.07922*.

Yue Wang, Weishi Wang, Shafiq Joty, and Steven CH Hoi. 2021. Codet5: Identifier-aware unified pre-trained encoder-decoder models for code understanding and generation. *arXiv preprint arXiv:2109.00859*.

Thomas Wolf, Lysandre Debut, Victor Sanh, Julien Chaumond, Clement Delangue, Anthony Moi, Pierric Cistac, Tim Rault, Rémi Louf, Morgan Funtowicz, et al. 2019. Huggingface's transformers: State-of-the-art natural language processing. *arXiv preprint arXiv:1910.03771*.

Ming Zhu, Aneesh Jain, Karthik Suresh, Roshan Ravindran, Sindhu Tipirneni, and Chandan K Reddy. 2022. Xlcost: A benchmark dataset for cross-lingual code intelligence. *arXiv preprint arXiv:2206.08474*.

A Appendix

A.1 Hyperparameter choice

For RoBERTa, we adopt best practices with a learning rate of 2×10^{-5}, 5 epochs, batch size of 32, weight decay of 0.01, and sequence length of 512. For CodeBERT, we follow the original paper's parameters, while adjusting the sequence length to 512 tokens for consistent comparisons. This involves a learning rate of 1×10^{-5}, a batch size of 32, and 8 epochs. Similarly, CodeT5+ adheres to its original parameters, but with a sequence length of 512 tokens and a batch size of 32 to ensure fairness.

Table 4: Hyperparameter settings for our language models

Hyperparameter	RoBERTa	CodeBERT	CodeT5+
Learning rate	2×10^{-5}	1×10^{-5}	2×10^{-5}
Epochs	5	8	10
Batch size	32	32	32
Weight decay	0.01	0.01	0.01
Sequence length	512	512	512

A.2 Breakdown of CodeSearchNet Results

Table 5 shows the breakdown of the CodeSearchNet by programming language. The numbers for in-distribution fine-tuning (fine-tuning for each individual language before testing) were taken from the original CodeBERT paper (Feng et al., 2020), where for each sample 999 distractors were chosen. Although this makes the comparison to our numbers (with only 99 distractors) unfair, we can still observe a substantial decrease in performance when a model is fine-tuned on out-of-distribution data.

A.3 GPT 3.5 Turbo Prompts

In the below sections, we report the prompts used for categorization and matching tasks for each of the test sets. GPT-3.5 was employed with default parameters, except for limit of 10 output tokens.

Table 5: Breakdown of the CodeSearchNet Results by Programming Language

Model	Ruby		Go		PHP		Java		JavaScript	
	Acc	MRR	Acc	MRR	Acc	MRR	Acc	MRR	Acc	MRR
Fine-tuned Models iid										
RoBERTa (Feng et al., 2020)	-	0.6245	-	0.6809	-	0.6576	-	0.6659	-	0.6060
CodeBERT (Feng et al., 2020)	-	0.6926	-	0.8400	-	0.7062	-	0.7484	-	0.7059
Fine-tuned Models ood										
RoBERTa	92.71	0.1551	99.18	0.0469	89.73	0.0917	90.69	0.1228	90.85	0.1109
CodeBERT	89.71	0.1451	94.55	0.0668	87.21	0.0742	91.24	0.0822	90.10	0.0850
CodeT5+ (encoder only)	87.47	0.1003	91.86	0.0158	85.03	0.0568	86.04	0.0594	86.30	0.0756
Zero-shot Models										
CodeT5+ (encoder only)	-	0.8398	-	0.8467	-	0.8000	-	0.7939	-	0.8185
GPT 3.5 Turbo	58.70	-	59.50	-	56.41	-	61.30	-	58.19	-
Ada 2	-	0.8942	-	0.9093	-	0.8684	-	0.8761	-	0.8782

A.3.1 Zero-shot code comment categorization

Task: Classify the code comment {Input} based on the categories provided below. If the comment doesn't fit into any of these categories, label it as 'No Relevant Class'. Categories: [Statistical Test], [Statistical Modeling], [Data Variable], [Visualization]

A.3.2 Matching

StatCodeSearch, CodeSearchNet and CodeSearchNet AdvTest

Given a code comment and a {Add the programming language name} programming language code snippet, determine if the comment accurately represents the code's function. Respond with 'True' if the code matches the comment and 'False' if it does not. The input format is defined as "comment" "[CODESPLIT]" "code". {Input}

CoSQA

Given a search query and a Python programming language code snippet, determine if the query accurately represents the code's function. Respond with 'True' if the code matches the query and 'False' if it does not. The input format is defined as "query" "[CODESPLIT]" "code". {Input}

A.4 GenBench Evaluation Card

In Table 6, we provide the evaluation card proposed by (Hupkes et al., 2023) for our experimental setups showcasing the different aspects of generalization our dataset studies.

Motivation			
Practical	*Cognitive*	*Intrinsic*	*Fairness*
□ △ ○			

Generalisation type					
Compositional	*Structural*	*Cross Task*	*Cross Language*	*Cross Domain*	*Robustness*
			□ △	△	○

Shift type			
Covariate	*Label*	*Full*	*Assumed*
□ △ ○			

Shift source			
Naturally occuring	*Partitioned natural*	*Generated shift*	*Fully generated*
□ △ ○			

Shift locus			
Train–test	*Finetune train–test*	*Pretrain–train*	*Pretrain–test*
	□ △ ○		□ △ ○

Table 6: GenBench Evaluation Card:
□CodeSearchNet
△StatCodeSearch
○CodeSearchNet Adv & CoSQA

Adapt and Decompose: Efficient Generalization of Text-to-SQL via Domain Adapted Least-To-Most Prompting

Aseem Arora, Shabbirhussain Bhaisaheb, Harshit Nigam,
Manasi Patwardhan, Lovekesh Vig, Gautam Shroff
TCS Research, India
{aseem.arora, shabbirhussain.b, h.nigam,
manasi.patwardhan, lovekesh.vig, gautam.shroff}@tcs.com

Abstract

Cross-domain and cross-compositional generalization of Text-to-SQL semantic parsing is a challenging task. Existing Large Language Model (LLM) based solutions rely on inference-time retrieval of few-shot exemplars from the training set to synthesize a run-time prompt for each Natural Language (NL) test query. In contrast, we devise an algorithm which performs offline sampling of a minimal set-of few-shots from the training data, with complete coverage of SQL clauses, operators and functions, and maximal domain coverage within the allowed token length. This allows for synthesis of a fixed Generic Prompt (GP), with a diverse set-of exemplars common across NL test queries, avoiding expensive test time exemplar retrieval. We further auto-adapt the GP to the target database domain (DA-GP), to better handle cross-domain generalization; followed by a decomposed Least-To-Most-Prompting (LTMP-DA-GP) to handle cross-compositional generalization. The synthesis of LTMP-DA-GP is an offline task, to be performed one-time per new database with minimal human intervention. Our approach demonstrates superior performance on the KaggleDBQA dataset, designed to evaluate generalizability for the Text-to-SQL task. We further showcase consistent performance improvement of LTMP-DA-GP over GP, across LLMs and databases of KaggleDBQA, highlighting the efficacy and model agnostic benefits of our prompt based adapt and decompose approach.

1 Introduction

Recently, Large Language Models (LLMs) such as GPT3(Brown et al., 2020a), Codex(Chen et al., 2021b), PaLM(Chowdhery et al., 2022), pretrained with massive volumes of data have shown improved performance for multiple reasoning tasks using in-context learning (Brown et al., 2020b; Huang and Chang, 2022), including program synthesis (Austin et al., 2021; Jain et al., 2021; Nijkamp et al., 2022) and semantic parsing (Shin and Durme, 2021; Drozdov et al., 2022; Shin and Durme, 2021; Shin et al., 2021). There are a few recent approaches where LLMs are specifically used for Text-to-SQL semantic parsing in a (i) zero-shot setting (Rajkumar et al., 2022a; Chang and Fosler-Lussier, 2023; Nan et al., 2023) where only the test Natural Language (NL) query constitutes the prompt, (ii) few-shot setting where exemplars similar to the test query in the target domain are retrieved from the available training data and appended to the test NL query to constitute the prompt (Poesia et al., 2022a; Chang and Fosler-Lussier, 2023; Nan et al., 2023; An et al., 2023). For this setting the available NL-SQL pairs would belong to domains that are different from the target database domain (iii) few-shot setting where exemplars are sampled NL-SQL queries available for the target-domain with maximum coverage of compositions (Rajkumar et al., 2022a; Qiu et al., 2022; Hosseini et al., 2022; Yang et al., 2022; Chang and Fosler-Lussier, 2023). In this paper, we are mainly interested in (ii) i.e. cross-domain generalization along with the scenario where the test queries may not have the set-of compositions covered in the training data (cross-composition generalizability). Moreover, considering a purely cross-domain setting, as opposed to (iii) above, we assume NO availability of exemplars belonging to the target databases. One solution to this setting is manual synthesis of few-shots for every new target database from scratch. However, this process is very tedious, time-consuming and also does not ensure diversity in the few-shots, with good coverage of SQL operators. Thus, there is a need for an efficient approach which can exploit available NL-SQL pairs from distinct domains, to intelligently sample few-shots and design prompts.

Synchromesh (Poesia et al., 2022a) and (Nan et al., 2023; An et al., 2023) have a similar setting, except they retrieve exemplars during run-time (during inference) by selecting NL queries as

Proceedings of the 1st GenBench Workshop on (Benchmarking) Generalisation in NLP, pages 25–47
December 6, 2023 ©2023 Association for Computational Linguistics

exemplars with similarity based on (a) NL query semantics (Nan et al., 2023) or (b) target SQLs (Target Similarity Tuning) (Poesia et al., 2022a) or (c) LLM generated 'skill' based NL representation, focusing on program compositions and ignoring the surface NL forms (An et al., 2023). This reliance on inference-time retrieval of similar few-shots from the available data to build a run-time prompt and generate SQL for a test NL query, results in a less efficient solution. As opposed to this, we devise an algorithm which samples a minimal set-of few-shots from the training data ensuring complete coverage of SQL clauses, operators and functions and maximum coverage of database domains, which fits into the token length restriction. We append these few-shots with the out-of-distribution test NL query to define what we term as a *Generic Prompt (GP)*, which is further used to generate the corresponding SQL. The *GP* is generated offline and is common across distinct test queries, resulting in a more time-efficient solution obviating the need for real time retrieval. We further auto-adapt the GP to (a) the target database domain, and refer to it as domain adapted GP (*DA-GP*), to better handle cross-domain generalization, (b) decompose it into a Least-To-Most-Prompting approach (Zhou et al., 2022) (*LTMP-GP*) to better handle cross-compositional generalization, and (c) combine the approaches (a) and (b) to exploit their complementary benefits (*LTMP-DA-GP*). In line with our motivation, formation of *LTMP-DA-GP* is an efficient solution, as it is an offline task to be performed one-time per new database and is mostly programmatic with minimal human intervention (only needed for validation of prompts). We further demonstrate a consistent performance improvement of (a) and (b) over the base *GP* and (c) over (a) and (b) on the databases of Kaggle-DBQA dataset (Lee et al., 2021a), designed to evaluate the generalizability of the Text-to-SQL task using distinct LLMs. Moreover, our approach not only yields an efficient solution, but also yields best performance for the used LLMs on KaggleDBQA. Following are our main contributions:

- To the best of our knowledge, apart from (Nan et al., 2023) ours is the only approach to implement offline programmatic prompt generation ensuring diversity of samples for NL-to-SQL task. Moreover, as opposed to (Nan et al., 2023), our *GP* based sampling technique guarantees complete coverage of SQL operators and maximum converge of database domains.
- Ours is the first approach of programmatic domain-adaptation of prompt, consistently showcasing performance improvement across multiple Kaggle-DBQA databases validating NL-to-SQL domain generalization capability.
- Ours is the first approach applying Least-to-Most-Prompting (Zhou et al., 2022) for compositional generalization of complex NL-to-SQL task, showcasing consistent performance improvement across LLMs.
- As compared to existing similarity based exemplar sampling approaches (Poesia et al., 2022b; Chang and Fosler-Lussier, 2023; An et al., 2023), our approach of offline prompts synthesis proves to be more efficient.
- Our pipeline yields the best performance on the *KaggleDBQA* dataset, reported in the literature for the used LLMs.

2 Datasets

Spider (Gan et al., 2022): Is a large-scale, complex, and cross-domain Text-to-SQL benchmark dataset with a total of 200 databases (140, 20, 40 in the training, development and test splits with 7000, 1034, and 2147 Text-to-SQL pairs). We use state-of-the-art models trained on Spider to benchmark performance of our approach against supervised approaches. We also use the training split of *Spider* to sample the exemplars, which serve as few-shots in our prompt (Section 4).

Spider-CG (Gan et al., 2022): This dataset is designed for evaluating Text-to-SQL compositional generalization performance. To synthesize this dataset, Text-to-SQL pairs from *Spider-Train* are transformed to corresponding sub-sentences and NatSQL pairs to form *Spider-SS* dataset. The sub-sentences are obtained using a sentence-split algorithm and the corresponding NatSQL, which is an intermediate representation of SQL, is manually annotated. We use the *Spider-SS* for the Least-To-Most-Prompting (LTMP) experiment, by retrieving the NL query decompositions in terms of sub-sentences and the corresponding intermediate NatSQL representations for few-shots sampled from *Spider-Train*, to synthesize prompts for each stage of LTMP (Section 4.4).

Kaggle-DBQA (Lee et al., 2021b): This is a cross-domain Text-to-SQL evaluation dataset with

Figure 1: Comparison of our Approach (A) GP (B) DA-GP (Stage 1, 2, 3) and (C) LTMP-DA-GP (Stage 1, 2, 3) with Prior Zero-shot, Query-Similarity based Few-shot Approaches

real world databases (DB). It covers a total of 8 DBs, viz. (i) Nuclear (10,22), (ii) Crime (9,18), (iii) Pesticide (16, 34), (iv) MathScore (9,19), (v) Baseball (12,27), (vi) Fires (12, 25), (vii) WhatCD (13,28), and (viii) Soccer (6,12), indicating fine-tuning and test examples, respectively. As we assume a purely cross-domain setting with no availability of in-domain few-shots, we do not use the fine-tuning samples but use only the test samples to evaluate our proposed LLM based pipelines. We prefer Kaggle-DBQA over other cross-domain and composition evaluation datasets such as spider-CG (Gan et al., 2022), because it is a real-web dataset and contains fewer test queries allowing us to showcase the efficacy of our approach using commercial LLMs with low cost overheads.

3 Large Language Models (LLMs)

The literature has demonstrated state-of-the-art few-shot performance for NL-to-SQL (Rajkumar et al., 2022a; Nan et al., 2023; Chang and Fosler-Lussier, 2023) tasks, with Codex (Chen et al., 2021a) (Code-da-Vincci) (Chen et al., 2021b) and GPT4[1] from OpenAI. However, Codex is discontinued by OpenAI [2] and the cost of GPT4 is very high. Instead, we use two LLMs to demonstrate the efficacy of the proposed pipeline, viz. OpenAI's GPT-3.5-Turbo (ChatGPT), which is 60x cheaper than GPT4 and Text-da-Vinci-003, which is 6x cheaper than GPT4, both with 175B parameters and 4096 token length restriction [3]. We have not used other open-source models pretrained on code, such as CodeT5+ (Wang et al., 2023) (768 token length) or Codegen (2048 token length) (Nijkamp et al., 2022) for our study as they do not offer the token length required for our prompt (4K).

[1]https://platform.openai.com/docs/models/gpt-4

[2]Starting 23rd March, 2023.

[3]https://platform.openai.com/docs/models/gpt-3-5

4 Approach

4.1 Database Schema Format

As the part of the prompt design, an important choice we make is the format of the schema of the Databases(DBs) to which the sampled few-shot exemplars and the test query belong. Each of our experiment, we keep the format of the DBs for the few-shots and the test (target) DB to be consistent. Existing approaches, yield state-of-the-art zero and few-shot results on *Spider-Dev* dataset and its variants using *CREATE TABLE* schema format with (i) TEN selected rows (Rajkumar et al., 2022b), (ii) THREE column values (Chang and Fosler-Lussier, 2023) or (iii) semantic augmentation with blocked column descriptions (Nan et al., 2023). These approaches can afford to use these elaborate schema formats because of the use of Codex and GPT4 LLMs with allowable $> 8K$ token lengths. As opposed to this, we use models with smaller allowable token length of maximum $4K$ (Section Section 3). To allow the the inclusion of few-shot exemplars in the *Generic Prompt* sampled by our algorithm (Section 4.2) along with the reasoning Least-to-Most-Prompting (LTMP) stages (*LTMP-GP*: Section 4.4), we compromise on the elaborate schema format to fit the prompt in the allowable token length. For the *GP* and *LTMP-GP* based pipelines we use the *CREATE TABLE* database schema format with Primary-Key and Foreign-Key constraints, but without the mention of column data-types and inclusion of row/column values and descriptions (Figure 1). With domain adaptation of the *GP* to the target database (Section 4.3), we require inclusion of only one (target) schema in the prompt allowing us to use an elaborate schema format. Thus, for the domain adaptation *DA-GP* and it's further enhancement with LTMP (LTMP-DA-GP: Section 4.5), we include the domain information to the *CREATE TABLE* format (Figure 1) in the form of (i) column data-types, (ii) randomly sampled FOUR values for categorical and date-time columns, (iii) range of values for numerical columns and (iv) additional column descriptions, wherever necessary.

4.2 Generic Prompt (GP) Design Algorithm

We have defined Algorithm 1 to sample the few-shots to form Generic Prompt (*GP*). The algorithm is designed to select exemplars from a dataset with available text-SQL annotations, to ensure complete coverage of SQL clauses, operators and functions and maximum coverage of domains (databases) which can fit into the allowable token length. We assume to have an annotated dataset $D = \{db_j, \{t_{ij}, s_{ij}, a_{ij}\}_{i=1}^{N_j}\}_{j=1}^{M}$, where t and s are the annotated text-SQL query pairs posed on databases db and a are the answers of the SQL queries after execution, N_j are the query pairs of database db_j, M are total number of databases. We have a test dataset $T = \{db_l, \{t_{kl}, s_{kl}, a_{kl}\}_{k=1}^{K_l}\}_{l=1}^{L}$ of $\sum_{l=1}^{L} K_l$ query pairs and L databases, such that $\{db_j\}_{j=1}^{M} \cap \{db_l\}_{l=1}^{L} = \phi$. Thus, as we consider completely cross-domain setting, we do not have any overlap between the training and test databases. We manually collect SQL operators, clauses and functions covered by queries $s_{ij} \in D$ to form a set-of primitive operations O, including (i) SQL Clauses ('FROM', 'HAVING', 'WHERE', 'ORDER BY', etc), (ii) SQL Operators such as arithmetic (+, -, *, /, %), comparison (=, !=, $<$, $>$, etc) and logical (ALL, AND, ANY, LIKE, etc) and (iii) SQL Functions (AVG, COUNT, MAX, MIN, etc).

To sample the few-shot exemplars E for the *GP*, we sort the databases $db_j \in D$ based on the operator coverage by the SQL queries s_{ij}. We perform query-pair (sample) traversal of this ordered list of databases. A sample $\{db_j, t_{ij}, s_{ij}\}$ becomes part of E, if s_{ij} covers at the least one uncovered primitive operation in O. If s_{ij} covers a super-set of primitive operations of any query s_x in an existing exemplar $\{db_x, t_x, s_x\} \in E$ then this exemplar is replaced by $\{db_i, t_{ij}, s_{ij}\}$. The algorithm terminates when all the possible primitive operations in O are covered by exemplars in E. This algorithm allows us to sample a minimal set of query-pairs as exemplars covering the complete set of primitive operations. This brings in diversity in the compositions of the SQL queries chosen as exemplars. The database ordering as per the primitive operator coverage, ensures minimal set of DB schema to be added in the GP, exhausting less number of tokens. However, selection of multiple DBs achieves diversity in the domains covered. We append the sampled few-shot exemplars with a NL test query, which is a sample $\{db_l, t_{lk}\} \in T$, retaining the consistency in the schema representation, forming the *GP* (Figure 1).

4.3 Domain Adaptation of GP (DA-GP)

As ours is a completely cross-domain setting, the *GP* consists of domains defined by database for which the few-shots are sampled from the train-dataset, which are distinct from the target database. We auto-adapt these few-shots to the domain of the

Algorithm 1: Generic Prompt Creation

```
Input    : D = {db_j, {t_ij, s_ij, a_ij}_{i=1}^{N_j}}_{j=1}^{M}
    // Dataset with databases, text, SQL
    queries and answer tuples
T = {db_l, {t_kl, s_kl, a_kl}_{k=1}^{K_l}}_{l=1}^{L} // Test Set
O = {Operators, Clauses, Functions} // Set
    of SQL Primitive Operators
Output   :GP // Generic Prompt
Initial Stage :
E ← Φ // Set of Exemplars
D ←Sort(Extract_Operators(db_j in D)) // Sort
    databases in D on operator coverage
for s_ij ∈ D do
    O_e ← Extract_Operators(s_ij) // Extract
        operators from training SQL
    if (o ∈ O_e) ∈ O then
        // an operator is not covered
        for s_x ∈ E do
            if Extract_Operators(s_x) ⊆ O_e then
                E ← E − {db_x, t_x, s_x}
                    // Remove existing
                    exemplar with operators
                    to be subset of current
                    exemplar operators
            end if
        end for
        E ← E + {db_j, t_ij, s_ij} // Add the
            tuple as an Exemplar
        O ← O − O_e // Remove covered
            operators
    end if
end for
GP ← E + {db_l, t_kl} ∈ T
```

target database, keeping the query compositions consistent. The hypothesis is that the adaptation should facilitate the LLMs to achieve better performance on the queries of the target domain. This task is performed in three stages.

Stage1: Generating Compositionally similar SQLs in the target domain: For each few-shot SQL query in the *GP* we feed the serialized source schema and SQL (without NL) along with the serialized target schema and prompt the LLM to generate SQL on the target schema which is compositionally similar to the source query, by explaining what is compositional similarity. We sample SQL queries from the beam, until we find an executable SQL query on the target DB, whose skeleton has the tree edit distance to be within a threshold to that of the skeleton of the original few-shot SQL query. This ensures compositional similarity (Figure 1).

Stage2: Generating text queries for the SQL queries: We feed each compositionally similar SQL, generated for each few-shot exemplar in the *GP*, to the LLM along with the target schema and prompts it to generate the NL question which describes the SQL query in text form. This step allows us to have a NL-SQL pair in the target domain (database) for each few-shot exemplar in the *GP*.

Stage 3: Using Domain Adapted GP to generate SQLs for the test NL queries: We form *Domain Adapted Generic Prompt(DA-GP)* using the target schema with the available domain information (Section 4.1) and the domain specific NL-SQL few-shot pairs. Note that *DA-GP* has one database schema consistent across the few-shots as well as the test query. We append the test NL query to *DA-GP* and feed it to the LLM to generate SQL.

4.4 Least-to-Most-Prompting with GP (LTMP-GP)

The *GP* covers all the primitive SQL Operations, Clauses and Functions. However, few-shots cover only a few compositions of these primitive operations. We perform LTMP to help the LLMs achieve generalizability on compositions unseen in the few-shots as well as in the pre-training data. To achieve this, we decompose the NL-to-SQL task into the following three sub-tasks and semi-auto-adapt each of the few-shot exemplars in the *GP* for each of the following sub-tasks (Figure 1). The hypothesis is that the decomposition of few-shots, helps exposing the underlying NL-SQL mappings at more primitive level, through the NAT-SQL based intermediate representations, which can be reused by the LLMs to synthesize SQLs for unseen compositions.

Stage 1: NL Query Decomposition: The few-shot NL queries in *GP* sampled from *Spider-Train*, along with their decompositions fetched from the *Spider-SS* (Section 2) forms the prompt for the first stage of LTMP. We append it with the test NL query to generate the decomposition for the same. For exploiting the reasoning capabilities of LLMs, for each few-shot, we manually include the Chain-Of-Thoughts (COT) behind the decomposition of the NL queries, in terms of explaining the choice of split point (semantic segmentation) of the NL.

Stage 2: Mapping of NatSQL to NL decomposition: The few-shot NL queries in *GP* sampled from *Spider-Train*, along with their decompositions and NAT-SQLs, which is an intermediate representations of ground truth SQLs, fetched from *Spider-SS* (Section 2) forms the prompt for the second stage of LTMP. For each few-shot, we explain the COT behind the mapping of each decomposed NL query to the NatSQL, in terms of selection of the SQL clause for the NatSQL (part of the skeleton of

Model	Approach	Database-wise Execution Accuracy (%Ex)								Total
		Geo Nuclear	Greater Manchester	Pesticide	Student Maths Score	The History of Baseball	US Wildfires	What CD Hiphop	World Soccer	% Ex
GPT-Turbo-3.5 (Benchmark)	Zero-Shot	27.27	33.33	19.35	10.93	11.11	32.00	7.69	41.67	21.11
	QP-TX †	31.82	44.44	29.03	15.79	11.11	28.00	34.62	8.33	26.11
	QP-TE †	27.27	27.78	22.58	15.79	25.93	44.00	26.82	33.33	27.78
	DIN-SQL †	-	-	-	-	-	-	-	-	27.00
Text-da-Vinci-003 (Benchmark)	Zero-Shot	27.27	22.22	29.03	15.79	18.52	20.00	7.69	8.33	19.44
	QP-TX †	27.27	33.33	19.35	10.93	11.11	32.00	7.69	41.67	21.11
	QP-TE †	27.27	33.33	19.35	10.93	11.11	32.00	7.69	41.67	21.11
	DIN-SQL †	45.45	33.33	20.59	21.05	18.52	50.00	21.43	25.00	29.18
	QP-SK	-	-	-	-	-	-	-	-	**36.80**
GPT-Turbo-3.5 **(Ours)**	GP	31.82	27.78	29.03	5.26	14.81	36.00	23.08	25.00	24.44
	DA-GP	40.91	33.33	**35.48**	10.53	22.22	20.00	15.38	25.00	25.56
	LTMP-GP	27.27	**50.00**	29.03	10.53	14.81	52.00	30.77	33.33	30.56
	LTMP-DA-GP	**50.00**	22.22	32.26	**15.79**	**22.22**	**60.00**	**30.77**	**33.33**	**33.89**
Text-da-Vinci-003 **(Ours)**	GP	31.82	22.22	35.48	10.53	11.11	20.00	15.38	16.67	21.11
	DA-GP	40.91	27.78	**45.16**	21.05	18.52	44.00	15.38	25.00	30.56
	LTMP-GP	59.09	44.44	41.18	21.05	22.22	52.00	21.43	25.00	36.41
	LTMP-DA-GP	**63.64**	**44.44**	41.18	**26.32**	**22.22**	**56.00**	**21.43**	**25.00**	**38.04**

Table 1: Kaggle DBQA - Results. Comparison with zero and few-shot approaches, QP-TX: Query specific TeXt-based Similarity(Poesia et al., 2022b), QP-TE:Query specific Tree-Edit-distance-based Similarity (Poesia et al., 2022b), QP-SK: Query specific Skill based Similarity (An et al., 2023), DIN-SQL (Pourreza and Rafiei, 2023), †Few-shots: 16, Result: **Overall Best**,**Best for the LLM**

Model	Approach	%EX
RATSQL (Gan et al., 2022)	Supervised Trained with *Spider-Train* (Gan et al., 2022)	13.56
T53B (Lan et al., 2023)		26.80
SmBOP (Rubin and Berant, 2020)		27.20
RASAT (Qi et al., 2022)		27.60
Picard (Scholak et al., 2021)		29.80
REDSQL (Li et al., 2023)		31.90
UL-20B (Lan et al., 2023)		34.90
RASAT (Rubin and Berant, 2020)	Supervised Trained on *UNITE* (Lan et al., 2023)	26.80
T53B (Lan et al., 2023)		33.80
Picard (Scholak et al., 2021)		**36.80**
GPT-Turbo-3.5 **(Ours)**	LTMP-DA-GP	33.89
Text-da-Vinci-003 **(Ours)**	LTMP-DA-GP	**38.04**

Table 2: Kaggle DBQA - Exec. Acc. **Best**, **Second Best**. Supervised Approaches Comparision

NatSQL) and schema linking including specific table(s) and Column(s) selected for the NL decomposition to form the NatSQL. We append the prompt with the test NL query followed by its decompositions generated in the prior stage, to generate the NatSQL for each decomposition.

Stage 3: Generating SQL from NatSQL: We auto-generate the third stage prompt of *LTMP-GP* to include the few-shot NL queries in the *GP* with their decompositions, corresponding NatSQLs and the ground truth SQLs. We append this with the test NL query, its decompositions and corresponding NatSQLs generated in the prior stages to generate the SQL for the test NL.

4.5 LTMP with DA-GP (LTMP-DA-GP)

To exploit the complementary advantages of domain adaptation (domain generalization) and least-to-most prompting (compositional generalization), we perform LTMP over *DA-GP* with executing all the three stages explained in the Section 4.4 to construct the *LTMP-DA-GP* . For this the domain adapted NL query decompositions and NAT-SQLs are manually created. We append the test NL query to the prompt of the first stage and the outputs of the prior stages to the subsequent stages recursively, as explained in Section 4.4, to finally generate the SQL as the result of the last stage.

5 Results and Discussion

5.1 Benchmarks

State-of-the-art supervised approaches: Include models (Table 2 trained with *Spider-Train* and *UNITE* (Lan et al., 2023) datasets and yielding SOTA results on *Spider-Dev* and its variants.

Zero-shot approaches: (Rajkumar et al., 2022b; Chang and Fosler-Lussier, 2023; Nan et al., 2023), yield SOTA results on *Spider-Dev* and its variants with Codex and GPT4 as LLMs. For fair comparison, we compute zero-shot *KaggleDBQA* results with our schema format and LLMs.

Existing few-shot approaches: Few-shots are sampled using Top-K samples from the train set using following sampling strategies found in the literature. For fair comparison, we choose the number few-shots (K) to be the same as the number of exemplars in the *GP*. (i) Test Query specific TeXt-based Similarity sampling (QP-TX) (Poesia et al., 2022b): having maximum semantic similarity (Reimers and Gurevych, 2019) with the test NL query, (ii) Test Query specific Tree-Edit-distance-based Similarity sampling (QP-TE) (Poesia et al., 2022b): having maximum target program based

	GP	DA	LTMP-DA	No.	Category	Illustrative Samples	%
Case 1	✗	✓	✓	1	Rectifying values	***NL**: Show all fires caused by campfires in Texas.* ***GT**: SELECT * FROM Fires WHERE STAT_CAUSE_DESCR = "Campfire" AND State = "TX"* ***GP**: SELECT * FROM Fires WHERE STAT_CAUSE_DESCR = 'Campfire' AND STATE = 'Texas'* ***DA**:SELECT * FROM Fires WHERE STAT_CAUSE_DESCR = 'Campfire' AND STATE = 'TX'* ***LTMP-DA**:SELECT * FROM Fires WHERE STAT_CAUSE_DESCR = "Campfire" AND STATE = "TX"*	5.38
				2	Rectifying columns	***NL**: How many number of units are there in sample 9628?* ***GT**: SELECT quantity FROM sampledata15 WHERE sample_pk = 9628* ***GP**: SELECT conunit FROM resultsdata15 WHERE sample_pk = 9628* ***DA-GP**:SELECT quantity FROM sampledata15 WHERE sample_pk = 9628* ***LTMP-DA**:SELECT quantity FROM sampledata15 WHERE sample_pk = 9628*	4.61
Case 2	✗	✗	✓	1	Extra SELECT + Operation on Column	***NL**: Which country lead the total capacity of the power plants it held?* ***GT**: SELECT Country FROM nuclear_power_plants GROUP BY Country ORDER BY sum(Capacity) DESC LIMIT 1* ***GP**: SELECT Country, SUM(Capacity) AS TotalCapacity FROM nuclear_power_plants GROUP BY Country ORDER BY TotalCapacity DESC LIMIT 1* ***DA**: SELECT Country, SUM(Capacity) AS TotalCapacity FROM nuclear_power_plants GROUP BY Country ORDER BY TotalCapacity DESC LIMIT 1* ***LTMP-DA**: SELECT Country FROM nuclear_power_plants GROUP BY Country ORDER BY SUM(Capacity) DESC LIMIT 1*	5.51
				2	Correcting Operations	***NL**: Which country has the least capacities of nuclear power plants?* ***GT**: SELECT Country FROM nuclear_power_plants GROUP BY Country ORDER BY sum(Capacity) LIMIT 1* ***GP**: SELECT Country, MIN(Capacity) FROM nuclear_power_plants GROUP BY Country ORDER BY Capacity ASC LIMIT 1* ***DA**: SELECT Country, MIN(Capacity) FROM nuclear_power_plants GROUP BY Country ORDER BY Capacity ASC LIMIT 1* ***LTMP-DA**:SELECT Country FROM nuclear_power_plants GROUP BY Country ORDER BY SUM(Capacity) ASC LIMIT 1*	0.69
				3	Rectifying Values;Extra Condition	***NL**: In 2014, how many wildfires were the result of mismanaged campfires?* ***GT**: SELECT count(*) FROM Fires WHERE STAT_CAUSE_DESCR LIKE "%Campfire%" AND FIRE_YEAR = 2014* ***GP**:SELECT COUNT(*) FROM Fires WHERE STAT_CAUSE_DESCR = 'Miscellaneous' AND STAT_CAUSE_CODE = 13 AND FIRE_YEAR = 2014* ***DA**:SELECT count(*) FROM Fires WHERE FIRE_YEAR = 2014 AND STAT_CAUSE_DESCR = 'Mismanaged Campfire'* ***LTMP-DA**: SELECT COUNT(*) FROM Fires WHERE FIRE_YEAR = 2014 AND STAT_CAUSE_DESCR = "Campfire"*	3.45
Case 3	✗	✗	✗	1	Additional column	***NL**: What's the most common type of crime?* ***GT**: SELECT Type FROM GreaterManchesterCrime GROUP BY Type ORDER BY count(*) DESC LIMIT 1;* ***GP**: SELECT Type, COUNT(*) AS Frequency FROM GreaterManchesterCrime GROUP BY Type ORDER BY Frequency DESC LIMIT 1* ***DA**: SELECT Type, COUNT(*) FROM GreaterManchesterCrime GROUP BY Type ORDER BY COUNT(*) DESC LIMIT 1* ***LTMP-DA**: SELECT Type, COUNT(*) FROM GreaterManchesterCrime GROUP BY Type ORDER BY COUNT(*) DESC LIMIT 1*	42.26
				2	Logically incorrect	***NL**: How many matches in Spain in 2010?* ***GT**: SELECT count(*) FROM football_data WHERE Season LIKE "%2010%" AND Country = "Spain";* ***GP**: SELECT COUNT(*) FROM betfront WHERE country = 'Spain' AND YEAR = 2010* ***DA**: SELECT COUNT(*) FROM football_data WHERE Country = 'Spain' AND YEAR(Datetime) = 2010* ***LTMP-DA**: SELECT COUNT(*) FROM football_data WHERE Country = 'Spain' AND YEAR = '2010'*	11.22
				3	Miscellaneous	***NL**: What are the downloaded numbers and their release types?* ***GT**: SELECT sum(totalSnatched), releaseType FROM torrents GROUP BY releaseType;* ***GP**: SELECT totalSnatched, releaseType FROM torrents* ***DA**: SELECT totalSnatched, releaseType FROM torrents* ***LTMP-DA**: SELECT totalSnatched, releaseType FROM torrents*	22.06
Case 4	✓	✗	✗	1	Semantics Misinterpretation	***NL**: State with highest average math score* ***GT**: SELECT state FROM NDECoreExcel_Math_Grade8 ORDER BY average_scale_score DESC LIMIT 1* ***GP**:SELECT state FROM NDECoreExcel_Math_Grade8 ORDER BY average_scale_score DESC LIMIT 1* ***DA**:SELECT state, MAX(average_scale_score) FROM NDECoreExcel_Math_Grade8 GROUP BY state* ***LTMP-DA**:SELECT state, MAX(average_scale_score) FROM NDECoreExcel_Math_Grade8 GROUP BY state ORDER BY MAX(average_scale_score) DESC LIMIT 1*	1.37
Case 5	✓	✓	✗	1	Fail to Understand Question; Incorrect Value	***NL**:What is the result in case 6B:E2:54:C6:58:D2?* ***GT**:SELECT Outcome FROM GreaterManchesterCrime WHERE CrimeID = "6B:E2:54:C6:58:D2"* ***GP**:SELECT Outcome FROM GreaterManchesterCrime WHERE CrimeID = "6B:E2:54:C6:58:D2"* ***DA**:SELECT Outcome FROM GreaterManchesterCrime WHERE CrimeID = '6B:E2:54:C6:58:D2'* ***LTMP-DA**:SELECT * FROM Table*	2.76
				2	Syntax Error	***NL**: What's the code for confirmation for the latest sample?* ***GT**: SELECT confmethod FROM resultsdata15 as T2 JOIN sampledata15 as T1 ON T1.sample_pk = T2.sample_pk ORDER BY year, month, day DESC LIMIT 1* ***GP**: SELECT confmethod FROM resultsdata15 ORDER BY sample_pk DESC LIMIT 1* ***DA**: SELECT confmethod FROM resultsdata15 ORDER BY sample_pk DESC LIMIT 1* ***LTMP-DA**: SELECT confmethod FROM resultsdata15 WHERE sample_pk = (SELECT sample_pk FROM sampledata15 ORDER BY year DESC, month DESC, day DESC LIMIT 1)*	0.69

Table 3: Qualitative analysis. NL:Natural Language, GT: Ground Truth ✓: Correct SQL and ✗: Incorrect SQL. % of Erroneous Test Queries

similarity with the test NL query. Following Synchromesh (Poesia et al., 2022b), we train Sentence BERT (Reimers and Gurevych, 2019)) as a scoring function to compute the tree-edit distance between the corresponding SQLs of the input NL queries (Target Semantic Tuning (TST)), (iii) Test Query specific Skill based similarity sampling (QP-SK): maximum skill based similarity (An et al., 2023). Here LLMs are used to retrieve skill based representations of the queries, by eliminating unimportant surface features. (iv) Diversity based sampling: (Nan et al., 2023) performs diversity sampling by picking up the exemplars near the centroids of the training sample clusters, formed using a combination of continuous NL embedding and discrete embedding with binary features representing syntactic elements of the SQL counterpart, including keywords, operators, and identifiers. Our *GP* based approach not only selects diverse samples, but also ensures SQL operator coverage. We have not benchmarked against this approach due to unavailability of the prompts or the code.

Chain-of-Thoughts (COT) approaches: DIN-SQL (Pourreza and Rafiei, 2023) performs the NL-to-SQL task by dividing it into stages, viz. schema linking, NL query classification based on difficulty, distinct well-curated COTs prompting for distinct difficulty levels, along with few-shots with COT explanations and self-refinement at the end. We use the prompts in the paper for computing results.

Note that for fair comparison, we have not benchmarked *KaggleDBQA* results against the of LLMs not used the experimentation (An et al., 2023; Chang and Fosler-Lussier, 2023; Nan et al., 2023) .

5.2 Experimentation and Results

We use the *Spider-train* set as the training set to fetch few-shots for our *GP* and *Kaggle-DBQA* test set to evaluate the performance. Our algorithm yields 16 exemplars as few-shots covering a total of 4 databases. The selected queries cover a total of 32 SQL operators and clauses. For more deterministic results, we set the LLM parameters temperature to be 0.

The results are illustrated in the Table 1. Our basic *GP* performs better than (i) some state-of-the-art supervised models, (ii) zero-shot and (iii) QP-TX. This is possible due to generalization capabilities of LLMs along with programmatically sampled diverse few-shots in GP. Our final adapted and decomposed *LTMP-DA-GP* consistently performs better than (i) All state-of-the-art supervised benchmarks and (ii) All few-shot benchmarks. This is due to the combined effect of diversity based sampling in GP (Nan et al., 2023; An et al., 2023) and effect of domain adaptation and LTMP. Except *US Wildfires* database *DA-GP*, consistently performs better than *GP* showcasing the effect of domain adaptation for domain generalizability. *LTMP-GP* consistently performs better than *GP*, showcasing the effect of LTMP for compositional generalizability. Except *Greater Manchester* and *Pesticide* DBs *LTMP-DA-GP* consistently improves over *LTMP-GP* and *DA-GP*, demonstrating complementary benefits of DA and LTMP for certain queries and thus proves the efficacy of our adapt and decompose pipeline. We find for *Greater Manchester* DB the GPT-Turbo-3.5 performance drops with LTMP-DA-GP as with additional DA information the model tries to reason better generating long COTs, leading unavailability of tokens left to generate the desired output.

5.3 Qualitative Analysis

We manually analyze the test-queries (Table 3). Case 1 Category (1) and (2) demonstrates samples where inclusion of domain knowledge in terms of table values and column descriptions rectifies the SQLs. Case 2 demonstrates LTMP rectifying samples due to better resolution of decomposed queries (e.g. 'Which country' and 'lead the total capacity of the power plants it held?') as opposed to the need of resolving complete query at once, with the prior approaches. Case 3 are erroneous samples, where (1) LTMP can not fix additional aggregation operation appearing in the SELECT clause, especially where the NLs can not be decomposed or generation of logically incorrect queries due to insufficient domain information such as: (2) query specific values (eg. 2010) not being present in the sampled values of the schema column descriptions (eg. season) in the prompt (wrong column 'Year' gets picked up due to its specified range as 2009-2013) and (3) absence of understanding of domain specific numerical formula 'downloaded numbers = sum(total snatched)' for songs for CD Hiphop DB. There are very few samples for Case 4 (1) where additional aggregation operation is added as a part of SELECT clause due to mis-interpretation of the NL query semantics. Eg. 'state with' is been interpreted as providing some additional information along with 'state' by LLM with DA as well as LTMP. Case 5 (1) LTMP fails to decompose the question due to complex value further propagating error in the following stages (2) Queries come out correct for GP and DA due to samples being arranged in order of time, however with decompositions LTMP tried to come up with a right query but fails due to adding extra DESC condition to each column as following a few-shot decomposition.

6 Conclusion

In this paper, we leverage LLMs for the cross-domain and cross-composition generalization of Text-to-SQL. As opposed to prior approaches, which rely on inference-time retrieval of exemplars similar to the test query; we devise an algorithm which samples diverse set-of exemplars with complete coverage of SQL operators, clauses and functions and maximal coverage of databases to form the *Generic Prompt (GP)*, which is common across every test sample obviating the need for dynamic exemplar retrieval and thus leading to an efficient approach. We further perform programmatic domain-adaptation of this prompt *DA-GP*, which consistently showcases performance improvement across multiple databases and LLMs better achieving domain generalization. We further decompose the exemplars of *DA-GP*, to execute a novel pipeline of Least-to-Most-Prompting (*LTMP-DA-GP*) for compositional generalization of the complex NL-to-SQL task. This pipeline showcases consistent improvement over *GP* across multiple databases and LLMs demonstrating complementary benefits of the adapt and decompose steps and thus proving the efficacy of our approach. Our pipeline, being offline with minimal human intervention, is not only efficient; but also yields the best performance reported in the literature with the experimented LLMs, on KaggleDBQA dataset designed to test generalizability of NL-to-SQL task.

7 Limitations

In the current solution, we design the *GP* such that the extended version *LTMP-GP*, after appending each few-shot with the corresponding query decomposition, their mapping to NAT-SQL followed by SQL, fits into the maximum token length of 4k tokens by Text-da-Vinci-003 and GPT-Turbo-3.5. However, for LLMs such as Bloom (Scao et al., 2022) and Falcon (Penedo et al., 2023), etc, which maintain a maximum context length of 2k tokens, the current solution would only be applicable after some truncation of *GP*, by removing some few-shots, to fit within the specified context length. This can impact the performance of the resulting *GP*. Due to the same reason, we were unable to incorporate column descriptions and values of the target schema within the *LTMP-GP* prompt, as doing so would exceed the 4k token limit. We might be able to alleviate these problem with the approaches such as (Ding et al., 2023; Bulatov et al., 2023), that aim at scaling sequence length issues in LLMs. Another limitation involves the necessity of human intervention in crafting the *LTMP-DA-GP* prompt based on the *DA-GP* prompt for each unique test schema leading to a semi-automated solution. However, this human-intervention is only one-time for a new database schema.

References

Shengnan An, Bo Zhou, Zeqi Lin, Qiang Fu, B. Chen, Nanning Zheng, Weizhu Chen, and Jian-Guang Lou. 2023. Skill-based few-shot selection for in-context learning. *ArXiv*, abs/2305.14210.

Jacob Austin, Augustus Odena, Maxwell Nye, Maarten Bosma, Henryk Michalewski, David Dohan, Ellen Jiang, Carrie J. Cai, Michael Terry, Quoc V. Le, and Charles Sutton. 2021. Program synthesis with large language models. *ArXiv*, abs/2108.07732.

Tom Brown, Benjamin Mann, Nick Ryder, Melanie Subbiah, Jared D Kaplan, Prafulla Dhariwal, Arvind Neelakantan, Pranav Shyam, Girish Sastry, Amanda Askell, et al. 2020a. Language models are few-shot learners. *Advances in neural information processing systems*, 33:1877–1901.

Tom B. Brown, Benjamin Mann, Nick Ryder, Melanie Subbiah, Jared Kaplan, Prafulla Dhariwal, Arvind Neelakantan, Pranav Shyam, Girish Sastry, Amanda Askell, Sandhini Agarwal, Ariel Herbert-Voss, Gretchen Krueger, T. J. Henighan, Rewon Child, Aditya Ramesh, Daniel M. Ziegler, Jeff Wu, Clemens Winter, Christopher Hesse, Mark Chen, Eric Sigler, Mateusz Litwin, Scott Gray, Benjamin Chess, Jack Clark, Christopher Berner, Sam McCandlish, Alec Radford, Ilya Sutskever, and Dario Amodei. 2020b. Language models are few-shot learners. *ArXiv*, abs/2005.14165.

Aydar Bulatov, Yuri Kuratov, and Mikhail S. Burtsev. 2023. Scaling transformer to 1m tokens and beyond with rmt.

Shuaichen Chang and Eric Fosler-Lussier. 2023. How to prompt llms for text-to-sql: A study in zero-shot, single-domain, and cross-domain settings. *ArXiv*, abs/2305.11853.

Mark Chen, Jerry Tworek, Heewoo Jun, Qiming Yuan, Henrique Ponde de Oliveira Pinto, Jared Kaplan, Harri Edwards, Yuri Burda, Nicholas Joseph, Greg Brockman, Alex Ray, Raul Puri, Gretchen Krueger, Michael Petrov, Heidy Khlaaf, Girish Sastry, Pamela Mishkin, Brooke Chan, Scott Gray, Nick Ryder, Mikhail Pavlov, Alethea Power, Lukasz Kaiser, Mohammad Bavarian, Clemens Winter, Philippe Tillet, Felipe Petroski Such, Dave Cummings, Matthias Plappert, Fotios Chantzis, Elizabeth Barnes, Ariel Herbert-Voss, William Hebgen Guss, Alex Nichol, Alex Paino, Nikolas Tezak, Jie Tang, Igor Babuschkin, Suchir Balaji, Shantanu Jain, William Saunders, Christopher Hesse, Andrew N. Carr, Jan Leike, Josh Achiam, Vedant Misra, Evan Morikawa, Alec Radford, Matthew Knight, Miles Brundage, Mira Murati, Katie Mayer, Peter Welinder, Bob McGrew, Dario Amodei, Sam McCandlish, Ilya Sutskever, and Wojciech Zaremba. 2021a. Evaluating large language models trained on code.

Mark Chen, Jerry Tworek, Heewoo Jun, Qiming Yuan, Henrique Ponde, Jared Kaplan, Harrison Edwards, Yura Burda, Nicholas Joseph, Greg Brockman, Alex Ray, Raul Puri, Gretchen Krueger, Michael Petrov, Heidy Khlaaf, Girish Sastry, Pamela Mishkin, Brooke Chan, Scott Gray, Nick Ryder, Mikhail Pavlov, Alethea Power, Lukasz Kaiser, Mohammad Bavarian, Clemens Winter, Philippe Tillet, Felipe Petroski Such, David W. Cummings, Matthias Plappert, Fotios Chantzis, Elizabeth Barnes, Ariel Herbert-Voss, William H. Guss, Alex Nichol, Igor Babuschkin, S. Arun Balaji, Shantanu Jain, Andrew Carr, Jan Leike, Joshua Achiam, Vedant Misra, Evan Morikawa, Alec Radford, Matthew M. Knight, Miles Brundage, Mira Murati, Katie Mayer, Peter Welinder, Bob McGrew, Dario Amodei, Sam McCandlish, Ilya Sutskever, and Wojciech Zaremba. 2021b. Evaluating large language models trained on code. *ArXiv*, abs/2107.03374.

Aakanksha Chowdhery, Sharan Narang, Jacob Devlin, Maarten Bosma, Gaurav Mishra, Adam Roberts, Paul Barham, Hyung Won Chung, Charles Sutton, Sebastian Gehrmann, et al. 2022. Palm: Scaling language modeling with pathways. *arXiv preprint arXiv:2204.02311*.

Jiayu Ding, Shuming Ma, Li Dong, Xingxing Zhang, Shaohan Huang, Wenhui Wang, Nanning Zheng, and Furu Wei. 2023. Longnet: Scaling transformers to 1,000,000,000 tokens.

Andrew Drozdov, Nathanael Scharli, Ekin Akyuurek, Nathan Scales, Xinying Song, Xinyun Chen, Olivier Bousquet, and Denny Zhou. 2022. Compositional semantic parsing with large language models. *ArXiv*, abs/2209.15003.

Yujian Gan, Xinyun Chen, Qiuping Huang, and Matthew Purver. 2022. Measuring and improving compositional generalization in text-to-sql via component alignment. *arXiv preprint arXiv:2205.02054*.

Arian Hosseini, Ankit Vani, Dzmitry Bahdanau, Alessandro Sordoni, and Aaron C. Courville. 2022. On the compositional generalization gap of in-context learning. *ArXiv*, abs/2211.08473.

Jie Huang and Kevin Chen-Chuan Chang. 2022. Towards reasoning in large language models: A survey.

Srinivasan Iyer, Ioannis Konstas, Alvin Cheung, Jayant Krishnamurthy, and Luke Zettlemoyer. 2017. Learning a neural semantic parser from user feedback. In *Proceedings of the 55th Annual Meeting of the Association for Computational Linguistics (Volume 1: Long Papers)*, pages 963–973, Vancouver, Canada. Association for Computational Linguistics.

Naman Jain, Skanda Vaidyanath, Arun Shankar Iyer, Nagarajan Natarajan, Suresh Parthasarathy, Sriram K. Rajamani, and Rahul Sharma. 2021. Jigsaw: Large language models meet program synthesis. *2022 IEEE/ACM 44th International Conference on Software Engineering (ICSE)*, pages 1219–1231.

Wuwei Lan, Zhiguo Wang, Anuj Chauhan, Henghui Zhu, Alexander Hanbo Li, Jiang Guo, Shenmin Zhang, Chung-Wei Hang, Joseph Lilien, Yiqun Hu, Lin Pan, Mingwen Dong, J. Wang, Jiarong Jiang, Stephen M. Ash, Vittorio Castelli, Patrick Ng, and Bing Xiang. 2023. Unite: A unified benchmark for text-to-sql evaluation. *ArXiv*, abs/2305.16265.

Chia-Hsuan Lee, Oleksandr Polozov, and Matthew Richardson. 2021a. KaggleDBQA: Realistic evaluation of text-to-SQL parsers. In *Proceedings of the 59th Annual Meeting of the Association for Computational Linguistics and the 11th International Joint Conference on Natural Language Processing (Volume 1: Long Papers)*, pages 2261–2273, Online. Association for Computational Linguistics.

Chia-Hsuan Lee, Oleksandr Polozov, and Matthew Richardson. 2021b. KaggleDBQA: Realistic evaluation of text-to-SQL parsers. In *Proceedings of the 59th Annual Meeting of the Association for Computational Linguistics and the 11th International Joint Conference on Natural Language Processing (Volume 1: Long Papers)*, pages 2261–2273, Online. Association for Computational Linguistics.

Haoyang Li, Jing Zhang, Cuiping Li, and Hong Chen. 2023. Resdsql: Decoupling schema linking and skeleton parsing for text-to-sql. *ArXiv*, abs/2302.05965.

Linyong Nan, Yilun Zhao, Weijin Zou, Narutatsu Ri, Jaesung Tae, Ellen Yue Zhang, Arman Cohan, and Dragomir R. Radev. 2023. Enhancing few-shot text-to-sql capabilities of large language models: A study on prompt design strategies. *ArXiv*, abs/2305.12586.

Erik Nijkamp, Bo Pang, Hiroaki Hayashi, Lifu Tu, Haiquan Wang, Yingbo Zhou, Silvio Savarese, and Caiming Xiong. 2022. Codegen: An open large language model for code with multi-turn program synthesis.

Guilherme Penedo, Quentin Malartic, Daniel Hesslow, Ruxandra Cojocaru, Alessandro Cappelli, Hamza Alobeidli, Baptiste Pannier, Ebtesam Almazrouei, and Julien Launay. 2023. The refinedweb dataset for falcon llm: Outperforming curated corpora with web data, and web data only.

Gabriel Poesia, Oleksandr Polozov, Vu Le, Ashish Tiwari, Gustavo Soares, Christopher Meek, and Sumit Gulwani. 2022a. Synchromesh: Reliable code generation from pre-trained language models. *ArXiv*, abs/2201.11227.

Gabriel Poesia, Oleksandr Polozov, Vu Le, Ashish Tiwari, Gustavo Soares, Christopher Meek, and Sumit Gulwani. 2022b. Synchromesh: Reliable code generation from pre-trained language models. *arXiv preprint arXiv:2201.11227*.

Mohammad Reza Pourreza and Davood Rafiei. 2023. Din-sql: Decomposed in-context learning of text-to-sql with self-correction. *ArXiv*, abs/2304.11015.

Jiexing Qi, Jingyao Tang, Ziwei He, Xiangpeng Wan, Yu Cheng, Chenghu Zhou, Xinbing Wang, Quanshi Zhang, and Zhouhan Lin. 2022. Rasat: Integrating relational structures into pretrained seq2seq model for text-to-sql. *ArXiv*, abs/2205.06983.

Linlu Qiu, Peter Shaw, Panupong Pasupat, Tianze Shi, Jonathan Herzig, Emily Pitler, Fei Sha, and Kristina Toutanova. 2022. Evaluating the impact of model scale for compositional generalization in semantic parsing. *ArXiv*, abs/2205.12253.

Nitarshan Rajkumar, Raymond Li, and Dzmitry Bahdanau. 2022a. Evaluating the text-to-sql capabilities of large language models. *ArXiv*, abs/2204.00498.

Nitarshan Rajkumar, Raymond Li, and Dzmitry Bahdanau. 2022b. Evaluating the text-to-sql capabilities of large language models. *arXiv preprint arXiv:2204.00498*.

Nils Reimers and Iryna Gurevych. 2019. Sentence-bert: Sentence embeddings using siamese bert-networks. In *Conference on Empirical Methods in Natural Language Processing*.

Ohad Rubin and Jonathan Berant. 2020. Smbop: Semi-autoregressive bottom-up semantic parsing. *arXiv preprint arXiv:2010.12412*.

Teven Le Scao, Angela Fan, Christopher Akiki, Ellie Pavlick, Suzana Ilić, Daniel Hesslow, Roman Castagné, Alexandra Sasha Luccioni, François Yvon, Matthias Gallé, et al. 2022. Bloom: A 176b-parameter open-access multilingual language model. *arXiv preprint arXiv:2211.05100*.

Torsten Scholak, Nathan Schucher, and Dzmitry Bahdanau. 2021. Picard: Parsing incrementally for constrained auto-regressive decoding from language models. *arXiv preprint arXiv:2109.05093*.

Richard Shin and Benjamin Van Durme. 2021. Few-shot semantic parsing with language models trained on code. *ArXiv*, abs/2112.08696.

Richard Shin, C. H. Lin, Sam Thomson, Charles C. Chen, Subhro Roy, Emmanouil Antonios Platanios, Adam Pauls, Dan Klein, Jas' Eisner, and Benjamin Van Durme. 2021. Constrained language models yield few-shot semantic parsers. *ArXiv*, abs/2104.08768.

Lappoon R. Tang and Raymond J. Mooney. 2001. Using multiple clause constructors in inductive logic programming for semantic parsing. In *European Conference on Machine Learning*.

Yue Wang, Hung Le, Akhilesh Deepak Gotmare, Nghi D. Q. Bui, Junnan Li, and Steven Hoi. 2023. Codet5+: Open code large language models for code understanding and generation. *ArXiv*, abs/2305.07922.

Jingfeng Yang, Haoming Jiang, Qingyu Yin, Danqing Zhang, Bing Yin, and Diyi Yang. 2022. SEQZERO: Few-shot compositional semantic parsing with sequential prompts and zero-shot models. In *Findings of the Association for Computational Linguistics: NAACL 2022*, pages 49–60, Seattle, United States. Association for Computational Linguistics.

Tao Yu, Rui Zhang, Kai Yang, Michihiro Yasunaga, Dongxu Wang, Zifan Li, James Ma, Irene Li, Qingning Yao, Shanelle Roman, et al. 2018. Spider: A large-scale human-labeled dataset for complex and cross-domain semantic parsing and text-to-sql task. *arXiv preprint arXiv:1809.08887*.

John M. Zelle and Raymond J. Mooney. 1996. Learning to parse database queries using inductive logic programming. In *AAAI/IAAI, Vol. 2*.

Denny Zhou, Nathanael Scharli, Le Hou, Jason Wei, Nathan Scales, Xuezhi Wang, Dale Schuurmans, Olivier Bousquet, Quoc Le, and Ed Huai hsin Chi. 2022. Least-to-most prompting enables complex reasoning in large language models. *ArXiv*, abs/2205.10625.

A Supplementary Material

A.1 Existing Work on LLM based NL-to-SQL

(Rajkumar et al., 2022a; Chang and Fosler-Lussier, 2023; Nan et al., 2023) has attempted to use LLMs for Text-to-SQL semantic parsing task in zero-shot as well as few-shot settings. For zero-shot setting, they experiment with various formats of the database schema, such as the APIDocs or SQL '*CREATE TABLE*' commands, with and without randomly selected data rows or columns from the database table (elaborated in Section 4.1). For the few-shot setting, (Rajkumar et al., 2022a; Qiu et al., 2022; Hosseini et al., 2022; Yang et al., 2022) focus on cross-composition generalization and provide the queries which are posed on the target database itself as exemplars (cross-domain setting is not considered). Thus, the assumption is that few queries are available for a new database. They work with datasets such as GeoQuery ((Tang and Mooney, 2001; Zelle and Mooney, 1996)) with data in US geography domain, Scholar ((Iyer et al., 2017)) with data in academic publications or a dataset designed for queries in E-commerce domain ((Yang et al., 2022)). In our approach, we assume no availability of annotated data in terms of SQL programs for the test database and thus, completely a cross-domain setting.

On the similar lines of our work, Synchromesh (Poesia et al., 2022a) and (Nan et al., 2023; An et al., 2023) assumes cross-domain setting. These approaches select few-shot exemplars from the training set based on (a) the semantic similarity with the NL test query (Nan et al., 2023) or (b) using Target Similarity Tuning (TST) where the NL queries with similar target programs are selected as exemplars (Poesia et al., 2022a) or (c) selecting similar NL queries as exemplars with their LLM generated 'skill' representation, which focuses on program compositions and ignores the surface NL forms (An et al., 2023). In addition to TST, Synchromesh (Poesia et al., 2022a) performs constrained semantic decoding (CSD), which reduces the implementation errors in the generated SQLs by ensuring that the generated tokens lead to correct programs following a pre-specified grammar. As constraint decoding is not the focus our approach, we compare our performance using Target Semantic Tuning (TST), without Constraint Semantic Decoding (CSD). All the above similarity based approaches have a reliance on inference-time retrieval of similar few-shot samples from the available data to build a run-time prompt and generate SQL for a test NL query leading to a less efficient solution. As opposed to this, we devise an algorithm to generate a prompt with diverse exemplars generic across test queries in offline fashion, resulting in a more time-efficient solution obviating the need for real time retrieval. Moreover, with further adaptation of this offline prompt with the adapt and decompose techniques, our approach yields better performance than existing similarity based sampling techniques (Poesia et al., 2022b; Chang and Fosler-Lussier, 2023; An et al., 2023).

(Nan et al., 2023) defines a 'diversity' based sampling method for few-shot exemplar selection, where the samples in the training set are clustered using a combination of continuous representation of the NL queries and discrete representation of SQL counterparts, to pickup the near-centroid samples are few-shots. They showcase that this diversity based sampling method performs better than similarity based sampling, which is further enhanced by similarity-diversity sampling. Our *GP* based sampling technique ensures diversity in the samples, by guaranteeing complete coverage of SQL operators and maximum converge of database domains.

A.2 Addressing LLM Memorization Concerns

(Rajkumar et al., 2022a) have addressed the concerns around possible memorization of existing datasets such as Spider(Yu et al., 2018) by large language models, which are trained on code data. The possibility of memorization arises as the the *Spider Dev* split file (*dev.sql*) resides on Github[4]. However, prompting LLMs with verbatim fragments of this file leads to generations which do not match with the file contents. For example, given a question in the format specified in the file, the table aliasing strategy followed in the generated SQLs does not match with the gold SQLs provided in the file. On the similar lines of (Rajkumar et al., 2022a), our prompting format of text queries (Explained in Section 4.1) is completely different than the format in which NL-SQL pairs are stored in the *Spider Dev* split file. Moreover, to avoid the concerns of memorization, we assess the performance of our pipelines using *Kaggle DBQA* (Lee et al., 2021b) dataset, for which the evaluation files are not residing on Github[5]. We also showcase with performance improvements with our approach over zero-shot setting on this dataset for distinct LLMs.

A.3 Prompts

In this section we provide the prompts generated by our pipeline including the (i) *GP* which is common across all the *KaggleDBQA* dataset (ii) *DA-GP* for *GeoNeuclear* database. The same prompt template can be used to recreate the prompts for other databases. (iii) *LTMP-GP* which is common across all the *KaggleDBQA* dataset (iv) *LTMP-DA-GP* for *GeoNeuclear* database. The same prompt template can be used to recreate the prompts for other databases.The Yellow part indicates the few-shot schemas, Blue part the test schema and queries and orange the domain information.

[4]https://github.com/taoyds/spider/tree/master/evaluation_examples

[5]https://github.com/chiahsuan156/KaggleDBQA

A.3.1 Generic Prompt (GP)

Note: PK and FK denote Primarky Key and Foreign Key, respectively, in all the below following schemas.
SQLite SQL tables, with their properties:
CREATE TABLE classroom (building, room_number, capacity, PK (building, room_number))
CREATE TABLE department (dept_name, building, budget, PK (dept_name))
CREATE TABLE course (course_id, title, dept_name, credits, PK (course_id), FK (dept_name) REFERENCES department (dept_name))
CREATE TABLE instructor (ID, name, dept_name, salary, PK (ID), FK (dept_name) references department (dept_name))
CREATE TABLE section (course_id, sec_id, semester), year, building, room_number, time_slot_id, PK (course_id, sec_id, semester, year), FK (course_id) references course (course_id), FK (building, room_number) references classroom (building, room_number))
CREATE TABLE teaches (ID, course_id, sec_id, semester, year, PK (ID, course_id, sec_id, semester, year), FK (course_id, sec_id, semester, year) references section (course_id, sec_id, semester, year), FK (ID) references instructor (ID))
CREATE TABLE student (ID, name, dept_name, tot_cred, PK (ID), FK (dept_name) references department (dept_name))
CREATE TABLE takes (ID, course_id, sec_id, semester, year, grade, PK (ID, course_id, sec_id, semester, year), FK (course_id,sec_id, semester, year) references section (course_id, sec_id, semester, year), FK (ID) references student (ID))
CREATE TABLE advisor (s_ID, i_ID, PK (s_ID), FK (i_ID) references instructor (ID), FK (s_ID) references student (ID))
CREATE TABLE time_slot (time_slot_id, day, start_hr, start_min, end_hr, end_min, PK (time_slot_id, day, start_hr, start_min))
CREATE TABLE prereq (course_id, prereq_id, PK (course_id, prereq_id), FK (course_id) references course (course_id), FK (prereq_id) references course (course_id))
#
Find the buildings which have rooms with capacity more than 50.
SELECT DISTINCT building FROM classroom WHERE capacity > 50
#
Find the name and building of the department with the highest budget.
SELECT dept_name, building FROM department ORDER BY budget DESC LIMIT 1
#
Find the title of courses that have two prerequisites?
SELECT T1.title FROM course AS T1 JOIN prereq AS T2 ON T1.course_id = T2.course_id GROUP BY T2.course_id HAVING count(*) = 2
#
How many courses that do not have prerequisite?
SELECT count(*) FROM course WHERE course_id NOT IN (SELECT course_id FROM prereq)
#
Find the total budgets of the Marketing or Finance department.
SELECT sum(budget) FROM department WHERE dept_name = 'Marketing' OR dept_name = 'Finance'
#
Find the department name of the instructor whose name contains 'Soisalon'.
SELECT dept_name FROM instructor WHERE name LIKE '#
Find the title of course that is provided by both Statistics and Psychology departments.
SELECT title FROM course WHERE dept_name = 'Statistics' INTERSECT SELECT title FROM course WHERE dept_name = 'Psychology'
#
Find the title of course that is provided by Statistics but not Psychology departments.
SELECT title FROM course WHERE dept_name = 'Statistics' EXCEPT SELECT title FROM course WHERE dept_name = 'Psychology'
#
Find courses that ran in Fall 2009 or in Spring 2010.
SELECT course_id FROM SECTION WHERE semester = 'Fall' AND YEAR = 2009 UNION SELECT course_id FROM SECTION WHERE semester = 'Spring' AND YEAR = 2010
#
Find the names and average salaries of all departments whose average salary is greater than 42000.

SELECT dept_name, AVG(salary) FROM instructor GROUP BY dept_name HAVING AVG (salary) > 42000
#
SQLite SQL tables, with their properties:
CREATE TABLE regions (REGION_ID, REGION_NAME, PK (REGION_ID))
CREATE TABLE countries (COUNTRY_ID, COUNTRY_NAME, REGION_ID, PK (COUNTRY_ID), FK (REGION_ID) REFERENCES regions (REGION_ID))
CREATE TABLE departments (DEPARTMENT_ID, DEPARTMENT_NAME, MANAGER_ID, LOCATION_ID, PK (DEPARTMENT_ID))
CREATE TABLE jobs (JOB_ID, JOB_TITLE, MIN_SALARY, MAX_SALARY, PK (JOB_ID))
CREATE TABLE employees (EMPLOYEE_ID, FIRST_NAME, LAST_NAME, EMAIL, PHONE_NUMBER, HIRE_DATE, JOB_ID, SALARY, COMMISSION_PCT, MANAGER_ID, DEPARTMENT_ID, PK (EMPLOYEE_ID), FK (DEPARTMENT_ID) REFERENCES departments(DEPARTMENT_ID), FK (JOB_ID) REFERENCES jobs(JOB_ID))
CREATE TABLE job_history (EMPLOYEE_ID, START_DATE, END_DATE, JOB_ID, DEPARTMENT_ID, PK (EMPLOYEE_ID,START_DATE), FK (EMPLOYEE_ID) REFERENCES employees(EMPLOYEE_ID), FK (DEPARTMENT_ID) REFERENCES departments(DEPARTMENT_ID), FK (JOB_ID) REFERENCES jobs(JOB_ID))
CREATE TABLE locations (LOCATION_ID, STREET_ADDRESS, POSTAL_CODE, CITY, STATE_PROVINCE, COUNTRY_ID, PK (LOCATION_ID), FK (COUNTRY_ID) REFERENCES countries(COUNTRY_ID))
#
display job Title, the difference between minimum and maximum salaries for those jobs which max salary within the range 12000 to 18000.
SELECT job_title, max_salary - min_salary FROM jobs WHERE max_salary BETWEEN 12000 AND 18000
#
display the employee ID for each employee and the date on which he ended his previous job.
SELECT employee_id, MAX(end_date) FROM job_history GROUP BY employee_id
#
return the smallest salary for every departments.
SELECT MIN(salary), department_id FROM employees GROUP BY department_id
#
display the department id and the total salary for those departments which contains at least two employees.
SELECT department_id, SUM(salary) FROM employees GROUP BY department_id HAVING count(*) >= 2
#
SQLite SQL tables, with their properties:
CREATE TABLE Rooms (RoomId PK, roomName, beds, bedType, maxOccupancy, basePrice, decor)
CREATE TABLE Reservations (Code PK, Room, CheckIn, CheckOut, Rate REAL, LastName, FirstName, Adults, Kids, FK (Room) REFERENCES Rooms(RoomId))
#
List how many times the number of people in the room reached the maximum occupancy of the room. The number of people include adults and kids.
SELECT count(*) FROM Reservations AS T1 JOIN Rooms AS T2 ON T1.Room = T2.RoomId WHERE T2.maxOccupancy = T1.Adults + T1.Kids;
#
SQLite SQL tables, with their properties:
CREATE TABLE Attribute_Definitions (attribute_id PK, attribute_name, attribute_data_type)
CREATE TABLE Catalogs (catalog_id PK, catalog_name, catalog_publisher, date_of_publication, date_of_latest_revision)
CREATE TABLE Catalog_Structure (catalog_level_number PK, catalog_id, catalog_level_name, FK (catalog_id) REFERENCES Catalogs(catalog_id))
CREATE TABLE Catalog_Contents (catalog_entry_id PK, catalog_level_number, parent_entry_id, previous_entry_id, next_entry_id, catalog_entry_name, product_stock_number, price_in_dollars, price_in_euros, price_in_pounds, capacity, length, height, width, FK (catalog_level_number) REFERENCES Catalog_Structure(catalog_level_number))
CREATE TABLE Catalog_Contents_Additional_Attributes (catalog_entry_id, catalog_level_number, attribute_id, attribute_value, FK (catalog_entry_id) REFERENCES Catalog_Contents(catalog_entry_id), FK (catalog_level_number) REFERENCES Catalog_Structure(catalog_level_number))
#

Find the names of the products with length smaller than 3 or height greater than 5.
SELECT catalog_entry_name FROM catalog_contents WHERE LENGTH < 3 OR width > 5
#
SQLite SQL tables, with their properties:
CREATE TABLE nuclear_power_plants (Id, Name, Latitude, Longitude, Country, Status, ReactorType, ReactorModel, ConstructionStartAt, OperationalFrom, OperationalTo, Capacity, LastUpdatedAt, Source)
#
Which country has the most capacities of nuclear power plants?
SELECT

A.3.2 Domain Adapted - Generic Prompt (DA-GP) (Stage-3)

SQLite SQL tables, with their properties:
#
CREATE TABLE nuclear_power_plants (Id, Name, Latitude, Longitude, Country, Status, ReactorType, ReactorModel, ConstructionStartAt, OperationalFrom, OperationalTo, Capacity, LastUpdatedAt, Source)
Columns in nuclear_power_plants with examples in each column and descriptions wherever required:
Id: 572, 560, 258, 433.
Name: Ågesta, Turkey Point4, Oskarshamn2, Ningde4.
Latitude: 55.084000, 55.604000, 41.188000, 45.800000. Description: latitude in decimal format
Longitude: 77.311000, 66.790000, 9.393000, 0.845000. Description: longitude in decimal format
Country: Canada, Germany, Taiwan, Province of China, Italy.
Status: Planned, Cancelled Construction, Under Construction, Suspended Construction.
ReactorType: HWGCR, GCR, LWGR, HTGR.
ReactorModel: Konvoi, VVER V-320, WH 2LP (DRYAMB), PHWR KWU.
ConstructionStartAt: 1977-02-01, 1968-05-18, 1965-04-12, 1972-11-01. Description: date when nuclear power plant construction was started
OperationalFrom: 2015-06-05, 1977-03-13, 1986-04-10, 1989-09-30. Description: date when nuclear power plant became operational (also known as commercial operation date)
OperationalTo: 2011-05-19, 2004-06-29, 1992-05-27, 2015-04-30. Description: date when nuclear power plant was shutdown (also known as permanent shutdown date)
Capacity: 1092, 125, 535, 1307. Description: nuclear power plant capacity (design net capacity in MWe)
LastUpdatedAt: 2015-05-24T04:50:59+03:00, 2015-05-24T04:51:11+03:00, 2017-02-10T23:58:48+02:00, 2018-03-10T13:41:49+02:00. Description: date and time when information was last updated
Source: WNA/wikipedia/IAEA, wikipedia, WNA, WNA/IAEA/GEO. Description: source of the information
#
Find the latitudes of nuclear power plants with capacity more than 50.
SELECT DISTINCT Latitude FROM nuclear_power_plants WHERE Capacity > 50;
#
Find the country and status of the nuclear power plant with the highest capacity.
SELECT Country, Status FROM nuclear_power_plants ORDER BY Capacity DESC LIMIT 1;
#
Find the name of nuclear power plants that have two entries in the database?
SELECT T1.Name FROM nuclear_power_plants AS T1 JOIN nuclear_power_plants AS T2 ON T1.Id = T2.Id GROUP BY T2.Id HAVING count(*) = 2;
#
How many nuclear power plants do not have a prerequisite?
SELECT COUNT(*) FROM nuclear_power_plants WHERE Id NOT IN (SELECT Id FROM prereq)
#
Find the total capacity of the nuclear power plants named Marketing or Finance.
SELECT sum(Capacity) FROM nuclear_power_plants WHERE Name = 'Marketing' OR Name = 'Finance'
#
Find the country associated with the nuclear power plant whose name contains 'Soisalon'.
SELECT Country FROM nuclear_power_plants WHERE Name LIKE '%Soisalon%'
#
Find the name of nuclear power plants that are located in both Statistics and Psychology countries.
SELECT Name FROM nuclear_power_plants WHERE Country = 'Statistics' INTERSECT SELECT Name FROM

nuclear_power_plants WHERE Country = 'Psychology'
#
Find the name of nuclear power plants that are located in Statistics but not Psychology countries.
SELECT Name FROM nuclear_power_plants WHERE Country = 'Statistics' EXCEPT SELECT Name FROM nuclear_power_plants WHERE Country = 'Psychology'
#
Find the Ids of nuclear power plants that were constructed in Fall 2009 or in Spring 2010.
SELECT Id FROM nuclear_power_plants WHERE ConstructionStartAt = 'Fall' AND LastUpdatedAt = 2009 UNION SELECT Id FROM nuclear_power_plants WHERE ConstructionStartAt = 'Spring' AND LastUpdatedAt = 2010
#
Find the countries and average capacities of all nuclear power plants whose average capacity is greater than 42000.
SELECT Country, AVG (Capacity) FROM nuclear_power_plants GROUP BY Country HAVING AVG (Capacity) > 42000
#
display the Name of the nuclear power plant and the difference between its capacity and the year it was constructed for those plants which capacity is within the range 12000 to 18000.
SELECT Name, Capacity - ConstructionStartAt FROM nuclear_power_plants WHERE Capacity BETWEEN 12000 AND 18000
#
display the ID for each nuclear power plant and the date on which it stopped operating.
SELECT Id, MAX(OperationalTo) FROM nuclear_power_plants GROUP BY Id
#
return the smallest capacity for each nuclear power plant.
SELECT MIN(Capacity), Id FROM nuclear_power_plants GROUP BY Id
#
display the id and the total capacity for those nuclear power plants which have at least two reactors.
SELECT Id, SUM(Capacity) FROM nuclear_power_plants GROUP BY Id HAVING count(*) >= 2
#
Count how many times the capacity of a nuclear power plant is equal to the sum of its status and reactor type.
SELECT COUNT(*) FROM nuclear_power_plants AS T1 JOIN nuclear_power_plants AS T2 ON T1.Id = T2.Id WHERE T2.Capacity = T1.Status + T1.ReactorType;
#
Find the names of the nuclear power plants with capacity smaller than 3 or capacity greater than 5.
SELECT Name FROM nuclear_power_plants WHERE Capacity < 3 OR Capacity > 5
#
Which country has the most capacities of nuclear power plants?
SELECT

A.3.3 Least-to-Most Prompting - Generic Prompt (LTMP-GP)

Note: PK and FK denote Primary Key and Foreign Key, respectively, in all the below following schemas.
SQLite SQL tables, with their properties:
#CREATE TABLE classroom (building, room_number, capacity, PK (building, room_number))
#CREATE TABLE department (dept_name, building, budget, PK (dept_name))
#CREATE TABLE course (course_id, title, dept_name, credits, PK (course_id), FK (dept_name) REFERENCES department (dept_name))
#CREATE TABLE instructor (ID, name, dept_name, salary, PK (ID), FK (dept_name) references department (dept_name))
#CREATE TABLE section (course_id, sec_id, semester), year, building, room_number, time_slot_id, PK (course_id, sec_id, semester, year), FK (course_id) references course (course_id), FK (building, room_number) references classroom (building, room_number))
#CREATE TABLE teaches (ID, course_id, sec_id, semester, year, PK (ID, course_id, sec_id, semester, year), FK (course_id, sec_id, semester, year) references section (course_id, sec_id, semester, year), FK (ID) references instructor (ID))
#CREATE TABLE student (ID, name, dept_name, tot_cred, PK (ID), FK (dept_name) references department

(dept_name))
#CREATE TABLE takes (ID, course_id, sec_id, semester, year, grade, PK (ID, course_id, sec_id, semester, year), FK (course_id,sec_id, semester, year) references section (course_id, sec_id, semester, year), FK (ID) references student (ID))
#CREATE TABLE advisor (s_ID, i_ID, PK (s_ID), FK (i_ID) references instructor (ID), FK (s_ID) references student (ID))
#CREATE TABLE time_slot (time_slot_id, day, start_hr, start_min, end_hr, end_min, PK (time_slot_id, day, start_hr, start_min))
#CREATE TABLE prereq (course_id, prereq_id, PK (course_id, prereq_id), FK (course_id) references course (course_id), FK (prereq_id) references course (course_id))
#
Q: Find the buildings which have rooms with capacity more than 50.
sub-questions:[Find the buildings, which have rooms with capacity more than 50.]
Intermediate representation: ['select distinct classroom.building', 'select where classroom.capacity > 50']
A: Lets think step by step. To get the SQL using the intermediate representations, we combine them to form:
SQL: SELECT DISTINCT building FROM classroom WHERE capacity > 50
#
Q: Find the name and building of the department with the highest budget.
sub-questions:[Find the name and building of the department, with the highest budget.]
Intermediate representation: ['select department.dept_name, department.building', 'select order by department.budge desc limit 1']
A: Lets think step by step. To get the SQL using the intermediate representations, we combine them to form:
SQL: SELECT dept_name, building FROM department ORDER BY budget DESC LIMIT 1
#
Q: Find the title of courses that have two prerequisites?
sub-questions:[Find the title of courses, that have two prerequisites?]
Intermediate representation: ['select course.title', 'select where count(prereq.*)=2 group by prereq.course_id']
A: Lets think step by step. To get the SQL using the intermediate representations, we combine them to form:
SQL: SELECT T1.title FROM course AS T1 JOIN prereq AS T2 ON T1.course_id = T2.course_id GROUP BY T2.course_id HAVING count(*) = 2
#
Q: How many courses that do not have prerequisite?
sub-questions:[How many courses, that do not have prerequisite?]
Intermediate representation: ['select count(Courses.*)', 'select where @.@ not in prereq.course_id']
A: Lets think step by step. To get the SQL using the intermediate representations, we combine them to form:
SQL: SELECT count(*) FROM course WHERE course_id NOT IN (SELECT course_id FROM prereq)
#
Q: Find the total budgets of the Marketing or Finance Department.
sub-questions:[Find the total budgets of the Marketing or Finance Department.]
Intermediate representation: ['select sum(department.budget) where department.dept_name = "Marketing" or department.dept_name="Finance"']
A: Lets think step by step. To get the SQL using the intermediate representations, we combine them to form:
SQL: SELECT sum(budget) FROM department WHERE dept_name = 'Marketing' OR dept_name = 'Finance'
#
Q: Find the department name of the instructor whose name contains 'Soisalon'.
sub-questions:[Find the department name of the instructor, whose name contains 'Soisalon'.]
Intermediate representation: ['select instructor.dept_name', 'select where instructor.name like "%Soisalon%"']
A: Lets think step by step. To get the SQL using the intermediate representations, we combine them to form:
SQL: SELECT dept_name FROM instructor WHERE name LIKE '%Soisalon%'
#
Q: Find the title of course that is provided by both Statistics and Psychology departments.
sub-questions:[Find the title of course, that is provided by both Statistics and Psychology departments.]
Intermediate representation: ['select course.title', 'select where course.dept_name="Statistics" and course.dept_name="Psychology"']
A: Lets think step by step. To get the SQL using the intermediate representations, we combine them to form:
SQL: SELECT title FROM course WHERE dept_name = 'Statistics' INTERSECT SELECT title FROM course WHERE dept_name = 'Psychology'

#
Q: Find the title of course that is provided by Statistics but not Psychology departments.
sub-questions:[Find the title of course, that is provided by Statistics, but not Psychology departments.]
Intermediate representation: ['select course.title', 'select where course.dept_name="Statistics"', 'select where course.dept_name!="Psychology"']
A: Lets think step by step. To get the SQL using the intermediate representations, we combine them to form:
SQL: SELECT title FROM course WHERE dept_name = 'Statistics' EXCEPT SELECT title FROM course WHERE dept_name = 'Psychology'
#
Q: Find courses that ran in Fall 2009 or in Spring 2010.
sub-questions:[Find courses, that ran in Fall 2009 or, in Spring 2010.]
Intermediate representation: ['select section.course_id', 'select where section.semester="Fall" and section.year=2009', 'select where section.semester="Spring" and section.year=2010']
A: Lets think step by step. To get the SQL using the intermediate representations, we combine them to form:
SQL: SELECT course_id FROM SECTION WHERE semester = 'Fall' AND YEAR = 2009 UNION SELECT course_id FROM SECTION WHERE semester = 'Spring' AND YEAR = 2010
#
Q: Find the names and average salaries of all departments whose average salary is greater than 42000.
sub-questions:[Find the names and average salaries of all departments, whose average salary is greater than 42000.]
Intermediate representation: ['select instructor.dept_name, avg(isntructor.slary) group by instructor.dept_name', 'select where avg(instructor.salary) > 42000']
A: Lets think step by step. To get the SQL using the intermediate representations, we combine them to form:
SQL: SELECT dept_name, AVG(salary) FROM instructor GROUP BY dept_name HAVING AVG (salary) > 42000
#
SQLite SQL tables, with their properties:
#CREATE TABLE regions (REGION_ID, REGION_NAME, PK (REGION_ID))
#CREATE TABLE countries (COUNTRY_ID, COUNTRY_NAME, REGION_ID, PK (COUNTRY_ID), FK (REGION_ID) REFERENCES regions (REGION_ID))
#CREATE TABLE departments (DEPARTMENT_ID, DEPARTMENT_NAME, MANAGER_ID, LOCATION_ID, PK (DEPARTMENT_ID))
#CREATE TABLE jobs (JOB_ID, JOB_TITLE, MIN_SALARY, MAX_SALARY, PK (JOB_ID))
#CREATE TABLE employees (EMPLOYEE_ID, FIRST_NAME, LAST_NAME, EMAIL, PHONE_NUMBER, HIRE_DATE, JOB_ID, SALARY, COMMISSION_PCT, MANAGER_ID, DEPARTMENT_ID, PK (EMPLOYEE_ID), FK (DEPARTMENT_ID) REFERENCES departments(DEPARTMENT_ID), FK (JOB_ID) REFERENCES jobs(JOB_ID))
#CREATE TABLE job_history (EMPLOYEE_ID, START_DATE, END_DATE, JOB_ID, DEPARTMENT_ID, PK (EMPLOYEE_ID,START_DATE), FK (EMPLOYEE_ID) REFERENCES employees(EMPLOYEE_ID), FK (DEPARTMENT_ID) REFERENCES departments(DEPARTMENT_ID), FK (JOB_ID) REFERENCES jobs(JOB_ID))
#CREATE TABLE locations (LOCATION_ID, STREET_ADDRESS, POSTAL_CODE, CITY, STATE_PROVINCE, COUNTRY_ID, PK (LOCATION_ID), FK (COUNTRY_ID) REFERENCES countries(COUNTRY_ID))
#
Q: display job Title, the diffrence between minimum and maximum salaries for those jobs which max salary within the range 12000 to 18000.
sub-questions:[display job Title, the diffrence between minimum and maximum salaries for those jobs, which max salary within the range 12000 to 18000.]
Intermediate representation: ['select jobs.JOB_TITLE, jobs.MAX_SALARY - jobs.MIN_SALARY', 'select where jobs.MAX_SALARY between 12000 and 18000']
A: Lets think step by step. To get the SQL using the intermediate representations, we combine them to form:
SQL: SELECT job_title, max_salary - min_salary FROM jobs WHERE max_salary BETWEEN 12000 AND 18000
#
Q: display the employee ID for each employee and the date on which he ended his previous job.
sub-questions:[display the employee ID for each employee and the date, on which he ended his previous job.]
Intermediate representation: ['select job_history.EMPLOYEE_ID, max(job_history.END_DATE) group by

job_history.EMPLOYEE_ID', 'select extra max (job_history.END_DATE)']
A: Lets think step by step. To get the SQL using the intermediate representations, we combine them to form:
SQL: SELECT employee_id, MAX(end_date) FROM job_history GROUP BY employee_id
#
Q: return the smallest salary for every departments.
sub-questions:[return the smallest salary for every departments.]
Intermediate representation: ['select min(employees.SALARY), employees.DEPARTMENT_ID group by employees.DEPARTMENT_ID']
A: Lets think step by step. To get the SQL using the intermediate representations, we combine them to form:
SQL: SELECT MIN(salary), department_id FROM employees GROUP BY department_id
#
Q: display the department id and the total salary for those department which contains at least two employees.
sub-questions:[display the department id and the total salary for those department, which contains at least two employees.]
Intermediate representation: ['select employees.DEPARTEMENT_ID, sum(employees.SALARY)', 'select where count (employees.*)>=2 group by employees.DEPARTMENT_ID']
A: Lets think step by step. To get the SQL using the intermediate representations, we combine them to form:
SQL: SELECT department_id, SUM(salary) FROM employees GROUP BY department_id HAVING count(*) >= 2
#
SQLite SQL tables, with their properties:
#CREATE TABLE Rooms (RoomId PK, roomName, beds, bedType, maxOccupancy, basePrice, decor)
#CREATE TABLE Reservations (Code PK, Room, CheckIn, CheckOut, Rate REAL, LastName, FirstName, Adults, Kids, FK (Room) REFERENCES Rooms(RoomId))
#
Q: List how many times the number of people in the room reached the maximum occupancy of the room. The number of people include adults and kids.
sub-questions:[List how many times the number of people in the room, the maximum occupancy of the room., The number of people include adults and kids.]
Intermediate representation: ['select count(Resrevations.*)', 'select where Rooms.maxOccupancy=Reservations.Adults','select extra Reservations.Adults']
A: Lets think step by step. To get the SQL using the intermediate representations, we combine them to form:
SQL: SELECT count(*) FROM Reservations AS T1 JOIN Rooms AS T2 ON T1.Room = T2.RoomId WHERE T2.maxOccupancy = T1.Adults + T1.Kids;
#
SQLite SQL tables, with their properties:
#CREATE TABLE Attribute_Definitions (attribute_id PK, attribute_name, attribute_data_type)
#CREATE TABLE Catalogs (catalog_id PK, catalog_name, catalog_publisher, date_of_publication, date_of_latest_revision)
#CREATE TABLE Catalog_Structure (catalog_level_number PK, catalog_id, catalog_level_name, FK (catalog_id) REFERENCES Catalogs(catalog_id))
#CREATE TABLE Catalog_Contents (catalog_entry_id PK, catalog_level_number, parent_entry_id, previous_entry_id, next_entry_id, catalog_entry_name, product_stock_number, price_in_dollars, price_in_euros, price_in_pounds, capacity, length, height, width, FK (catalog_level_number) REFERENCES Catalog_Structure(catalog_level_number))
#CREATE TABLE Catalog_Contents_Additional_Attributes (catalog_entry_id, catalog_level_number, attribute_id, attribute_value, FK (catalog_entry_id) REFERENCES Catalog_Contents(catalog_entry_id), FK (catalog_level_number) REFERENCES Catalog_Structure(catalog_level_number))
#
Q: Find the names of the products with length smaller than 3 or height greater than 5.
sub-questions:[Find the names of the products, with length smaller than 3 or, height greater than 5.]
Intermediate representation: ['select Catalog_Contents.catalog_entry_name, 'select where Catalog_Contents.length < 3','select where Catalog_Contents.width > 5']
A: Lets think step by step. To get the SQL using the intermediate representations, we combine them to form:
SQL: SELECT catalog_entry_name FROM catalog_contents WHERE LENGTH < 3 OR width > 5
#
SQLite SQL tables, with their properties:

CREATE TABLE nuclear_power_plants (Id, Name, Latitude, Longitude, Country, Status, ReactorType, ReactorModel, ConstructionStartAt, OperationalFrom, OperationalTo, Capacity, LastUpdatedAt, Source)
#
Q: Which country has the most capacities of nuclear power plants?
A:

A.4 Least-to-Most Prompting - Domain Adapted - Generic Prompt (LTMP-DA-GP)

SQLite SQL tables, with their properties:
#
CREATE TABLE nuclear_power_plants (Id, Name, Latitude, Longitude, Country, Status, ReactorType, ReactorModel, ConstructionStartAt, OperationalFrom, OperationalTo, Capacity, LastUpdatedAt, Source)
Columns in nuclear_power_plants with examples in each column and descriptions wherever required:
Id: 572, 560, 258, 433.
Name: Ågesta, Turkey Point-4, Oskarshamn-2, Ningde-4.
Latitude: 55.084000, 55.604000, 41.188000, 45.800000. Description: latitude in decimal format
Longitude: -77.311000, 66.790000, 9.393000, 0.845000. Description: longitude in decimal format
Country: Canada, Germany, Taiwan, Province of China, Italy.
Status: Planned, Cancelled Construction, Under Construction, Suspended Construction.
ReactorType: HWGCR, GCR, LWGR, HTGR.
ReactorModel: Konvoi, VVER V-320, WH 2LP (DRYAMB), PHWR KWU.
ConstructionStartAt: 1977-02-01, 1968-05-18, 1965-04-12, 1972-11-01. Description: date when nuclear power plant construction was started
OperationalFrom: 2015-06-05, 1977-03-13, 1986-04-10, 1989-09-30. Description: date when nuclear power plant became operational (also known as commercial operation date)
OperationalTo: 2011-05-19, 2004-06-29, 1992-05-27, 2015-04-30. Description: date when nuclear power plant was shutdown (also known as permanent shutdown date)
Capacity: 1092, 125, 535, 1307. Description: nuclear power plant capacity (design net capacity in MWe)
LastUpdatedAt: 2015-05-24T04:50:59+03:00, 2015-05-24T04:51:11+03:00, 2017-02-10T23:58:48+02:00, 2018-03-10T13:41:49+02:00. Description: date and time when information was last updated
Source: WNA/wikipedia/IAEA, wikipedia, WNA, WNA/IAEA/GEO. Description: source of the information
#
Q: Find the latitudes of nuclear power plants with capacity more than 50.
sub-questions:['Find the latitudes of nuclear power plants', 'with capacity more than 50.']
Intermediate representation: ['select distinct nuclear_power_plants.Latitude', 'select where nuclear_power_plants.Capacity > 50']
A: Lets think step by step. To get the SQL using the intermediate representations, we combine them to form:
SQL: [SELECT DISTINCT Latitude FROM nuclear_power_plants WHERE Capacity > 50]
#
Q: Find the country and status of the nuclear power plant with the highest capacity.
sub-questions:['Find the country and status of the nuclear power plant', 'with the highest capacity.']
Intermediate representation: ['select nuclear_power_plants.Country, nuclear_power_plants.Status', 'select order by nuclear_power_plants.Capacity desc limit 1']
A: Lets think step by step. To get the SQL using the intermediate representations, we combine them to form:
SQL: [SELECT Country, Status FROM nuclear_power_plants ORDER BY Capacity DESC LIMIT 1]
#
Q: Find the name of nuclear power plants that have two entries in the database?
sub-questions:['Find the name of nuclear power plants', 'that have two entries in the database?']
Intermediate representation: ['select nuclear_power_plants.Name', 'select where count(nuclear_power_plants.*)=2 group by nuclear_power_plants.Id']
A: Lets think step by step. To get the SQL using the intermediate representations, we combine them to form:
SQL: [SELECT T1.Name FROM nuclear_power_plants AS T1 JOIN nuclear_power_plants AS T2 ON T1.Id = T2.Id GROUP BY T2.Id HAVING count(*) = 2]
#
Q: How many nuclear power plants do not have a prerequisite?
sub-questions:['How many nuclear power plants', 'do not have a prerequisite?']

Intermediate representation: ['select count(nuclear_power_plants.*)', 'select where @.@ not in prereq.Id']
A: Lets think step by step. To get the SQL using the intermediate representations, we combine them to form:
SQL: [SELECT COUNT(*) FROM nuclear_power_plants WHERE Id NOT IN (SELECT Id FROM prereq)]
#
Q: Find the total capacity of the nuclear power plants named Marketing or Finance.
sub-questions:['Find the total capacity of the nuclear power plants named Marketing or Finance.']
Intermediate representation: ['select sum(nuclear_power_plants.Capacity) where nuclear_power_plants.Name = "Marketing" or nuclear_power_plants.Name="Finance"']
A: Lets think step by step. To get the SQL using the intermediate representations, we combine them to form:
SQL: [SELECT sum(Capacity) FROM nuclear_power_plants WHERE Name = 'Marketing' OR Name = 'Finance']
#
Q: Find the country associated with the nuclear power plant whose name contains 'Soisalon'.
sub-questions:['Find the country associated with the nuclear power plant', 'whose name contains "Soisalon"'.]
Intermediate representation: ['select nuclear_power_plants.Country', 'select where nuclear_power_plants.name like "%Soisalon%"']
A: Lets think step by step. To get the SQL using the intermediate representations, we combine them to form:
SQL: [SELECT Country FROM nuclear_power_plants WHERE Name LIKE '%Soisalon%']
#
Q: Find the name of nuclear power plants that are located in both Statistics and Psychology countries.
sub-questions:['Find the name of nuclear power plants', 'that are located in both Statistics and Psychology countries.']
Intermediate representation: ['select nuclear_power_plants.Name', 'select where nuclear_power_plants.Country="Statistics" and nuclear_power_plants.Country="Psychology"']
A: Lets think step by step. To get the SQL using the intermediate representations, we combine them to form:
SQL: [SELECT Name FROM nuclear_power_plants WHERE Country = 'Statistics' INTERSECT SELECT Name FROM nuclear_power_plants WHERE Country = 'Psychology']
#
Q: Find the name of nuclear power plants that are located in Statistics but not Psychology countries.
sub-questions:['Find the name of nuclear power plants', 'that are located in Statistics but not Psychology countries.']
Intermediate representation: ['select nuclear_power_plants.Name', 'select where nuclear_power_plants.Country="Statistics"', 'select where nuclear_power_plants.Country!="Psychology"']
A: Lets think step by step. To get the SQL using the intermediate representations, we combine them to form:
SQL: [SELECT Name FROM nuclear_power_plants WHERE Country = 'Statistics' EXCEPT SELECT Name FROM nuclear_power_plants WHERE Country = 'Psychology']
#
Q: Find the Ids of nuclear power plants that were constructed in Fall 2009 or in Spring 2010.
sub-questions:['Find the Ids of nuclear power plants', 'that were constructed in Fall 2009 or, in Spring 2010.']
Intermediate representation: ['select nuclear_power_plants.Id', 'select where nuclear_power_plants.ConstructionStartAt="Fall" and nuclear_power_plants.LastUpdatedAt=2009', 'select where nuclear_power_plants.ConstructionStartAt="Spring" and nuclear_power_plants.LastUpdatedAt=2010']
A: Lets think step by step. To get the SQL using the intermediate representations, we combine them to form:
SQL: [SELECT Id FROM nuclear_power_plants WHERE ConstructionStartAt = 'Fall' AND LastUpdatedAt = 2009 UNION SELECT Id FROM nuclear_power_plants WHERE ConstructionStartAt = 'Spring' AND LastUpdatedAt = 2010"]
#
Q: Find the countries and average capacities of all nuclear power plants whose average capacity is greater than 42000.
sub-questions:['Find the countries and average capacities of all nuclear power plants, whose average capacity is greater than 42000.']
Intermediate representation: ['select nuclear_power_plants.Country, avg(isntructor.Capacity) group by nuclear_power_plants.Country', 'select where avg(nuclear_power_plants.Capacity) > 42000']
A: Lets think step by step. To get the SQL using the intermediate representations, we combine them to form:
SQL: [SELECT Country, AVG (Capacity) FROM nuclear_power_plants GROUP BY Country HAVING AVG (Capacity) > 42000]
#
Q: display the Name of the nuclear power plant and the difference between its capacity and the year it was

constructed for those plants which capacity is within the range 12000 to 18000.
sub-questions:['display the Name of the nuclear power plant and the difference between its capacity and the year it was constructed for those plants', 'which capacity is within the range 12000 to 18000.']
Intermediate representation: ['select nuclear_power_plants.Name, nuclear_power_plants.Capacity - nuclear_power_plants.ConstructionStartAt', 'select where nuclear_power_plants.Capacity between 12000 and 18000']
A: Lets think step by step. To get the SQL using the intermediate representations, we combine them to form:
SQL: [SELECT Name, Capacity - ConstructionStartAt FROM nuclear_power_plants WHERE Capacity BETWEEN 12000 AND 18000]
#
Q: display the ID for each nuclear power plant and the date on which it stopped operating.
sub-questions:['display the ID for each nuclear power plant and the date', 'on which it stopped operating.']
Intermediate representation: ['select nuclear_power_plants.Id, max(nuclear_power_plants.OperationalTo) group by nuclear_power_plants.Id', 'select extra max (nuclear_power_plants.OperationalTo)']
A: Lets think step by step. To get the SQL using the intermediate representations, we combine them to form:
SQL: [SELECT Id, MAX(OperationalTo) FROM nuclear_power_plants GROUP BY Id]
#
Q: return the smallest capacity for each nuclear power plant.
sub-questions:['return the smallest capacity for each nuclear power plant.']
Intermediate representation: ['select min(nuclear_power_plants.Capacity), nuclear_power_plants.Id group by nuclear_power_plants.Id']
A: Lets think step by step. To get the SQL using the intermediate representations, we combine them to form:
SQL: [SELECT MIN(Capacity), Id FROM nuclear_power_plants GROUP BY Id]
#
Q: display the id and the total capacity for those nuclear power plants which have at least two reactors.
sub-questions:['display the id and the total capacity for those nuclear power plants', 'which have at least two reactors.']
Intermediate representation: ['select nuclear_power_plants.Id, sum(nuclear_power_plants.Capacity)', 'select where count (nuclear_power_plants.*)>=2 group by nuclear_power_plants.Id']
A: Lets think step by step. To get the SQL using the intermediate representations, we combine them to form:
SQL: [SELECT Id, SUM(Capacity) FROM nuclear_power_plants GROUP BY Id HAVING count(*) >= 2]
#
Q: Count how many times the capacity of a nuclear power plant is equal to the sum of its status and reactor type.
sub-questions:['Count how many times the capacity of a nuclear power plant', 'is equal to the sum of its status', 'and reactor type.']
Intermediate representation: ['select count(nuclear_power_plants.*)', 'select where nuclear_power_plants.Capacity=nuclear_power_plants.Status + nuclear_power_plants.ReactorType','select extra nuclear_power_plants.Capacity']
A: Lets think step by step. To get the SQL using the intermediate representations, we combine them to form:
SQL: [SELECT COUNT(*) FROM nuclear_power_plants AS T1 JOIN nuclear_power_plants AS T2 ON T1.Id = T2.Id WHERE T2.Capacity = T1.Status + T1.ReactorType]
#
Q: Find the names of the nuclear power plants with capacity smaller than 3 or capacity greater than 5.
sub-questions:['Find the names of the nuclear power plants with capacity', 'smaller than 3 or', 'capacity greater than 5.']
Intermediate representation: ['select nuclear_power_plants.Name, 'select where nuclear_power_plants.Capacity < 3','select where nuclear_power_plants.Capacity > 5']
A: Lets think step by step. To get the SQL using the intermediate representations, we combine them to form:
SQL: [SELECT Name FROM nuclear_power_plants WHERE Capacity < 3 OR Capacity > 5]
#
Q: Which country has the most capacities of nuclear power plants?
sub-questions:['Which country has the most capacities of nuclear power plants?']
Intermediate representation: ['select nuclear_power_plants.Country, sum(nuclear_power_plants.Capacity) group by nuclear_power_plants.Country', 'select order by sum(nuclear_power_plants.Capacity) desc limit 1']
A:

B GenBench Evaluation Card

Motivation			
Practical *Sec. 1*	*Cognitive*	*Intrinsic*	*Fairness*

Generalisation type					
Compositional *Sec. 2*	*Structural*	*Cross Task*	*Cross Language*	*Cross Domain* *Sec. 2*	*Robustness*

Shift type			
Covariate	*Label*	*Full*	*Assumed* *Sec. 2*

Shift source			
Naturally occuring *Sec. 2*	*Partitioned natural*	*Generated shift*	*Fully generated*

Shift locus			
Train–test	*Finetune train–test*	*Pretrain–train*	*Pretrain–test* *Sec. 4*

Evaluating Neural Language Models as Cognitive Models of Language Acquisition

Héctor Javier Vázquez Martínez[1] **Annika Heuser**[1] **Charles Yang**[1,2] **Jordan Kodner**[3]
[1]University of Pennsylvania, Deptartment of Linguistics
[2]University of Pennsylvania, Deptartment of Computer and Information Science
[3]Stony Brook University, Dept. of Linguistics & Inst. for Advanced Computational Science
hjvm@sas.upenn.edu aheuser@sas.upenn.edu
charles.yang@ling.upenn.edu jordan.kodner@stonybrook.edu

Abstract

The success of neural language models (LMs) on many technological tasks has brought about their potential relevance as scientific theories of language despite some clear differences between LM training and child language acquisition. In this paper we argue that some of the most prominent benchmarks for evaluating the syntactic capacities of LMs may not be sufficiently rigorous. In particular, we show that the template-based benchmarks lack the structural diversity commonly found in the theoretical and psychological studies of language. When trained on small-scale data modeling child language acquisition, the LMs can be readily matched by simple baseline models. We advocate for the use of the readily available, carefully curated datasets that have been evaluated for gradient acceptability by large pools of native speakers and are designed to probe the structural basis of grammar specifically. On one such dataset, the LI-Adger dataset, LMs evaluate sentences in a way inconsistent with human language users. We conclude with suggestions for better connecting LMs with the empirical study of child language acquisition.

1 Introduction

The growth of neural language models (LMs) for NLP over the past decade has been followed by a growth in research on the potential of these models to provide insights into the cognitive aspects of human language acquisition, representation, and processing (Linzen and Baroni, 2021). Good, even human-like, performance on NLP tasks does not necessarily imply that LMs solve these in human-like ways, so computational linguists have designed a wide variety of experimental paradigms to probe specific properties of the models' linguistic knowledge (Linzen et al., 2016a; Chowdhury and Zamparelli, 2018; Gulordava et al., 2018; Wilcox et al., 2018; McCoy et al., 2020; Hu et al., 2020; Warstadt et al., 2020; Papadimitriou et al., 2021; Huebner et al., 2021) These range from ways of classifying or extracting structures from internal representations (e.g., Hewitt and Manning, 2019; Tenney et al., 2019; Tucker et al., 2021; Papadimitriou et al., 2021), to building tasks inspired by psycholinguistic processing studies and classic acceptability rating task that theoretical linguists use to infer grammatical knowledge (e.g., Linzen et al., 2016a; Warstadt et al., 2020; Huebner et al., 2021; Sinclair et al., 2022).

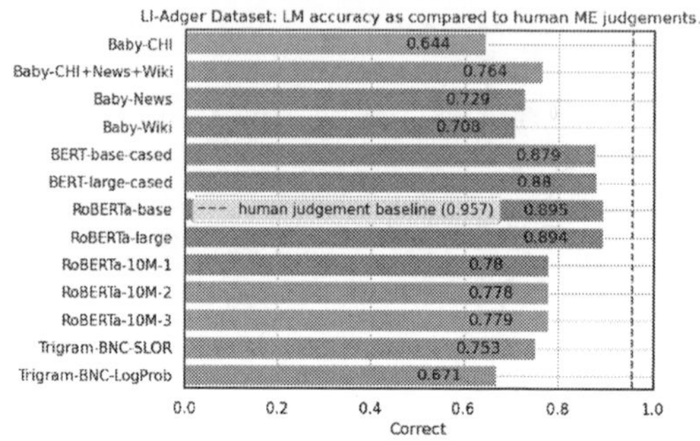

Figure 1: LM performance on the LI-Adger dataset. Human performance is marked by the vertical line. Baby=BabyBERTa, CHI=AO-CHILDES, News=AO-NEWSELA, Wiki=Wikipedia-1.

Of these approaches, acceptability rating may be the most popular. Large acceptability rating data sets focusing on syntax, semantics, and morphology, such as BLiMP (Warstadt et al., 2020), SyntaxGym (Gauthier et al., 2020), and CoLA (Warstadt et al., 2019) lend themselves to benchmarking, and these sit alongside myriad smaller scale studies focused on specific lingusitic phenomena (e.g., Linzen et al., 2016b; Marvin and Linzen, 2018; Wilcox et al., 2018). Results have been impressive for the most part. It appears, from the logic of these studies, that many state-of-the-art neural models are capable of inducing human-like grammatical knowledge on unannotated data – like children during language acquisition.

Proceedings of the 1st GenBench Workshop on (Benchmarking) Generalisation in NLP, pages 48–64
December 6, 2023 ©2023 Association for Computational Linguistics

1.1 Implications for Language Acquisition?

Neural model training differs from human language acquisition in key ways, perhaps most obviously, in that most models are trained on orders of magnitude more input (in plain text form) than humans receive (in spoken or signed form)– BERT was trained on about 3.3B forms, and Chinchilla on 1.4T, while an English-learning child only receives about 10M word per year, for a total vocabulary measured in the hundreds at age three (Fenson et al., 1994; Bornstein et al., 2004).

Recent studies have begun to address this. Can we build models that learn from input on the scale of language acquisition? Would these models then inform our understanding of human language acquisition? Warstadt and Bowman (2022) favor this perspective. They argue that a computational model that performs well on behavioral probing benchmarks when trained on ablated input, that is at least as limited as a human learner's input, is evidence that the model is a good proxy for human linguistic knowledge. Huebner et al. (2021) showed that a specially tuned model trained on only 5M tokens of child-directed speech (CDS) performs well on a purpose-designed data set. And in 2023, an aptly-named shared task, the CoNLL/CMCL BabyLM Challenge,[1] is asking participants to train on only 100M words (about the input of an adolescent) before testing on acceptability benchmarks.

1.2 Goals of the Paper

A push towards extracting performance on smaller training data is a welcome change for the field. In addition to its possible cognitive implications, the drive will also benefit efficient NLP and NLP for low-resource languages. However, while we look forward to the impending engineering advances, we also urge caution in the approaches used to draw scientific conclusions about the nature of neural models' linguistic knowledge. In particular, we take issue with Warstadt and Bowman (2022)'s assertion that "positive results from model learners are more meaningful than negative results."

Their reasoning follows that of an existence proof. If a model that strictly lacks any advantages over humans nevertheless succeeds at a task that requires human-like linguistic knowledge, then it is proof that there exists at least one model with human-like linguistic knowledge. A failure only tells us that this model failed for some reason that may or may not be relevant to the question at hand.

However, this line of reasoning requires faith in the evaluation. If there are any potentially unrecognized non-human-like ways to succeed at the task, or if the task does not truly reflect acquisition, or the task does not actually test a relevant structural property of language, then a positive result becomes inconclusive at best. Unexpected shortcuts emerging from unforeseen biases in evaluation abound across NLP (Chao et al., 2018; McCoy et al., 2019; Wang et al., 2022), so this is a realistic concern. Even the underlying reasoning that "if a (neural) model X behaves like cognitive system Y, then it is equivalent to Y" may be fraught (Guest and Martin, 2023).

In this paper,[2] we evaluate LMs as models of language acquisition on two benchmarking data sets: the widely used Benchmark of Linguistic Minimal Pairs (BLiMP; Warstadt et al., 2020), which also forms part of the evaluation for the BabyLM Challenge, and Zorro (Huebner et al., 2021), a data set inspired by BLiMP with restricted vocabulary for acquisition-inspired models trained only on CDS.

Section 2 reviews the nature of linguistic knowledge and child language acquisition. In Section 3, we introduce the BLiMP and Zorro benchmarks and subject them to baseline tests by simple non-human-like models. These establish several weaknesses in the organization and content of both benchmarks. In Section 4, we evaluate neural models on a more challenging data set derived directly from theoretical linguistics papers. We find that LMs are not necessarily human-like in terms of within- and across-model variability. Finally, Section 5 concludes with a discussion of the logical problem of behavioral probing. We argue for **(a)** benchmarks that better probe the structural knowledge of syntax, **(b)** tests that reflect the developmental findings of language acquisition, and **(c)** more baseline models.

2 Knowledge of Language and its Acquisition

One of the goals of linguistic theory is to characterize the properties that distinguish grammatical from ungrammatical sentences in a language. The empirical study of grammaticality, however, mainly relies on native speakers' acceptability judgments, which interact with other cognitive and perceptual

[1] https://babylm.github.io/

[2] Our evaluation code and data are available at https://github.com/hjvm/benchmarking_acquisition.git

systems and generally produce gradient results. For example, longer and more complex sentences, even when fully grammatical, are rated as less acceptable than shorter and simpler sentences. Nevertheless, large-scale investigations have established the structural basis of a categorical grammar (Sprouse and Hornstein, 2013). For example, syntactic constraints that prohibit certain transformational processes are shown to have a "super-additive" effect that go beyond acceptability rating due to sentence length and other non-structural factors. Furthermore, acceptability judgments collected at scale are highly consistent with the data reported in the theoretical literature typically gathered informally with few consultants (Sprouse and Almeida, 2012; Sprouse et al., 2013; Sprouse and Almeida, 2017).

The structural basis of language and its uniformity across the linguistic community can be better appreciated from the perspective of child language acquisition. Recent years have seen renewed interest in individual differences across child learners (Kidd et al., 2018), especially with respect to vocabulary acquisition (Frank et al., 2021). It is at least possible that children differ in their cognitive abilities for language and learning, but it is empirically obvious that they differ in their experience with language. Longitudinal records of child language development have made it possible to track both children's vocabulary growth, and the development of the structural aspects of their grammar. In the Providence Corpus (Demuth et al., 2006), for example, six children were recorded at regular intervals from age 1 to 3. On average, fewer than 20% of the first 100 words are shared between any two children. The overlap merely rises to about 40% for the first 1,000, which is the upper limit of a three-year old's vocabulary size (Hart and Risley, 1995; Bornstein et al., 2004). Yet these children's grammars are highly uniform even at this stage. Major syntactic categories, word order and argument structure, and the core morphological rules are firmly established before age three (Brown, 1973) on the basis of at most around 10M words per year (Hart and Risley, 1995) and a vocabulary size of only a few hundred types (Fenson et al., 1994), and all children produce similar grammatical errors during this time. Recent decades have also seen a convergence between the psychological and formal study of language development and the quantitative study of language variation in early childhood. The sociolinguist, Bill Labov, remarks that "The end result is a high degree of uniformity in both the categorical and variable aspects of language production, where individual variation is reduced below the level of linguistic significance" (2012).

The acquisition of vocabulary and grammar provide clues for investigating the capacities of LMs. Vocabulary learning is a matter of rote learning. This includes not just the arbitrary pairing of sounds and meanings, but also morphological processes (e.g., irregularity) and syntactic structures (e.g., sub-categorization, collocations, etc.). There is no escape from experience: more data results in better learning. But, the structural aspects of the grammar are different. They require form generalizations over the vocabularies.

The distinction between rote learning and structural learning (words vs. rules) is not well reflected by existing LM benchmarks including those discussed in this paper. In practice, these benchmarks are a mixture of tests for both vocabulary learning and grammar learning. Moreover, they are stochastically generated by templates: as such, a large number of test sentences are immediately available, but they lack the structural diversity that has proven revealing in the theoretical study of grammar.

Furthermore, the sentences are sometimes highly unnatural and semantically/pragmatically uncontrolled, which is precisely the confounding factor that linguists seek to neutralize when attempting to uncover the structural basis of language. Warstadt et al. (2020) are aware that their templates generate unnatural sentences, presenting the BLiMP sentence '`Sam ran around some glaciers.`' as an example. We found similar issues in Zorro, such as '`the lie on the foot is flat .`,' the first sentence in Zorro's `across_prepositional_phrase` paradigm (`lie` is a noun). The BLiMP authors state that this is not a problem because it affects both sentences in a pair, but how can we rule out unintended interactions between the grammatical phenomenon under evaluation and the semantic implausibility? Sprouse et al. (2018) find that this semantic implausibility may affect judgments of sentence wellformedness, even in the Forced Choice (FC) task used to collect the human baselines in BLiMP.

Indeed, there are already a large amount of carefully curated linguistic materials that are not only structurally diverse but also have minimized lexical and semantic confounds. Furthermore, these datasets (e.g., the Adger/LI dataset; Section 4) have been evaluated for acceptability at an individual level by a large pool of native speaker subjects and show very high convergence rates across individuals. They will be especially informative if we are to explore the structural knowledge of LMs.

3 Re-examining the Benchmarks

BLiMP (Warstadt et al., 2020)

Warstadt et al. (2020) introduce the Benchmark of Linguistic Minimal Pairs (BLiMP)[3] as a means of evaluating the linguistic knowledge of neural language models. BLiMP extends the reasoning of earlier studies (e.g., Linzen et al., 2016b; Marvin and Linzen, 2018; Wilcox et al., 2018) which use a minimal pair paradigm to approximate acceptability judgments. Instead of prompting for a acceptability judgments on individual sentences, as is most commonly done for human subjects, they present an LM with two sentences that only differ in one structural or lexical property. For a given minimal pair m_i consisting of an acceptable sentence $s_{i,1}$ and an unacceptable sentence $s_{i,2}$, if an LM evaluates $P(s_{i,1}) > P(s_{i,2})$, then the model has succeeded on m_i. An LM is scored according to the percentage of all the minimal pairs for which it identified the acceptable sentence. The minimal pair approach allows for the direct evaluation of LMs without training a binary classifier on top of them as was necessary for previous acceptability benchmarks (e.g., CoLA; Warstadt et al., 2019).

Minimal pairs need to be carefully constructed to control for length and lexical frequencies. BLiMP aims to accomplish this with automatic generation from templates, but as we discuss, it often yields sentences with low structural diversity and implausible semantics. The benchmark corpus includes data sets for 12 linguistic phenomena, including ANAPHOR AGREEMENT, ARGUMENT STRUCTURE, BINDING, CONTROL/RAISING, and others listed in the Appendix. These are further divided into 67 paradigms, each containing 1000 sentences pairs, which are meant to test variants of the phenomena, for example the phenomenon DETERMINER-NOUN AGR. contains 6 paradigms for adjacent agreement, agreement with irregular nouns, and agreement with adjectives intervening. BLiMP has become a standard NLP benchmark for this task and will be used as part of the test data for the upcoming BabyLM Challenge.

[3]https://github.com/alexwarstadt/blimp

Zorro (Huebner et al., 2021)

Huebner et al. (2021) explicitly aim to evaluate the relationship between LMs and the acquisition of grammar. They introduce BabyBERTa_AO-CHILDES "an acquisition-friendly version of RoBERTa," trained on English child-directed/produced speech (CDS) approximating the total input of a typical English-learning six-year-old. They train variants on only CDS from AO-CHILDES (Huebner and Willits, 2021), a pre-processed version of English CHILDES (MacWhinney, 1991), as well as variants on larger datasets from other sources.

Because BabyBERTa_AO-CHILDES (henceforth BabyBERTa) was trained on much less text than typical large transformer models are, its vocabulary is much smaller. To mitigate the impact of out-of-vocabulary (OOV) items on their tests, the authors introduce a new grammaticality test suite, Zorro,[4] in the style of BLiMP. Sentence pairs are generated for one paradigm each for 11 of BLiMP's 12 phenomena, along with two additional phenomena. However, we show that the Zorro sentences are not only lexically simpler as intended, but their templates are also far less complex and even less varied than the sentences in the corresponding BLiMP phenomena. Full lists of paradigms for each data set can be found in the Appendix, and the full data sets themselves are made available by the benchmarks' original authors.

3.1 Linear Baselines

As noted earlier, BLiMP and Zorro tests are stochastically generated with category-based templates. This way, a large number of examples can be generated and tested, but the drawback is that all examples are essentially the same structure. Moreover, many of the structures are simple, falling considerably below the coverage of modern syntactic analyses. In fact, many examples appear solvable by strictly linear methods. The observation that such template-generated examples can be solved this way is not new to to field. For example, Kam et al. (2008) demonstrated that a bigram model will predict the grammatical sentence from template-produced pairs featuring auxiliary inversion (a structural phenomenon) as well as neural models of the time.

To take an example from BLiMP, within its SUBJECT-VERB AGR phenomenon, four of six

[4]https://github.com/phueb/Zorro/

paradigms evaluate string-adjacent subject verb agreement that could be captured by a bigram model. The remaining two include intervening distractor nouns, but in both these and the string-adjacent paradigms, the target noun is consistently the first/leftmost noun. A single linear rule, albeit a long-distance one, is sufficient to succeed on this phenomenon. In ANAPHORA AGREEMENT, none of the sentences has any distractors at all: the test is solely about whether the anaphor (e.g., *himself/herself*) agrees with the first, and only, noun in the sentence preceding it. Success on such simple tests tells us little about the genuine grammatical capacity of LMs and distorts or dilutes summary metrics calculated over the benchmark.

We evaluate this problem quantitatively with two studies of linear rules that do not incorporate structural knowledge. We find that many, but certainly not all, paradigms are solvable with non-human-like linear approaches. These paradigms therefore do not contribute to the overall goal of evaluating whether an LM possesses linguistic knowledge. Additionally, we find that the paradigms of Zorro tend to be structurally even simpler and less internally varied than the parallel paradigms of BLiMP. It is a weaker benchmark even when accounting for the intended lexical simplicity.

3.1.1 *N*-Gram Models

The original BLiMP paper reports the accuracy of a 5-gram model trained on the 3.1B token Gigaword Corpus (Graff et al., 2003) in addition to three neural LMs and human performance. They find that the 5-gram model scores above chance (50%) on all but two phenomena but is outclassed by most of the neural LMs on most paradigms. Performance for all LMs can vary widely across paradigms within one phenomenon. In some cases, there is a clear split between the 5-gram and neural models, suggesting that the latter capture some structural property of the paradigm that the 5-gram model does not, but in other cases, the 5-gram model performs well, demonstrating that linear rules can be sufficient for completing those tasks.

Revisiting SUBJECT-VERB AGR. as an illustrative example, the Gigaword 5-gram model performs only slightly behind the neural models on each string-adjacent paradigm but far below chance in the distractor paradigms. However, the neural models also perform up to 20.5 points better in the adjacent paradigms than the distractor paradigms. The two distractor paradigms demonstrate that the neural models have learned a long-distance pattern (whether that be structural or "agree with the left-most noun"), but the adjacent paradigms cannot show this. They, and about half of the BLiMP paradigms, are uninformative in this way.

We extend this approach to the language acquisition setting by training a 5-gram model only on AO-CHILDES and evaluating on both BLiMP and Zorro. We compare these results to BabyBERTa on these data sets.[5] To further manage lexical effects while adding minimal complexity to the model, we evaluate both a 5-gram word model (5-word), and a 5-gram model trained only on POS tags (5-tag). AO-CHILDES was tagged using GPoSTTL, a rule-based POS tagger with tokenizer and lemmatizer based on the Brill Tagger (Brill, 1992). This was used to train sklearn's CRF POS-tagger, which was then used to label the benchmark corpora. This approach was taken to avoid bringing additional knowledge from a tagger trained on larger corpora into the benchmark corpora. The downside is that the tagger is not particularly accurate on the ungrammatical benchmark sentences, which may hurt performance for the 5-tag model. In addition to the 5-word and 5-tag models, we evaluate an oracle which marks a correct prediction if either 5-word or 5-tag makes a correct prediction. Our use of POS is motivated from a developmental perspective. Syntactic categories can be formed purely distributionally as early as infancy (Mintz, 2003; Shi and Melançon, 2010; Reeder et al., 2013) and children almost never make mistakes in their use of syntactic categories (Valian, 1986). It is thus plausible to assume that the acquisition of grammatical knowledge builds on a developmentally prior stage of syntactic category learning.

The results of the 5-gram experiments are summarized in Table 1 and laid out in detail in the Appendix. We draw three conclusions from these. First, the 5-gram models perform surprisingly well relative to the BabyBERTa transformer despite its extremely non-human-like simplicity when trained on the same AO-CHILDES data. Either 5-word or 5-tag, trained on the same data as BabyBERTa, outperformed BabyBERTa on 11 of 23 Zorro paradigms and 21 of 67 BLiMP paradigms. BabyBERTa's performance appears less impressive when presented alongside even this very weak

[5]Refer to Appendix for full details. We downloaded the publicly available model checkpoints from the BabyBERTa GitHub repository and replicated the BLiMP and Zorro results hosted on the Zorro GitHub repository

Zorro	BabyBERTa	5-Word	5-Tag	Either	Oracle
# Best	–	8/23	8/23	11/23	14/23
Avg Acc	78.91%	63.44%	57.59%	–	83.43%
BLiMP	**BabyBERTa**	**5-Word**	**5-Tag**	**Either**	**Oracle**
# Best	–	18/67	10/67	23/67	48/67
Avg Acc	60.72%	50.72%	37.93%	–	68.32%

Table 1: Performance summaries for 5-grams relative to BabyBERTa on Zorro and BLiMP. Number of paradigms in which a 5-gram model outperforms BabyBERTa and overall average accuracy across paradigms are reported. Either = either 5-word or 5-tag outpeformed BabyBERTa on the entire paradigm. Oracle = sentence pairs were marked correct if either 5-word or 5-tag made the correct prediction.

baseline. The AO-CHILDES 5-gram models perform more poorly on BLiMP than the Gigaword 5-gram model, but it still achieves high accuracy on several paradigms scattered across the phenomena.

Second, 5-gram oracle outperforms 5-word, 5-tag, and BabyBERTa. The 5-gram oracle is not a fair direct comparison but provides a summary metric for correlation between 5-word and 5-tag. A high oracle score relative to the two 5-gram models indicates that they do not make the same errors. That is, errors are not necessarily attributable to the string-local limitations of 5-grams *per se* but rather to 5-gram sparsity or errors in tagging. The high oracle score is another sign that the paradigms often capture surface properties rather than structural properties that would stump 5-gram models.

Third, the 5-gram models outperform BabyBERTa on proportionately more Zorro paradigms than BLiMP paradigms. Additionally, the AO-CHILDES 5-word model achieved 78.91% performance on Zorro, while the Gigaword 5-gram model only reached 60.5% on BLiMP. If Zorro were merely accounting for the smaller vocabulary in the AO-CHILDES training data, we should expect much more similar performance on both of these measures. Taken together, these suggest that Zorro is a substantially weaker benchmark that BLiMP, and it more greatly overestimates the apparent positive results of the acquisition-inspired BabyBERTa.

3.1.2 Hand-Written Simple Rules

In addition to reporting results on 5-gram models, we created simple hand-written rules which demonstrate that the probes are solvable in principle without reference to linguistic structure. While we do not claim that such rules are akin to the state of knowledge in LMs, it is also difficult to completely rule out this possibility. On the one hand, it is still unclear how to interpret the representation of linguistic knowledge in LMs. On the other, the vast majority of training data, at least child-directed for language acquisition, is structurally simple and can in fact be handled by rule-like pattern matchers. In English CDS, the distribution of anaphora is exceedingly straightforward: almost all instances of *himself* are preceded in the sentence by the subject pronoun *he* and a (male) noun phrase with no co-referential competitors. For comparison, Zorro `adjunct_island` can be solved perfectly by always selecting the sentence where the third-last word is *the*, and many of the paradigms can be solved by tracking the index of a specific word. Others can be solved by checking for the presence of a certain word. For example, the `superlative` paradigm can be solved by accepting the sentence that contains either *more* or *fewer*. For both Zorro and BLiMP, more than one paradigm can often be solved with the exact same rule. We write simple linear rules for each Zorro and BLiMP paradigm. See the Appendix for a full list of rules.

In summary, these rules yielded 93.97% accuracy on Zorro and solved 14 of 23 Zorro paradigms with 100% accuracy. Each `agreement_` paradigm is solved with at least 96% accuracy, with the remainder due to two irregular nouns, *feet* and *children*, which do not end in the *-s* referenced by these rules. The lowest performance is 52.75% on `anaphor_agreement-pronoun_gender`, a paradigm that requires an LM to 'know' the canonical gender of English names in order to choose *himself* or *herself*. The test sentence pairs were not quite balanced, so always guessing *himself* earns more than 50%.

BLiMP proved more challenging. The rules only yielded 84.35% accuracy on average and achieved perfect scores on 14 of 67 rules. The overall high score of the hand-written simple linear rules suggests that BLiMP suffers from the same issues regarding lack of sentence variety that Zorro does, but the lower accuracy indicates that the problem is not quite as severe. In principle, we could have composed more complex rules which achieved perfect accuracy on all paradigms, however, these simpler rules better illustrate our points. The success of non-human-like simple linear rules on most paradigms on both benchmarks further emphasizes that success on the template-based behavioral task does not necessarily imply that an LM possesses linguistic knowledge.

Sentence ID	Sentence	ME Z-score
32.3.Culicover.7a.g.01	John tried to win.	1.453262
32.3.Culicover.7b.*.01	John tried himself to win.	-0.86729
33.2.bowers.7b.g.07	Sarah counted the change accurately.	1.230412
33.2.bowers.7b.*.07	Sarah accurately counted the change.	1.20698
ch8.150.*.01	Melissa seems that is happy.	-1.14131
ch8.151.g.01	It seems that Melissa is happy.	1.000644
ch8.152.g.01	Melissa seems to be happy.	1.196088

Table 2: Top: Two pairwise phenomena from the Linguistic Inquiry (LI) dataset. Bottom: One multi-condition phenomenon from the Adger dataset. The ME Z-score is the averaged Z-score transformation of the human Magnitude Estimation judgments for each of the sentences across all the experimental participants.

4 An Alternative: The LI-Adger Dataset

The LI-Adger dataset is a comprehensive collection of 519 sentence types, 300 collected by Sprouse et al. (2013) from *Linguistic Inquiry (LI) 2001-2010*,[6] a major theoretical journal in linguistics, and 219 collected by Sprouse and Almeida (2012) from Adger's (2003) *Core Syntax* textbook.[7] Each sentence type includes eight hand-constructed, semantically plausible sentences, assembled into 150 pairwise (LI) and 105 multi-condition (Adger) phenomena where each minimal pair is lexically matched. We provide an example of each in Table 2.

The LI-Adger dataset improves upon the prior two datasets in three key ways. Firstly, unlike BLiMP and Zorro, the LI-Adger sentences are controlled for semantic implausibility, which has been shown to be a strong confounding factor when eliciting human judgments (Sprouse et al., 2018). Second, the 255 total pairwise and multi-condition phenomena achieve much more diverse coverage of syntactic phenomena than the 67 paradigms in BLiMP, and the 23 paradigms in Zorro. Third, the human judgments were collected using the Magnitude Estimation (ME) task (and Likert Scale (LS) in the case of the LI sentences) in addition to Forced-Choice (FC) as in the BLiMP human baselines. We believe this to be a crucial advantage because the FC task treats sentence acceptability as functionally categorical: A sentence is only acceptable or not relative to its minimal pair counterpart, whereas tasks such as ME allow us to make comparisons within and across minimal pairs, thereby treating sentence acceptability as a gradient measure.

With this dataset, we conduct the following two tests. First, in line with Vázquez Martínez (2021), we sort the LI-Adger dataset into 2391 unique minimal pairs. We then collect pseudo log-likelihood scores for each sentence from several models evaluated by Huebner et al. (2021), and score them using the same criteria as BLiMP and Zorro. As a baseline for the models, we include Log-Likelihood and Syntactic Log-Odds Ratio (SLOR; Pauls and Klein, 2012; Lau et al., 2017) scores by a trigram model trained on the British National Corpus (BNC; 100M words) by Sprouse et al. (2018).

We include the results of this test in Figure 1. We observe that all models are further from the human baseline as compared to those in BLiMP (no human baselines were reported for Zorro). But more importantly, we observe that the trigram model scored using SLOR performs on par with the BabyBERTa models and approaches the performance of RoBERTa (Liu et al., 2019) trained on 10M words. If we were to adopt the "positive results from model learners are more meaningful than negative results" argument, then the trigram model is as suitable a model of language acquisition as BabyBERTa is.

Raw accuracy notwithstanding, we proceed to conduct a novel test of judgment variability on our collection of LMs. We take advantage of the structure of the LI-Adger dataset in the following way: There are 519 sentence types, and for each type there are eight sentences that retain the same syntactic structure but vary lexical items at the locus of the syntactic structure tested (e.g., the head of a verb phrase from which extraction takes place). These datasets thus allow us to contrast the consistency of human judgment across and within construction types against that of the LMs.

We z-score the LM judgments to make them comparable to the human judgments. Then, for each set of eight sentences, we take the mean and standard deviation of all the judgments for humans and each LM. We find that the models are much more variable in their judgments: The human judgments, on average, vary by 0.288 standard devia-

[6]https://www.jonsprouse.com/data/Lingua2013/SSA.data.zip

[7]https://www.jonsprouse.com/data/JoL2012/SA2012.data.zip

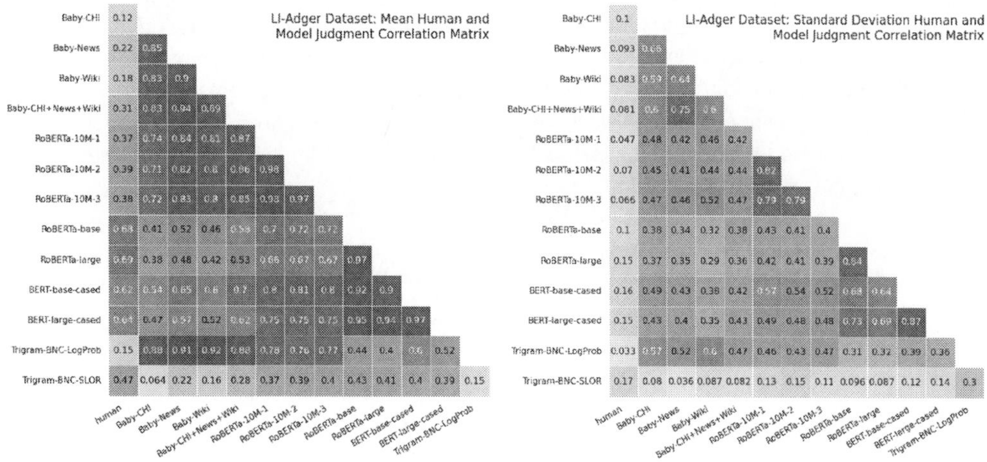

Figure 2: Correlation matrices of human judgments and LM output means (top) and standard deviations (bottom) on each sentence type on the LI-Adger dataset. Baby=BabyBERTa, CHI=AO-CHILDES, News=AO-NEWSELA, Wiki=Wikipedia-1.

tion (std. dev.) units within a given set of sentences. On the other hand, the LM that least varies is BabyBERTa Wiki, varying by 0.451 std. dev. units on average. The rest of the models nearly double the variability of the human judgments, ranging from 0.518 for RoBERTa-10M-1 to 0.554 for BERT-large-cased. Variability appears to increase rather than decrease as training size and performance increase. Surprisingly, the trigram model, when scored using log probabilities, is the closest in variability to the human judgments at 0.331 std. dev. units, but also the furthest when scored using SLOR with a variability of 0.599. Once again we find that a positive result on one test or another is not enough to draw positive conclusions.

For further illustration, we correlate the means and standard deviations of 512 sentence types across each LM and humans and plot the results in Figure 2. Both in terms of mean and standard deviations, we observe generally high correlations between the various neural LMs, but much lower correlations between the LMs and humans. This suggests that whatever the LMs are doing, good or bad, does not appear to be human. Interestingly, the BabyBERTa LMs show very high correlations with the naive trigram log-likelihood scores and very low with trigram SLOR scores, raising further suspicions that these small acquisition-inspired LMs behave like a very non-human-like model.

5 Discussion

It is widely recognized that children acquire language in ways that appear quite different from LM training. There is a growing realization that the cognitive relevance of LMs can only be established in a comparable setting. Bringing down training size requirements stands not to not only improve the applicability of such models to the study of language acquisition but also to efficient NLP on low-resource languages.

However, in this paper, we observed several weaknesses in BLiMP and Zorro, two minimal pair benchmarks for evaluating the linguistic knowledge of neural language models. We believe that it is worth critically revisiting the underlying assumption that positive results on such benchmarks are a demonstration of human-like representations or human-like language acquisition, especially if an evaluation can be solved in unintended ways, or if it does not reflect an adequately broad range of linguistic structures. It is unlikely that a behavioral probe, such as these large binarized benchmarks, can fully capture the complexity of linguistic knowledge. To this end, we made a case for also evaluating with curated benchmarking datasets: the gradient acceptability judgments from human subjects makes these effective probes for the structural basis of grammar. Together with a range of tests, from carefully constructed tests of grammaticality to probes correlating the internal state of LMs with their predictions need to complement theoretical, psycholinguistic, and neurolinguistic studies before a meaningful cognitive claim about the nature of neural language models can be made.

We end with some broader discussion about language acquisition and the cognitive interpretation of computational models. While it is now widely recognized that children learn language with only a fraction of the data needed for large LM training, merely reducing the amount of training data alone – such as the 100M word threshold in the BabyLM Challenge – still falls short of the requirement for an adequate model of language acquisition. While it is true that a native speaker's knowledge of language can be established on the basis of approximately 100 million words, child language research makes clear that not all aspects of linguistic knowledge are learned at the same time. Some, such as inflectional morphology, case marking, word order, and major transformations are acquired very early in all languages studied so far (e.g., Brown, 1973; Slobin, 2022) at an order of magnitude fewer words of input, while others are learned rather late: These include derivational morphology (Jarmulowicz, 2002), passivization (Pinker et al., 1987), control and cleft structures (Chomsky, 1969) and the dative constructions (Gropen et al., 1989) in the case of English, but these may emerge much earlier in other languages. This suggests that successful learning in the limit (e.g., 100M word) is not sufficient. For example, while a neural model of English past tense (Kirov and Cotterell, 2018) eventually learns the "add -ed" rule, it does so with over 3,000 verb lemmas. By contrast, children learn that rule before or around 3 (Kuczaj, 1977), when their vocabulary only contains around 300 or so verbs (Marcus et al., 1992). To serve as cognitive models of language, it is thus important to compare the training trajectory of LMs as a function of the training data volume against the developmental benchmarks of specific linguistic phenomena which have been amply documented in the empirical literature on child language.

Limitations

Our study is about the limitations of evaluation, so it is to be expected that our study has its limits as well. Most obviously, ours and any study would benefit from testing and reporting on a wider range of neural models and a wider range of baselines. And like most work in this area, our evaluations were only performed on English. We recommend the use of the LI-Adger data set. Like any behavioral probe, including the ones which we criticize, it can be subject to ambiguous interpretation. It has some substantial advantages, as we discuss in this paper, but also a couple of additional drawbacks. It is smaller than BLiMP or Zorro, and it has not been annotated by phenomenon. Nevertheless, it provides additional insights that those benchmarks do not. As in the paper, we recommend its use in conjunction with a wide range of other evaluation methods.

References

David Adger. 2003. *Core syntax: A minimalist approach*, volume 20. Oxford University Press Oxford.

Marc H Bornstein, Linda R Cote, Sharone Maital, Kathleen Painter, Sung-Yun Park, Liliana Pascual, Marie-Germaine Pêcheux, Josette Ruel, Paola Venuti, and Andre Vyt. 2004. Cross-linguistic analysis of vocabulary in young children: Spanish, Dutch, French, Hebrew, Italian, Korean, and American English. *Child development*, 75(4):1115–1139.

Eric Brill. 1992. A simple rule-based part of speech tagger. In *Proceedings of the Third Conference on Applied Natural Language Processing*, ANLC '92, page 152–155, USA. Association for Computational Linguistics.

Roger Brown. 1973. *A first language: The early stages.* Harvard University Press, Cambridge, MA.

Wei-Lun Chao, Hexiang Hu, and Fei Sha. 2018. Being negative but constructively: Lessons learnt from creating better visual question answering datasets. In *Proceedings of the 2018 Conference of the North American Chapter of the Association for Computational Linguistics: Human Language Technologies, Volume 1 (Long Papers)*, pages 431–441, New Orleans, Louisiana. Association for Computational Linguistics.

Carol Chomsky. 1969. *The acquisition of syntax in children from 5 to 10.* MIT Press.

Shammur Absar Chowdhury and Roberto Zamparelli. 2018. RNN simulations of grammaticality judgments on long-distance dependencies. In *Proceedings of the 27th International Conference on Computational Linguistics*, pages 133–144, Santa Fe, New Mexico, USA. Association for Computational Linguistics.

Katherine Demuth, Jennifer Culbertson, and Jennifer Alter. 2006. Word-minimality, epenthesis, and coda licensing in the acquisition of English. *Language and Speech*, 49(2):137–173.

Larry Fenson, Philip S Dale, J Steven Reznick, Elizabeth Bates, Donna J Thal, Stephen J Pethick, Michael Tomasello, Carolyn B Mervis, and Joan Stiles. 1994. Variability in early communicative development. *Monographs of the Society for Research in Child Development*, pages i–185.

Michael C Frank, Mika Braginsky, Daniel Yurovsky, and Virginia A Marchman. 2021. *Variability and consistency in early language learning: The Wordbank project.* MIT Press, Cambridge, MA.

Jon Gauthier, Jennifer Hu, Ethan Wilcox, Peng Qian, and Roger Levy. 2020. SyntaxGym: An online platform for targeted evaluation of language models. In *Proceedings of the 58th Annual Meeting of the Association for Computational Linguistics: System Demonstrations*, pages 70–76, Online. Association for Computational Linguistics.

David Graff, Junbo Kong, Ke Chen, and Kazuaki Maeda. 2003. English gigaword. *Linguistic Data Consortium, Philadelphia*, 4(1):34.

Jess Gropen, Steven Pinker, Michelle Hollander, Richard Goldberg, and Ronald Wilson. 1989. The learnability and acquisition of the dative alternation in english. *Language*, pages 203–257.

Olivia Guest and Andrea E Martin. 2023. On logical inference over brains, behaviour, and artificial neural networks. *Computational Brain & Behavior*, pages 1–15.

Kristina Gulordava, Piotr Bojanowski, Edouard Grave, Tal Linzen, and Marco Baroni. 2018. Colorless green recurrent networks dream hierarchically. In *Proceedings of the 2018 Conference of the North American Chapter of the Association for Computational Linguistics: Human Language Technologies, Volume 1 (Long Papers)*, pages 1195–1205, New Orleans, Louisiana. Association for Computational Linguistics.

Betty Hart and Todd R Risley. 1995. *Meaningful differences in the everyday experience of young American children.* Paul H Brookes Publishing, Baltimore, MD.

John Hewitt and Christopher D. Manning. 2019. A structural probe for finding syntax in word representations. In *Proceedings of the 2019 Conference of the North American Chapter of the Association for Computational Linguistics: Human Language Technologies, Volume 1 (Long and Short Papers)*, pages 4129–4138, Minneapolis, Minnesota. Association for Computational Linguistics.

Jennifer Hu, Jon Gauthier, Peng Qian, Ethan Wilcox, and Roger Levy. 2020. A systematic assessment of syntactic generalization in neural language models. In *Proceedings of the 58th Annual Meeting of the Association for Computational Linguistics*, pages 1725–1744, Online. Association for Computational Linguistics.

Philip A. Huebner, Elior Sulem, Fisher Cynthia, and Dan Roth. 2021. BabyBERTa: Learning more grammar with small-scale child-directed language. In *Proceedings of the 25th Conference on Computational Natural Language Learning*, pages 624–646, Online. Association for Computational Linguistics.

Philip A Huebner and Jon A Willits. 2021. Using lexical context to discover the noun category: Younger children have it easier. In *Psychology of learning and motivation*, volume 75, pages 279–331. Elsevier.

Linda D Jarmulowicz. 2002. English derivational suffix frequency and children's stress judgments. *Brain and Language*, 81(1-3):192–204.

Xuân-Nga Cao Kam, Iglika Stoyneshka, Lidiya Tornyova, Janet D Fodor, and William G Sakas. 2008. Bigrams and the richness of the stimulus. *Cognitive science*, 32(4):771–787.

Evan Kidd, Seamus Donnelly, and Morten H Christiansen. 2018. Individual differences in language acquisition and processing. *Trends in cognitive sciences*, 22(2):154–169.

Christo Kirov and Ryan Cotterell. 2018. Recurrent neural networks in linguistic theory: Revisiting Pinker and Prince (1988) and the past tense debate. *Transactions of the Association for Computational Linguistics*, 6:651–665.

Stan A. Kuczaj. 1977. The acquisition of regular and irregular past tense forms. *Journal of Verbal Learning and Verbal Behavior*, 16(5):589–600.

William Labov. 2012. What is to be learned. *Review of Cognitive Linguistics*, 10(2):265–293.

Jey Han Lau, Alexander Clark, and Shalom Lappin. 2017. Grammaticality, acceptability, and probability: A probabilistic view of linguistic knowledge. *Cognitive science*, 41(5):1202–1241.

Tal Linzen and Marco Baroni. 2021. Syntactic structure from deep learning. *Annual Review of Linguistics*, 7:195–212.

Tal Linzen, Emmanuel Dupoux, and Yoav Goldberg. 2016a. Assessing the ability of LSTMs to learn syntax-sensitive dependencies. *Transactions of the Association for Computational Linguistics*, 4:521–535.

Tal Linzen, Emmanuel Dupoux, and Yoav Goldberg. 2016b. Assessing the ability of lstms to learn syntax-sensitive dependencies. *Transactions of the Association for Computational Linguistics*, 4:521–535.

Yinhan Liu, Myle Ott, Naman Goyal, Jingfei Du, Mandar Joshi, Danqi Chen, Omer Levy, Mike Lewis, Luke Zettlemoyer, and Veselin Stoyanov. 2019. Roberta: A robustly optimized bert pretraining approach. *arXiv preprint arXiv:1907.11692.*

Brian MacWhinney. 1991. *The CHILDES language project: Tools for analyzing talk.* Lawrence Erlbaum, Mahwah, NJ.

Gary F Marcus, Steven Pinker, Michael Ullman, Michelle Hollander, T John Rosen, Fei Xu, and Harald Clahsen. 1992. Overregularization in language acquisition. *Monographs of the society for research in child development.*

Rebecca Marvin and Tal Linzen. 2018. Targeted syntactic evaluation of language models. In *Proceedings of the 2018 Conference on Empirical Methods in Natural Language Processing*, pages 1192–1202, Brussels, Belgium. Association for Computational Linguistics.

R. Thomas McCoy, Robert Frank, and Tal Linzen. 2020. Does syntax need to grow on trees? sources of hierarchical inductive bias in sequence-to-sequence networks. *Transactions of the Association for Computational Linguistics*, 8:125–140.

Tom McCoy, Ellie Pavlick, and Tal Linzen. 2019. Right for the wrong reasons: Diagnosing syntactic heuristics in natural language inference. In *Proceedings of the 57th Annual Meeting of the Association for Computational Linguistics*, pages 3428–3448, Florence, Italy. Association for Computational Linguistics.

Toben H Mintz. 2003. Frequent frames as a cue for grammatical categories in child directed speech. *Cognition*, 90(1):91–117.

Isabel Papadimitriou, Ethan A. Chi, Richard Futrell, and Kyle Mahowald. 2021. Deep subjecthood: Higher-order grammatical features in multilingual BERT. In *Proceedings of the 16th Conference of the European Chapter of the Association for Computational Linguistics: Main Volume*, pages 2522–2532, Online. Association for Computational Linguistics.

Adam Pauls and Dan Klein. 2012. Large-scale syntactic language modeling with treelets. In *Proceedings of the 50th Annual Meeting of the Association for Computational Linguistics (Volume 1: Long Papers)*, pages 959–968.

Steven Pinker, David S Lebeaux, and Loren Ann Frost. 1987. Productivity and constraints in the acquisition of the passive. *Cognition*, 26(3):195–267.

Patricia A Reeder, Elissa L Newport, and Richard N Aslin. 2013. From shared contexts to syntactic categories: The role of distributional information in learning linguistic form-classes. *Cognitive psychology*, 66(1):30–54.

Rushen Shi and Andréane Melançon. 2010. Syntactic categorization in french-learning infants. *Infancy*, 15(5):517–533.

Arabella Sinclair, Jaap Jumelet, Willem Zuidema, and Raquel Fernández. 2022. Structural persistence in language models: Priming as a window into abstract language representations. *Transactions of the Association for Computational Linguistics*, 10:1031–1050.

Dan Isaac Slobin. 2022. *The Crosslinguistic Study of Language Acquisition: Volume 3*, volume 3. Psychology Press.

Jon Sprouse and Diogo Almeida. 2012. Assessing the reliability of textbook data in syntax: Adger's core syntax. *Journal of Linguistics*, 48(3):609–652.

Jon Sprouse and Diogo Almeida. 2017. Design sensitivity and statistical power in acceptability judgment experiments. *Glossa*, 2(1):1.

Jon Sprouse and Norbert Hornstein. 2013. *Experimental syntax and island effects*. Cambridge University Press, Cambridge.

Jon Sprouse, Carson T Schütze, and Diogo Almeida. 2013. A comparison of informal and formal acceptability judgments using a random sample from linguistic inquiry 2001–2010. *Lingua*, 134:219–248.

Jon Sprouse, Beracah Yankama, Sagar Indurkhya, Sandiway Fong, and Robert C Berwick. 2018. Colorless green ideas do sleep furiously: gradient acceptability and the nature of the grammar. *The Linguistic Review*, 35(3):575–599.

Ian Tenney, Dipanjan Das, and Ellie Pavlick. 2019. BERT rediscovers the classical NLP pipeline. In *Proceedings of the 57th Annual Meeting of the Association for Computational Linguistics*, pages 4593–4601, Florence, Italy. Association for Computational Linguistics.

Mycal Tucker, Peng Qian, and Roger Levy. 2021. What if this modified that? syntactic interventions with counterfactual embeddings. In *Findings of the Association for Computational Linguistics: ACL-IJCNLP 2021*, pages 862–875, Online. Association for Computational Linguistics.

Virginia Valian. 1986. Syntactic categories in the speech of young children. *Developmental psychology*, 22(4):562.

Héctor Vázquez Martínez. 2021. The acceptability delta criterion: Testing knowledge of language using the gradience of sentence acceptability. In *Proceedings of the Fourth BlackboxNLP Workshop on Analyzing and Interpreting Neural Networks for NLP*, pages 479–495, Punta Cana, Dominican Republic. Association for Computational Linguistics.

Tianlu Wang, Rohit Sridhar, Diyi Yang, and Xuezhi Wang. 2022. Identifying and mitigating spurious correlations for improving robustness in NLP models. In *Findings of the Association for Computational Linguistics: NAACL 2022*, pages 1719–1729, Seattle, United States. Association for Computational Linguistics.

Alex Warstadt and Samuel R Bowman. 2022. What artificial neural networks can tell us about human language acquisition. In *Algebraic Structures in Natural Language*, pages 17–60. CRC Press.

Alex Warstadt, Alicia Parrish, Haokun Liu, Anhad Mohananey, Wei Peng, Sheng-Fu Wang, and Samuel R. Bowman. 2020. BLiMP: The benchmark of linguistic minimal pairs for English. *Transactions of the Association for Computational Linguistics*, 8:377–392.

Alex Warstadt, Amanpreet Singh, and Samuel R. Bowman. 2019. Neural network acceptability judgments. *Transactions of the Association for Computational Linguistics*, 7:625–641.

Ethan Wilcox, Roger Levy, Takashi Morita, and Richard Futrell. 2018. What do RNN language models learn about filler–gap dependencies? In *Proceedings of the 2018 EMNLP Workshop BlackboxNLP: Analyzing and Interpreting Neural Networks for NLP*, pages 211–221, Brussels, Belgium. Association for Computational Linguistics.

Appendix

Phenomenon	Paradigm	BabyBERTa	5-Gram			Simple
		AO-CHILDES	Word	Tag	Oracle	Rule
agreement_subject_verb	across_rel_clause	64.85	50.95	46.35	**68.95**	**96.20**
	in_simple_question	92.35	61.15	90.9	**93.9**	**98.30**
	in_question_with_aux	90.85	59	80.15	**90.9**	**98.05**
	across_prep_phrase	72.85	50	50	62.6	**98.40**
agreement_determiner_noun	between_neighbors	91.3	83.05	49.85	88.6	**98.60**
	across_1_adjective	89.85	50.45	50.05	75.05	**97.20**
filler-gap	wh_question_object	98.75	42.8	**100**	**100**	**100**
	wh_question_subject	75.7	**88.3**	**76.55**	**97.1**	**100**
island-effects	coord_struct_constr	97.05	43.35	55.6	83.85	**100**
	adjunct_island	56.15	**66.1**	**58.8**	**83.85**	**100**
quantifiers	existential_there	92.9	80.25	38.4	89.55	**100**
	superlative	64.55	45.1	**82**	**96.05**	**100**
npi_licensing	only_npi_licensor	74.1	**79.4**	3.7	**79.4**	**100**
	matrix_question	65.25	47.5	28.65	58	**100**
argument_structure	swapped_arguments	91	**92.15**	81.7	**98.85**	**100**
	transitive	60.05	**64.15**	32.65	**78.6**	58.05
	dropped_argument	79.9	**85.05**	**83.6**	**95.75**	**100**
irregular	verb	69.65	62.9	**93.6**	**96.35**	**88.40**
anaphor_agreement	pronoun_gender	51.75	49.15	1.95	50.95	**52.75**
ellipsis	n_bar	55.3	**66.6**	**63.6**	**89.9**	**100**
binding	principle_a	89.4	45.9	3.6	47.75	**100**
case	subjective_pronoun	94.7	**99.55**	**97.95**	**100**	**100**
local_attractor	in_question_with_aux	96.65	55.65	95	**99.05**	**100**
AVERAGE		78.91%	63.44%	57.59%	83.43%	93.97%
Fraction $\geq$ BabyBERTa		–	8/23	8/23	14/23	22/23

Table 3: Word and tag-level 5-gram models trained on AO-CHILDES plus 5-Gram Oracle and Simple Linear Rule Oracle for Zorro. 5-Gram and Simple Rule scores that are greater than BabyBERTa_AO-CHILDES are bolded

Phenomenon	Paradigm	Rule
agreement_subject_verb	across_rel_clause	2nd word ends in *s* iff 3rd last is in {*are*, *were*, *do*}
	in_simple_question	Word 2 right of {*are*, *were*} ends in *s*.
		Word 2 right of {*is*, *are*} does not
	in_question_with_aux	4th word ends in *s* iff 2nd is in {*are*, *were*, *do*}
	across_prep_phrase	2nd word ends in *s* iff 3rd last is in {*are*, *were*, *do*}
agreement_determiner_noun	between_neighbors	If {*these*, *those*} in sentence, next word ends in *s*.
		If {*this*, *that*} in sentence, next word does not
	across_1_adjective	If {*these*, *those*} in sentence, word 2 right ends in *s*.
		If {*this*, *that*} in sentence, word 2 right does not
filler-gap	wh_question_object	2nd word is *the*
	wh_question_subject	*who* does not immediately precede *the*
island-effects	coord_struct_constr	4th word is *and*
	adjunct_island	3rd last word is *the*
quantifiers	existential_there	Contains one of {*many*, *some*, *no*, *few*, *a*, *an*}
	superlative	Contains one of {*more*, *fewer*}
npi_licensing	only_npi_licensor	1st word is *only*
	matrix_question	Contains one of {*does*, *will*, *should*, *could*, *did*, *wouldo*}
argument_structure	swapped_arguments	1st word is *the*
	transitive	2nd last word does not end in *e*
	dropped_argument	1st word is *the*
irregular	verb	word following *had* ends in *n* or no word ends in *n*
anaphor_agreement	pronoun_gender	Sentence contains *himself*
ellipsis	n_bar	*Sentence where *and* appears farther right
binding	principle_a	4th last word ends with *ing*
case	subjective_pronoun	1st word is *the*
local_attractor	in_question_with_aux	4th word does not end with *'s*

Table 4: Simple Linear Rule descriptions for Zorro. Rules that require sentences to be compared are marked with an asterisk.

Phenomenon	Paradigm	BabyBERTa AO-CHILDES	5-Gram Word	 Tag	 Oracle	Simple Rule
anaphor_agreement	anaphor_gender_agreement	65.6	26.3	8	33.9	**73.9**
	anaphor_number_agreement	73.7	52.9	5.7	55.5	**80.1**
argument_structure	causative	58.5	55.2	30.7	**68.8**	**85.6**
	drop_argument	63.2	50.9	52.9	**80.8**	**77.1**
	inchoative	50.7	**56**	37.1	**73.8**	**57.1**
	intransitive	52.1	48.2	49.6	**76.3**	**73.55**
	passive_1	50.2	**52.1**	12.9	**56.4**	**59.5**
	passive_2	54	**48.4**	18.1	**56.8**	**59.6**
	transitive	55.3	51.6	36.1	**67.6**	**57.85**
binding	principle_A_case_1	43.6	**100**	7.1	**100**	**100**
	principle_A_case_2	99.9	41.5	13	48.3	99.2
	principle_A_c_command	58.7	35.7	4.2	38.1	**71.35**
	principle_A_domain_1	96.5	38.4	3.1	40.7	**100**
	principle_A_domain_2	51.4	**61.7**	2.7	**62.8**	**58.3**
	principle_A_domain_3	46.8	44.5	29.7	**61.1**	**50.4**
	principle_A_reconstruction	40.9	32.1	**53.9**	**68**	**74.1**
control_raising	existential_there_object_raising	59.1	30.5	23.4	46.5	**67.95**
	existential_there_subject_raising	51	43.4	17	**53.6**	**77**
	expletive_it_object_raising	63.3	61.2	48.3	**79.6**	**69.5**
	tough_vs_raising_1	72.2	59.1	49.6	**83.2**	**87.1**
	tough_vs_raising_2	34.4	**41.3**	18.4	**54.1**	**92.5**
determiner_noun_ agreement = a	a_irregular_1	66.6	48.8	37.4	61.3	**68.45**
	a_irregular_2	87.4	74.3	12.3	77.1	73.7
	a_with_adjective_1	76.3	48.2	49.7	63.8	**95.95**
	a_with_adj_irregular_1	82.9	49	49.7	56.3	74.45
	a_with_adj_irregular_2	67	49.5	18.3	58.2	**71.8**
	a_with_adj_2	80.4	49.8	19.9	59.7	**95.6**
	a_1	72.2	64.1	48.1	**74.5**	**95.55**
	a_2	87.4	65.2	11	68.1	**96.75**
ellipsis	ellipsis_n_bar_1	58.7	**64.1**	**63.5**	**86.4**	**85.65**
	ellipsis_n_bar_2	42.8	39.9	**70.5**	**80.9**	**99.95**
filler_gap_dependency	wh_questions_object_gap	73	37	**82.4**	**89.2**	**99.95**
	wh_questions_subject_gap	79.9	49	**81.4**	**89.4**	**99.9**
	wh_vs_that_no_gap	90.9	77.2	83.8	**94.9**	**99.95**
	wh_vs_that_no_gap_long_distance	92.1	74.9	87	**95.8**	**99.7**
	wh_vs_that_with_gap	29.1	22.7	15	**33**	**100**
	wh_vs_that_with_gap_long_distance	14.9	**25.8**	12.8	**32.8**	**99.9**
irregular_forms	irregular_past_participle_adjectives	59.8	**99.4**	12.2	**99.4**	**100**
	irregular_past_participle_verbs	59.8	**99.4**	12.2	**99.4**	**100**
island_effects (coordinate_structure_ constraint = y)	adjunct_island	63.8	58.4	55.5	**82.5**	**94.5**
	y_complex_left_branch	36.2	11.8	19.6	26.9	**97.05**
	y_object_extraction	56.5	41.9	37.1	**63.7**	**86.35**
	left_branch_island_echo_question	52.4	16.3	30.1	38.7	**100**
	left_branch_island_simple_question	66.6	24.5	30.3	43.8	**97.9**
	sentential_subject_island	46.1	37.3	42.8	**62.9**	**82.65**
	wh_island	47.1	**69**	**93.4**	**97.3**	**100**
npi_licensing	matrix_question_npi_licensor_present	56.4	41.1	39.5	**65.7**	**97.4**
	npi_present_1	27	**56**	26.7	**69.6**	**100**
	npi_present_2	20.3	**56.4**	**25.8**	**70.5**	**100**
	only_npi_licensor_present	71.6	**98.4**	2.4	**98.5**	**100**
	only_npi_scope	72.1	**80.4**	**79.4**	**97.2**	**100**
	sentential_negation_npi_licensor_present	73.8	**100**	0	**100**	**100**
	sentential_negation_npi_scope	81.9	40	65.3	79.6	**100**
quantifiers	existential_there_quantifiers_1	93.7	79.1	26.4	87.4	**97.3**
	existential_there_quantifiers_2	35.7	19.6	**36**	**50.6**	**96.85**
	superlative_quantifiers_1	49.5	**73**	**89.8**	**96.4**	**100**
	superlative_quantifiers_2	61.2	51.9	0.1	52	**100**
s-selection	animate_subject_passive	45.5	**48.4**	24	**58.4**	**65.25**
	animate_subject_trans	59.7	50	57.1	**78.2**	**84.65**
subject_verb_agreement	distractor_agreement_relational_noun	29	26.2	21.4	**42.1**	**50.25**
	distractor_agreement_relative_clause	35.6	28.3	30.4	**49.8**	**55.85**
	irregular_plural_subject_verb_agreement_1	67.9	33.4	51.7	62.5	53.2
	irregular_plural_subject_verb_agreement_2	66.2	51	51.9	**70.7**	59.3
	regular_plural_subject_verb_agreement_1	68.8	39.9	51.1	**72**	64.35
	regular_plural_subject_verb_agreement_2	60.1	51	55.6	**76.9**	**73.15**
AVERAGE		60.72%	50.72%	37.93%	68.32%	84.35%
Fraction $\geq$ BabyBERTa		–	18/67	10/67	48/67	62/67

Table 5: Word and tag-level 5-gram models trained on AO-CHILDES plus 5-Gram Oracle and Simple Linear Rule Oracle for BLiMP. 5-Gram and Simple Rule scores that are greater than BabyBERTa_AO-CHILDES are bolded

Phenomenon	Paradigm	Rule
anaphor_agreement	anaphor_gender_agreement	Does not contain *itself*
	anaphor_number_agreement	Number of words that end in *s* is even
argument_structure	causative	Does not contain one of {*appear, vanish, exist,*
	transitive	*sigh, rust, cheer, clash, fall, fell, waste*}
	drop_argument	Last word is not one of {*to,*
	inchoative	*with, about, from,*
	intransitive	*at, through, by, like*}
	passive_1	None of {*communicat, suffer, compet, shout, laugh,*
	passive_2	*scream, complain, compromis, grin, chat*} in sentence
binding	principle_A_case_1	*Is the shorter of the two sentences
	principle_A_case_2	*Is the longer of the two sentences
	principle_A_	(Last word ends in *s* and (1st word is any of pl_det
	c_command	or the 2nd word is *lot*)) or 2nd to last word ends in *s*)
	principle_A_domain_1	*Is the shorter of the two sentences
	principle_A_domain_2	*Is the shorter of the two sentences
	principle_A_domain_3	Does not contain *that*
	principle_A_reconstruction	4th word does not end in *ed* nor *'t*
control_raising	a_obj_raising	Does not contain one of verb_set
	a_subj	Contains one of subj_words or {*appear, sure,*
(existential_	subj_raising	*threaten, look*}
there = a)	expletive_it_object_raising	Does not contain one of verb_set
	tough_vs_raising_1	Does not contain one of subj_words, nor *apt*
	tough_vs_raising_2	Contains one of subj_words, or *apt*
determiner_noun_	a_irregular_1	Does not end in *that* followed by (one of
agreement = b	b_irregular_2	{*people, women, men, children*} or a word ending
	b_with_adj_irregular_1	in *ses*) nor in {*those, these*} followed by (a word
	b_with_adj_irregular_2	ending in *is* or not with *s* at all)
	b_with_adjective_1	Does not end in *that* followed by a word ending in
	b_with_adj_2	a letter other than *i* followed by *s* nor in
	b_1	{*those, these*} followed by (a word ending in
	b_2	*is* or not with *s* at all)
ellipsis	ellipsis_n_bar_1	Last word in num_quant
	ellipsis_n_bar_2	Last word has already occurred in sentence
filler_gap_	wh_questions_object_gap	Does not contain *wh*
dependency	wh_questions_subject_gap	Does not contain *wh*
	wh_vs_that_no_gap = c	Does not contain *wh*
	c_long_distance	Does not contain *wh*
	wh_vs_that_with_gap = d	Contains *wh*
	d_long_distance	Contains *wh*
irregular_forms	irregular_past_	If 1st word is *the*, then 2nd word ends in *n*,
	part_adj	otherwise 2nd word must not end in *n*
	irregular_past_part_verbs	*Is the shorter of the two sentences
island_effects	adjunct_island	Last word is not *about* and does not end in *ing*
	e_complex_left_branch	2nd word is not in mod_aux
(coordinate_structure_	e_object_extraction	2nd to last word is not *and*
constraint = e)	f_echo_question	Does not start with *Wh*
(left_branch_	f_simple_question	2nd word is not in mod_aux
island = f)	sentential_subject_island	Ends in *ing* or *ed* or *with*
	wh_island	*wh*, capitalized or not, occurs twice in sentence
npi_licensing	matrix_question_g	1st word in mod_aux
	npi_present_1	Does not contain the word *ever*
(npi_licensor_	npi_present_2	Does not contain the word *ever*
present = g)	only_g	1st word is *only*
(npi_scope = h)	only_h	1st word is *only*
	sentential_negation_g	Does not contain the word *ever*
	sentential_negation_h	Does not contain the word *ever*
quantifiers	a_quantifiers_1	Does not contain {*each, most, all, every*} while
	a_quantifiers_2	also containing {*one-ten*}
	superlative_quantifiers_1	*Is the longer of the two sentences
	superlative_quantifiers_2	1st word is not *no*
s-selection	animate_subject_passive	Contains one of people_groups
	animate_subject_trans	*Is the shorter of the two sentences
subject_verb_agreement	i_relational_noun	*Is the longer of the two sentences
	i_relative_clause	The number of words that ends in *s* is odd
(distractor_	irregular_j_1	Contains no word ending in a letter other than *i* and
agreement = i)		followed by *s* that is followed by a word ending in *s*
(plural_subject_	irregular_j_2	None of {*people, women, men, children*} is
verb_agreement = j)		followed by a word ending in *s*
	regular_j_1	*Is the shorter of the two sentences
	regular_j_2	The number of words that ends in *s* is odd

Table 6: Linear Rule descriptions for BLiMP. Rules that require sentences to be compared are marked with an asterisk. Rules sometimes span across multiple rows. If one paradigm name is split across these rows, then the rule only corresponds to that paradigm. Otherwise the rule corresponds to all the paradigms listed in these rows. All variables (e.g. verb_set, subj_words) are defined in table 7.

Name	Content
`verb_set`	{*ask, press, entic, prod, obligat, convinc, badger, compel, sway, order*}
`subj_words`	{*certain, soon, likely, unlikely, bound, about*}
`num_quant`	{*one-ten, many, few, several, more, some, lot, fewer*}
`mod_aux`	{*had, should, is, was, can, has, will, would, could, do, does, might, were, did*}
`people_groups`	{*men, woman, children, teacher, lad, offspring, student, customer, girl, boy*}

Table 7: The sets of words represented by the variables used in table 6

Understanding Code Semantics: An Evaluation of Transformer Models in Summarization

Debanjan Mondal* **Abhilasha Lodha*** **Ankita Sahoo*** **Beena Kumari***
University of Massachusetts Amherst
{debanjanmond,alodha,asahoo,beenakumari}@umass.edu

Abstract

This paper delves into the intricacies of code summarization using advanced transformer-based language models. Through empirical studies, we evaluate the efficacy of code summarization by altering function and variable names to explore whether models truly understand code semantics or merely rely on textual cues. We have also introduced adversaries like dead code and commented code across three programming languages (Python, Javascript, and Java) to further scrutinize the model's understanding. Ultimately, our research aims to offer valuable insights into the inner workings of transformer-based LMs, enhancing their ability to understand code and contributing to more efficient software development practices and maintenance workflows.

1 Introduction

Code summarization is a task that involves generating coherent and semantically relevant summaries that effectively describe the intended function of the software. In the dynamic realm of software development and maintenance, an adept grasp of program functionalities is of paramount importance. In this context, the integration of natural language summaries derived from source code emerges as a potent instrument, streamlining developers' efforts and augmenting program comprehension.

While current state-of-the-art code summarization models are developed and evaluated on clean and curated datasets, the real-world coding environment is far from standardized. Developers often deviate from standard coding practices, leading to inconsistent naming conventions. Additionally, actual codebases often feature commented sections, serving as legacy code or reserved for future use cases. Our research aims to simulate these real-world scenarios and assess whether models truly comprehend the inherent code semantics, rather than merely relying on textual cues.

The prevailing approaches to code summarization typically employ an encoder-decoder framework, encompassing the conversion of code into a hidden space and its subsequent transformation into natural language. For instance, CodeT5 (Wang et al., 2021), a unified pretrained encoder-decoder Transformer model, leverages the semantics encoded in identifiers. In this research, we investgate the effectiveness of these models by tweaking the function and variable names in the existing code summarization datasets. Furthermore, we introduce additional challenges, such as commented code and dead code, to elevate the complexity of data samples and scrutinize the models' summarization processes. Dead code refers to unreachable code segments, devoid of functional importance, which language interpreters (e.g., Python and Javascript) ignore. We seek to evaluate whether models effectively disregard such code segments. All our experiments are reproducible and we will release our code and data upon publication.

The driving motivation behind this research lies in enhancing code comprehension and reducing the efforts entailed in software development and maintenance. By unraveling how Language Models comprehend code, we aim to contribute insights that pave the way for more effective software development practices. Our study, through experimentation and analysis, strives to provide valuable directions for improving the capabilities of Language Models in understanding and summarizing code, despite the challenges posed by real-world coding scenarios.[*]

2 Related Work

Automated code summarization is a useful tool for software developers and has been an active re-

[*]Equal contribution.

[*]Our code is publicly available at: Github

Proceedings of the 1st GenBench Workshop on (Benchmarking) Generalisation in NLP, pages 65–75
December 6, 2023 ©2023 Association for Computational Linguistics

serach field for quite some time. Recently large language models have shown significant improvements in natural language tasks. Inspired by this, several pretrained language models have been developed for the programming language tasks. The encoder-decoder models have been found to be more successful in Programming Language (PL) tasks, whereas fully decoder models perform significantly better in Natural Language (NL) domain.

Models like CodeBERT (Feng et al., 2020), PLBART (Ahmad et al., 2021), GraphCodeBERT (Guo et al., 2021), CodeT5 (Wang et al., 2021), CoTexT (Phan et al., 2021) have shown impressive performances in the CodeXGLUE (Lu et al., 2021) benchmark. Unlike natural language, it's necessary to capture the rich code semantics in the programming language. Most Programming Language Models (PLMs) in this domain are pretrained on a large corpus of NL-PL pair in several programming languages with a masked token prediction objective. To capture the code semantics, various models have used different approaches. For example, CodeT5 uses an additional masked identifier prediction and GraphCodeBERT incorporates the data flow extracted from the code. These PLMs have shown impressive results in downstream tasks like code summarization. Ahmed and Devanbu (2022a) explored the code summarization in project-specific domain. Sun et al. (2022) used an extractive and abstractive framework from source code summarization. Ahmed and Devanbu (2022b) showed that multilingual training can amply performance for low resource languages in different downstream tasks including code summarization. (Chen et al., 2022) provided further insights for low resource languages like Ruby.

As indicated by Guo et al. (2021) in GraphCodeBERT, indicators play a key role in code summarization. However, it's more desirable that our model relies more on code semantics and syntax rather than method names and identifiers. Developers follow their own naming conventions which can affect the model performance. In a closely related work, Sontakke et al. (2022) have shown that Semantic Preserving Transformations like removing code comments, replacing function names and local variable names to generic names significantly affects the BLEU score of the models like PLBART. We want to extend this exploration to other models like CodeT5, CodeBERT etc. We also aim to increase the scope of semantic preserving transformations by including dead code and commented code to check the model's understanding of the code.

3 Dataset

There are several different code summarization datasets available. But we prefered CodeXGLUE (Lu et al., 2021) over others for these reasons -

- CodeXGLUE has been meticulously deduplicated, as demonstrated in (Shi et al., 2022). This ensures that any duplication within the dataset does not artificially inflate performance metrics.
- CodeXGLUE offers a wide range of six languages. This allowed us to conduct experiments and compare results across different programming languages.

We can categorize the six languages available in CodeXGLUE into three groups based on the size of their combined datasets (including train, validation, and test sets). Please note that the following information pertains to the combined dataset size:

- In the High Resource category, both Python and PHP have approximately 300,000 code-summary pairs each.
- In the Mid Resource category, Java and Go consist of around 180,000 code-summary pairs.
- In the Low Resource category, Javascript comprises 65,000 pairs, while Ruby only has 27,000 code-summary pairs.

To analyze the impact of data transformation across resource categories, we selected one language from each category. Therefore, for our experiments, we utilized the languages Python, Java, and Javascript. The detailed statistics about train, validation and test splits is presented in Table 1.

3.1 Data Transformation

We will focus on code transformations that will preserve the code functionality. In the programming paradigm, this is known as **obfuscation**. In this study, we focused on 3 kinds of transformations. These are visually explained in Figure 1:

- **Renaming Identifiers:** Although the software development industry emphasizes the importance of meaningful and descriptive names for functions and variables, developers often use random function and variable names. To replicate such scenario, we replaced function and variable names with generic but unique names. However while doing so, we had to keep in mind that the control flow of the overall program should not be affected. We leveraged the Abstract Syntax Tree (AST) of the source code to identify and edit identifiers. Implementation details and interesting corner cases vary across programming languages and will be discussed subsequently.

- **Commented Code:** It is very common in software engineering to encounter commented codes inside a function. These may be legacy codes which are not used anymore, or code snippets that might be used in future. To simulate such situation, we added commented codes. For each source code, we randomly sampled a function within the same data split, created commented version of it and added it after a function definition. Finding a suitable place to add comments is tricky and sometimes it can potentially change the program functionality. For our experiments, we add the comments starting from the next line after function definition.

- **Dead Code:** Adding code after return statements is another transformation that we explored in our experiments. Python and Javascript interpreters ignore anything added after return statements, and we wanted to check if the models have developed the ability to do so. Since Java compiler throws error if we add anything after return, we excluded Java from this study.

Code transformation implementation details about specific programming languages have been presented in A.2.

4 Models and Evaluation

4.1 Models

In this study we ran our experiments on 2 models:

- **CodeT5:** Upon examining the leaderboard of CodeXGLUE[2], and comparing metrics from various research papers, we discovered that CodeT5 (Wang et al., 2021) achieves state-of-the-art results for the code summarization task on this benchmark. Due to limitations in the size of our available GPUs, we opted to utilize the CodeT5 small[3] (60M parameters) and base[4] (223M parameters) models, while excluding the CodeT5 Large model (770M parameters) from our analysis. It is worth noting that CodeT5 incorporates an identifier aware denoising objective during its pretraining, making it more inclined to utilize textual cues from identifiers. We wanted to evaluate its robustness in our experiments.

- **CodeBERT:** For comparison across different architectures, we chose the CodeBERT (Feng et al., 2020) (173M parameters) model. Unlike CodeT5, CodeBERT is an encoder only model which is pretrained on the CodeSearchNet (Husain et al., 2020) dataset. For sequence-to-sequence generation problems like code summarization, the authors provide an Encoder-Decoder framework where they initialize the encoder with the pretrained CodeBERT, but they randomly initialize the decoder with a transformer model. Note that the decoder weights are not trained during the pretraining phase. For our experiments we use the CodeBERT Base[5] model.

Languages	Transformation	Train Data	Validation Data	Test Data
Python	Original	251820	13914	14918
	Renamed Identifiers	251820	13914	14918
	Commented Code	251820	13914	14918
	Dead Code	251820	13914	14918
Javascript	Original	58025	3885	3291
	Renamed Identifiers	38254	2730	2157
	Commented Code	38254	2730	2157
	Dead Code	21897	1548	1213
Java	Original	164923	5183	10955
	Renamed Identifiers	164888	5182	10953
	Commented Code	164923	5183	10955

Table 1: Dataset Size Information for different splits.

The finetuning code utilized for our project was obtained from the public GitHub repository of CodeT5.[6] The CodeT5 authors also included the finetuning code for CodeBERT. We reused the finetuned checkpoint of CodeT5 base that

[2]https://microsoft.github.io/CodeXGLUE/

[3]https://huggingface.co/Salesforce/codet5-small

[4]https://huggingface.co/Salesforce/codet5-base

[5]https://huggingface.co/microsoft/codebert-base

[6]https://github.com/salesforce/CodeT5

Transformation Type	Original Code	Modified Code
Renaming Identifiers	def standard(cls, element): # We remove all special # characters and return the # formatted string. return (Regex(element, cls.regex_replace, replace_with="@funilrys") .replace() .replace("@funilrys", ""))	def func1(arg1, arg2): return Regex(arg2, arg1.regex_replace, replace_with='@funilrys') .replace() .replace('@funilrys', '')
Dead code	def collection_to_df (collection): return pd.concat([record.series for record in collection], axis=1).T	def collection_to_df (collection): return pd.concat([record.series for record in collection], axis=1).T style = tag.get('style') if style and 'text-decoration:underline' in style: tag.wrap(self.soup .new_tag('u'))
Commented Code	def str_lower(x): sl = _to_string_sequence(x).lower() return column.ColumnStringArrow(sl.b ytes, sl.indices, sl.length, sl.offset, string_sequence=sl)	def str_lower(x): # def fromRaw(cls, skype=None, # raw={}): # return cls(skype, raw, # **cls.rawToFields(raw)) sl = _to_string_sequence(x).lower() return column.ColumnStringArrow(sl.b ytes, sl.indices, sl.length, sl.offset, string_sequence=sl)

Figure 1: Examples of different kind of transformations discussed in Section 3.1.

was available. As for CodeT5 small and CodeBERT, we performed the finetuning process on clean CodeXGLUE data, using the hyperparameters specified in the repository. The finetuned checkpoints on clean data for every model and every language serve as our baseline. Note that, the BLEU scores (Papineni et al., 2002) of our finetuned checkpoints on the clean CodeXGLUE test data has slight discrepancies with the BLEU scores reported in the original papers. However, the difference was not more than one decimal point. This may be attributed to the difference between GPU architectures. We report the scores mentioned in the original papers as the train clean - test clean scores.

5 Experiments

For all our experiments, we use the NVIDIA Tesla M40 GPUs. While finetuning for all types of data (Clean, Corrupted and Combined), we used the clean data finetuning hyperparameters that were available in the CodeT5 repository. However, for CodeT5 Base model, we had to reduce the batch size from 48 to 16 to fit in our GPU. All other hyperparameters remain the same. With this setup, we perform the following experiments.

- **Identifier Corruption:** We conducted individual finetuning of the models using clean, corrupted, and combined train data (clean + corrupted). Subsequently, we evaluated these three types of models on both clean and corrupted test data. We used CodeBERT, CodeT5 Small and CodeT5 Base models for this experiment.

- **Commented Code Corruption:** For this corruption type, we performed separate finetuning of the model using clean data and commented code corrupted data. Finally, we evaluated these two types of models on both clean data and commented code corrupted data. We only evaluated the CodeT5 Small and CodeT5 base models in this particular setup.

- **Dead Code Corruption:** Similar to the previous corruption type, we carried out separate finetuning of the model using clean data and dead code corrupted data. Subsequently, we evaluated these two types of models on both clean data and dead code corrupted data. Once again, we only evaluated the CodeT5 Small and CodeT5 base models in this setup.

5.1 Evaluation

Evaluation metrics are crucial for assessing the effectiveness of a code summarization model. In our study, we utilized both automatic and human evaluations.

1. **BLEU** (Papineni et al., 2002): It is a precision-based metric that measures the overlap between the words (and/or n-grams) in the machine-generated summaries and the human reference summaries. We calculated smoothed BLEU-4 (considering upto 4-grams) scores for each of the generated summaries and then averaged across all the summaries. We used the same evaluation script as CodeT5 which in turn reused the original evaluation script provided in the CodeXGLUE (Lu et al., 2021) benchmark. The BLEU scores obtained from different experiments for Python, Java, and JavaScript are presented in Table 2, 3, and 4.

2. **Human Evaluation:** Additionally, we performed a manual evaluation by annotating 200 random samples for both Python and JavaScript. Further details of the human evaluation process are discussed in the Section 7.

6 Discussion

Our experiments try to answer the following essential questions on models' understandability.

6.1 Research Question 1: *Does a model trained on clean data perform well on the identifier corrupted data?*

For all languages and models, the performance of a model trained on clean data tends to diminish when faced with corrupted test data, as compared to its performance on clean test data. The drop in performance for all models and languages is at least 4 points in terms of BLEU score. This phenomenon may be attributed to the model's reliance on textual hints found within function and variable names during training, rather than grasping the true essence of the code's functionality and achieving generalization. The comparison is visually shown in Figure 2.

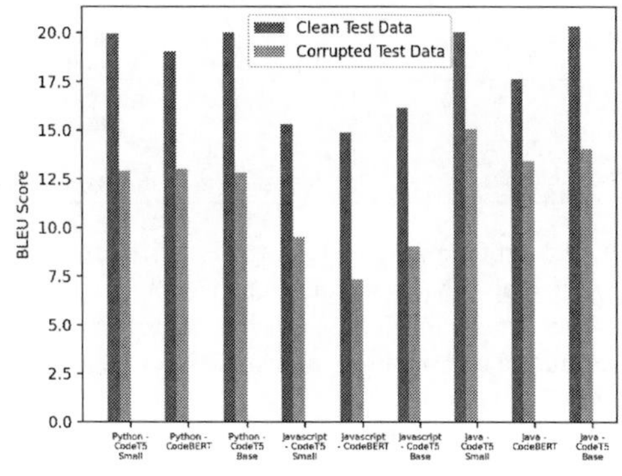

Figure 2: Comparing performance on clean and corrupted test data for models trained on clean data.

6.2 Research Question 2: *Does the model trained on identifier corrupted data perform well on clean data?*

A surprising observation arises when examining the performance of the model trained only on corrupted data. It demonstrates a commendable level of proficiency not only on corrupted test data (which is expected) but also on clean test data. This is visually explained in Figure 3. For all languages and models, the performance on clean test data between the model trained on clean data and corrupted data is less than 1 point in terms of BLEU score, except for CodeBERT in javascript. We hypothesize that when we train on the corrupted data, the model is forced to understand the code functionality in a generalized manner, thereby enabling it to perform well even in the clean dataset.

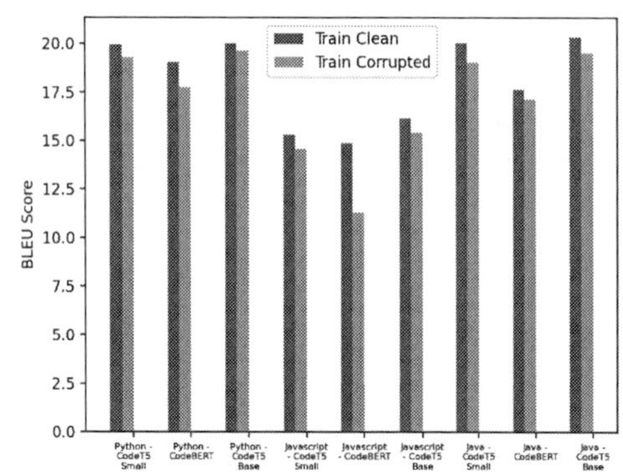

Figure 3: Comparing performance on clean test data and for models trained on clean data and corrupted data.

Train Data	Test Data	Python			Javascript			Java		
		CodeT5 Small	CodeBERT	CodeT5 Base	CodeT5 Small	CodeBERT	CodeT5 Base	CodeT5 Small	CodeBERT	CodeT5 Base
Clean	Clean	19.96	19.06	20.01	15.32	14.90	16.16	20.02	17.65	20.31
	Corrupted	12.92	13.03	12.81	9.51	7.34	9.04	15.06	13.42	14.05
Corrupted	Clean	19.28	17.75	19.64	14.55	11.30	15.41	19.05	17.16	19.50
	Corrupted	16.21	15.52	16.50	12.68	10.76	13.13	17.27	16.20	17.36
Combined	Clean	19.73	18.93	20.05	15.27	13.01	15.83	19.82	18.01	19.70
	Corrupted	16.17	15.76	16.51	12.46	11.29	12.86	17.14	16.19	17.44

Table 2: Smooth BLEU-4 scores for different train-test combinations for clean and identifier corrupted data. When models are trained using clean data, their performance deteriorates when tested on identifier corrupted data. However, when models are trained on a combination of both clean and corrupted data, they demonstrate satisfactory performance on both types of test data - clean and corrupted.

Train Data	Test Data	Python		Javascript	
		CodeT5 Small	CodeT5 Base	CodeT5 Small	CodeT5 Base
Clean	Clean	19.96	20.01	15.32	16.16
	Dead Code	18.55	19.83	15.20	15.52
Dead Code	Clean	19.74	18.66	14.69	15.32
	Dead Code	18.92	19.19	15.62	16.70

Table 3: Smooth BLEU-4 scores for different language and train-test combinations for dead code corruption.

6.3 Research Question 3: *How is the performance of the model trained on the combined data?*

Our combined dataset contained both clean data and identifier corrupted data. The model trained on a combined dataset exhibits impressive performance not only on clean data but also on identifier corrupted data. Its performance on the clean test data is very similar to and sometimes even surpasses the performance of the model only trained on the clean data. Similar observations are seen for the corrupted test data. Notably, this pattern is consistent across all the models and languages. This shows that if we curate our dataset correctly, the model can generalize across clean and corrupted datasets. The BLEU score performance comparisons are visually explained in Figures 4 and 5.

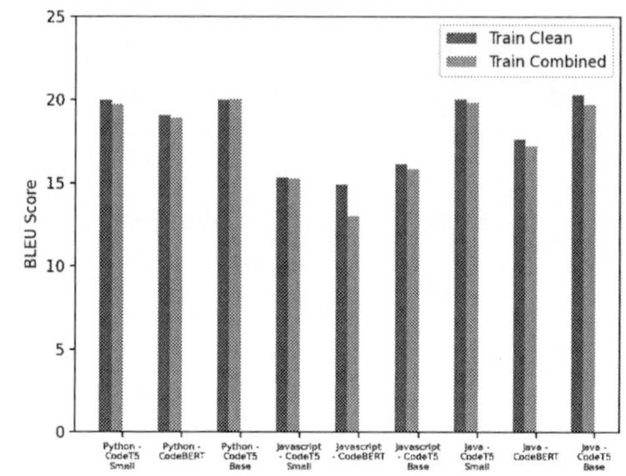

Figure 4: Comparing performance on clean test data for models trained on clean data and combined data.

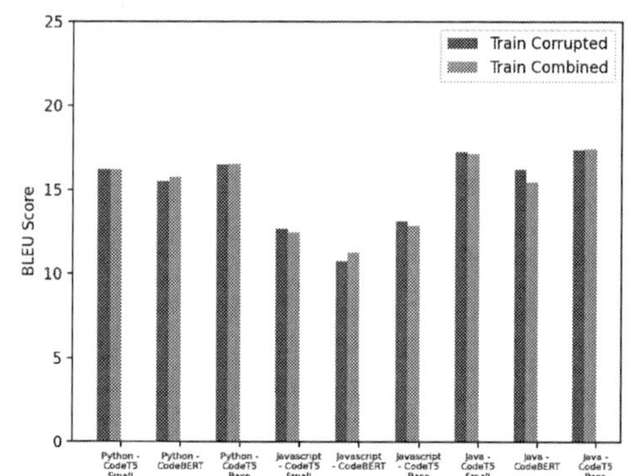

Figure 5: Comparing performance on corrupted test data for models trained on corrupted data and combined data.

6.4 Research Question 4: *What is the effect of commented code perturbations on the model's capabilities?*

We observe that the model trained on a dataset consisting of commented code showcases comparable and impressive performance on both clean code data and commented code data. However, a model trained exclusively on clean data displays satisfactory performance on the clean test set, albeit experiencing a notable decline in performance when evaluated on the commented code test set (presented in Figure 6). A potential explanation is that the absence of comments in the clean code training data prevents the model from learning the syntax associated with comments. However, when the model is trained on code that includes comments, it captures the code syntax information despite the comments not directly influencing the code's functionality.

Train Data	Test Data	Python		Javascript		Java	
		CodeT5 Small	**CodeT5 Base**	**CodeT5 Small**	**CodeT5 Base**	**CodeT5 Small**	**CodeT5 Base**
Clean	Clean	19.96	20.01	15.32	16.16	20.02	20.31
	Commented	16.15	16.26	14.61	14.21	15.06	18.83
Commented	Clean	19.07	17.90	15.00	15.07	19.77	20.23
	Commented	18.32	18.75	15.90	15.73	19.57	20.17

Table 4: Smooth BLEU-4 scores for different language and train-test combinations for commented code corruption.

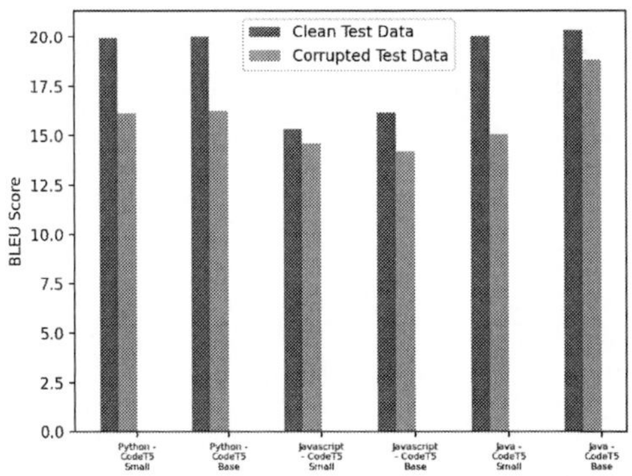

Figure 6: Comparing performance on clean and commented test data for models trained on clean data.

6.5 Research Question 5: *What is the effect of dead code perturbations on the model's capabilities?*

Upon analysis, we determine that a model trained on a dataset that includes non-functional dead code demonstrates impressive and similar performance when applied to both clean code and the aforementioned dead code. We make the same observation for a model trained on clean data and evaluated on both clean and non-functional code test datasets. We thus conclude that the addition of dead code doesn't have any significant impact on the generated summaries.

7 Human Evaluation

In order to gain deeper insights into specific errors, a manual evaluation was conducted on a randomly selected subset of 200 examples from the identifier corrupted dataset. The evaluation compared the performance of two CodeT5 Base models: the model trained on the combined dataset (including identifier corrupted codes) and the baseline model trained on clean data. The evaluation involved analyzing code, gold truth, baseline model summaries, and combined data trained model summaries. We prepare one such set for both Python and Javascript (Refer Table 5). To avoid human bias, the annotators were given the summaries in a random order without any access to the information about which model generated them.

Language	Clean Data Model	Combined Data Model	Ties	Total
Python	21	143	36	200
Javascript	15	148	37	200

Table 5: Statistics of the aggregated manual evaluation data determining which model's summary was better.

The evaluation process included two individuals independently annotating the same set of data and marking the annotations as *Prediction 1*, *Prediction 2*, or *Tie* (both models). The chosen option implies that the selected annotation is more closely aligned with the gold truth and code. The inter-annotator agreement can be observed in the Table 6.

In cases where there was a disagreement between the annotators, *Ties* were resolved using the following strategies:

- If one annotation was marked as a *Tie* and the other was marked as *Prediction 1* or *Prediction 2*, we considered the *Prediction 1* or *Prediction 2* annotation as the final annotation in the aggregated dataset.
- If one annotation was marked as *Prediction 1* and the other as *Prediction 2*, the two annotators engaged in a discussion to reach a consensus for the final annotation for the summaries.

The observations revealed that the summaries generated by the model trained on the combined data were more relevant to the code and closer to the desired outcome (gold truth) compared to the baseline model. There were several notable issues with the summaries generated by the baseline model, which are discussed in the Figure 7.

The computed BLEU scores for the two models, where one was trained on clean data and the other on combined data, are as follows: For Python, the bleu scores on the identifier corrupted dataset are **12.92** and **16.17**, while for Javascript, the scores are **9.04** and **12.86**, respectively. These scores align with the manual evaluation results, indicating that the model trained on combined data outperforms the model trained solely on clean data in code summarization.

8 Conclusion

By studying advanced code summarization models, we discover how making changes that preserve the meaning of the code affects the quality of the summaries they generate. Additionally, we provide evidence that if we train the large language models like CodeT5 properly, making changes that disrupt the meaning of function and variable names have little impact on the resulting summaries. Our observations remain consistent across three distinct programming languages: Java, Python, and JavaScript. These findings raise important concerns about how well these models truly understand code, highlighting the need for better training methods and carefully curated datasets that improve their understanding. We propose using different types of code transformations, such as introducing renamed identifiers, adding comments, or dead code, as ways to enhance the training of these models. Furthermore, there is an exciting opportunity to apply these findings to different programming languages, so that we can learn more about their general applicability.

Limitations

While this study presents valuable insights into code summarization using CodeBERT and CodeT5, certain limitations merit consideration.

Firstly, the experimentation focused exclusively on CodeBERT and CodeT5 due to practical GPU restrictions. While Large Language Model (LLMs) based approaches hold immense potential, their exclusion from the evaluation due to GPU limitations might restrict the generalizability of findings.

Secondly, the reliance on BLEU evaluation metrics, although widely used, introduces its own limitations(Roy et al., 2021). BLEU captures the word-level overlap between generated and reference summaries, but it may not holistically reflect the quality of the summary in all cases. The intricate semantics and contextual intricacies present in code may not be fully captured by BLEU scores alone.

Moreover, while human evaluation was conducted on a subset of 200 samples, the comprehensiveness of this assessment could have been further extended. A more expansive human evaluation, covering a broader array of code samples, could provide a richer understanding of the models' actual performance.

In future studies, overcoming these limitations could involve wider experimentation across a spectrum of Language Models, a more robust human evaluation, and exploring alternative evaluation metrics that better align with the complex nature of code summarization.

References

Wasi Ahmad, Saikat Chakraborty, Baishakhi Ray, and Kai-Wei Chang. 2021. Unified pre-training for program understanding and generation. In *Proceedings of the 2021 Conference of the North American Chapter of the Association for Computational Linguistics: Human Language Technologies*, pages 2655–2668, Online. Association for Computational Linguistics.

Toufique Ahmed and Premkumar Devanbu. 2022a. Learning code summarization from a small and local dataset.

Toufique Ahmed and Premkumar Devanbu. 2022b. Multilingual training for software engineering. In *Proceedings of the 44th International Conference on Software Engineering*, ICSE '22, page 1443–1455, New York, NY, USA. Association for Computing Machinery.

Fuxiang Chen, Fatemeh Fard, David Lo, and Timofey Bryksin. 2022. On the transferability of pre-trained language models for low-resource programming languages.

Zhangyin Feng, Daya Guo, Duyu Tang, Nan Duan, Xiaocheng Feng, Ming Gong, Linjun Shou, Bing Qin, Ting Liu, Daxin Jiang, and Ming Zhou. 2020. CodeBERT: A pre-trained model for programming and natural languages. In *Findings of the Association for Computational Linguistics: EMNLP 2020*, pages 1536–1547, Online. Association for Computational Linguistics.

Daya Guo, Shuo Ren, Shuai Lu, Zhangyin Feng, Duyu Tang, Shujie LIU, Long Zhou, Nan Duan, Alexey Svyatkovskiy, Shengyu Fu, Michele Tufano, Shao Kun Deng, Colin Clement, Dawn Drain, Neel Sundaresan, Jian Yin, Daxin Jiang, and Ming Zhou. 2021. Graphcode{bert}: Pre-training code representations with data flow. In *International Conference on Learning Representations*.

Hamel Husain, Ho-Hsiang Wu, Tiferet Gazit, Miltiadis Allamanis, and Marc Brockschmidt. 2020. Codesearchnet challenge: Evaluating the state of semantic code search.

Shuai Lu, Daya Guo, Shuo Ren, Junjie Huang, Alexey Svyatkovskiy, Ambrosio Blanco, Colin Clement, Dawn Drain, Daxin Jiang, Duyu Tang, Ge Li, Lidong Zhou, Linjun Shou, Long Zhou, Michele Tufano, MING GONG, Ming Zhou, Nan Duan, Neel Sundaresan, Shao Kun Deng, Shengyu Fu, and Shujie LIU. 2021. CodeXGLUE: A machine learning benchmark dataset for code understanding and generation. In *Thirty-fifth Conference on Neural Information Processing Systems Datasets and Benchmarks Track (Round 1)*.

Kishore Papineni, Salim Roukos, Todd Ward, and Wei-Jing Zhu. 2002. Bleu: a method for automatic evaluation of machine translation. In *Proceedings of the 40th Annual Meeting of the Association for Computational Linguistics*, pages 311–318, Philadelphia, Pennsylvania, USA. Association for Computational Linguistics.

Long Phan, Hieu Tran, Daniel Le, Hieu Nguyen, James Anibal, Alec Peltekian, and Yanfang Ye. 2021. Cotext: Multi-task learning with code-text transformer.

Devjeet Roy, Sarah Fakhoury, and Venera Arnaoudova. 2021. Reassessing automatic evaluation metrics for code summarization tasks.

Ensheng Shi, Yanlin Wang, Lun Du, Junjie Chen, Shi Han, Hongyu Zhang, Dongmei Zhang, and Hongbin Sun. 2022. On the evaluation of neural code summarization. In *Proceedings of the 44th International Conference on Software Engineering*. ACM.

Ankita Nandkishor Sontakke, Manasi Patwardhan, Lovekesh Vig, Raveendra Kumar Medicherla, Ravindra Naik, and Gautam Shroff. 2022. Code summarization: Do transformers really understand code? In *Deep Learning for Code Workshop*.

Weisong Sun, Chunrong Fang, Yuchen Chen, Quanjun Zhang, Guanhong Tao, Tingxu Han, Yifei Ge, Yudu You, and Bin Luo. 2022. An extractive-and-abstractive framework for source code summarization.

Yue Wang, Weishi Wang, Shafiq Joty, and Steven C.H. Hoi. 2021. CodeT5: Identifier-aware unified pre-trained encoder-decoder models for code understanding and generation. In *Proceedings of the 2021 Conference on Empirical Methods in Natural Language Processing*, pages 8696–8708, Online and Punta Cana, Dominican Republic. Association for Computational Linguistics.

A Appendix

A.1 Additional information on human annotation

Language	Raw Agreement	Cohen's Kappa
Python	74.5%	0.62
Javascript	82.0%	0.73

Table 6: Inter-annotator Agreement Statistics.

A.2 Data Transformation Procedure

A.2.1 Python

- **Renaming Identifiers:** We use Python's *ast* package to parse the code and create AST. Then we transform the ast using *NodeTransformer*[7] class. Finally the modified ast is unparsed and saved to the output file.

- **Commented Code:** Commented code is added after the function definition by randomly selecting a function code snippet from the same data split and adding comment symbols (#) before each line of the selected code snippet.

- **Dead Code:** The code in this section adds extra code snippets after return statements in Python source code. The extra code snippet is taken from the function body of a randomly selected function in the same data split. It uses the *libcst*[8] library to identify the location of the return statement.

A.2.2 Javascript

- **Renaming Identifiers:** To achieve this, the *esprima*[9] library was employed to obtain the AST structure. Some codes are excluded from our dataset because the library fails to obtain the AST for those specific codes. The AST was traversed using *Depth-First Search (DFS)* to extract node details of Identifiers related to variables and functions. Subsequently, the *estraverse*[10] library was utilized to traverse

[7] https://docs.python.org/3/library/ast.html#ast.NodeTransformer

[8] https://libcst.readthedocs.io/en/latest/

[9] https://www.npmjs.com/package/esprima

[10] https://www.npmjs.com/package/@types/estraverse

<table>
<tr><th>Corrupted Code</th><th>Type of issues in the summary</th><th>Gold truth</th><th>Summary generated by model trained on clean data</th><th>Summary generated by the model trained on combined data</th></tr>
<tr><td>function func0(variable0, variable1,
variable2) {
const variable3 =
copyArray(this.subscribers(variable0,
variable1));
let variable4;
const variable5 = variable3.length;
if (variable5 === 0) {
return false;
}
variable2 =
preprocessorsPublishData(variable2);
while (!!(variable4 = variable3.shift())) {
_executeHandler(variable4,
variable2, variable0, variable1);
}
return true;}</td><td>Repetitive summary generated by model trained on clean data</td><td>Publish the event in one channel .</td><td>This function is the function that is called when the function is called .</td><td>Publishes data to all subscribers .</td></tr>
<tr><td>def func1(arg1, arg2):
var1 = asyncio.get_event_loop()
var2 = AsyncSatel(arg1, arg2, var1, [1,
2, 3, 4, 5, 6, 7, 8, 12, 13, 14, 15, 16, 17,
18, 19, 20, 21, 22, 23, 25, 26, 27, 28, 29,
30], [8, 9, 10])
loop.run_until_complete(stl.connect())
loop.create_task(stl.arm('3333', 1))
loop.create_task(stl.disarm('3333'))
loop.create_task(stl.keep_alive())
loop.create_task(stl.monitor_status())
loop.run_forever()
loop.close()</td><td>Irrelevant / Generic summary of the code generated by model trained on clean data</td><td>Basic demo of the monitoring capabilities .</td><td>Same as func2 .</td><td>Example demo .</td></tr>
<tr><td>function func0(variable0, variable1,
variable2) {
if (Array.isArray(variable1)) {
variable1.forEach(v =>
store[variable0].langs[v] = variable2);
return;
}
store[variable0].langs[variable1] =
variable2;
}</td><td>Usage of variable and function names in the summary of model trained on clean data</td><td>Register Loader of different Language</td><td>set variable0 to variable1 with variable2</td><td>Adds a language to the store .</td></tr>
<tr><td>function func0(variable0, variable1) {
var variable2 = lex();
if (variable2.type !== (variable1 ?
Token.Identifier : Token.Keyword) ||
variable2.value !== variable0) {
throwUnexpected(variable2);
}
}</td><td>Irrelevant / incoherent summary generated in case of Tie</td><td>Expect the next token to match the specified keyword . If not an exception will be thrown .</td><td>ECMA - 262 12 . 2</td><td>ECMA - 262 13 . 3 . 3</td></tr>
<tr><td>def func1(arg1, arg2, arg3, *arg4, **arg5):
if (arg2 is None):
(arg2, var1) =
self._get_client_creds_from_request(arg3
)
log.debug('Authenticate client %r.',
arg2)
var2 = (request.client or
self._clientgetter(arg2))
if (not var2):
log.debug('Authenticate failed, client
not found.')
return False
request.client = var2
return True</td><td>Relevant summary generated in case of Tie</td><td>Authenticate a non - confidential client .</td><td>Authenticate a client .</td><td>Authenticate a client .</td></tr>
</table>

Figure 7: Examples of different summaries generated by the models in manual evaluation.

the AST and rename each identified node accordingly. Finally, the modified code was generated using *escodegen*[11] and saved as the output.

- **Commented Code:** The commented code is inserted following the function signature. This is performed after getting the AST and using the AST to identify the end of function signature. The code used for commenting is chosen randomly from a collection of code snippets found in another JSON object, with comment symbols (//) added to each line.

[11] `https://www.npmjs.com/package/escodegen`

- **Dead Code:** Similar to commented code example, a function body code is randomly selected from a collection of code snippets in the same data split. This code is then appended to the original code after the return statement.

A.2.3 Java

- **Renaming Identifiers:** To modify the function names, and variable names, AST was generated for each code input samples using *JavaParser*[12] package. The AST was traversed to extract the function and variable name nodes, which was then modified to generalized names. It is taken care of to replace the occurrence of same variable and function names with the modified name throughout the code sample using a hash map.

- **Commented Code:** For adding commented code, we searched for the first opening curly braces "{" and the commented code was inserted within /* ... */ and added after the aforementioned curly braces. The commented code snippets were randomly sampled from the same data split of Java code samples.

- **Dead Code:** Addition of codes after return statement in Java throws compile error, therefore dead code was not added to Java code samples.

[12] `https://javaparser.org/`

Temporal Generalizability in Multimodal Misinformation Detection

Nataliya Stepanova
University of Edinburgh
npstepanova@gmail.com

Björn Ross
University of Edinburgh
b.ross@ed.ac.uk

Abstract

Misinformation detection models degrade in performance over time, but the precise causes of this remain under-researched, in particular for multimodal models. We present experiments investigating the impact of temporal shift on performance of multimodal automatic misinformation detection classifiers. Working with the r/Fakeddit dataset, we found that evaluating models on temporally out-of-domain data (i.e. data from time stretches unseen in training) results in a non-linear, 7-8% drop in macro F1 as compared to traditional evaluation strategies (which do not control for the effect of content change over time). Focusing on two factors that make temporal generalizability in misinformation detection difficult, content shift and class distribution shift, we found that content shift has a stronger effect on recall. Within the context of coarse-grained vs. fine-grained misinformation detection with r/Fakeddit, we find that certain misinformation classes seem to be more stable with respect to content shift (e.g. Manipulated and Misleading Content). Our results indicate that future research efforts need to explicitly account for the temporal nature of misinformation to ensure that experiments reflect expected real-world performance.

1 Introduction

Misinformation proliferation in sectors from public health to politics has shaped public attitudes, undermining trust in reputable organizations and science as a whole. The threat of misinformation is so severe that Lin (2019) qualifies "cyber-enabled information warfare" as an existential risk that can undermine the structure of public discourse, with its potential harm to civilization on par with climate change and nuclear warfare. Although misinformation is not a novel phenomenon, its impact on society has been exacerbated by the advent of social media, which has increased the rate and ease of misinformation spread (Murayama, 2021). As such, automated misinformation detection models are vital in mitigating misinformation's destabilizing effects on society.

In the case of multimodal data, such as an image with a text caption, we must also consider the interaction between modalities (e.g. does the caption contradict the image?), which makes multimodal misinformation detection a harder task (Abdali, 2022). Nevertheless, accounting for multimodality is vital for real-world applications, since a large portion of information shared online is multimodal.

While some Machine Learning (ML) methods can be comparable to human annotators in labelling fake news (Pérez-Rosas et al., 2017), building a multimodal model that is generalizable, explainable and scalable remains a challenge. In the current work, we explore model performance on future, unseen data (temporal generalizability). Undoubtedly, the topics most subject to misinformation change rapidly with time, as does the misinformation itself. As such, a real-world model trained for optimal performance at a specific time point will likely continue to degrade in performance over time. However, most surveyed literature did not directly account for this expected drop in performance, testing models on data collected from the same time period as training data. This practice inflates expected model performance for future applications, referred to by Murayama (2021) as an issue with the model's "velocity".

Thus, we undertook experiments to quantify temporal generalizability of multimodal misinformation detection models. Our goals are twofold:

GOAL 1: Quantify the expected drop in performance when a multimodal classifier trained on the r/Fakeddit dataset is tested on out-of-temporal-domain content.

GOAL 2: Isolate the effect of content shift on the expected performance drop, specifically disentangling trends with reference to the r/Fakeddit misinformation classes.

Proceedings of the 1st GenBench Workshop on (Benchmarking) Generalisation in NLP, pages 76–88
December 6, 2023 ©2023 Association for Computational Linguistics

2 Literature Review

2.1 Detecting Misinformation

Works such as Murayama (2021) and Wardle et al. (2018) provide an overview of different definitions of "fake news" and related concepts (misinformation, rumor, satire, propaganda, etc.). But the question of how to define "misinformation" is still an on-going area of research. For example, Abdali (2022) listed binary ground truth (true vs. false) and lack of granularity in labels in existing datasets as a data-related challenge in the field. To avoid the issue of coarse labeling, some researchers formulate the misinformation detection task as a regression problem. For our purposes, we use "misinformation" interchangeably with "fake news" to refer to content that contains some element of untruth, regardless of intention.

Fake news classification research is closely related to tasks such as fact verification, fact checking, rumor/stance detection, and sentiment extraction (Oshikawa et al., 2020). A classic ML fake news detection model represents input content (e.g. text and/or image) with manually selected features and feeds these into a classification or regression model (Zhou and Zafarani, 2020). The advent of powerful deep learning models like BERT (Devlin et al., 2019) for text or ResNet (He et al., 2016) for images made it possible to step away from manually crafted features toward learned representations extracted from hidden layers.

For multimodal information, the main question lies in whether to process each individual modality and then combine the predictions (ensemble methods), or whether to extract cross-modal features that account for inter-modal interactions (Abdali, 2022). In ensemble methods, one can fuse the modalities at the raw input level – "early fusion", after extracting modality-specific features (e.g. through vector concatenation) – "intermediate fusion", or instead fuse predictions of each modality-specific model – "late fusion" (Boulahia et al., 2021). Examples of cross-modal features used include measures of similarity between the input text and images (Giachanou et al., 2020). Another explored avenue for extracting cross-modal interactions consists of using attention mechanisms. However, attention-based models are not as easily explainable, with regions to attend to often discovered through trial and error (Abdali, 2022).

2.2 Evaluation and Temporal Generalizability

The problem of model generalizability to unseen data is a known challenge in ML, often addressed through methods such as domain adaptation and transfer learning (e.g. see Kouw and Loog (2018)). Works such as Suprem et al. (2019) and Žliobaitė (2010) have used continuous/incremental learning to train models to respond to "concept drift". In the context of misinformation detection, what is defined as "in-domain" and "out-of-domain" can vary. Experiments posed by Nan et al. (2021) and Min et al. (2022) define "domain" as "subject/topic of data", e.g., training models on political sources and testing on social content. In this paper, we treat different time periods as different "domains", since content even within the same subject/topic changes so rapidly. We refer to a model's ability to perform on data from a time period not seen in training as its "temporal generalizability".

Bozarth and Budak (2020) explored such "temporal generalizability" of misinformation detection models by comparing evaluation strategies: **classic** (common N-fold cross-validation across the entire dataset), **forecast** (evaluating on future data from a time period past the end of training), **bydomain** (evaluation against content not seen in training). They found that "classic" evaluation (which was most often encountered in surveyed literature) yielded higher performance than "forecast" evaluation (which closely mimics what happens with production models). Horne et al. (2019) similarly found that performance of fake news classifiers worsens over time, although they note that certain features (e.g. content-based features like style of writing) are more robust to temporal changes. Alkhalifa et al. (2023) observed a more pronounced model deterioration with time for "open-domain" content (e.g. social media) as opposed to "closed-domains" (e.g. book reviews).

Improving temporal generalizability has been explored on text-only models: Zhu et al. (2022) used an "entity debiasing framework", Suprem and Pu (2022) proposed a new method based on K-Means clustering, while Murayama et al. (2021) showed that using masking during text-based model training resulted in a better generalization accuracy. The generalizability of multimodal models has not been explored to the same extent as for unimodal (specifically text-only) models. Moreover, to the best of our knowledge, no prior temporal generalizability study has used the r/Fakeddit dataset.

3 Methods

3.1 Data: r/Fakeddit

We used the r/Fakeddit dataset, introduced by Nakamura et al. (2020) as a "multimodal benchmark dataset for fine-grained fake news detection". Compared to other multimodal datasets, it is one of the largest publicly available,[1] and contains both binary and fine-grained labels. Data was sampled from 22 subreddits (refer to Table 8 in the Appendix for specifics). Of its 1 million samples, roughly 650K are multimodal, containing text (title of Reddit post) and an associated image. These span June 1, 2008 to November 15, 2019 and are the focus of our investigations. Labels consist of three levels of granularity: 2-, 3- or 6-way (see Figure 1).

2-way	3-way	6-way	Sample Clean Text	Sample Image	Subreddit
True 38.8%	True 38.8%	True 38.8%	a white fire truck		mildly interesting
	Half Fake 2.49%	Misleading Content 3.9%	dutch war british election poster southampton		propaganda posters
		False Connection 18.7%	the happiest thing in the craft store		pareiodolia
False 61.2%	False 58.7%	Satire 5.9%	life oceans that have been on tv		theonion
		Manipulated Content 30.6%	one small step		psbattle artwork
		Imposter Content 2.1%	wp as a brit i can become a vegetarian		subreddit simulator

Figure 1: Example r/Fakeddit data for all possible 2-, 3-, and 6-way classes with relative class sizes.

r/Fakeddit is imbalanced, with the imbalance getting more pronounced as the classification gets more fine-grained. In the 2-way labels, 255,913 (38.81%) of posts are labelled as True and 403,451 (61.19%) False. The 3-way labeling is roughly the same as for 2-way labeling, just a portion of the Fake samples is listed as Half Fake (2.49% of data). The most fine-grained 6-way labeling, with 5 sub-classes for fake content, contains the most imbalances. In this report, we focus only on 2-way and 6-way classification, as our 3-way models behaved extremely similarly to the 2-way models, likely due to the relatively small size of the Half Fake class.

Preprocessing We keep the pre-processed text of Nakamura et al. (2020). Images were preprocessed following the practices of He et al. (2016), Krizhevsky et al. (2012), and Simonyan and Zisserman (2015): we resized and randomly cropped images to force image dimensions to 224x224, then normalized each pixel value using the mean and standard deviation of RGB values in the ImageNet dataset (default in Pytorch).[2]

3.2 Train-Validation-Test Data Splits

We prepared three train-val-test splits, changing the temporal range of information available to models.

Original (OG) Data Split: A random partitioning of the dataset into train, val, and test sets provided by the r/Fakeddit authors. All three spanned the entire decade of available data (see Table 1).

Split	Time Covered	# Posts	% Data
Train	06.2008-11.2019	544,288	82.56%
Val	07.2008-10.2019	57,551	8.72%
Test	06.2008-10.2019	57,525	8.72%

Table 1: Original train-val-test split statistics.

Temporal Data Split: All three splits cover a separate time period. We sorted all available data by creation timestamp and separated it into three consecutive chunks corresponding in size to the OG train, val, and test splits (to control for dataset size). Splitting the data this way ensured that models would be both validated and evaluated on temporally out-of-domain data.

Split	Time Covered	% Data	Months
Train	06.2008-04.2019	82.56%	131
Val	04.2019-07.2019	8.72%	3
Test	07.2019-11.2019	8.72%	4

Table 2: Temporal train-val-test split statistics.

Multiple Test Splits Over Time: Has 5 consecutive test splits, designed to quantify the change in performance as the test set gets further removed from the training data. Although the raw count of data points in our train and validation sets had to

[1]Refer to https://github.com/entitize/Fakeddit

[2]https://pytorch.org/vision/stable/transforms.html#scriptable-transforms

decrease, we controlled for the *relative* proportion (82% to 9%) of samples in them (see Table 3). We made the test splits roughly equal to that of the validation set. We controlled for the temporal coverage (not size) of the test sets because in a hypothetical real-life scenario it would be preferable to know how soon after deployment (not after how many runs) a model should be retrained.

Split	Time Covered	% of Data	Days
Train	06.2008-05.2017	54.05%	3,287
Val	06.2017-11.2017	5.71%	155
Test 1	11.2017-04.2018	5.97%	153
Test 2	05.2018-09.2018	7.57%	155
Test 3	09.2018-02.2019	2.48%	155
Test 4	02.2019-07.2019	14.02%	152
Test 5	07.2019-11.2019	10.19%	128

Table 3: Data split stats for multiple test splits.

3.3 Model Architecture and Training

Our multimodal models followed one version of the "ensemble method" described by Abdali (2022):

1. Text and image were processed individually to extract modality-specific features
2. Feature vectors were concatenated ("intermediate fusion", see Boulahia et al. (2021))
3. The resulting concatenated vector was fed into a neural network classifier

To process cleaned submission titles, we used a variant of the popular transformer-based pre-trained language model BERT (Devlin et al., 2019). BERT has successfully been used to embed input for misinformation detection models (see Nakamura et al. (2020) and Segura-Bedmar and Alonso-Bartolome (2022)). We used a pre-trained RoBERTa model (variant *all-distilroberta-v1*)[3] to obtain 768-dim embeddings for sample text.

We used a pre-trained network called ResNet-50 to extract image features (He et al., 2016). The ResNet architecture won the ILSVRC 2015 image classification task and has since remained a popular backbone for computer vision models. It has also made its way into misinformation classifiers, demonstrating potential for transfer learning. For example, Nakamura et al. (2020) found that using ResNet-50 for classification with r/Fakeddit

[3]https://huggingface.co/sentence-transformers/all-distilroberta-v1

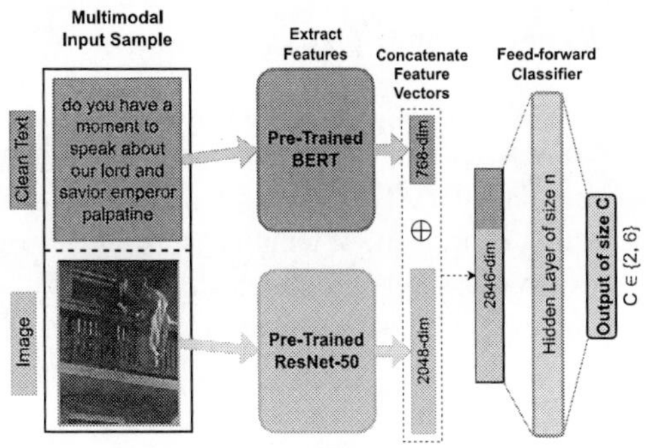

Figure 2: Ensemble multimodal model for 2-way and 6-way classification. The best-performing hidden layer size, n, was found through hyperparameter tuning.

resulted in a better performance than using VGG16 (Simonyan and Zisserman, 2015) or EfficientNet (Tan and Le, 2019), both alternative deep convolutional neural networks (CNNs) commonly used for computer vision. We similarly used ResNet-50's penultimate layer weights to represent each input image with 2048-dim vectors.

Text and image features were combined through simple concatenation. This concatenated vector was fed through a one-hidden-layer feed-forward neural network for classification (see Figure 2).

To train our models, we first loosely followed both Nakamura et al. (2020) and Segura-Bedmar and Alonso-Bartolome (2022) to choose hyperparameters. We used cross-entropy loss and the Adam optimizer. Each model was selected after conducting extensive hyperparameter tuning over hidden layer size (n) and learning rate (lr). We tested all possible pairs of the following: $n = 2^i, i \in \{5, 6, 7, 8, 9, 10, 11, 12, 14\}$, and $lr \in \{0.01, 0.001, 0.0001, 0.00001\}$. We used batches of size 256 and trained for a max of 20 epochs, with early stopping where validation accuracy did not improve over 4 consecutive epochs. Each final model was selected by choosing the hyperparameter setting that maximized accuracy on the validation set (see Appendix for specifics).

3.4 Evaluation

In an imbalanced class setting, a micro F1 score can be inflated by high performance on high frequency classes, whereas macro F1 is a better reflection of model performance across all classes, regardless of size. We use both metrics to evaluate our models for Experiment 1. For Experiment 2, we report micro F1 change over time, as that is representative of real-world performance after deployment.

4 Experiment 1: OG vs. Temporal

Our first experiment quantified the drop in performance when evaluating on temporally "out-of-domain" data (GOAL 1). We built multimodal models using the original vs. temporal splits for 2-way and 6-way classification. For each type of prediction and data split, we evaluated a Baseline model that randomly classified test samples proportionally to their rate of occurrence in the training set.

4.1 Results: 2-Way Classification

We report micro and macro F1 (see Table 4) and confusion matrices (see Figure 3) both for the model trained on the original train-val-test split and the temporal split. Our confusion matrices are normalized over the True/Actual labels (all rows sum to 1.0), so entries along the main diagonal represent recall per class.

	Trained		Baseline	
	OG	Temp.	OG	Temp.
Micro F1	0.85	0.81	0.52	0.56
Macro F1	0.85	0.78	0.50	0.50

Table 4: Exp. 1 evaluation metrics for 2-way models.

When the train-val-test split was changed to be temporal, we saw a 4% decrease in Micro F1 and 7% decrease in Macro F1. Both OG and Temporal models outperformed their respective Baselines.

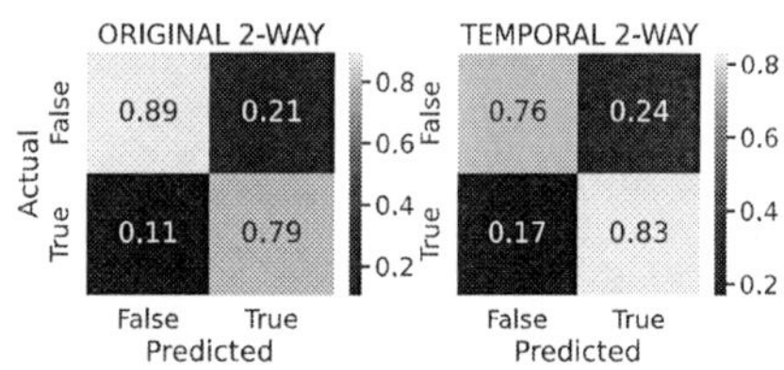

Figure 3: Confusion matrices: OG vs. temporal 2-way.

Looking at the confusion matrices, per-class recall dropped 13% for the Fake class and increased 4% for the True class. The Temporal model was generally predicting more samples into the True class (values in column 2 for both rows are greater than column 1). Detection of Fake samples worsened more than that of True samples.

4.2 Results: 6-Way Classification

We report micro and macro F1 scores in Table 5 and confusion matrices (normalized over the True labels) for 6-way models, both for the original (see Figure 4) and temporal (see Figure 5) splits.

	Trained		Baseline	
	OG	Temp.	OG	Temp.
Micro F1	0.76	0.72	0.29	0.28
Macro F1	0.60	0.52	0.17	0.17

Table 5: Exp. 1 evaluation metrics for 6-way models.

When the train-val-test split was changed to temporal, the 6-way model drop in performance was similar to the 2-way models. Micro F1 dropped by 4% and macro F1 by 8%. Both OG and Temporal models, nevertheless, performed substantially better than their respective Baselines. The Temporal model performed worse on lower frequency classes, hence macro F1 was affected more than micro F1.

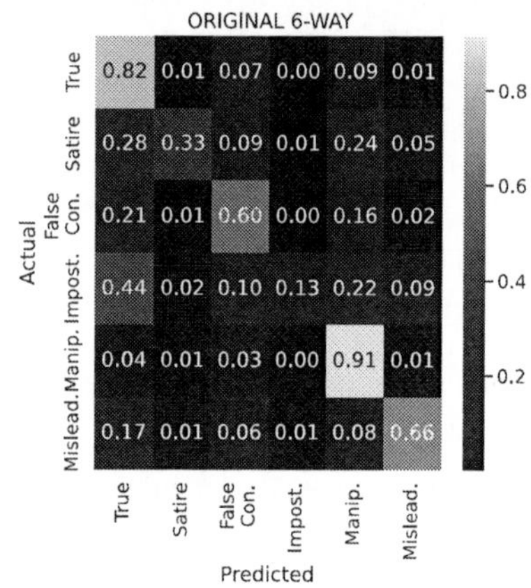

Figure 4: Confusion matrix for original 6-way model.

The OG 6-way model achieved the best per-class recall on True and Manipulated Content classes, potentially since they comprise the majority of training data (39% and 31%, respectively). Perhaps more surprising was the model's ability to achieve 66% recall on Misleading Content, which comprises only 4% of the training set (21K samples). The worst per-class recall performance was on Imposter Content (13%). 44% of True samples was predicted to Imposter Content, making it the most evasive misinformation class (followed by Satire at 28% misclassification to True). Perhaps this type of data is hard to detect, or there were simply not enough samples for the model to learn (11K samples for Imposter Content and 32K for Satire).

The temporal split decreased per-class recall on almost all classes but Satire (7% increase) and Imposter Content (2% increase). We also observed a general trend of predicting most samples into the True class, regardless of the actual label (see the

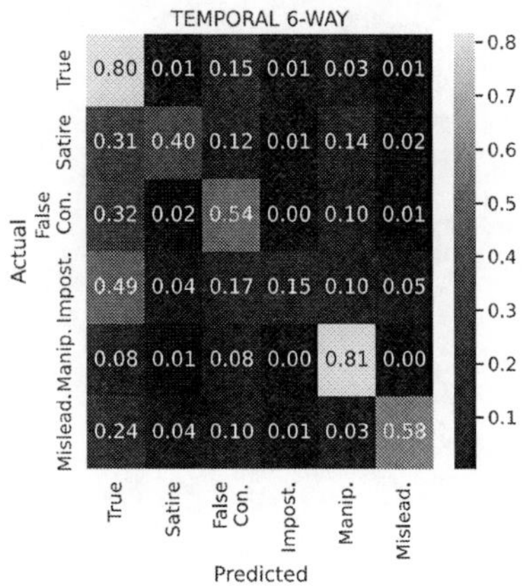

Figure 5: Confusion matrix for temporal 6-way model.

increase across the entire first column) – likely because the True class comprised 69% of the testing set as opposed to 33% of training. The best recall performance was again achieved by the True and Manipulated Content classes. This suggests that unlike the other types of Fake samples, Manipulated images are easiest to detect over time. This makes intuitive sense, as while the subject of photoshopped images might change over time, photoshopping techniques remain relatively stable.

5 Experiment 2: Multiple Test Splits

Our second experiment delved even further into GOAL 1. We quantified the rate of decay in model performance by increasing the number of test splits to five. We probed at the reasons for change in performance (GOAL 2) by comparing our resulting model (**Exp. 2 Normal**) against two variations. There are two reasons performance could change:

1. **Content shift**; e.g. the subject of posts from Apr. 2018 is different than Feb. 2019
2. **Class distribution shift**; e.g. the distribution of True vs. Fake posts changes over time

To isolate the effects of content shift, we evaluated on subsampled sets of the 5 test splits, enforcing the same class distribution and controlling for its effect (**Exp. 2 Balanced**). To isolate the effects of class distribution, we created a **Dummy** classifier that predicted proportionally to class distributions observed in training. Since the dummy classifier did not use content features for prediction, any observed effects over the 5 test splits reflected the class distribution's effect on performance.

5.1 Results: 2-way Classification

We present micro F1 for all three compared models across the 5 test splits for 2-way classification in Table 6. We follow by a per-class, per-test-split, per-model breakdown of F1, precision, and accuracy scores in Figure 6, isolating the effects of content vs. class distribution shift on each metric.

	Model + Evaluation		
	Exp. 2 Normal	**Exp. 2 Balanced**	**Dummy**
Test 1	0.82	0.60	0.76
Test 2	0.79	0.59	0.70
Test 3	0.48	0.46	0.48
Test 4	0.48	0.45	0.50
Test 5	0.40	0.42	0.47

Table 6: 2-way accuracy (micro F1). Exp. 2 Normal represents "real-life" performance, Exp. 2 Balanced isolates content shift effects, and Dummy isolates class distribution shift effects.

In Exp. 2 Normal, accuracy decreased with time, dropping dramatically after Test Split 2. Starting from Test Split 3, it performed worse than a Dummy model. The falling performance of both Exp. 2 Balanced and Dummy models suggest that the drop is due to both content shift and a change in class distributions. Since Test Split 3 starts ~450 days from the end of training (~300 days from val), in a real-life scenario our models would likely need to be retrained about once a year.

Looking at Figure 6, we can observe the effects of content shift in column 2 (Exp. 2 Balanced). Recall was unaffected for both True and False classes (compare bottom tiles in columns 1 vs. 2), while precision and F1 fell for both. We turn to column 3 for the effects of class distribution shift (Dummy performance). The relative percentage of the False class in the test sets decreased substantially across the test splits: 76% for Test Split 1, to 73%, 41%, 37%, and finally 31% for Test Split 5. Recall was unaffected by class distribution, whereas precision decreased as the Fake class got smaller.

Overall, the trends in precision of Exp. 2 Normal were most similar to that of the Dummy model, suggesting that class distribution shift has a stronger impact on precision than recall. The trends in recall of Exp. 2 Normal were most similar to that of Exp. 2 Balanced, suggesting that content distribution shift has a stronger effect on recall rather than precision. These two effects combine to give a cumulative negative effect on F1 – worsening

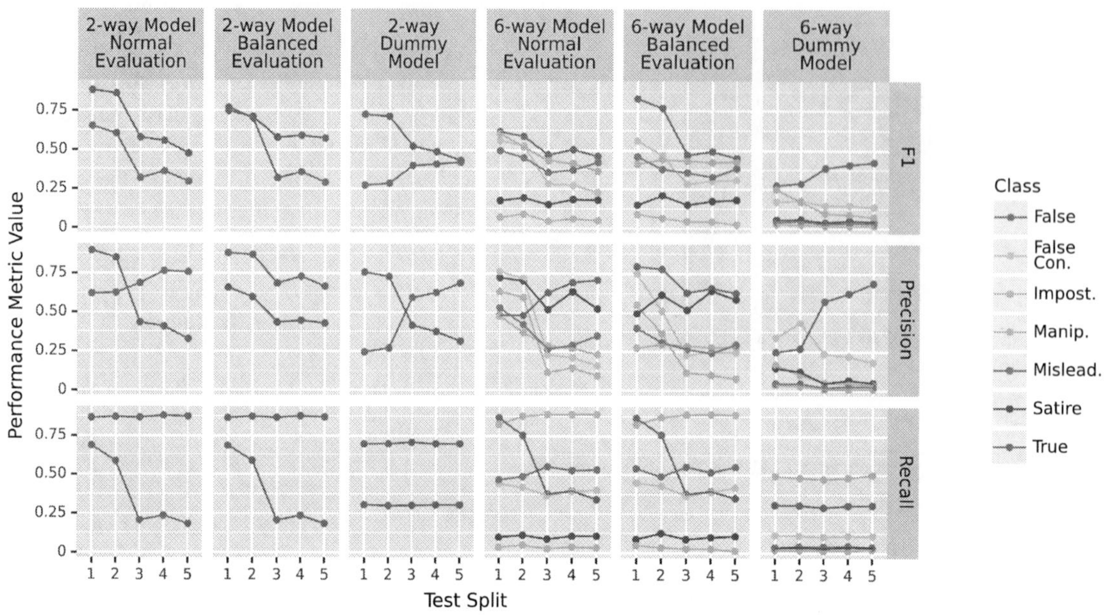

Figure 6: Precision, recall and F1 for 2-way and 6-way models over 5 temporal tests splits. "Normal" model evaluation reports the results as they would be observed in a real-life scenario, whereas "Balanced" model evaluation isolates the effects of content shift and Dummy isolates the effects of class distribution shift.

precision due to class distribution shift and worsening recall due to content shift. Interestingly, the observed per-class and per-metric trends in Exp. 2 Normal can be roughly seen as a sum of the trends in Exp. 2 Balanced and the Dummy model.

5.2 Results: 6-way Classification

We present 6-way micro F1 for all three compared models in Table 7. A breakdown of F1, precision and accuracy scores is again in Figure 6.

	Model + Evaluation		
	Exp. 2 Normal	**Exp. 2 Balanced**	**Dummy**
Test 1	0.54	0.20	0.68
Test 2	0.51	0.19	0.62
Test 3	0.38	0.24	0.38
Test 4	0.40	0.24	0.40
Test 5	0.36	0.25	0.37

Table 7: 6-way accuracy (same as micro F1).

The 6-way pattern of accuracy change in Exp. 2 Normal and Dummy was very similar as for 2-way models. Performance fell the most between Test Splits 2 and 3 (to an approximately at-chance performance – see Exp. 1 Baselines). Unlike 2-way classification, the Dummy model outperformed the trained Exp. 2 Normal model from Test Split 1, suggesting that finer-grained misinformation classification may be more temporally unstable than coarser-grained. After the Test Split 3, performance remained relatively stable. However, the Exp. 2 Balanced model performed abysmally through all test splits, starting from the first one, and there was not much change throughout the test splits. This suggests that the drop in performance in the Normal model can be mostly attributed to class distribution shift and not content shift.

Looking at Figure 6, the Exp. 2 Normal model was more similar to Exp. 2 Balanced than the Dummy model with respect to Recall, again suggesting that content shift affects recall. The change in precision for the Dummy model went hand-in-hand with how the relative class distributions changed (the True class got relatively larger with each successive test split, the False Connection class peaked at Test Split 1 and then fell along with the rest, just like the precision values changed).

With Exp. 2 Balanced, True and False Connection classes fell systematically across all splits. However, Manipulated and Misleading content classes performed relatively stably. This either suggests that, potentially, the features our models learned to identify these misinformation classes persist more stably over time than others.

6 Discussion

6.1 Our Contributions

In the r/Fakeddit dataset, a temporal data split resulted in a **4% drop in macro F1 and 7-8% drop in micro F1 for 2-way and 6-way multimodal models** (compare GOAL 1).

For GOAL 2, to isolate the effect of content shift on the performance drop, we found that **content shift seems to affect recall more than precision**. Additionally, **finer-grained misinformation classes do not behave in the same way with regards to temporal generalizability**. Notably, Manipulated and Misleading content classes seemed to be more stable.

Our results for Experiment 1 underline the importance of considering the performance drop in misinformation classification models on a new temporal domain. Our results for Experiment 2 further isolate a period of time where performance drops substantially, suggesting that models may suffer from a sudden and dramatic decrease in performance (as opposed to a gradual worsening of classification accuracy). Specifically in reference to the r/Fakeddit dataset, it seems like there was a qualitative change in content posted between September 2018 and February 2019, where we see the sudden drop in performance (to Baseline levels). Investigating whether this change is due to a specific singular event or has to do with general content shift over time is out of the scope of this paper. In the real-world, guidance from social scientists and/or political scientists who are aware of current online discourse would help identify periods of time when content is expected to change, affecting the performance of deployed models.

Our findings in Experiment 2 with respect to disentangling the effects of content vs. class distribution shift underline the importance of accounting not only for how content might change over time, but also how models will perform in varying class distribution settings. Throughout the experimentation process, we found that when we split the r/Fakeddit dataset temporally, the variation in relative class distribution varied widely across the temporal splits. It is unclear whether this has to do with the way the authors of r/Fakeddit collected the data, or with the underlying distribution of content on Reddit in general. Regardless, in the real world it is very possible that the data collected at time point *X* will vary widely from the data collected at time point *Y*. As such, researchers have to explicitly prepare for how their models will perform in different class distributions settings.

It makes theoretical sense why recall is not affected by class distribution shift and therefore is a useful metric for isolating the effects of content shift. Recall is equal to $\frac{TP}{TP+FN}$, where TP = true positives and FN = false negatives for a certain class. Assuming the content distribution stays the same, an α increase in total data points of a class will correspond to an analogous α increase in both TP and FN, and the scaling factor will cancel out in the recall calculation. The same does not apply to Precision, which is $\frac{TP}{TP+FP}$, with FP = false positives. Whereas TP and FN came from the same class, FP are by definition from a different one, therefore any scaling effects of the two different classes will compound rather than cancel.

6.2 Implications for Research and Industry

As our experiments showed, deployed models can expect a sudden and significant drop in performance, indicating that future research efforts need to explicitly account for the temporal nature of misinformation to ensure that experiments reflect expected real-world performance. Although there is existing research in this space (e.g. Chen and Hasan (2021) look at the temporal generalizability of COVID-19 misinformation detection models), many studies do not account for content change over time. A deeper analysis of why model performance was not always generalizable was hindered by a lack of understanding of what our models were learning. To that end, further research should also look at how models learn what is fake, and whether it is possible to make the decision-making process less dependent on temporal context.

Approaches to misinformation detection can be separated into categories based on how they learn. Zhou et al. (2020) and Shiao and Papalexakis (2021) discuss four: content-based, propagation-based, knowledge-based and source-based models. Our models were implicitly operating off of a content-based approach, relying on latent text and image features to embed samples into a semantic space representing truth-value. Perhaps knowledge-based models are more generalizable, but only if the knowledge base is iteratively updated with the passage of time. Further research would benefit from considering what types of updating (e.g. feature extraction or knowledge base) would be most feasible from an industry perspective.

7 Limitations

Our multimodal models perform worse than related works on r/Fakeddit (Nakamura et al., 2020; Segura-Bedmar and Alonso-Bartolome, 2022). We tried exactly recreating the architecture of Nakamura et al. (2020), but model performance was still lower. Noting that our investigation would benefit from being comparable to related studies, we attempted to locate the source of the discrepancy in performance but were unsuccessful. We think that our difficulty with reproducing existing results is not uncommon, and future research would benefit greatly from studies that explicitly outline guidelines on how to exactly reproduce their architecture (as in Zaeem et al. (2020), Shu et al. (2019)).

Due to computational limitations, we did not fine-tune the feature extraction process on our dataset, instead relying on pretrained RoBERTa and ResNet-50. Building models that are specifically tailored to misinformation datasets for feature extraction might increase performance, though it is unclear if this would change the impact of a temporal data split. Future research could explore whether temporal generalizability is largely dependent on the dataset being used, and whether the obtained results would be different if another dataset was analyzed instead.

Additionally, we did not extensively investigate what validation strategy would work the best for temporal generalizability. Instead, we naively separated the training and validation set temporally from each other, and used that for hyperparameter tuning. Further work could look into training methods specifically designed for maximal temporal generalizability in misinformation detection.

We study the temporal generalizability of multimodal misinformation detection models in one specific language, for one specific platform. Although the experiments presented in this paper are inspired by real-world applications (e.g. deploying a misinformation detection model on a social media platform), it is worth noting that the r/Fakeddit dataset contains some particularities that make it difficult to generalize to broader misinformation detection in other languages and settings. Some of the samples labeled as "Fake" are harmless (e.g. certain memes), although technically they are "untrue" or "manipulated". This raises the question of whether the results presented here are generalizable to datasets that focus on more "serious" topics of information (e.g. COVID-19 or certain political topics). For example, some photoshopped images are evidently meant to entertain, and, although technically they constitute "misinformation", it seems unintuitive to seriously treat them as such. This raises the research question of how to effectively define "misinformation" that both makes sense semantically and also is maximally useful for automated models deployed in the real world, dealing with topics of substantial weight.

8 Ethical considerations

We use the existing r/Fakeddit dataset. Since this was released as a benchmarking dataset for misinformation detection models, our use of this dataset is consistent with the use cases it was intended for. The dataset may contain personal data or offensive content so we ensure that the examples reported in this paper do not make any individuals identifiable or include offensive content. We were not able to find information on the licence associated with this dataset but since it was released for the purpose of benchmarking we assume that our use of this dataset is acceptable.

We study when misinformation detection systems fail to perform well. A malicious actor could potentially exploit this knowledge to decide what kind of misinformation to spread, however, we believe that our results will be far more useful to those who are hoping to improve the temporal generalizability of their systems.

References

Sara Abdali. 2022. Multi-modal misinformation detection: Approaches, challenges and opportunities. *arXiv preprint arXiv:2203.13883*.

Rabab Alkhalifa, Elena Kochkina, and Arkaitz Zubiaga. 2023. Building for tomorrow: Assessing the temporal persistence of text classifiers. *Information Processing & Management*, 60(2):103200.

Said Yacine Boulahia, Abdenour Amamra, Mohamed Ridha Madi, and Said Daikh. 2021. Early, intermediate and late fusion strategies for robust deep learning-based multimodal action recognition. *Machine Vision and Applications*, 32(6):1–18.

Lia Bozarth and Ceren Budak. 2020. Toward a better performance evaluation framework for fake news classification. *Proceedings of the International AAAI Conference on Web and Social Media*, 14(1):60–71.

Yuanzhi Chen and Mohammad Hasan. 2021. Navigating the kaleidoscope of COVID-19 misinformation using deep learning. In *Proceedings of the 2021*

Conference on Empirical Methods in Natural Language Processing, pages 6000–6017, Online and Punta Cana, Dominican Republic. Association for Computational Linguistics.

Jacob Devlin, Ming-Wei Chang, Kenton Lee, and Kristina Toutanova. 2019. BERT: Pre-training of deep bidirectional transformers for language understanding. In *Proceedings of the 2019 Conference of the North American Chapter of the Association for Computational Linguistics: Human Language Technologies, Volume 1 (Long and Short Papers)*, pages 4171–4186, Minneapolis, Minnesota. Association for Computational Linguistics.

Anastasia Giachanou, Guobiao Zhang, and Paolo Rosso. 2020. Multimodal fake news detection with textual, visual and semantic information. In *International Conference on Text, Speech, and Dialogue*, pages 30–38. Springer.

Kaiming He, Xiangyu Zhang, Shaoqing Ren, and Jian Sun. 2016. Deep residual learning for image recognition. In *Proceedings of the IEEE conference on computer vision and pattern recognition*, pages 770–778.

Benjamin D Horne, Jeppe Nørregaard, and Sibel Adali. 2019. Robust fake news detection over time and attack. *ACM Transactions on Intelligent Systems and Technology (TIST)*, 11(1):1–23.

Wouter M Kouw and Marco Loog. 2018. An introduction to domain adaptation and transfer learning. *arXiv preprint arXiv:1812.11806*.

Alex Krizhevsky, Ilya Sutskever, and Geoffrey E Hinton. 2012. Imagenet classification with deep convolutional neural networks. *Advances in neural information processing systems*, 25.

Herbert Lin. 2019. The existential threat from cyber-enabled information warfare. *Bulletin of the Atomic Scientists*, 75(4):187–196.

Erxue Min, Yu Rong, Yatao Bian, Tingyang Xu, Peilin Zhao, Junzhou Huang, and Sophia Ananiadou. 2022. Divide-and-conquer: Post-user interaction network for fake news detection on social media. In *Proceedings of the ACM Web Conference 2022*, pages 1148–1158.

Taichi Murayama. 2021. Dataset of fake news detection and fact verification: A survey. *arXiv preprint arXiv:2111.03299*.

Taichi Murayama, Shoko Wakamiya, and Eiji Aramaki. 2021. Mitigation of diachronic bias in fake news detection dataset. In *Proceedings of the Seventh Workshop on Noisy User-generated Text (W-NUT 2021)*, pages 182–188, Online. Association for Computational Linguistics.

Kai Nakamura, Sharon Levy, and William Yang Wang. 2020. Fakeddit: A new multimodal benchmark dataset for fine-grained fake news detection. In *Proceedings of the Twelfth Language Resources and Evaluation Conference*, pages 6149–6157, Marseille, France. European Language Resources Association.

Qiong Nan, Juan Cao, Yongchun Zhu, Yanyan Wang, and Jintao Li. 2021. Mdfend: Multi-domain fake news detection. In *Proceedings of the 30th ACM International Conference on Information & Knowledge Management*, pages 3343–3347.

Ray Oshikawa, Jing Qian, and William Yang Wang. 2020. A survey on natural language processing for fake news detection. In *Proceedings of the Twelfth Language Resources and Evaluation Conference*, pages 6086–6093, Marseille, France. European Language Resources Association.

Verónica Pérez-Rosas, Bennett Kleinberg, Alexandra Lefevre, and Rada Mihalcea. 2017. Automatic detection of fake news. *arXiv preprint arXiv:1708.07104*.

Isabel Segura-Bedmar and Santiago Alonso-Bartolome. 2022. Multimodal fake news detection. *Information*, 13(6).

William Shiao and Evangelos E Papalexakis. 2021. Ki2te: Knowledge-infused interpretable embeddings for covid-19 misinformation detection. In *KnOD@ WWW*.

Kai Shu, Limeng Cui, Suhang Wang, Dongwon Lee, and Huan Liu. 2019. defend: Explainable fake news detection. In *Proceedings of the 25th ACM SIGKDD international conference on knowledge discovery & data mining*, pages 395–405.

Karen Simonyan and Andrew Zisserman. 2015. Very deep convolutional networks for large-scale image recognition. In *3rd International Conference on Learning Representations, ICLR 2015, San Diego, CA, USA, May 7-9, 2015, Conference Track Proceedings*.

Abhijit Suprem, Aibek Musaev, and Calton Pu. 2019. Concept drift adaptive physical event detection for social media streams. In *World Congress on Services*, pages 92–105. Springer.

Abhijit Suprem and Calton Pu. 2022. Evaluating generalizability of fine-tuned models for fake news detection. *arXiv Preprint posted online May*, 15.

Mingxing Tan and Quoc Le. 2019. Efficientnet: Rethinking model scaling for convolutional neural networks. In *International conference on machine learning*, pages 6105–6114. PMLR.

Claire Wardle et al. 2018. Information disorder: The essential glossary. *Harvard, MA: Shorenstein Center on Media, Politics, and Public Policy, Harvard Kennedy School*.

Razieh Nokhbeh Zaeem, Chengjing Li, and K Suzanne Barber. 2020. On sentiment of online fake news. In *2020 IEEE/ACM International Conference on*

Advances in Social Networks Analysis and Mining (ASONAM), pages 760–767. IEEE.

Xinyi Zhou, Atishay Jain, Vir V Phoha, and Reza Zafarani. 2020. Fake news early detection: A theory-driven model. *Digital Threats: Research and Practice*, 1(2):1–25.

Xinyi Zhou and Reza Zafarani. 2020. A survey of fake news: Fundamental theories, detection methods, and opportunities. *ACM Computing Surveys (CSUR)*, 53(5):1–40.

Yongchun Zhu, Qiang Sheng, Juan Cao, Shuokai Li, Danding Wang, and Fuzhen Zhuang. 2022. Generalizing to the future: Mitigating entity bias in fake news detection. In *Proceedings of the 45nd International ACM SIGIR Conference on Research and Development in Information Retrieval*. Association for Computing Machinery.

Indrė Žliobaitė. 2010. Learning under concept drift: an overview. *arXiv preprint arXiv:1010.4784*.

A Appendix

This appendix first provides additional implementation details, specifically optimal found hyperparameter settings. We follow with details on the subreddits in the dataset and the performance of the 6-way models broken down by subreddit.

As described in section 3.3, we conducted hyperparameter tuning over hidden layer size (n) and learning rate (lr), testing all possible pairs of the following: $n = 2^i, i \in \{5, 6, 7, 8, 9, 10, 11, 12, 14\}$, and $lr \in \{0.01, 0.001, 0.0001, 0.00001\}$. Each final model was selected by choosing the hyperparameter setting that maximized accuracy on the validation set, with optimal learning rate being 0.0001 across the board, $n = 16384$ for OG 2-way and $n = 8192$ for OG 6-way, $n = 8192$ for Temporal 2-way and $n = 1024$ for Temporal 6-way.

The final choice of subreddit and associated truth values went through a rigorous multi-step quality assurance process to justify the use of subreddit-level labels (as opposed to labeling each sample individually), see Nakamura et al. (2020) for a detailed overview of this process and Table 8 for the labels assigned to each subreddit.

Additionally, since all samples from a specific subreddit received the same label (a type of domain-level ground truth, where the domain a sample comes from determines its truth value), refer to Table 9 for a per-subreddit breakdown of 6-way classification accuracy for the original vs. temporal models.

subreddit	Label 2-way	3-way	6-way
mildlyinteresting	True	True	True
photoshopbattles	True	True	True
nottheonion	True	True	True
upliftingnews	True	True	True
neutralnews	True	True	True
usanews	True	True	True
pic	True	True	True
usnews	True	True	True
fakealbumcovers	Fake	Fake	Satire
theonion	Fake	Fake	Satire
satire	Fake	Fake	Satire
waterfordwhispersnews	Fake	Fake	Satire
propagandaposters	Fake	Half Fake	Misleading Content
fakefacts	Fake	Fake	Misleading Content
savedyouaclick	Fake	Fake	Misleading Content
psbattle_artwork	Fake	Fake	Manipulated Content
pareidolia	Fake	Fake	False Connection
fakehistoryporn	Fake	Fake	False Connection
misleadingthumbnails	Fake	Fake	False Connection
confusing_perspective	Fake	Fake	False Connection
subredditsimulator	Fake	Fake	Imposter Content
subsimulatorgpt2	Fake	Fake	Imposter Content

Table 8: 2-way, 3-way, and 6-way subreddit-level labels for r/Fakeddit (every sample from a specific subreddit is labeled the same way).

subreddit	6-way Label	Per-Subreddit Accuracy Original	Temporal
mildlyinteresting	True	88.00	80.29
photoshopbattles	True	80.54	83.13
nottheonion	True	89.68	91.26
upliftingnews	True	93.85	94.28
usanews	True	90.29	94.30
pic	True	64.66	71.64
usnews	True	91.16	91.18
neutralnews	True	89.88	NA
fakealbumcovers	Satire	55.56	57.06
theonion	Satire	45.83	35.51
satire	Satire	25.57	19.78
waterfordwhispersnews	Satire	25.00	20.00
pareidolia	False Connection	60.81	60.59
fakehistoryporn	False Connection	74.62	66.18
misleadingthumbnails	False Connection	46.40	54.85
confusing_perspective	False Connection	31.10	33.16
propagandaposters	Misleading Content	75.66	79.72
savedyouaclick	Misleading Content	47.04	46.53
fakefacts	Misleading Content	NA	0.00
subredditsimulator	Imposter Content	29.48	36.51
subsimulatorgpt2	Imposter Content	15.38	7.22
psbattle_artwork	Manipulated Content	87.24	86.52

Table 9: Percent of correctly classified samples per subreddit for original vs. temporal BERT 6-way models.

Motivation					
Practical □ △	*Cognitive*	*Intrinsic*	*Fairness*		
Generalisation type					
Compositional	*Structural*	*Cross Task*	*Cross Language*	*Cross Domain* □ △	*Robustness*
Shift type					
Covariate	*Label*	*Full*	*Assumed* □ △		
Shift source					
Naturally occuring □ △	*Partitioned natural*	*Generated shift*	*Fully generated*		
Shift locus					
Train–test □ △	*Finetune train–test*	*Pretrain–train*	*Pretrain–test*		

Table 10: GenBench evaluation card for Exp. 1 (□) and Exp. 2 (△).

Robust Generalization Strategies for Morpheme Glossing in an Endangered Language Documentation Context

Michael Ginn and **Alexis Palmer**
University of Colorado
michael.ginn@colorado.edu and alexis.palmer@colorado.edu

Abstract

Generalization is of particular importance in resource-constrained settings, where the available training data may represent only a small fraction of the distribution of possible texts. We investigate the ability of morpheme labeling models to generalize by evaluating their performance on unseen genres of text, and we experiment with strategies for closing the gap between performance on in-distribution and out-of-distribution data. Specifically, we use weight decay optimization, output denoising, and iterative pseudo-labeling, and achieve a 2% improvement on a test set containing texts from unseen genres. All experiments are performed using texts written in the Mayan language Uspanteko.

1 Introduction

With over half of the world's languages endangered (Seifart et al., 2018), language documentation is one of several strategies for preservation. Traditionally, many documentation projects have aimed to create grammatical descriptions, dictionaries, and annotated text corpora, in the form of interlinear glossed text (IGT; see section 2.1). The annotated texts can be used in the creation of reference tools and pedagogical materials, as well as providing input data for downstream tasks such as machine translation (Zhou et al., 2019), morphological paradigm induction (Moeller et al., 2020), dependency parsing (Georgi et al., 2012), and other tasks (Georgi, 2016), making it particularly valuable for low-resource languages.

Annotation of large corpora can be time-consuming and monotonous, so there is a desire for systems to automatically produce IGT, annotating plain text with labels describing the part-of-speech, morphology, and syntax of each word in the corpus (Ginn et al., 2023). These systems can be used in conjunction with human annotators to create annotated corpora rapidly, ensuring consistency and reducing the amount of human effort required. Importantly, reducing annotation time also frees up language experts to work on other types of language preservation or revitalization activities.

However, generalization for automated annotation systems remains a critical problem. Preexisting corpora of annotated text are often small, contain transcriptions of spoken language from a small number of distinct speakers, and focus on specific types of language such as story-telling and oration. Thus, systems trained on these corpora have difficulty generalizing to out-of-distribution (OOD) language, limiting their utility and robustness.

As acquiring additional annotated data is generally expensive and difficult, it is preferable to design models that generalize well to OOD data. In this work, we design models for one type of text annotation: labeling each morpheme in a text with its grammatical function. We envision these models being used alongside human annotators to provide suggestions and annotate text more quickly and consistently than by human labeling alone.

We examine three strategies to improve the robustness of these morpheme labeling models with limited data:

1. We optimize weight decay to improve generalization of large models.
2. We apply a separate denoiser model to improve performance on out-of-vocabulary inputs.
3. We apply self-supervised learning on unlabeled texts.

Our experiments evaluate model performance on texts of different genres than the texts in the training set, in order to investigate their ability to generalize to future, out-of-distribution texts. We find that these strategies achieve small performance improvements on in- and out-of-distribution texts,

Proceedings of the 1st GenBench Workshop on (Benchmarking) Generalisation in NLP, pages 89–98
December 6, 2023 ©2023 Association for Computational Linguistics

and may be valuable for building more robust morpheme labeling models. Our code is available on GitHub.[1]

2 Background

2.1 Interlinear Glossed Text

In language documentation projects, annotated text typically uses a standardized format such as Interlinear Glossed Text (IGT) (Comrie et al., 2008), although the exact glossing conventions vary across projects. An example IGT sentence in Uspanteko is provided in 1.

(1) Ti- j- ya' -tq -a' juntiir
INC- E3S- *give* -PL -ENF *everything*
They give us everything
(Pixabaj et al., 2007)

The first line of the example is a **transcription** in the target language. Words may be transcribed as-is, or divided into morphemes (meaning-bearing units of language), as in the example.

The second line of the example gives a **gloss** for each morpheme. Glosses typically indicate either the translation of a morpheme or its grammatical function. For example, the *-tq-* morpheme is glossed as PL (plural). Stem morphemes, such as *ya'*, are glossed either with their translation (as here) or with a gloss indicating the stem type (such as VT for "transitive verb"). Our systems gloss stems using the latter approach.

The third line provides a translation of the sentence in a high-resource language, such as English.

Although there exist some large mixed-language corpora of IGT such as ODIN (Lewis and Xia, 2010) and IMTVault (Nordhoff and Krämer, 2022), the availability of IGT data is limited. For many languages, only small IGT corpora are available, and different corpora may (and do) use various annotation conventions. Depending on the wishes of the language community, such corpora may or may not be available for wider use or distribution.

2.2 Task

In this research, the task our systems address is to predict the gloss line of IGT given the transcription, segmented into morphemes. Each morpheme should be glossed with its grammatical function; to keep the output vocabulary small, we gloss stems with part-of-speech labels instead of translations.

[1]https://github.com/michaelpginn/igt-glossing

Using the example in item 1, the input to the system would be the sequence

"Ti j ya' tq a' [SEP] juntiir"

and the intended output would be

"INC E3S VT PL ENF [SEP] ADV"

where stems such as "ya'" and "juntiir" are glossed with the stem type, here VT for transitive verb and ADV for adverb.

2.3 Related Work

Existing scholarship has used a variety of approaches for automated gloss prediction, including rule-based methods (Bender et al., 2014), active learning (Palmer et al., 2010, 2009), conditional random fields (Moeller and Hulden, 2018; McMillan-Major, 2020), and neural models (Moeller and Hulden, 2018; Zhao et al., 2020). Ginn and Palmer (2023) experiment with morphologically-inspired loss functions to improve low-resource glossing models. However, to our knowledge, there has been no evaluation or experimentation with generalization of these models.

One of the 2023 SIGMORPHON shared tasks involved creating models for automated gloss prediction (Ginn et al., 2023), with participant systems employing strategies such as leveraging the translation line for stem glossing (Okabe and Yvon, 2023), pretraining on large multilingual corpora (He et al., 2023), and straight-through gradient estimation (Girrbach, 2022).

Although the majority of machine learning research has traditionally evaluated models on in-distribution data, the ability to generalize to out-of-distribution data is desirable for natural language models (Linzen, 2020; Lake et al., 2017). This is particularly important for low-resource languages where collecting a wide distribution of data can be expensive or even infeasible.

3 Data & Methodology

3.1 Data

This work uses a corpus of IGT data for Uspanteko, a low-resource Mayan language, originally from the OKMA documentation project (Pixabaj et al., 2007) and adapted by Palmer et al. (2009). Morphemes are glossed with 68 different labels, plus a separator label. Each text was produced through recording speakers, transcribing text, and glossing with morpheme tags and translations. The corpus used includes 17 different speakers.

For this research, we experiment with generalization to unseen texts that represent different genres of text. This consideration is very practical for documentation projects, where the available training corpora are often the result of a single data collection project, and sometimes contain only one or two genres or registers of speech.

The Uspanteko corpus contains 27 texts in four different genres: stories, histories, personal anecdotes, and advice. We use the story and history texts as our in-distribution (ID) data, as we hypothesize that stories and histories have similar grammar and vocabulary. We use personal anecdotes and advice as our out-of-distribution (OOD) data. One intuitive difference between these sets is that stories and histories tend to talk about others, while an anecdote is about the speaker (and thus tends to use first-person voice) and advice is about the listener (second-person voice). There is only one instance where a document created by the same speaker appears in both the ID and OOD splits.

We randomly divide the ID data into training and evaluation sets and divide the OOD data into evaluation and final testing sets. The splits are listed in Table 1.

Set	Genre(s)	# Sentences
Training	Story, History	5049
Eval (ID)	Story, History	2128
Eval (OOD)	Personal, Advice	2128
Test (OOD)	Personal, Advice	2128

Table 1: Data splits, including in-distribution (ID) and out-of-distribution (OOD) data

To verify that these splits represent accurate distributions, we pretrained a masked language model on the training set (described in subsection 3.2) and calculated the perplexity for the ID and OOD eval sets.

Set	Perplexity
Eval (ID)	77.78
Eval (OOD)	94.03

Table 2: Perplexity of pretrained language model on data splits

Of course, genre and register only represent one form of out-of-distribution data. Data may also be out-of-distribution due to different speakers, dialects of a language, time period, and other factors.

All transcription data is segmented into morphemes. Thus, the task is to predict a gloss label for each morpheme in a sequence.

3.2 Pretraining

Existing pretrained models are rarely available for low-resource languages such as Uspanteko. Thus, we pretrain a new masked language model (MLM) on the training set before fine-tuning to the task at hand (on the same data set). We use a smaller variation of the RoBERTa architecture (Liu et al., 2019) to prevent over-fitting and reduce resources used. The model uses 3 hidden layers, hidden layers of size 100, and 5 attention heads, as in Gessler and Zeldes (2023), and we found in preliminary experiments that there is no significant difference in performance from a full-size RoBERTa model.

The model is pretrained using the parameters listed in Table 3. We employ a dynamic masking strategy (Liu et al., 2019) where 15% of tokens are masked, of which 80% use a *MASK* token, 10% use a random token, and 10% use the original token.

Parameter	Value
Optimizer	AdamW
β_1	0.9
β_2	0.999
ϵ	1E−8
Weight decay	0
Batch size	64
Gradient accumulation steps	3
Epochs	50
GPU	NVIDIA V100

Table 3: Training Hyperparameters
AdamW from Loshchilov and Hutter (2017b)

We refer to this pretrained model as USPMLM. For each experiment, USPMLM was fine-tuned on a token classification task. Because the words in the Uspanteko data are already segmented into morphemes, we are able to model this as a token classification task, predicting a gloss for each morpheme. If segmentation were not available, we would have to model the problem with a sequence-to-sequence approach or use some strategy to predict morpheme segmentation. Still, in the token classification approach, the surrounding context for each morpheme is important to making high-quality predictions, and we cannot predict a gloss for each morpheme in a vacuum.

3.3 Evaluation

Models are evaluated on both the in-distribution and out-of-distribution evaluation sets. We follow the evaluation strategy used in the SIGMORPHON shared task, calculating the overall accuracy for every morpheme, ignoring word separators, and requiring glosses to be correctly aligned to morphemes.

4 Experiments

For a baseline model, we fine-tune USPMLM on the token classification task. Fine-tuning uses the same hyperparameters listed in Table 3. We also compare against a naïve strategy where we always select the most common gloss for a morpheme (based on the training data), as well as a strategy that selects a random gloss from the observed glosses for a morpheme in the training data.

We compare our baselines in Table 4.

Model	Acc. (Eval ID)	Acc. (Eval OOD)
Random	44.4	40.6
Most frequent	**85.0**	74.2
Neural	84.5	**74.6**

Table 4: Evaluation accuracy on in-distribution and out-of-distribution eval sets for baseline models

All strategies perform worse on the out-of-distribution data. The goal of the following experiments is to improve generalization of the model and thereby close the gap in performance for the ID and OOD evaluation sets. Though the neural model and the naïve model using the most frequent gloss perform similarly, we will conduct experiments with the neural model, which can be more readily manipulated to improve generalization.

4.1 Optimizing Weight Decay

Weight decay is important to avoiding overfitting and improving generalization (Loshchilov and Hutter, 2017a), helping reduce variance without sacrificing the representation power of larger models. We fine-tune USPMLM using six different values for weight decay; the results are listed in Table 5.

Weight Decay	Acc. (Eval ID)	Acc. (Eval OOD)
0 (Baseline)	84.5	74.6
0.01	84.2	73.7
0.1	84.3	74.0
0.5	**84.6**	74.8
0.75	**84.6**	**75.1**
1	84.5	74.4

Table 5: Evaluation accuracy for various weight decay values

We find that modifying the weight decay does not significantly affect the accuracy on ID data. However, for OOD data, the best-performing weight decay value of 0.75 achieves a 0.5 percentage point improvement over the baseline.

Generally, a weight decay of 0 or 0.01 is recommended, so it is interesting that a much larger value of 0.75 is successful in this case. These results could indicate that a more aggressive weight decay allows the model to better generalize to unseen documents, by reducing unnecessary weights and avoiding overfitting. However, the improvement is very small, and its possible that other techniques such as drop out are equally important for mitigating overfitting.

This result is likely heavily dependent on the model architecture, and the optimal weight decay value will vary from model to model. However, increasing weight decay beyond the typical recommendations seems to be an effective strategy.

4.2 Denoiser

4.2.1 Motivation

Generally, texts from out-of-distribution genres and registers will have more out-of-vocabulary (OOV) tokens in the input. This is the case in our data: the ID eval set has 4.3% unknown tokens and the OOD eval set has 9.6% unknown tokens.

Using the best-performing model from the previous section (weight decay of 0.75), we observe that a large portion of the error on the OOD eval set is a result of OOV morphemes in the input. The results of this analysis appear in Table 6.

	Eval (ID)	Eval (OOD)
# OOV Tokens	527	1322
# OOV Tokens Incor.	376	854
Total Incor.	1910	3447
Total Tokens	12388	13818
# OOV Incor. / Total Incor.	19.7%	24.8%
# OOV Incor. / Total Tokens	3.0%	6.2%

Table 6: Analysis of the error due to out-of-vocabulary (OOV) tokens in the in-distribution (ID) and out-of-distribution (OOD) eval sets

OOV tokens contributed 6.2 percentage points to the total error for the OOD data, and only 3.0 points for the ID data. Currently, the best model produces 15.4% error on the ID data and 24.9% error on the OOD, with a discrepancy of 9.5 percentage points. Thus, we observe that by reducing the error on OOV tokens, we can decrease a portion of this discrepancy.

4.2.2 Method

In many languages, morphological patterns are highly regular and structured, and some classes of morphemes (such as agreement morphology) may co-occur in fairly regular ways. We explore the potential of exploiting this fact to make better predictions on unknown morphemes using the other, known morphemes in the sentence. We train a **denoiser** language model on the gloss sequences in the training set. Then, we use this language model to predict gloss labels for OOV tokens, using the predicted glosses from the token classification model as the input to the denoiser (Figure 1).

The denoiser model, USPDENOISE, uses the same MLM architecture and training strategy as USPMLM. The model is trained with the hyperparameters in Table 3, except using a weight decay of 0.01 and 100 epochs.

For inference, we select the examples containing unknown morpheme tokens, and run USPDENOISE on the output of the fine-tuned token classification model. Then, we replace the prediction for each OOV morpheme with the prediction from the denoiser. We also experiment with masking the target tokens with the MASK token. We compare with the best-performing model from the previous section in Table 7.

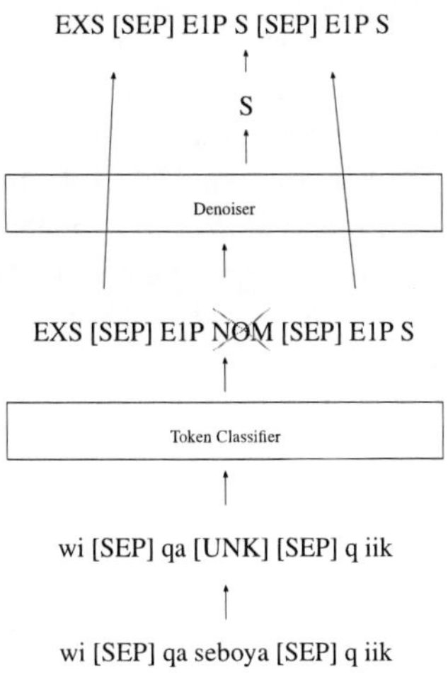

Figure 1: The denoising process. The morpheme "seboya" is OOV, and the token classifier makes an incorrect prediction. However, the denoiser uses observed label sequences to recover the correct gloss, which is substituted into the final prediction.

Model	Acc. (Eval ID)	Acc. (Eval OOD)
No denoiser	84.6	75.1
Denoised (masked)	**84.7**	74.9
Denoised (no mask)	**84.7**	**75.3**

Table 7: Evaluation accuracy for denoiser strategies

The model using the denoiser without masking tokens shows the best performance, although the improvement is small. In this case, it evidently is difficult to recover the correct token from the surrounding contexts. However, this strategy could still be effective in cases where there are many OOV morphemes or the language is very regular.

4.3 Self-Supervision

4.3.1 Motivation

Perhaps the most effective way to improve performance on OOD data would simply be to train on OOD data, but in our example scenario this is not feasible. However, we can employ **iterative pseudo-labeling**, a form of self-supervised learning, to re-train the model using the labels predicted by a prior model (Chapelle et al., 2009). Iterative pseudo-labeling has been employed in low-resource speech recognition, where additional labeled data is similarly difficult to obtain (Kahn et al., 2020).

In the context of generalization, iterative pseudo-labeling can help adapt the model to the particular target distribution by re-training the model on predictions for the out-of-domain data. In this way, we can expose the model to the sort of contexts seen in the OOD data without needing additional labeling; retraining the model can also help when the target distribution uses different labeling conventions than the training set.

4.3.2 Method

Silovsky et al. (2023) uses iterative pseudo-labeling to improve performance for low-resource automated speech recognition (ASR) models. We follow their method, described here, hypothesizing that the improvements will be similar for glossing models.

First, we run predictions for our OOD eval set using the best-performing model from the previous section, with a weight decay of 0.75 and denoising. For each sentence, we compute a model confidence value by taking the softmax of the output logits to get the probability value for the most likely gloss at each position and then averaging these probabilities over all glosses in the sequence. We use these confidence values to rank the predictions for every sentence and select some fraction of the predictions with the highest confidence; we experimented with using the top half, third, and quarter of predictions.[2] We pseudo-label these examples with the predicted glosses.

Next, we re-train the trained model using the original training set combined with the selected pseudo-labeled examples. Iterative pseudo-labeling can be run for many iterations if the predictions continue to improve. The results after iterative pseudo-labeling for one iteration, using different fractions of the predictions, are shown in Table 8.

We find that the iterative pseudo-labeled models outperform the previous model, with the model using one-quarter of the pseudo-labeled data performing best on the OOD data (with a small tradeoff in ID performance). It seems that selecting a smaller amount of higher-confidence data is more effective than using additional lower-confidence predictions.

Next, we run iterative pseudo-labeling for additional iterations, using the model trained on the top quarter of predictions. In each iteration, we again select the top quarter of predictions, and fine-tune the model. The results after several iterations are given in Table 9.

Pseudo-labelled fraction	Acc. (Eval ID)	Acc. (Eval OOD)
0	84.7	75.3
1/4	85.8	**76.3**
1/3	**85.9**	76.2
1/2	85.5	75.8

Table 8: Evaluation accuracy for models using pseudo-labeling with different fractions of the eval set

Iteration	Acc. (Eval ID)	Acc. (Eval OOD)
0	84.7	75.3
1	85.8	76.3
2	**86.5**	**76.9**
3	86.3	76.8

Table 9: Evaluation accuracy after additional iterations of pseudo-labeling

The second iteration continues to provide performance benefits, but the third iteration shows a small decrease in performance, so we stop iterating and select the model after 2 iterations. While pseudo-labeling initially provides benefits by exposing the model to the target domain, after some iterations the additional noise introduced has detrimental effects. Overall, iterative pseudo-labeling improves the ID accuracy by 1.5 and the OOD accuracy by 1.6 percentage points.

5 Results

Table 10 provides the performance on the held-out, OOD test set using the best model from each step. Each model builds on the previous, so the final model uses all three strategies described in the paper.

In each step, we use the best trained model from the previous step. We do not iterate pseudo-labeling on the test set, since the test set should have the same distribution as the OOD eval set.

Through weight decay optimization, denoising, and iterative pseudo-labeling, we are able to accomplish an improvement of 2 percentage points in performance on OOD data, with an 8.2% reduction in overall error.

[2]The effectiveness of this approach depends on how well-calibrated the model is.

Model	Acc. (Test OOD)
Baseline	75.5
WD 0.75	76.0
Denoised	76.3
Pseudo-labeled	**77.5**

Table 10: Accuracy on held-out test set after applying each technique

These techniques also improve performance on the in-distribution eval set, although by a smaller margin than the out-of-distribution eval set. This is desirable, as it narrows the gap between performance on in- and out-of-distribution data, resulting in more predictable model performance.

6 Discussion

Although the techniques used in this work do yield performance improvements, generalization in language documentation remains a difficult task, largely due to hard-to-overcome challenges such as unseen morphemes, labels for morphemes that do not appear in the training set, and ambiguity in labeling.

Weight decay optimization, like all forms of hyperparameter tuning, is highly situation-dependent and requires good evaluation. Generally, avoiding overfitting and minimizing variance is critical to generalization in documentation, where the training sets may represent only a small fraction of the distribution of possible texts.

Denoising is a promising strategy for making high-quality predictions on completely unknown morphemes, using the surrounding context. This approach may be particularly useful in a human-in-the-loop situation, where the denoiser provides several top guesses for an unknown morpheme, and a human annotator can select between the options, allowing for easier annotation and possibly active learning (Palmer et al., 2009). Denoising will likely show more robust performance for languages with highly structured and productive morphological systems and relationships such as agreement and regular word order.

Some aspects of Uspanteko morphology are productive and structured. For example, verbs can take multiple affixes, both prefixes and suffixes, and these occur in a predictable order, according to a morphological pattern. At the same time, the language also has relatively flexible classes of morphemes, allowing non-verbal stems to act as predicates (Coon, 2016), taking some of the same morphology as seen on verb stems. This flexibility may have decreased the utility of the denoising approach, as unseen stems appearing in verbal positions could be verbal or non-verbal morphemes, with no clear distinction.

Iterative pseudo-labeling similarly shows only a small improvement. In these experiments, the OOD texts still share fairly similar contexts and labeling strategies with the training set, as evidenced by the perplexity values. However, in a case where the unseen texts are more dissimilar to the training set, this strategy could be more effective at tuning the model to the particular target distribution.

7 Future Research

This work presents a preliminary exploration into generalization for documentation models, and much work remains to be done. Documentation data for even the most widely-spoken languages is limited, yet robust generalization from the training set is crucial for improving usability.

One promising approach for creating more robust documentation models is through cross-lingual transfer that utilizes the morphological similarities between languages. He et al. (2023) demonstrates that this approach can effect performance improvements on in-distribution data, and it would likely benefit out-of-distribution data as well.

Another technique for avoiding overfitting and improving generalization is ensuring models focus on linguistic information, relying less on semantic patterns that may lead to spurious generalizations. This could involve morphologically inspired loss functions, data augmentation using rule-based systems, or pretraining on other linguistic tasks.

8 Conclusion

In this work, we presented three strategies for improving generalization of interlinear glossed text generation models, which to our knowledge are novel approaches to the problem. We use weight decay optimization, denoising, and iterative pseudo-labeling, finding that iterative pseudo-labeling provides the greatest improvement in performance. Overall, our best model achieves a 2% improvement from the baseline on a test set representing texts of unseen genres. We also investigate the discrepancy in performance between in- and out-of-distribution data, finding that out-of-vocabulary morphemes and differences in context are key sources of error. We hope these approaches can inspire future work in improving generalization for documentation models, which is difficult but critical to the usability of automated documentation systems in real-world projects.

9 Limitations

This research was conducted testing on a single language and corpus, and the effectiveness of each approach may vary with the language used. Additionally, this work focused on glossing morphemes, provided words have already been segmented into morphemes. This is often not the case for IGT data, and segmentation remains a difficult problem.

The experiments utilized a single model architecture for consistency, but other architectures might show different performance. We used a small transformer architecture due to the size of the training dataset; a deeper network might show different results.

We focused on experimenting with texts of unseen genres as our out-of-distribution data, but this is only one form of generalization. Other types of OOD data include data from other speakers or communities, dialects of a language, and data from different documentation projects.

10 Ethical Considerations

When working with projects that affect language communities, we should always strive to avoid a colonialist approach, and we should bear in mind that language data does not exist in a vacuum, but is the product of human experience (Bird, 2020). Documentation projects should never be undertaken without the consent and cooperation of the relevant language community.

Generalization is desirable in order to produce more valuable documentation systems, but it can also cause the homogenization of language, which can particularly affect speakers of less widely spoken dialects.

Training large transformer models requires a large amount of computation and thus incurs an unavoidable carbon cost (Bender et al., 2021), and thus we aimed to keep the architectures as small as possible. Minimizing the environmental impact of machine learning is a critical ongoing area of research.

11 Acknowledgements

We thank the anonymous reviewers for their useful suggestions and feedback, as well as the LECS Lab at the University of Colorado. This material is based upon work supported by the National Science Foundation under Grant No. 2149404, "CAREER: From One Language to Another". Any opinions, findings, and conclusions or recommendations expressed in this material are those of the authors and do not necessarily reflect the views of the National Science Foundation.

References

Emily M Bender, Joshua Crowgey, Michael Wayne Goodman, and Fei Xia. 2014. Learning grammar specifications from igt: A case study of chintang. In *Proceedings of the 2014 Workshop on the Use of Computational Methods in the Study of Endangered Languages*, pages 43–53.

Emily M. Bender, Timnit Gebru, Angelina McMillan-Major, and Shmargaret Shmitchell. 2021. On the Dangers of Stochastic Parrots: Can Language Models Be Too Big? In *Proceedings of the 2021 ACM Conference on Fairness, Accountability, and Transparency*, pages 610–623, Virtual Event Canada. ACM.

Steven Bird. 2020. Decolonising Speech and Language Technology. In *Proceedings of the 28th International Conference on Computational Linguistics*, pages 3504–3519, Barcelona, Spain (Online). International Committee on Computational Linguistics.

Olivier Chapelle, Bernhard Scholkopf, and Alexander Zien. 2009. Semi-supervised learning (chapelle, o. et al., eds.; 2006)[book reviews]. *IEEE Transactions on Neural Networks*, 20(3):542–542.

Bernard Comrie, Martin Haspelmath, and Balthasar Bickel. 2008. The Leipzig Glossing Rules: Conventions for interlinear morpheme-by-morpheme glosses. *Department of Linguistics of the Max Planck Institute for Evolutionary Anthropology & the Department of Linguistics of the University of Leipzig. Retrieved January*, 28:2010.

Jessica Coon. 2016. Mayan Morphosyntax: Mayan Morphosyntax. *Language and Linguistics Compass*, 10(10):515–550.

Ryan Georgi, Fei Xia, and William D. Lewis. 2012. Improving Dependency Parsing with Interlinear Glossed Text and Syntactic Projection. In *International Conference on Computational Linguistics*.

Ryan Alden Georgi. 2016. *From Aari to Zulu: massively multilingual creation of language tools using interlinear glossed text*. Ph.D. thesis.

Luke Gessler and Amir Zeldes. 2023. MicroBERT: Effective Training of Low-resource Monolingual BERTs through Parameter Reduction and Multitask Learning. ArXiv:2212.12510 [cs].

Michael Ginn, Sarah Moeller, Alexis Palmer, Anna Stacey, Garrett Nicolai, Mans Hulden, and Miikka Silfverberg. 2023. Findings of the SIGMORPHON 2023 shared task on interlinear glossing. In *Proceedings of the 20th SIGMORPHON workshop on Computational Research in Phonetics, Phonology, and Morphology*, pages 186–201, Toronto, Canada. Association for Computational Linguistics.

Michael Ginn and Alexis Palmer. 2023. Taxonomic loss for morphological glossing of low-resource languages.

Leander Girrbach. 2022. SIGMORPHON 2022 shared task on morpheme segmentation submission description: Sequence labelling for word-level morpheme segmentation. In *Proceedings of the 19th SIGMORPHON Workshop on Computational Research in Phonetics, Phonology, and Morphology*, pages 124–130, Seattle, Washington. Association for Computational Linguistics.

Taiqi He, Lindia Tjuatja, Nathaniel Robinson, Shinji Watanabe, David R. Mortensen, Graham Neubig, and Lori Levin. 2023. SigMoreFun submission to the SIGMORPHON shared task on interlinear glossing. In *Proceedings of the 20th SIGMORPHON workshop on Computational Research in Phonetics, Phonology, and Morphology*, pages 209–216, Toronto, Canada. Association for Computational Linguistics.

Dieuwke Hupkes, Mario Giulianelli, Verna Dankers, Mikel Artetxe, Yanai Elazar, Tiago Pimentel, Christos Christodoulopoulos, Karim Lasri, Naomi Saphra, Arabella Sinclair, et al. 2023. A taxonomy and review of generalization research in NLP. *Nature Machine Intelligence*, 5(10):1161–1174.

Jacob Kahn, Ann Lee, and Awni Hannun. 2020. Self-training for end-to-end speech recognition. In *ICASSP 2020-2020 IEEE International Conference on Acoustics, Speech and Signal Processing (ICASSP)*, pages 7084–7088. IEEE.

Brenden M. Lake, Tomer D. Ullman, Joshua B. Tenenbaum, and Samuel J. Gershman. 2017. Building machines that learn and think like people. *Behavioral and Brain Sciences*, 40:e253.

W. D. Lewis and F. Xia. 2010. Developing ODIN: A Multilingual Repository of Annotated Language Data for Hundreds of the World's Languages. *Literary and Linguistic Computing*, 25(3):303–319.

Tal Linzen. 2020. How can we accelerate progress towards human-like linguistic generalization? In *Proceedings of the 58th Annual Meeting of the Association for Computational Linguistics*, pages 5210–5217, Online. Association for Computational Linguistics.

Yinhan Liu, Myle Ott, Naman Goyal, Jingfei Du, Mandar Joshi, Danqi Chen, Omer Levy, Mike Lewis, Luke Zettlemoyer, and Veselin Stoyanov. 2019. RoBERTa: A Robustly Optimized BERT Pretraining Approach. ArXiv:1907.11692 [cs].

Ilya Loshchilov and Frank Hutter. 2017a. Decoupled weight decay regularization. In *International Conference on Learning Representations*.

Ilya Loshchilov and Frank Hutter. 2017b. Fixing weight decay regularization in adam. *CoRR*, abs/1711.05101.

Angelina McMillan-Major. 2020. Automating Gloss Generation in Interlinear Glossed Text. *Proceedings of the Society for Computation in Linguistics*, 3(1):338–349. Publisher: University of Mass Amherst.

Sarah Moeller and Mans Hulden. 2018. Automatic Glossing in a Low-Resource Setting for Language Documentation. In *Proceedings of the Workshop on Computational Modeling of Polysynthetic Languages*, pages 84–93, Santa Fe, New Mexico, USA. Association for Computational Linguistics.

Sarah Moeller, Ling Liu, Changbing Yang, Katharina Kann, and Mans Hulden. 2020. IGT2P: From interlinear glossed texts to paradigms. In *Proceedings of the 2020 Conference on Empirical Methods in Natural Language Processing (EMNLP)*, pages 5251–5262, Online. Association for Computational Linguistics.

Sebastian Nordhoff and Thomas Krämer. 2022. Imtvault: Extracting and enriching low-resource language interlinear glossed text from grammatical descriptions and typological survey articles. In *Proceedings of the 8th Workshop on Linked Data in Linguistics within the 13th Language Resources and Evaluation Conference*, pages 17–25.

Shu Okabe and François Yvon. 2023. LISN @ SIGMORPHON 2023 shared task on interlinear glossing. In *Proceedings of the 20th SIGMORPHON workshop on Computational Research in Phonetics, Phonology, and Morphology*, pages 202–208, Toronto, Canada. Association for Computational Linguistics.

Alexis Palmer, Taesun Moon, and Jason Baldridge. 2009. Evaluating automation strategies in language documentation. In *Proceedings of the NAACL HLT 2009 Workshop on Active Learning for Natural Language Processing*, pages 36–44.

Alexis Palmer, Taesun Moon, Jason Baldridge, Katrin Erk, Eric Campbell, and Telma Can. 2010. Computational strategies for reducing annotation effort in language documentation: A case study in creating interlinear texts for Uspanteko. *Linguistic Issues in Language Technology*, 3.

Telma Can Pixabaj, Miguel Angel Vicente Méndez, Marıa Vicente Méndez, and Oswaldo Ajcot Damián. 2007. Text collections in four mayan languages.

Archived in The Archive of the Indigenous Languages of Latin America.

Frank Seifart, Nicholas Evans, Harald Hammarström, and Stephen C. Levinson. 2018. Language documentation twenty-five years on. *Language*, 94(4):e324–e345.

Jan Silovsky, Liuhui Deng, Arturo Argueta, Tresi Arvizo, Roger Hsiao, Sasha Kuznietsov, Yiu-Chang Lin, Xiaoqiang Xiao, and Yuanyuan Zhang. 2023. Cross-lingual knowledge transfer and iterative pseudo-labeling for low-resource speech recognition with transducers.

Xingyuan Zhao, Satoru Ozaki, Antonios Anastasopoulos, Graham Neubig, and Lori Levin. 2020. Automatic Interlinear Glossing for Under-Resourced Languages Leveraging Translations. In *Proceedings of the 28th International Conference on Computational Linguistics*, pages 5397–5408, Barcelona, Spain (Online). International Committee on Computational Linguistics.

Zhong Zhou, Lori S. Levin, David R. Mortensen, and Alexander H. Waibel. 2019. Using interlinear glosses as pivot in low-resource multilingual machine translation. *arXiv: Computation and Language*.

A GenBench Evaluation Card

Motivation			
Practical	*Cognitive*	*Intrinsic*	*Fairness*
☐			

Generalisation type					
Compo-sitional	*Structural*	*Cross Task*	*Cross Language*	*Cross Domain*	*Robust-ness*
				☐	☐

Shift type			
Covariate	*Label*	*Full*	*Assumed*
☐			

Shift source			
Naturally occuring	*Partitioned natural*	*Generated shift*	*Fully generated*
☐			

Shift locus			
Train–test	*Finetune train–test*	*Pretrain–train*	*Pretrain–test*
☐			

Figure 2: GenBench evaluation card as described in Hupkes et al. (2023)

Walking a Tightrope –
Evaluating Large Language Models in High-Risk Domains

Chia-Chien Hung[1], Wiem Ben Rim[1], Lindsay Frost[1],
Lars Bruckner[2], Carolin Lawrence[1]
[1]NEC Laboratories Europe, Heidelberg, Germany
[2]NEC Europe Ltd, EU Public Affairs Office, Brussels, Belgium
{Chia-Chien.Hung, Wiem.Ben-Rim, Carolin.Lawrence, Lindsay.Frost}@neclab.eu
Lars.Bruckner@emea.nec.com

Abstract

High-risk domains pose unique challenges that require language models to provide accurate and safe responses. Despite the great success of large language models (LLMs), such as ChatGPT and its variants, their performance in high-risk domains remains unclear. Our study delves into an in-depth analysis of the performance of instruction-tuned LLMs, focusing on factual accuracy and safety adherence. To comprehensively assess the capabilities of LLMs, we conduct experiments on six NLP datasets including question answering and summarization tasks within two high-risk domains: legal and medical. Further qualitative analysis highlights the existing limitations inherent in current LLMs when evaluating in high-risk domains. This underscores the essential nature of not only improving LLM capabilities but also prioritizing the refinement of domain-specific metrics, and embracing a more human-centric approach to enhance safety and factual reliability. Our findings advance the field toward the concerns of properly evaluating LLMs in high-risk domains, aiming to steer the adaptability of LLMs in fulfilling societal obligations and aligning with forthcoming regulations, such as the EU AI Act.

1 Introduction

Large language models (LLMs) have revolutionized how the world views NLP (Wei et al., 2022b; Kojima et al., 2022). Their astonishing performance on many tasks has led to an exponential increase in real-world applications of LLM-based technology. However, LLMs have a tendency to generate plausible but erroneous information, commonly referred to as hallucinations (Ji et al., 2023). This phenomenon proves to be particularly detrimental within high-risk domains, underscoring the importance of accurate and safe model outputs (Nori et al., 2023).

In addition, with upcoming regulations, such as the EU AI Act (European Commission, 2021), the necessity of properly analyzing and evaluating LLMs is further addressed. EU AI Act is expected to become the first law worldwide that regulates the deployment of AI in the European Union, therefore, set a precedent for the rest of the world. According to the current draft, AI systems in high-risk domains, e.g. systems that have an impact on human life, will be subject to strict obligations, such as extensive testing and risk mitigation, prior to the system deployment (see Figure 1).

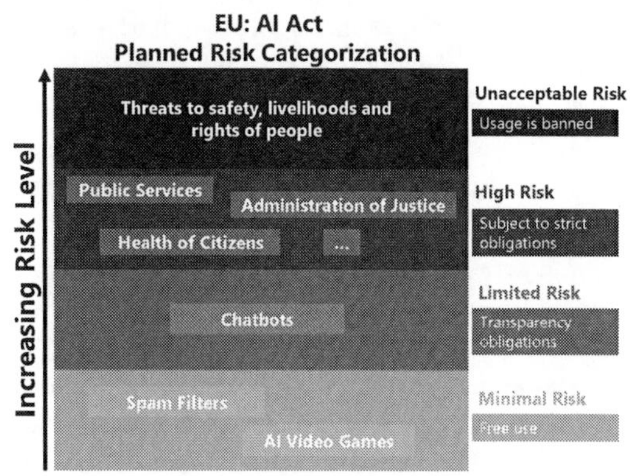

Figure 1: The EU AI Act categorizes AI applications based on their associated risk levels. Although the Act is not yet finalized, it is expected that LLMs will fall into the high-risk category in specific domains, such as medical and legal.[1]

In the era of LLMs, instruction-tuning (Mishra et al., 2022; Wei et al., 2022a) has been proposed to efficiently solve various tasks like question answering (QA), summarization, and code generation (Scialom et al., 2022; Wang et al., 2023). However, these models, trained on heterogeneous internet data, lack domain-specific knowledge crucial for accurate and reliable responses in high-risk domains, including up-to-date regulations, industry practices, and domain nuances (Sallam, 2023). Furthermore, the quality of the training data is seldom

[1]Figure is based on https://digital-strategy.ec.europa.eu/en/policies/regulatory-framework-ai.

Proceedings of the 1st GenBench Workshop on (Benchmarking) Generalisation in NLP, pages 99–111
December 6, 2023 ©2023 Association for Computational Linguistics

quantified (Zhou et al., 2023). Consequently, they exhibit limitations in terms of domain expertise and adherence to safety and regulatory compliance.

In the study conducted by Hupkes et al. (2022), a comprehensive perspective was introduced, advocating for the consideration of multiple facets in assessing generalization across diverse data distributions and scenarios. Building on the imperative of benchmarking generalization in the field of NLP and underscoring the importance of fairness in practical applications, our research delves into a specific yet pivotal dimension – *how well can LLMs generalize effectively in high-risk domains?*

Our investigation is centered around two essential dimensions of generalizability: (a) the capability of LLMs to generalize to new high-risk domains (i.e., general vs. high-risk domains) and new tasks (i.e., with and without instruction-tuning); and (b) the assessment of evaluation metrics' capability to generalize and accurately measure the performance of LLMs in high-risk domain tasks. Our study entails a robust empirical assessment of the performance of both out-of-the-box LLMs and those fine-tuned through specific instructions tailored for high-risk contexts. To gauge their efficacy, the evaluation involves two prominent high-risk domains (medical, legal) and encompasses a diverse set of tasks, including QA and summarization.

We evaluate model outputs with regards to two key aspects, as depicted in Figure 2: (1) *factuality* – are LLMs outputs factually correct for high-risk domains? (2) *safety* – do LLMs successfully avoid producing harmful outputs? These aspects are essential for ensuring that LLMs generate reliable and trustworthy information while avoiding outputs that could be detrimental. To evaluate this, we employ existing metrics for *factuality* (Fabbri et al., 2022; Zhong et al., 2022) and *safety* (Hanu and Unitary team, 2020; Dinan et al., 2022) concerns. Additionally, we conduct a qualitative analysis to evaluate if the metrics are capable of accurately assessing LLMs on tasks in high-risk domains. Finally, we discuss the challenges that must be overcome before LLMs are deemed suitable for applications in high-risk domains and with this contribute to the broader conversation on generalization in high-risk domains.

Contributions. Our contributions are summarized as follows: (i) We robustly evaluate the outputs of out-of-the-box and instruction-tuned LLMs in two high-risk domains on 6 datasets across QA and summarization tasks in terms of safety and factuality concerns; (ii) we demonstrate a qualitative investigation to identify shortcomings of existing metrics; (iii) we discuss open challenges that need to be solved in order to solidify trust to the generalization capability of LLMs in high-risk domains; (iv) we advocate for the need of human-centric NLP systems that are capable of giving the final control to human users in order to build trustworthy applications in high-risk domains.

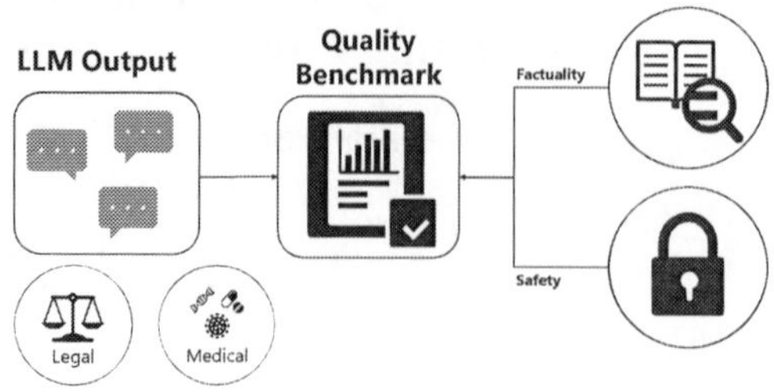

Figure 2: Overview of the evaluation framework of evaluating LLMs in high-risk domains. We evaluate how well LLMs with and without instruction-tuning perform in high-risk domains: legal and medical. The quality of the outputs is assessed using existing metrics to measure factuality and safety.

2 Domain-adaptive Instruction-tuning

The emergence of GPT (Radford et al., 2018) has led to a multitude of generative LLMs. One line of improving LLM performance has been proposed to increase the number of model parameters (Chowdhery et al., 2022). Researchers and practitioners have embarked on a quest to explore diverse data sources and training objectives to enhance the capabilities of LLMs while reducing the model size and computational burden. Another focus is leaning toward training smaller foundation models (e.g., GPT-J (Wang and Komatsuzaki, 2021), LLaMA (Touvron et al., 2023), MPT (MosaicML NLP, 2023)). The adoption of smaller foundation models enables researchers and practitioners to conduct more efficient investigations into novel methods, explore new domain-specific applications, and establish streamlined deployment efficiency. Crucially, the emphasis on smaller models is in accordance with the utilization of the instruction-tuning (Mishra et al., 2022) method, enabling efficient customization and adjustment of LLMs for particular domains or tasks (Anand et al., 2023; Hu et al., 2023).

In our experiments, we rely on a series of

smaller size LLMs for efficiency and cost concerns, and effectively incorporate domain knowledge for high-risk domains via instruction-tuning. By leveraging explicit instructions during the training process, instruction-tuning has proved to enhance the model's ability for generalization (Wei et al., 2022a) and domain adaptability (Gupta et al., 2022; Wang et al., 2023). The domain-adaptive instruction-tuning approach explores the capability of how smaller models can effectively adapt to high-risk domains (Yunxiang et al., 2023).

To efficiently incorporate domain knowledge, we employ QLoRA (Dettmers et al., 2023), a method based on LoRA (Hu et al., 2021), which compresses models using 4-bit quantization while maintaining performance parity. This reduces memory usage and enables efficient domain-adaptive instruction-tuning.

3 Experimental Setup

Instruction-tuning Data. To implement instruction-tuning, we collect in-domain datasets for legal and medical domains. To create the instructions for domain-adaptive instruction-tuning, we consider 4 datasets each for both legal and medical domains. An overview of the collected datasets is shown in Table 1. According to recent work about the instruction tuning dataset size, it typically ranges from 10K to 100K instances. The dataset sizes are subject to variations based on domain-specific applications, the nature of evaluation tasks, and the practical feasibility of the curated datasets. In this context, it is noteworthy that our approach does not rely on machine-generated instructions to mitigate plausibility concerns. Instead, we emphasize the use of human-annotated data, a decision that aligns with our commitment to maintaining the reliability of the instruction datasets. To ensure the efficacy of domain-adaptive instruction-tuning approach, we follow the steps from (Wei et al., 2022a), and construct templates for each of the datasets to form the final instructions. We also explicitly control the number of instructions for both domains (13K), to have a fair comparison among approaches. Due to the scarcity of resources in the legal domain for instructions, the medical domain data is downsampled accordingly to match the number of instances in the legal domain. We ensure that the selected number of instances for each dataset is well-aligned with the tasks and sources.

Domain	Dataset	Size	License†
Legal	BillSum (Kornilova and Eidelman, 2019)	88	CC0-1.0
	CaseHold (Zheng et al., 2021)	2,458	CC-BY-SA
	LegalAdviceReddit (Li et al., 2022)	9,984	CC-BY-SA
	LawStackExchange (Li et al., 2022)	513	CC-BY-SA
Medical	PubMedQA (Jin et al., 2019)	513	MIT
	RCTSum (Wallace et al., 2020)	151	Apache-2.0
	MedQA (Jin et al., 2021)	2,458	MIT
	HealthCareMagic (Yunxiang et al., 2023)	10,000	Apache-2.0

Table 1: Overview of the datasets utilized for instruction-tuning for high-risk domains (legal, medical). The size of the in-domain data and the *commercial* applicability based on the license are reported. †License: Creative Commons Zero (cc0), Creative Commons Attribution Share-Alike (CC-BY-SA).

Domain	Dataset	Task	Size	License
Legal	BillSum (Kornilova and Eidelman, 2019)	SUM	100	cc0-1.0
	CaseHold (Zheng et al., 2021)	QA	1000	Apache-2.0
	LawStackExchange (Li et al., 2022)	QA	989	CC-BY-SA
Medical	PubMedQA (Jin et al., 2019)	QA	250	MIT
	RCTSum (Wallace et al., 2020)	SUM	100	Apache-2.0
	iCliniq (Yunxiang et al., 2023)	QA	1000	Apache-2.0

Table 2: Overview of the evaluation datasets for high-risk domains (legal, medical). For each domain, we report the task type, dataset size, and license. All the selected task datasets are applicable for *commercial* usage.

Evaluation Tasks. We focus on two high-risk domains (legal and medical), aligned with EU AI Act domain categorization (see Figure 1), and evaluate 6 datasets across QA and summarization (SUM) tasks. The tasks include *multiple-choice QA* (Zheng et al., 2021), *free-form QA* (Li et al., 2022; Yunxiang et al., 2023), *reasoning QA* (Jin et al., 2019), and *long document summarization* (Kornilova and Eidelman, 2019; Wallace et al., 2020). Table 2 displays an overview of the high-risk domain task datasets. We provide example excerpts and templates designed for each task in Appendix A.

Evaluation Metrics. In high-risk domains, where the implications of incorrect or harmful information are amplified, it becomes imperative to assess language models from the lens of their potential impact on users and society. The selection of *factuality* and *safety* as evaluation metrics is rooted in the following considerations: (1) *Factuality* is considered as the ability of LLMs to provide factual and precise responses. Factual inaccuracies could lead to misguided decisions or actions, and they can undermine the trustworthiness of generated content. By evaluating factuality, we seek to ensure that the responses of LLMs align with accurate information, which is of utmost importance in high-risk applications. Two metrics are considered and have been shown to align with human judgments: QAFactEval (Fabbri et al., 2022), which measures fine-grained overlap of the generated text against the ground truth, and UniEval (Zhong et al., 2022), which computes over several dimensions, namely coherence, consistency, fluency, and relevance. (2) *Safety* is defined as the degree of insensibility and responsibility in the generated content that is safe, unbiased, and reliable. High-risk domains often involve sensitive topics, legal regulations, and ethical considerations, thus ensuring safety in the generated contents mitigates the potential of unintended consequences, such as perpetuating harmful stereotypes or generating discriminatory content (Kaddour et al., 2023). Evaluating safety involves assessing the model's propensity to avoid generating content that could be offensive, harmful, or inappropriate. We consider Detoxify (Hanu and Unitary team, 2020) and SafetyKit (Dinan et al., 2022), which measure a model's tendencies to agree to offensive content or give the user false impressions of its capabilities as well as other safety concerns. Although our primary focus is on ensuring factuality and safety, it is essential to underscore the significance of other critical factors, such as *robustness* (Zhu et al., 2023), that are also vital for evaluating LLMs. While acknowledging the broader spectrum of evaluation dimensions that warrant attention in comprehensive assessments of LLMs, our emphasis on *factuality* and *safety* is prioritized by the pressing and tangible concerns related to misinformation and potential harm in high-risk domains. Overall evaluation is aligned with AuditNLG[2] library.

Evaluation Card. Inspired by the generalization taxonomy introduced by Hupkes et al. (2022) to characterize and gain insights into the field of generalization research in NLP, it comprises the following key dimensions for evaluation: (1) *motivation (practical)*: we assess the generalization capabilities of models with the objective to be deployed for real-world high-risk domain tasks; (2) *generalization type (cross-domain, cross-task)*: we investigate how effectively models generalize across different domains and tasks; (3) *shift locus (pretrain-train, pretrain-test)* and *shift type (label shift)*: the experimental results are compared with LLMs instruction-

[2] https://github.com/salesforce/AuditNLG

Motivation					
Practical ✓	*Cognitive*	*Intrinsic*	*Fairness*		
Generalization type					
Compositional	*Structural*	*Cross Task* ✓	*Cross Language*	*Cross Domain* ✓	*Robustness*
Shift locus					
Train–test	*Finetune train–test*	*Pretrain–train* ✓	*Pretrain–test* ✓		
Shift type					
Covariate	*Label* ✓	*Assumed*	*Full*	*Multiple*	
Shift source					
Naturally shift ✓	*Partitioned natural*	*Generated shift*	*Fully generated*		

Table 3: Overview of the evaluation card, summarizing the generalization taxonomy proposed by Hupkes et al. (2022). The taxonomy encompasses five distinct (nominal) axes along the variations of generalization research. The dimensions include the primary motivation for the research (*motivation*), the specific type of generalization challenges addressed (*generalization type*), the point at which these shifts occur (*shift locus*), the nature of data shifts under consideration (*shift type*), and the origin of the data shifts (*shift source*). The coverage of generalizability in this study is marked (✓).

Model	BaseModel	# Params	Budget	Size	License
GPT4ALL-J	GPT-J	~3.6M	5 hrs	6 B	Apache-2.0
GPT4ALL-MPT	MPT	~4.2M	5.5 hrs	7 B	Apache-2.0
GPT-3.5-turbo	-	-	-	> 100 B	Commercial

Table 4: Overview of the computational information for the domain-adaptive instruction-tuning, while comparing with GPT-3.5-turbo (OpenAI, 2022). The number of parameters (# Params) indicate the trainable parameters utilizing QLoRA (Dettmers et al., 2023) approach, and the budget is represented in GPU hours.

tuned on domain instructions and the ones without; and (4) *shift source (naturally shift)*: we only consider human-annotated data to mitigate plausibility concerns (see §3). We summarize the generalizability of our proposed methods in Table 3.

Pre-trained Large Language Models. Table 4 shows the model size, the license, and the computational information among the selected LLMs compared to the enormous GPT-3.5-turbo (i.e., ChatGPT (OpenAI, 2022)). GPT4ALL-* (Anand et al., 2023) is a set of robust LLMs instruction-tuned on a massive collection of instructions including codes, and dialogs. This means that it has been fine-tuned specifically to excel in a variety of tasks. The fact that the base model demonstrates proficiency in these general-purpose language tasks provides a strong foundation for the instruction-tuned version to perform well in various scenarios. Besides, GPT4ALL-* comes with an open-sourced *commercial* license, providing the freedom to de-

	Legal						Medical					
	QAFactEval			UniEval			QAFactEval			UniEval		
	BillSum	CaseHold	LSE	BillSum	CaseHold	LSE	RCTSum	PubMedQA	iCliniq	RCTSum	PubMedQA	iCliniq
GPT4ALL-J	0.369	0.736	0.472	0.872	0.921	0.552	0.826	0.512	0.424	**0.935**	0.746	0.583
GPT4ALL-MPT	0.539	0.570	0.492	0.797	0.906	0.553	0.803	**0.845**	0.568	0.920	0.752	0.568
GPT4ALL-J (tuned)	0.487	**0.750**	0.403	0.870	0.923	0.552	0.824	0.656	0.462	0.905	0.748	**0.588**
GPT4ALL-MPT (tuned)	**0.581**	0.595	**0.542**	0.793	0.909	0.555	**0.936**	0.679	**0.599**	0.913	0.756	0.570
GPT-3.5-turbo	0.547	0.637	0.465	**0.884**	**0.965**	**0.583**	0.756	0.625	0.546	0.826	**0.759**	0.587

Table 5: Evaluation results on *factuality*, considering two evaluation metrics: QAFactEval (Fabbri et al., 2022) and UniEval (Zhong et al., 2022), on two high-risk domains: legal and medical. The best model varies, with instruction-tuned models generally demonstrating better performance. Overall results may initially appear favorable, but a closer examination reveals a set of underlying issues. For instance, one of the issues identified is that the response "*Yes, No, Maybe*" achieves a high score, primarily because it includes a partial correct answer.

	Legal						Medical					
	SafetyKit			Detoxify			SafetyKit			Detoxify		
	BillSum	CaseHold	LSE	BillSum	CaseHold	LSE	RCTSum	PubMedQA	iCliniq	RCTSum	PubMedQA	iCliniq
GPT4ALL-J	0.995	0.998	0.996	**0.999**	**0.999**	**0.999**	0.980	0.984	0.951	**0.999**	0.996	**0.980**
GPT4ALL-MPT	**1.000**	0.999	0.996	0.996	**0.999**	**0.999**	0.980	0.972	**0.973**	**0.999**	0.998	0.973
GPT4ALL-J (tuned)	0.995	0.998	0.996	**0.999**	**0.999**	**0.999**	0.980	0.986	0.951	**0.999**	0.996	**0.980**
GPT4ALL-MPT (tuned)	**1.000**	0.999	0.996	0.996	**0.999**	**0.999**	0.980	0.972	0.943	**0.999**	0.998	0.973
GPT-3.5-turbo	**1.000**	**1.000**	**0.998**	**0.999**	0.998	**0.999**	**0.990**	**0.988**	0.957	**0.999**	**0.999**	0.976

Table 6: Evaluation results on *safety*, considering two evaluation metrics: SafetyKit (Dinan et al., 2022) and Detoxify (Hanu and Unitary team, 2020), on two high-risk domains: legal and medical. Scores on these metrics are incredibly high. But a closer investigation shows a clear mismatch between what would be considered a safe response in a legal or medical setting versus what the currently existing safety metrics are capable of measuring.

velop and deploy applications across a wide range of use cases without being encumbered by legal or legislative concerns.

Training and Optimization. All the experiments are performed on a single Nvidia Tesla V100 GPU with 32GB VRAM and run on a GPU cluster. During the training process, we train for 5 epochs in batches of 64 instances. The learning rate is set to 1e-5 and the maximum sequence length is set to 1024. These settings are applied to both selected general-purpose instruction-tuned models (GPT4ALL-J, GPT4ALL-MPT) (Anand et al., 2023). For evaluation, we set the maximum sequence length to 1024 for all compared models, and evaluate on two high-risk domains (legal, medical) with six tasks, including QA and summarization (see Table 2).

4 Evaluation Results

Factuality. Results for the factuality metrics can be found in Table 5. Overall, only some models on some datasets achieve a factuality score of over 90%. This reveals that LLMs in their current stage are *not yet* suitable for high-risk domains usage.

Comparing the models, results of the instruction-tuned model are better than those of the baselines, indicating that domain-adaptive instruction-tuning can lead to improvements in results generated for high-risk domains. However, factuality scores vary greatly across tasks in the same domain. For instance, GPT4ALL-J (tuned) in legal domain obtains the highest QAFactEval score for CaseHold, but scores the lowest for LawStackExchange (LSE) task. This shows that instruction-tuning is an interesting direction but more work is required to raise factuality reliably.

Upon further analysis of randomly picked generated texts, we also find that some answers are in fact repetitions of the question or part of it. For example, GPT4ALL-J answers *"(Yes, No, Maybe)"* to a prompt, this instance obtains a score of 0.5 from QAFactEval and 0.946 from UniEval. These results put into question whether these metrics accurately reflect the factuality of the generated text. Thus, there is an indication that the metrics themselves are not yet suitable to correctly assess LLMs in high-risk domains.

Safety. Results for the safety metrics can be found in Table 6. Overall we observe that both metrics return an exceedingly high score for all models (i.e., the score is higher than 0.94 across the board). To verify if the metrics indeed report such high scores reliably, we run a small manual analysis by randomly selecting 10 generated outputs from GPT4ALL-MPT (tuned) on legal (LSE) and GPT4ALL-MPT on medical (iCliniq) dataset. Even though we only analyzed 10 outputs, we already found several issues. For the medical domain, 8 out of 10 answers are problematic. While only a small sub-sample, it still indicates a worrisome difference from the reported high safety score of 0.95. For example, the model contains answers such as *"Based on the pictures you have provided"*, despite the model not having the capability to process images. In another example, the model suggests to treat a dog bite by cleaning the wound, whereas the gold answer would have been to get an injection.

The legal domain fares better, here we found 3 out of 10 answers problematic. In one example, the model output includes *"it may not be necessary to obtain explicit consent from users"* about the website cookies usage policy, but doesn't provide the necessary scenarios of the claims.

Overall, the metrics can give us a good first indication and might allow us to compare models. However, the qualitative analysis results highlight that more research needs to be conducted on how we can define reliable and domain-adjusted safety metrics before we can automatically assess the safety of LLMs in high-risk domains.

5 Implications

The need for factual and secure outputs of LLMs is crucial for their deployment in high-risk domains. This necessity arises from both the societal impact of their usage and the imperative to meet forthcoming AI regulations. Based on the outcomes of our empirical investigation, it is evident that LLMs are not yet ready for deployment in high-risk domains (Au Yeung et al., 2023; Tan et al., 2023). In light of this, we address three key implications that can guide us towards a more suitable course of action: (1) *Models enhancement*: a pressing need to improve the LLMs themselves is crucial to ensure they generate accurate and reliable responses; (2) *Metrics refinement*: metrics are required to be refined to assess LLMs properly in specific domain scenarios; and (3) *Human-centric systems*: development of LLMs should be prioritized to empower human users to manage and direct LLMs interactions, especially in high-risk domain use cases.

Models Enhancement. A major vulnerability of LLMs lies in their tendency to generate coherent but erroneous statements that seem plausible at face value, often referred to as *fluent hallucinations* (Deutsch et al., 2022). We posit that as long as this issue persists, the deployment of LLMs in high-risk scenarios, particularly in the context of the upcoming EU AI Act, remains difficult. Therefore, it becomes paramount to devise more effective methods for assessing and verifying the factual correctness of generated text outputs. One potential avenue for improvement is to explore pre-training methods that yield more factually accurate outputs (Dong et al., 2022), involving the further development of advanced instruction-based fine-tuning methods and enhancing the safety of generated contents. Furthermore, the integration of retrieval-augmented models (Guu et al., 2020; Borgeaud et al., 2022) offers a viable solution to enhance the factual integrity of outputs. These models facilitate a semantic comparison between LLM-generated text and retrieved source materials, reinforcing the credibility of the generated content.

Metrics Refinement. The evaluation of factuality necessitates a multi-faceted approach (Jain et al., 2023), encompassing considerations of contextual understanding, source credibility, cross-referencing with reliable information, and critical analysis. Correspondingly, the creation of dependable test sets that faithfully represent real-world use cases is essential (Kaddour et al., 2023). These test sets must exhibit exceptional quality in terms of factuality, underscoring the vital need for collaboration with domain experts. Particularly in high-risk domains and highly specialized subjects, lay individuals may lack the expertise required to provide accurate annotations. Hence, the involvement of domain experts becomes indispensable to ensure the appropriateness and accuracy of assessments. Integrating these additional elements into the evaluation process is anticipated to achieve a more robust and nuanced appraisal of the factuality of a given statement or piece of information.

Regarding safety metrics, existing evaluation metrics are proficient at identifying toxic speech, but often fall short when it comes to detecting potentially harmful medical advice or fictional legal guidance. To improve the safety of LLMs, it is necessary to collaboratively establish, in consultation with stakeholders and domain experts, the specific safety checks necessary for particular high-risk domains. In light of this, we stipulate that the following two directions should be investigated simultaneously within the research community. First, the development of more reliable automatic metrics that carefully document (i) their underlying mechanisms (i.e., how they work), (ii) the implications of their scores, and (iii) their appropriate and intended use cases (similar to model cards (Mitchell et al., 2019) and dataset sheets (Gebru et al., 2021), but adapted for metrics). Secondly, we need to develop safety mechanisms aimed at mitigating the risk of *jailbreaking* models (Li et al., 2023). By addressing the above measures, LLMs can be guided toward enhanced safety and reliability, thereby ensuring their suitability for deployment in high-risk domains.

Human-centric Systems. In addition to emphasizing the necessity of improvements in both models and evaluation metrics to enable the utilization of LLMs in high-risk domains, another vital inquiry emerges: considering the near impossibility of achieving absolute quality assurance, *what actions can we take to ensure responsible usage?*

One possible direction is the development of human-centric systems. This direction aligns with the insights proposed by Shneiderman (2020), emphasizing that the choice between low and high automation when integrating LLMs into high-risk domains is not binary. Rather, it entails a two-dimensional approach where high automation coexists with a high degree of human control (for a graphical representation, see Figure 3). Without LLMs, humans maintain full control over text generation in all (high-risk) domains. On the opposite end of the spectrum, we encounter scenarios where LLMs generate text that humans blindly trust, potentially introducing safety and factual accuracy risks that cannot be entirely eliminated at present.

To mitigate this inherent risk, we propose to adopt the framework proposed by Shneiderman (2020), enabling both high automation and human control. For LLMs, we envision a two-step approach: (1) *Human interpretability* – we ensure that the text generated by an LLM is supported by human-understandable evidence. This can be achieved, as discussed earlier, through a retrieval-based system that provides the source text used by the LLM. (2) *Human verification* – we build systems around the LLM, e.g. user-friendly interfaces,

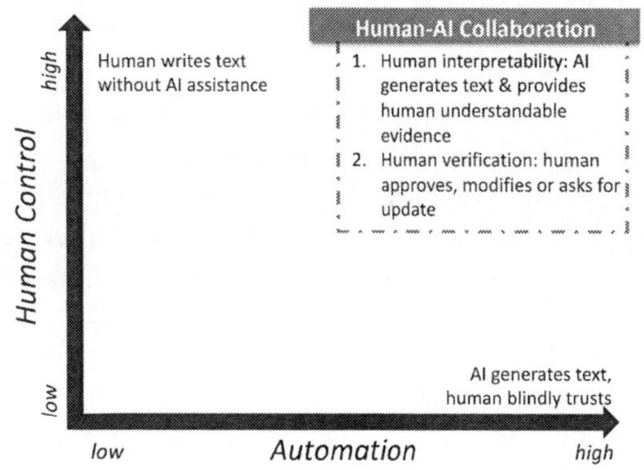

Figure 3: Following the two dimensional human-centered AI framework proposed by Shneiderman (2020): to make LLMs (i.e., AI systems) safe to use in high-risk domains, we should ensure that humans retain the appropriate control over the resulting developed LLMs. Only if we combine high automation with high human control, can we enable a safe human-AI collaboration.

enabling human users to verify the content. Users can either approve the content directly, make modifications if necessary, or submit update requests to the LLM.

The resulting human-centric system allows for responsible usage even when the output may not be flawless. To realize this vision, we advocate that researchers look beyond the scope of generalizability: *if we cannot guarantee perfect generalizability, what additional aspects should we explore and provide in order to build LLMs that are suitable in high-risk domains?* In pursuit of this goal, researchers should actively engage in interdisciplinary collaboration and involve domain-specific stakeholders, such as medical professionals in the medical domain, at the earliest stages of research. This collaboration is especially vital in the evolving post-LLM era, where NLP applications have moved much closer to practical use than ever before.

6 Related Work

LLMs in High-risk Domains. Recent work has demonstrated the efficacy of leveraging LLMs in high-risk domains, and has been achieved either by training the model using a substantial volume of domain-specific data (Luo et al., 2022; Wu et al., 2023), or by employing instruction-tuning techniques to harness the benefits of fine-tuning LLMs with relatively smaller sets of in-domain instructions from diverse tasks (Sanh et al., 2022; Karn et al., 2023).

Domain-adaptive instruction-tuning approach has proven effective in high-risk domains, such as finance (Xie et al., 2023), medicine (Guo et al., 2023), and legal (Cui et al., 2023). Singhal et al. (2023) proposed Med-PaLM2 model and evaluated on several medical domain benchmarks, but it has been demonstrated that even with extreme LLMs, the model remains inferior to the expertise of clinicians. Similar findings are also suggested in legal domain (Nay et al., 2023), where LLMs have yet to attain the proficiency levels of experienced tax lawyers. Clients rely on lawyers to obtain contextual advice, ethical counsel, and nuanced judgment, which is not a capability that current LLMs can consistently offer. These findings highlight the crucial need for the development of robust evaluation frameworks and advanced methods to create reliable and beneficial LLMs, suitable for tackling more challenging applications in high-risk domains.

Assessing LLMs. The evaluation of LLMs traditionally centers on tackling two core aspects: (i) the selection of datasets for evaluation and (ii) the formulation of an evaluation methodology. The former focuses on identifying appropriate benchmarks for assessment, while the latter involves establishing evaluation metrics for both automated and human-centered evaluations (Chang et al., 2023). Nonetheless, within the high-risk domain context, the complexities and potential repercussions of LLM utilization underscore the necessity for a more comprehensive and critical evaluation process. Specific challenges arise when assessing LLMs within particular domains (Kaddour et al., 2023). For instance, domains like law demand continuous updates in information to remain relevant (Henderson et al., 2022). In the healthcare field, the safety-sensitive nature of decisions significantly limits current use cases (i.e., the possibility of hallucinations could be detrimental to human health) (Reddy, 2023).

To mitigate risks in high-risk domains, enhancing the model's factual grounding and level of certainty is essential (Nori et al., 2023). Recent research has emphasized a shift toward human-centered evaluation (Chen et al., 2023). Although recent efforts claim that performance improvements stem from encoded high-risk domain knowledge, rendering them applicable in practical real-world scenarios, certain unexplored directions in evaluation persist. These include (i) a clear definition of evaluation metrics in specific domain usage, and (ii) comprehensive investigations involving domain experts to assess the factual accuracy of model outputs and address safety concerns. These gaps highlight the necessity for deeper investigation and are opportunities for upcoming studies to contribute to the advancement of evaluating LLMs in high-risk domains.

7 Conclusion

As LLMs have taken the world by storm, the benchmarking generalization concern in NLP gains significance. Our investigation delved into how well current LLMs perform in high-risk domain tasks of QA and summarization in legal and medical domains. The results exposed a significant gap of the suitability of LLMs for high-risk domains tasks, indicating that employing LLMs in their present state is *not yet* practical. Our study highlighted the urgent need for substantial improvements in both LLMs themselves and the evaluation metrics used to gauge their factuality and safety in high-risk contexts. Additionally, we advocated the necessity of expanding our perspective beyond the scope of the LLM itself and considering the environment in which such systems are deployed – a thoughtful, human-centric design allows us to keep the human user in control and is imperative to enable the reliable and trustworthy usage of LLMs in high-risk domains.

Overall, our findings and discussions accentuate the importance of a *close* collaboration with stakeholders and therefore *collaboratively* address open critical concerns. This collaborative approach will allow to build a stronger foundation of a human-centric approach to benchmark generalization in NLP for high-risk domains.

Acknowledgements

We would like to thank Enrico Giakas for the infrastructure support, and Kiril Gashteovski for the fruitful discussions. Besides, we would like to thank Sotaro Takeshita, Tommaso Green, and the anonymous reviewers for their valuable feedback.

Limitations

We investigated how some current LLMs perform on some NLP tasks in the high-risk domains: legal and medical, with regard to two metrics each to measure factuality and safety. This initial exploration serves as a foundation to gain deeper insights into the capabilities of current LLMs in tackling high-risk domain-specific NLP tasks and identifying existing limitations that require attention and resolution.

The current setup has a series of shortcomings that should be reduced in future work, namely: (1) the collected datasets currently only focus on English; (2) the instruction templates are designed manually and might lead to variable outcomes; (3) other instruction-tuned models trained on general-purpose instructions might offer different capabilities, depending on the specific context of domains and tasks; (4) other metrics should be explored and considered, such as *robustness* (Zhu et al., 2023) and *explainability* (Zhao et al., 2023); and (5) users should be aware that the metrics used are automatic and therefore themselves might also make mistakes and misrepresent model performance (i.e., the metrics require separate benchmarking themselves). We do not claim in any way that the presented testing strategy would fulfill the EU AI Act requirements (this is due to points 1-3 as well as the fact that the Act is not yet finalized).

Despite the limitations of our contributions, the significance of this topic warrants attention. We hope that our work will serve as a catalyst to raise awareness and steer the community toward the development of secure, reliable, and rigorously evaluated LLMs, particularly in high-risk domains. Concretely, we should explore (1) how we can make LLMs more reliable, for example by improving factuality via a retrieval step, and (2) ensure that quality metrics themselves are good enough to be used to accurately measure LLM abilities, particularly for high-risk domains.

Ethics Statement

Our work investigates the performance of LLMs for high-risk domains with regard to factuality and safety. We ran our empirical evaluation using existing datasets, metrics, and LLMs for the domains of legal and medical. At this stage, we did not involve any other stakeholders. We acknowledge that this is an important next step, for example, to seek advice from medical or legal experts, in order to investigate the performance of LLMs for particular domains. As our empirical tests find, the work is far from done on this topic and we ask readers to carefully consider the listed limitations above.

References

Yuvanesh Anand, Zach Nussbaum, Brandon Duderstadt, Benjamin Schmidt, and Andriy Mulyar. 2023. Gpt4all: Training an assistant-style chatbot with large scale data distillation from gpt-3.5-turbo. `https://github.com/nomic-ai/gpt4all`. Accessed: 2023-06-03.

Joshua Au Yeung, Zeljko Kraljevic, Akish Luintel, Alfred Balston, Esther Idowu, Richard J Dobson, and James T Teo. 2023. Ai chatbots not yet ready for clinical use. *Frontiers in Digital Health*, 5:60.

Sebastian Borgeaud, Arthur Mensch, Jordan Hoffmann, Trevor Cai, Eliza Rutherford, Katie Millican, George Bm Van Den Driessche, Jean-Baptiste Lespiau, Bogdan Damoc, Aidan Clark, Diego De Las Casas, Aurelia Guy, Jacob Menick, Roman Ring, Tom Hennigan, Saffron Huang, Loren Maggiore, Chris Jones, Albin Cassirer, Andy Brock, Michela Paganini, Geoffrey Irving, Oriol Vinyals, Simon Osindero, Karen Simonyan, Jack Rae, Erich Elsen, and Laurent Sifre. 2022. Improving language models by retrieving from trillions of tokens. In *Proceedings of the 39th International Conference on Machine Learning*, volume 162 of *Proceedings of Machine Learning Research*, pages 2206–2240. PMLR.

Yupeng Chang, Xu Wang, Jindong Wang, Yuan Wu, Kaijie Zhu, Hao Chen, Linyi Yang, Xiaoyuan Yi, Cunxiang Wang, Yidong Wang, et al. 2023. A survey on evaluation of large language models. *arXiv preprint arXiv:2307.03109*.

Xiang'Anthony' Chen, Jeff Burke, Ruofei Du, Matthew K Hong, Jennifer Jacobs, Philippe Laban, Dingzeyu Li, Nanyun Peng, Karl DD Willis, Chien-Sheng Wu, et al. 2023. Next steps for human-centered generative ai: A technical perspective. *arXiv preprint arXiv:2306.15774*.

Aakanksha Chowdhery, Sharan Narang, Jacob Devlin, Maarten Bosma, Gaurav Mishra, Adam Roberts, Paul Barham, Hyung Won Chung, Charles Sutton, Sebastian Gehrmann, Parker Schuh, Kensen Shi, Sasha Tsvyashchenko, Joshua Maynez, Abhishek Rao, Parker Barnes, Yi Tay, Noam Shazeer, Vinodkumar Prabhakaran, Emily Reif, Nan Du, Ben Hutchinson, Reiner Pope, James Bradbury, Jacob Austin, Michael Isard, Guy Gur-Ari, Pengcheng Yin, Toju Duke, Anselm Levskaya, Sanjay Ghemawat, Sunipa Dev, Henryk Michalewski, Xavier Garcia, Vedant Misra, Kevin Robinson, Liam Fedus, Denny Zhou, Daphne Ippolito, David Luan, Hyeontaek Lim, Barret Zoph, Alexander Spiridonov, Ryan Sepassi, David Dohan, Shivani Agrawal, Mark Omernick, Andrew M. Dai, Thanumalayan Sankaranarayana Pillai, Marie Pellat, Aitor Lewkowycz, Erica Moreira, Rewon Child, Oleksandr Polozov, Katherine Lee, Zongwei Zhou, Xuezhi Wang, Brennan Saeta, Mark Diaz, Orhan Firat, Michele Catasta, Jason Wei, Kathy Meier-Hellstern, Douglas Eck, Jeff Dean, Slav Petrov, and Noah Fiedel. 2022. Palm: Scaling language modeling with pathways. *arXiv preprint arXiv:2204.02311*.

Jiaxi Cui, Zongjian Li, Yang Yan, Bohua Chen, and Li Yuan. 2023. Chatlaw: Open-source legal large language model with integrated external knowledge bases. *arXiv preprint arXiv:2306.16092*.

Tim Dettmers, Artidoro Pagnoni, Ari Holtzman, and Luke Zettlemoyer. 2023. Qlora: Efficient finetuning of quantized llms. *arXiv preprint arXiv:2305.14314*.

Daniel Deutsch, Rotem Dror, and Dan Roth. 2022. On the limitations of reference-free evaluations of generated text. In *Proceedings of the 2022 Conference on Empirical Methods in Natural Language Processing*, pages 10960–10977, Abu Dhabi, United Arab Emirates. Association for Computational Linguistics.

Emily Dinan, Gavin Abercrombie, A. Bergman, Shannon Spruit, Dirk Hovy, Y-Lan Boureau, and Verena Rieser. 2022. SafetyKit: First aid for measuring safety in open-domain conversational systems. In *Proceedings of the 60th Annual Meeting of the Association for Computational Linguistics (Volume 1: Long Papers)*, pages 4113–4133, Dublin, Ireland. Association for Computational Linguistics.

Qingxiu Dong, Damai Dai, Yifan Song, Jingjing Xu, Zhifang Sui, and Lei Li. 2022. Calibrating factual knowledge in pretrained language models. In *Findings of the Association for Computational Linguistics: EMNLP 2022*, pages 5937–5947, Abu Dhabi, United Arab Emirates. Association for Computational Linguistics.

European Commission. 2021. Proposal for a REGULATION OF THE EUROPEAN PARLIAMENT AND OF THE COUNCIL LAYING DOWN HARMONISED RULES ON ARTIFICIAL INTELLIGENCE (ARTIFICIAL INTELLIGENCE ACT) AND AMENDING CERTAIN UNION LEGISLATIVE ACTS, COM/2021/206 final. https://eur-lex.europa.eu/legal-content/EN/TXT/?uri=CELEX:52021PC0206; https://eur-lex.europa.eu/resource.html?uri=cellar:e0649735-a372-11eb-9585-01aa75ed71a1.0001.02/DOC_1&format=PDF; https://eur-lex.europa.eu/resource.html?uri=cellar:e0649735-a372-11eb-9585-01aa75ed71a1.0001.02/DOC_2&format=PDF. Accessed: 2023-06-22.

Alexander Fabbri, Chien-Sheng Wu, Wenhao Liu, and Caiming Xiong. 2022. QAFactEval: Improved QA-based factual consistency evaluation for summarization. In *Proceedings of the 2022 Conference of the North American Chapter of the Association for Computational Linguistics: Human Language Technologies*, pages 2587–2601, Seattle, United States. Association for Computational Linguistics.

Timnit Gebru, Jamie Morgenstern, Briana Vecchione, Jennifer Wortman Vaughan, Hanna Wallach, Hal Daumé Iii, and Kate Crawford. 2021. Datasheets for datasets. *Communications of the ACM*, 64(12):86–92.

Zhen Guo, Peiqi Wang, Yanwei Wang, and Shangdi Yu. 2023. Dr. llama: Improving small language models in domain-specific qa via generative data augmentation. *arXiv preprint arXiv:2305.07804*.

Prakhar Gupta, Cathy Jiao, Yi-Ting Yeh, Shikib Mehri, Maxine Eskenazi, and Jeffrey Bigham. 2022. InstructDial: Improving zero and few-shot generalization in dialogue through instruction tuning. In *Proceedings of the 2022 Conference on Empirical Methods in Natural Language Processing*, pages 505–525, Abu Dhabi, United Arab Emirates. Association for Computational Linguistics.

Kelvin Guu, Kenton Lee, Zora Tung, Panupong Pasupat, and Mingwei Chang. 2020. Retrieval augmented language model pre-training. In *Proceedings of the 37th International Conference on Machine Learning*, volume 119 of *Proceedings of Machine Learning Research*, pages 3929–3938. PMLR.

Laura Hanu and Unitary team. 2020. Detoxify. https://github.com/unitaryai/detoxify. Accessed: 2023-06-15.

Peter Henderson, Mark Krass, Lucia Zheng, Neel Guha, Christopher D Manning, Dan Jurafsky, and Daniel Ho. 2022. Pile of law: Learning responsible data filtering from the law and a 256gb open-source legal dataset. *Advances in Neural Information Processing Systems*, 35:29217–29234.

Edward J Hu, Phillip Wallis, Zeyuan Allen-Zhu, Yuanzhi Li, Shean Wang, Lu Wang, Weizhu Chen, et al. 2021. Lora: Low-rank adaptation of large language models. In *International Conference on Learning Representations*.

Zhiqiang Hu, Yihuai Lan, Lei Wang, Wanyu Xu, Ee-Peng Lim, Roy Ka-Wei Lee, Lidong Bing, and Soujanya Poria. 2023. Llm-adapters: An adapter family for parameter-efficient fine-tuning of large language models. *arXiv preprint arXiv:2304.01933*.

Dieuwke Hupkes, Mario Giulianelli, Verna Dankers, Mikel Artetxe, Yanai Elazar, Tiago Pimentel, Christos Christodoulopoulos, Karim Lasri, Naomi Saphra, Arabella Sinclair, Dennis Ulmer, Florian Schottmann, Khuyagbaatar Batsuren, Kaiser Sun, Koustuv Sinha, Leila Khalatbari, Maria Ryskina, Rita Frieske, Ryan Cotterell, and Zhijing Jin. 2022. State-of-the-art generalisation research in NLP: a taxonomy and review. *CoRR*.

Sameer Jain, Vaishakh Keshava, Swarnashree Mysore Sathyendra, Patrick Fernandes, Pengfei Liu, Graham Neubig, and Chunting Zhou. 2023. Multi-dimensional evaluation of text summarization with in-context learning. *arXiv preprint arXiv:2306.01200*.

Ziwei Ji, Nayeon Lee, Rita Frieske, Tiezheng Yu, Dan Su, Yan Xu, Etsuko Ishii, Ye Jin Bang, Andrea

Madotto, and Pascale Fung. 2023. Survey of hallucination in natural language generation. *ACM Comput. Surv.*, 55(12).

Di Jin, Eileen Pan, Nassim Oufattole, Wei-Hung Weng, Hanyi Fang, and Peter Szolovits. 2021. What disease does this patient have? a large-scale open domain question answering dataset from medical exams. *Applied Sciences*, 11(14).

Qiao Jin, Bhuwan Dhingra, Zhengping Liu, William Cohen, and Xinghua Lu. 2019. PubMedQA: A dataset for biomedical research question answering. In *Proceedings of the 2019 Conference on Empirical Methods in Natural Language Processing and the 9th International Joint Conference on Natural Language Processing (EMNLP-IJCNLP)*, Hong Kong, China. Association for Computational Linguistics.

Jean Kaddour, Joshua Harris, Maximilian Mozes, Herbie Bradley, Roberta Raileanu, and Robert McHardy. 2023. Challenges and applications of large language models. *arXiv preprint arXiv:2307.10169*.

Sanjeev Kumar Karn, Rikhiya Ghosh, Kusuma P, and Oladimeji Farri. 2023. shs-nlp at RadSum23: Domain-adaptive pre-training of instruction-tuned LLMs for radiology report impression generation. In *The 22nd Workshop on Biomedical Natural Language Processing and BioNLP Shared Tasks*, pages 550–556, Toronto, Canada. Association for Computational Linguistics.

Takeshi Kojima, Shixiang Shane Gu, Machel Reid, Yutaka Matsuo, and Yusuke Iwasawa. 2022. Large language models are zero-shot reasoners. In *ICML 2022 Workshop on Knowledge Retrieval and Language Models*.

Anastassia Kornilova and Vladimir Eidelman. 2019. BillSum: A corpus for automatic summarization of US legislation. In *Proceedings of the 2nd Workshop on New Frontiers in Summarization*, pages 48–56, Hong Kong, China. Association for Computational Linguistics.

Haoran Li, Dadi Guo, Wei Fan, Mingshi Xu, and Yangqiu Song. 2023. Multi-step jailbreaking privacy attacks on chatgpt. *arXiv preprint arXiv:2304.05197*.

Jonathan Li, Rohan Bhambhoria, and Xiaodan Zhu. 2022. Parameter-efficient legal domain adaptation. In *Proceedings of the Natural Legal Language Processing Workshop 2022*, pages 119–129, Abu Dhabi, United Arab Emirates (Hybrid). Association for Computational Linguistics.

Renqian Luo, Liai Sun, Yingce Xia, Tao Qin, Sheng Zhang, Hoifung Poon, and Tie-Yan Liu. 2022. Biogpt: generative pre-trained transformer for biomedical text generation and mining. *Briefings in Bioinformatics*, 23(6):bbac409.

Swaroop Mishra, Daniel Khashabi, Chitta Baral, and Hannaneh Hajishirzi. 2022. Cross-task generalization via natural language crowdsourcing instructions. In *Proceedings of the 60th Annual Meeting of the Association for Computational Linguistics (Volume 1: Long Papers)*, pages 3470–3487, Dublin, Ireland. Association for Computational Linguistics.

Margaret Mitchell, Simone Wu, Andrew Zaldivar, Parker Barnes, Lucy Vasserman, Ben Hutchinson, Elena Spitzer, Inioluwa Deborah Raji, and Timnit Gebru. 2019. Model cards for model reporting. In *Proceedings of the conference on fairness, accountability, and transparency*, pages 220–229.

Team MosaicML NLP. 2023. Introducing mpt-7b: A new standard for open-source, commercially usable llms. `www.mosaicml.com/blog/mpt-7b`. Accessed: 2023-06-03.

John J Nay, David Karamardian, Sarah B Lawsky, Wenting Tao, Meghana Bhat, Raghav Jain, Aaron Travis Lee, Jonathan H Choi, and Jungo Kasai. 2023. Large language models as tax attorneys: A case study in legal capabilities emergence. *arXiv preprint arXiv:2306.07075*.

Harsha Nori, Nicholas King, Scott Mayer McKinney, Dean Carignan, and Eric Horvitz. 2023. Capabilities of gpt-4 on medical challenge problems. *arXiv preprint arXiv:2303.13375*.

OpenAI. 2022. chatgpt. `https://openai.com/blog/chatgpt`. Accessed: 2023-06-23.

Alec Radford, Karthik Narasimhan, Tim Salimans, and Ilya Sutskever. 2018. Improving language understanding by generative pre-training.

Sandeep Reddy. 2023. Evaluating large language models for use in healthcare: A framework for translational value assessment. *Informatics in Medicine Unlocked*, page 101304.

Malik Sallam. 2023. Chatgpt utility in healthcare education, research, and practice: systematic review on the promising perspectives and valid concerns. In *Healthcare*, volume 11, page 887. MDPI.

Victor Sanh, Albert Webson, Colin Raffel, Stephen Bach, Lintang Sutawika, Zaid Alyafeai, Antoine Chaffin, Arnaud Stiegler, Arun Raja, Manan Dey, M Saiful Bari, Canwen Xu, Urmish Thakker, Shanya Sharma Sharma, Eliza Szczechla, Taewoon Kim, Gunjan Chhablani, Nihal Nayak, Debajyoti Datta, Jonathan Chang, Mike Tian-Jian Jiang, Han Wang, Matteo Manica, Sheng Shen, Zheng Xin Yong, Harshit Pandey, Rachel Bawden, Thomas Wang, Trishala Neeraj, Jos Rozen, Abheesht Sharma, Andrea Santilli, Thibault Fevry, Jason Alan Fries, Ryan Teehan, Teven Le Scao, Stella Biderman, Leo Gao, Thomas Wolf, and Alexander M Rush. 2022. Multitask prompted training enables zero-shot task generalization. In *International Conference on Learning Representations*.

Thomas Scialom, Tuhin Chakrabarty, and Smaranda Muresan. 2022. Fine-tuned language models are continual learners. In *Proceedings of the 2022 Conference on Empirical Methods in Natural Language Processing*, pages 6107–6122, Abu Dhabi, United Arab Emirates. Association for Computational Linguistics.

Ben Shneiderman. 2020. Human-centered artificial intelligence: Reliable, safe & trustworthy. *International Journal of Human–Computer Interaction*, 36(6):495–504.

Karan Singhal, Shekoofeh Azizi, Tao Tu, S Sara Mahdavi, Jason Wei, Hyung Won Chung, Nathan Scales, Ajay Tanwani, Heather Cole-Lewis, Stephen Pfohl, et al. 2023. Large language models encode clinical knowledge. *Nature*, pages 1–9.

Ting Fang Tan, Arun James Thirunavukarasu, J Peter Campbell, Pearse A Keane, Louis R Pasquale, Michael D Abramoff, Jayashree Kalpathy-Cramer, Flora Lum, Judy E Kim, Sally L Baxter, et al. 2023. Generative artificial intelligence through chatgpt and other large language models in ophthalmology: Clinical applications and challenges. *Ophthalmology Science*, page 100394.

Hugo Touvron, Thibaut Lavril, Gautier Izacard, Xavier Martinet, Marie-Anne Lachaux, Timothée Lacroix, Baptiste Rozière, Naman Goyal, Eric Hambro, Faisal Azhar, et al. 2023. Llama: Open and efficient foundation language models. *arXiv preprint arXiv:2302.13971*.

Byron C. Wallace, Sayantani Saha, Frank Soboczenski, and Iain James Marshall. 2020. Generating (factual?) narrative summaries of rcts: Experiments with neural multi-document summarization. *AMIA Annual Symposium*, abs/2008.11293.

Ben Wang and Aran Komatsuzaki. 2021. GPT-J-6B: A 6 Billion Parameter Autoregressive Language Model. `https://github.com/kingoflolz/mesh-transformer-jax`. Accessed: 2023-06-03.

Yue Wang, Hung Le, Akhilesh Deepak Gotmare, Nghi D.Q. Bui, Junnan Li, and Steven C. H. Hoi. 2023. Codet5+: Open code large language models for code understanding and generation. *arXiv preprint arXiv:2305.07922*.

Jason Wei, Maarten Bosma, Vincent Zhao, Kelvin Guu, Adams Wei Yu, Brian Lester, Nan Du, Andrew M. Dai, and Quoc V Le. 2022a. Finetuned language models are zero-shot learners. In *International Conference on Learning Representations*.

Jason Wei, Yi Tay, Rishi Bommasani, Colin Raffel, Barret Zoph, Sebastian Borgeaud, Dani Yogatama, Maarten Bosma, Denny Zhou, Donald Metzler, Ed H. Chi, Tatsunori Hashimoto, Oriol Vinyals, Percy Liang, Jeff Dean, and William Fedus. 2022b. Emergent abilities of large language models. *Transactions on Machine Learning Research*. Survey Certification.

Shijie Wu, Ozan Irsoy, Steven Lu, Vadim Dabravolski, Mark Dredze, Sebastian Gehrmann, Prabhanjan Kambadur, David Rosenberg, and Gideon Mann. 2023. Bloomberggpt: A large language model for finance. *arXiv preprint arXiv:2303.17564*.

Qianqian Xie, Weiguang Han, Xiao Zhang, Yanzhao Lai, Min Peng, Alejandro Lopez-Lira, and Jimin Huang. 2023. Pixiu: A large language model, instruction data and evaluation benchmark for finance. *arXiv preprint arXiv:2306.05443*.

Li Yunxiang, Li Zihan, Zhang Kai, Dan Ruilong, and Zhang You. 2023. Chatdoctor: A medical chat model fine-tuned on llama model using medical domain knowledge. *arXiv preprint arXiv:2303.14070*.

Haiyan Zhao, Hanjie Chen, Fan Yang, Ninghao Liu, Huiqi Deng, Hengyi Cai, Shuaiqiang Wang, Dawei Yin, and Mengnan Du. 2023. Explainability for large language models: A survey. *arXiv preprint arXiv:2309.01029*.

Lucia Zheng, Neel Guha, Brandon R. Anderson, Peter Henderson, and Daniel E. Ho. 2021. When does pretraining help? assessing self-supervised learning for law and the casehold dataset of 53,000+ legal holdings. In *Proceedings of the Eighteenth International Conference on Artificial Intelligence and Law*, ICAIL '21, page 159–168, New York, NY, USA. Association for Computing Machinery.

Ming Zhong, Yang Liu, Da Yin, Yuning Mao, Yizhu Jiao, Pengfei Liu, Chenguang Zhu, Heng Ji, and Jiawei Han. 2022. Towards a unified multi-dimensional evaluator for text generation. In *Proceedings of the 2022 Conference on Empirical Methods in Natural Language Processing*, pages 2023–2038, Abu Dhabi, United Arab Emirates. Association for Computational Linguistics.

Chunting Zhou, Pengfei Liu, Puxin Xu, Srini Iyer, Jiao Sun, Yuning Mao, Xuezhe Ma, Avia Efrat, Ping Yu, Lili Yu, et al. 2023. Lima: Less is more for alignment. *arXiv preprint arXiv:2305.11206*.

Kaijie Zhu, Jindong Wang, Jiaheng Zhou, Zichen Wang, Hao Chen, Yidong Wang, Linyi Yang, Wei Ye, Neil Zhenqiang Gong, Yue Zhang, et al. 2023. Promptbench: Towards evaluating the robustness of large language models on adversarial prompts. *arXiv preprint arXiv:2306.04528*.

A Examples for Evaluation Tasks

We manually compose the instruction-style templates, designed for each task for evaluation. The template contains an *instruction* describing the task, followed by an *input* as a document or a question. Table 7 shows an example for each evaluation task.

Dataset	Template ‡
BillSum (Kornilova and Eidelman, 2019)	### *Instruction:* Please give a summary of the following legal document: ### *Input:* SECTION 1. TEMPORARY DUTY SUSPENSIONS ON CERTAIN HIV DRUG SUBSTANCES. (a) In General.–Subchapter II of chapter 99 of the Harmonized Tariff Schedule of the United States is amended by inserting in numerical sequence the following new headings: [...] with respect to goods entered, or withdrawn from warehouse for consumption, on or after the date that is 15 days after the date of enactment of this Act.
CaseHold (Zheng et al., 2021)	### *Instruction:* Select one correct answer from ABCDE to match the <HOLDING> statement, not to list all answers. ### *Input:* Statement: has "jurisdiction to render judgment on an action by an interested party objecting [...] A bidder has a direct economic interest if the alleged errors in the procurement caused it to suffer a competitive injury or prejudice. Myers Investigative & Sec. Servs., Inc. v. United States, 275 F.3d 1366, 1370 (Fed.Cir.2002) (<HOLDING>). In a post-award bid protest, the protestor A: holding that an antitrust injury is a necessary element of a 2 claim B: holding that actual prejudice is not a necessary element of an insurers untimely notice defense C: holding that an assertion of prejudice is not a showing of prejudice D: recognizing that allegation of state action is a necessary element of a 1983 claim E: holding that prejudice or injury is a necessary element of standing
LawStackExchange (Li et al., 2022)	### *Instruction:* Please give an answer to the question: ### *Input:* How do we claim the estate of someone who died under a different name in a different country?
PubMedQA (Jin et al., 2019)	### *Instruction:* Answer the question with (yes, no, maybe) and provide the reason based on the given context. ### *Input:* Question: Does oxybutynin hydrochloride cause arrhythmia in children with bladder dysfunction? Context: METHOD: This study represents a subset of a complete data set, considering only those children aged admitted to the Pediatric Surgery and Pediatric Nephrology Clinics during the period January 2011 to July 2012. RESULT: In this study, we have determined that the QT interval changes significantly depending on the use of oxybutynin. The QT changes increased cardiac arrhythmia in children.
RCTSum (Wallace et al., 2020)	### *Instruction:* Summarize the document based on the given title and abstract. ### *Input:* Title: Efficacy of prophylactic antibiotics for the prevention of endomyometritis after forceps delivery. Abstract: The purpose of this prospective randomized controlled clinical trial was to determine whether prophylactic antibiotics reduce the incidence of endomyometritis after forceps delivery. Of the 393 patients studied, 192 received 2 gm of intravenous cefotetan after forceps delivery, and 201 patients received no antibiotics. There were seven cases of endomyometritis in the group given no antibiotic and none in the cefotetan group, a statistically significant difference (P less than .01). We conclude that prophylactic antibiotics are effective in reducing the incidence of endomyometritis after forceps delivery. We believe this is the first published study demonstrating this benefit.
iCliniq (Yunxiang et al., 2023)	### *Instruction:* Please give an answer to the question: ### *Input:* Hello doctor, when should I take probiotics?

Table 7: Templates designed for each evaluation task. ‡For brevity, we record partial inputs for long documents with [...].

Latent Feature-based Data Splits to Improve Generalisation Evaluation: A Hate Speech Detection Case Study

Maike Züfle[1] and **Verna Dankers**[1] and **Ivan Titov**[1,2]
[1]ILCC, University of Edinburgh
[2]ILLC, University of Amsterdam
m.s.zufle@sms.ed.ac.uk vdankers@ed.ac.uk ititov@inf.ed.ac.uk

Abstract

With the ever-growing presence of social media platforms comes the increased spread of harmful content and the need for robust hate speech detection systems. Such systems easily overfit to specific targets and keywords, and evaluating them without considering distribution shifts that might occur between train and test data overestimates their benefit. We challenge hate speech models via new train-test splits of existing datasets that rely on the clustering of models' hidden representations. We present two split variants (SUBSET-SUM-SPLIT and CLOSEST-SPLIT) that, when applied to two datasets using four pretrained models, reveal how models catastrophically fail on blind spots in the latent space. This result generalises when developing a split with one model and evaluating it on another. Our analysis suggests that there is no clear surface-level property of the data split that correlates with the decreased performance, which underscores that task difficulty is not always humanly interpretable. We recommend incorporating latent feature-based splits in model development and release two splits via the GenBench benchmark.[1]

1 Introduction

Developing generalisable hate speech detection systems is of utmost importance due to the environment in which they are deployed. Social media usage is rapidly increasing, and the detection of harmful content is challenged by non-standard language use, implicitly expressed hatred, a lack of consensus on what constitutes hateful content, and the lack of high-quality training data (Yin and Zubiaga, 2021a). When developing hate speech detection models in the lab, it is, therefore, vital to simulate evaluation scenarios requiring models to generalise outside the training context. 'In the wild', NLP models may encounter text from different periods

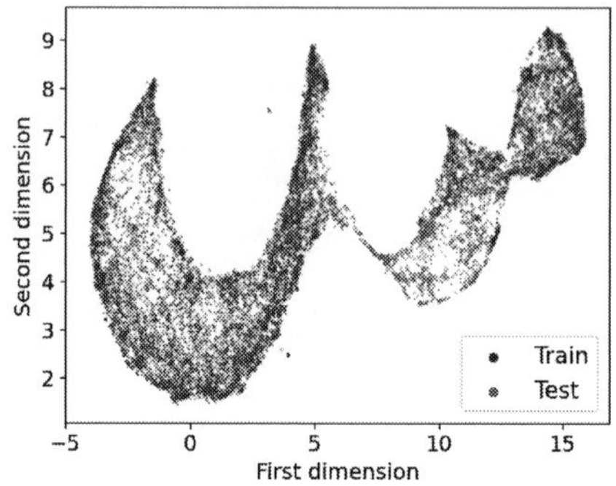

Figure 1: A UMAP projection of BERT's representations, showing the proposed train-test split, that is constructed by grouping clusters in the latent space.

(Lazaridou et al., 2021), authors (Huang and Paul, 2019) or dialects (Ziems et al., 2022), including unseen words (Elangovan et al., 2021) and words whose spelling changed or was obfuscated (Serra et al., 2017). Performing successfully on this data despite such distributional changes is called *out-of-distribution* (o.o.d.) generalisation.

How can the ability to generalise best be measured? Despite recent work illustrating that i.i.d. testing does not adequately reflect models' generalisability (e.g. Søgaard et al., 2021), evaluation using randomly sampled test sets is still the status quo (Rajpurkar et al., 2016; Wang et al., 2018, 2019; Muennighoff et al., 2023). Potentially, this is because obtaining and annotating new data is expensive, and it is hard to define what o.o.d. data is (Arora et al., 2021). For *humans*, properties like input length (Varis and Bojar, 2021) or spelling mistakes (Ebrahimi et al., 2018) might determine difficulty. But this need not be the same for *models*. Evaluating models using a notion of model-dependent difficulty is gaining some traction (e.g. Godbole and Jia, 2022) but still remains largely unexplored.

Contributing to that line of work, we propose a method that reuses existing datasets but splits them in a new way by relying on models' latent features.

[1]Our implementation is available at https://github.com/MaikeZuefle/Latent-Feature-Splits

Proceedings of the 1st GenBench Workshop on (Benchmarking) Generalisation in NLP, pages 112–129
December 6, 2023 ©2023 Association for Computational Linguistics

We cluster hidden representations using k-means and distribute clusters over the train and test set to create a data split. An illustrative example of such a split is shown in Fig. 1. We present two variants (SUBSET-SUM-SPLIT and CLOSEST-SPLIT). While this method is in principle applicable to any classification problem, we experiment with four language models and two hate speech datasets (that include Reddit, Twitter and Gab data). The results suggest that these splits approximate worst-case performance. Models fail catastrophically on the new test sets, while their performance on independent test data is on par with other systems trained on i.i.d. training sets. The difficulty is relatively stable across different models. We analyse the data splits through correlation analyses, and do not find one clear surface-level property of the data split to be predictive of split difficulty. This underscores that model-based difficulty can be quite elusive. We release two of our data splits for inclusion in the GenBench benchmark.

The remainder of this work is structured as follows: Section 2 elaborates on related work, followed by the introduction of the hate speech datasets (Section 3) and the proposed splitting method (Section 4). Section 5 presents model evaluation results, Section 6 analyses the splits in detail, and we conclude in Section 7. The GenBench eval card can be found in Appendix A.

2 Related Work

This section discusses related work on o.o.d. generalisation evaluation (Section 2.1), followed by a discussion on why generalisation is a persisting challenge in hate speech detection (Section 2.2).

2.1 Generalisation evaluation

It is now well-established within NLP that models with high or even human-like scores (e.g. Chowdhery et al., 2022) on i.i.d. splits do not generalise as robustly as the results would suggest. This has been demonstrated using synthetic data (i.a. Lake and Baroni, 2018; McCoy et al., 2019; Kim and Linzen, 2020) and for natural language tasks (i.a. Sinha et al., 2021; Søgaard et al., 2021; Razeghi et al., 2022). Alternative methods of evaluation have become more prominent, such as testing with different domains (e.g. Tan et al., 2019; Kamath et al., 2020; Yang et al., 2022) and adversarial testing, using both human-written (Kiela et al., 2021) and automatically generated adversarial examples (e.g. Zhang et al., 2020; Chen et al., 2019; Gururangan et al., 2018; Ebrahimi et al., 2018).

However, these types of evaluation require collecting or creating new data points, which is not always feasible for datasets that have been in use for years. Re-splitting existing datasets in a non-i.i.d. manner makes more efficient use of existing datasets, and, accordingly, new data splits have been developed, that typically use a feature of the input or the output to separate train from test examples. Splits that rely on the input use, for example, word overlap (Elangovan et al., 2021), linguistic structures (Søgaard, 2020), the timestamp (Lazaridou et al., 2021), or the context of words in the data (Keysers et al., 2019) to generate a split. Similarly, Broscheit et al. (2022) maximise the Wasserstein distances of train and test examples. Alternatively, one can evaluate generalisation using output-based non-i.i.d. splits: Naik et al. (2018) analyse the predictions of a model to find challenging phenomena, and Godbole and Jia (2022) re-split a dataset based on the predicted log-likelihood for each example.

The splitting method we propose relies neither on the discrete input tokens nor the output, but instead uses the internal representations of finetuned models.

2.2 Hate speech detection

With the rise of social media platforms, hate speech detection gained traction as a computational task (Jahan and Oussalah, 2023), leading to a wide range of benchmark datasets. Most of these datasets rely on data from social media platforms, such as Reddit (Qian et al., 2019; Vidgen et al., 2021), Twitter (ElSherief et al., 2021), Gab (Qian et al., 2019; Mathew et al., 2020), or Stormfront (de Gibert et al., 2018). This work is restricted to hate speech classification using a Reddit dataset (Qian et al., 2019) and a Twitter and Gab dataset (Mathew et al., 2020), which we will elaborate on in Section 3.

Recent advances in NLP such as the introduction of large language models have led to impressive results in hate speech detection (Fortuna and Nunes, 2018; Vidgen et al., 2019). Nonetheless, non-i.i.d. generalisation is a persisting challenge (Yin and Zubiaga, 2021b), because models tend to overfit to specific topics (Nejadgholi and Kiritchenko, 2020; Bourgeade et al., 2023), social media users (Arango et al., 2019), or keywords, such as slurs or pejorative terms (Dixon et al., 2018; Kennedy et al., 2020; Talat et al., 2018; Palmer et al., 2020; Kurrek et al., 2020). When such overt terms are missing, models often fail to detect hate speech (ElSherief et al., 2021). In response to these generalisation issues, recent works combine existing hate speech datasets (Fortuna et al., 2018; Salminen et al., 2020; Chiril et al., 2022; Bourgeade et al., 2023), which is a challenging task in itself considering the inconsistent definition of hate-speech across datasets (Nejadgholi and Kiritchenko, 2020).

Augmenting datasets or evaluating whether a model overfits to particular users or data sources requires annotated data. However, these characteristics are often unavailable due to privacy requirements or because the annotations were not included in the dataset release. Therefore, this work aims to find a data split that can evaluate generalisation without such annotations, relying instead only on a model's internal representations.

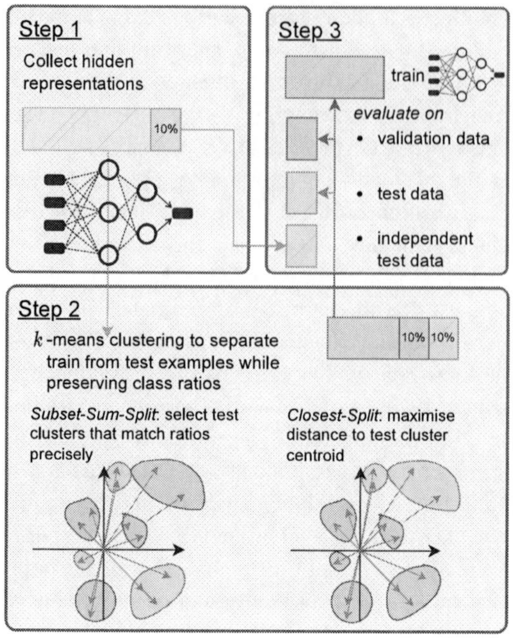

Figure 2: Overview of the proposed splitting method.

3 Data

We develop and evaluate our splitting method using the following two hate speech datasets.

3.1 Reddit

We use a widely used topic-generic Reddit dataset, proposed by Qian et al. (2019). The dataset includes 22,317 examples. Each example in the dataset is labelled as either *hate* (23.5%) or *noHate* (76.5%). The dataset was collected from ten different subreddits by retrieving potential hate speech posts using hate keywords taken from ElSherief et al. (2018). The hate keywords correspond roughly to the following categories: *archaic*, *class*, *disability*, *ethnicity*, *gender*, *nationality*, *religion*, and *sexual orientation*. The data is structured in conversations that consist of at most 20 comments by the same or different authors. These comments were manually annotated with *hate* or *noHate*, with each annotator assigned five conversations.

3.2 HateXplain

The second dataset is HateXplain (Mathew et al., 2020), which is also topic-generic and widely used. It contains 20,148 examples from Twitter and Gab. Posts from the combined collection were filtered based on a lexicon of hate keywords and phrases by Davidson et al. (2017); Mathew et al. (2019); Ousidhoum et al. (2019). The selected posts were then manually annotated. HateXplain examples are labelled as either *hateful* (31%), *offensive* (29%) or *normal* (40%), as proposed by Davidson et al. (2017). Offensive speech differs from hate speech in that it uses offensive terms without directing them against any person or group in particular. All offensive and hate examples are annotated with the community that they target. These communities include, among others, *Africans*, *Jewish People*, *Homosexuals* and *Women*, and we use them for further analysis of our data splits in Section 6.

4 Methodology

Our proposed splitting strategy, for which we introduce two variants, is detailed in Section 4.1. We evaluate our splits through comparisons to a random splitting baseline and on external test sets. We discuss the corresponding experimental setups in Section 4.2.

4.1 Constructing Data Splits

The construction of the data splits involves three steps, that are depicted in Fig. 2. In step 1, the method extracts the latent representations of inputs from a language model that was finetuned on the task using one of the hate speech datasets mentioned above. In step 2, the data is clustered based on these representations and clusters are assigned to either the train or the test set. In step 3, language models are then trained and evaluated on this new split. In addition to the obtained test set, the language models are also evaluated on independent test data, that was set aside for this purpose.[2]

The key idea behind the approach is that language models implicitly capture salient features of the input in their hidden representations, where inputs with similar properties are close together (Thompson and Mimno, 2020; Grootendorst, 2022). Assigning clusters to the train and test set thus accomplishes separation based on latent features, and by finetuning we ensure that the clusters separate examples based on *task-specific* features.

Obtaining Hidden Representations We finetune a language model for the given task, using the independent test data as validation set to optimise hyperparameters. We then obtain latent representations for each input example, leveraging the representation of the `[CLS]` token after the final layer as a representation of the input, as is commonly done (e.g. May et al., 2019; Qiao et al., 2019).

Since for high-dimensional data, distance metrics fail to accurately capture the concept of proximity (Beyer et al., 1999; Aggarwal et al., 2001) and tend to overly rely on individual dimensions (Timkey and van Schijndel, 2021) we conduct experiments with low-dimensional representations and full-dimensional ones. To this end, we either project the full representations into d_U-dimensional spaces using UMAP post-training (McInnes et al., 2020), or obtain d_B-dimensional representations by introducing a bottleneck in the model between the last hidden layer and the classification layer. The bottleneck is a linear layer that compresses the hidden representations, forcing the model to encode the most salient latent features into a low-dimensional space before classifying the examples.

Clustering and Splitting the Data Each representation from step 1 gives the position of an input example in the latent space. The examples are clustered in this space using the k-means algorithm (Lloyd, 1982).

Hyperparameters of the k-means clustering can be found in Table 3. After clustering, each cluster is assigned to either the train or the test set, keeping two constraints: A fixed test data size (we choose 10%) and train and test set need to have equal class distributions. Without equal class distributions, it would be unclear whether changes in performance are due to the increased difficulty of the test set, or the changes in label imbalance. A partition of the dataset that fulfils these constraints will be referred to as *target* in this work.

To reach the target test set, two algorithms, SUBSET-SUM-SPLIT and CLOSEST-SPLIT, are designed to decide how to split the clusters. Both algorithms lead to an under-representation of parts of the latent space in the model's training set, but whilst SUBSET-SUM-SPLIT might under-represent smaller, potentially distant pockets of the latent space, CLOSEST-SPLIT under-represents a single connected region. The algorithms are explained in detail below.

Method 1: SUBSET-SUM-SPLIT The constraints on the class and test ratios explained above, and the additional constraint of keeping whole clusters together can be described by the Subset Sum Problem (Kellerer et al., 2004). In this setting, the Subset Sum Problem can be modified to a *multidimensional* Subset Sum Problem: The multidimensional target consists of the number of desired test examples for each class in the dataset. The task is then to select a subset of the clusters, such that the number of examples for each class sums up to the desired target. To improve the chances of reaching the desired target, the Subset Sum Problem is solved for $k = 3$ to $k = 50$ clusters and the solution closest to the desired target using the smallest k is taken as the test set. If the closest solution does not match the exact target sum, examples from another randomly selected cluster are used to complete the test set. Note that the clusters in the test set do not necessarily lie close to each other in the latent space, as this is not a constraint for this algorithm.

Method 2: CLOSEST-SPLIT In contrast to the SUBSET-SUM-SPLIT, the CLOSEST-SPLIT aims to put as much distance as possible between the train and test clusters. This leads to an even bigger under-representation of parts of the latent space in the training set. Once the clusters have been computed, their centroids are calculated. The cluster that lies farthest away from all the other clusters is identified and added to the test set. If the size of the farthest cluster exceeds the target test set size, the next farthest cluster is taken instead. Cosine similarity between cluster centroids is used as the distance measure. Then *nearest neighbour* clustering with the cluster centroids is performed, as long as the size of the test set does not exceed the target size. When this nearest-neighbour clustering is finished,

[2]Note that the split thus only includes 90% of the data. Setting aside the 10% is for quality control of the models and could be omitted when future work applies our method.

individual examples that are closest to one of the test set centroids are added to the test set until the target size is reached. As for the SUBSET-SUM-SPLIT, the algorithm is performed for $k = 3$ to $k = 50$ clusters. k is selected such that the number of individual examples added is minimised.

4.2 Evaluating Splits' Difficulty

Models We use four transformer language models to obtain and evaluate the data splits: BERT-Base(-Cased) (Devlin et al., 2019), its smaller variant BERT-Medium (Turc et al., 2019; Bhargava et al., 2021), HateBERT (Caselli et al., 2021), a BERT-Base-Uncased model that was further pretrained on abusive Reddit data using the MLM objective, and RoBERTa-Base (Liu et al., 2019). From these models, we extract the full hidden representations, hidden representations via a bottleneck, for $d_B \in \{10, 50, 200\}$, and hidden representations post-processed using UMAP, for $d_U \in \{10, 50, 200\}$.

Model Evaluation Having obtained data splits based on four language models and hidden dimensions with different sizes, the first way of evaluating models is by finetuning the language models on their respective SUBSET-SUM-SPLIT and CLOSEST-SPLIT. The hyperparameters used for finetuning are listed in Table 4, Appendix B, and we estimate d_U and d_B by varying their values for the Reddit dataset. We compare the results obtained with the proposed data splits to a baseline split, which takes the same examples but splits them randomly while maintaining class proportions. Random splits are generated using three different seeds, and the proposed data splits are obtained with three different clustering seeds. For each data split involved, the models are trained with three seeds that determine the classifier's initialisation and the presentation order of the data. The results are averaged accordingly.

The evaluation metrics are accuracy and F1-scores. For the Reddit dataset, the F1-score is the score of the *hate* class, whereas for HateXplain, the F1-score is macro-averaged over the three classes.

To better understand the robustness of the results, we perform an additional set of experiments on the most challenging data splits observed, to answer the following questions:

1. *Is split difficulty driven by the input or by task-specific latent features?* For the Reddit data, we split the dataset based on task-agnostic hidden representations obtained from pretrained models to analyse whether task-specific representations (i.e. representations finetuned on the task) are needed to create challenging data splits.
2. *Do models trained on new splits perform on par with conventional models on independent data?* Using HateXplain, we test the finetuned models on the independent test data that was set aside earlier to ensure that the newly obtained train data is still informative enough for test data sampled according to the original distribution.
3. *Is the difficulty of the data splits model-independent?* We also examine whether a split obtained by the hidden representations of a specific model is also challenging for other models using HateXplain data.

model	Reddit Hate F1	HateXplain Macro F1
BERT-base	81.96 ± 0.5	66.0 ± 0.36
BERT-medium	81.58 ± 0.66	60.18 ± 0.42
HateBert	82.34 ± 0.59	66.25 ± 0.35
RoBERTa	82.15 ± 0.61	64.1 ± 0.9

Table 1: Results for the Reddit and HateXplain dataset on random splits using 90% of the data. Random splits are generated using three different seeds and models are trained with three initialisation seeds. Mean and standard errors are reported.

5 Results

We now turn to evaluating models' performance on our newly proposed splits.

5.1 Performance on Challenging Splits

We compare the performance of models trained on a random split to models trained on the CLOSEST-SPLIT and SUBSET-SUM-SPLIT. The random split performances are presented in Table 1. For the binary Reddit dataset, performance on random splits is high for all four models with F1-scores for the hate class of around 82%. The performance on the three-way HateXplain dataset is comparably lower, with macro F1-scores of around 65%. For both datasets, these results are on par with (or surpass) baselines from prior work, upon which we elaborate in Appendix D.1.[3]

Hyperparameter Estimation For both splits, we conduct a hyperparameter estimation to select d_U

[3] Note that these results are obtained with 90% of the data as explained in Section 4.2. The reader is referred to Table 5 and Table 6 for accuracy results, results on 100% of the data and results on the standard split.

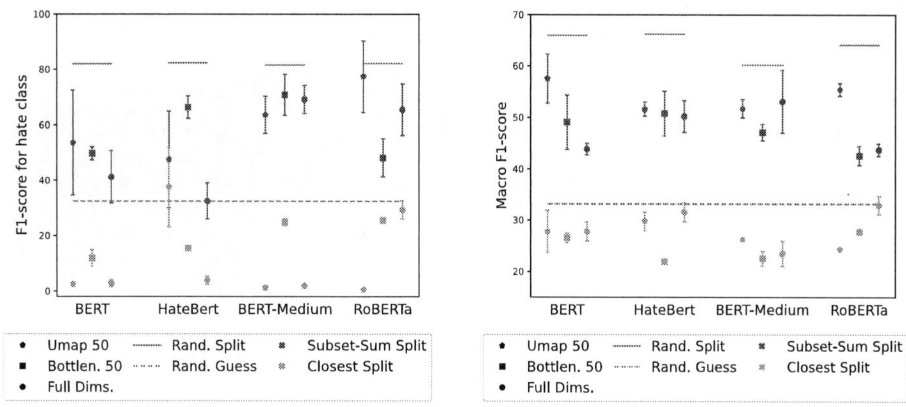

(a) Reddit Dataset

(b) HateXplain Dataset

Figure 3: Performance of models trained on the SUBSET-SUM-SPLIT and CLOSEST-SPLIT . The errorbars show the standard error between cluster seeds. Horizontal lines indicate performance for models trained and tested on a random split.

and d_B using the Reddit dataset, for which the results are shown in Fig. 9, Appendix D.2. Across the board, all values considered challenge the models more than the random split, but full dimensions, $d_U = 50$ and $d_B = 50$ lead to a large decrease with relatively small variance between cluster seeds.

In addition to varying the dimensionalities, we consider using the models' pretrained representations (without further finetuning) to examine whether the latent features must be task-specific to challenge our models. Task-specific representations are, indeed, vital, as is shown in Fig. 8, Appendix D.2.

New Data Splits Reveal Catastrophic Failure Both SUBSET-SUM-SPLIT and CLOSEST-SPLIT lead to an under-representation of parts of the latent space in the model's training set and we hypothesised that this leads to a challenging data split. Indeed, the empirical results show significant performance drops when training models on these splits in comparison to random splits.

Fig. 3a shows the performance drops for the Reddit dataset. For the SUBSET-SUM-SPLIT, F1-scores for the hate class drop significantly for all four models, but with a high variation between different cluster seeds. For the CLOSEST-SPLIT, test set performance drops even further and more consistently without much variation between cluster seeds: F1-scores for the hate class are mostly between 0 and 25%. [4]

[4]These results are not specific to the examination of F1-scores; the same tendencies can be observed when looking at the accuracy (Appendix D.3).

Fig. 3b displays performances for HateXplain, which similarly shows a drop in performance for SUBSET-SUM-SPLIT and CLOSEST-SPLIT. CLOSEST-SPLIT leads to F1-scores that are on par with or below random guessing, resulting from drops of around 36%.

Overall, the CLOSEST-SPLIT is more challenging than the SUBSET-SUM-SPLIT. Moreover, the bottleneck-based splits generally lead to the most stable results, i.e., the variance between different cluster seeds is the lowest. In some cases performance drops below the random guessing baseline; this happens when a model fails to predict some class completely, defaulting instead to one of the other classes. In summary, the new splits lead to drastic performance drops for both datasets and across all four models.

5.2 Independent Test Set Performance

We now take the most challenging split observed (CLOSEST-SPLIT with $d_B = 50$) and further analyse the behaviour of models trained on this split for the HateXplain dataset, which is the most widely used dataset as well as the most challenging one.

From the results in Section 5.1 it is clear that CLOSEST-SPLIT reveals weaknesses in these models, since the models struggle to generalise to the split's test data. The question remains whether the test set obtained by the new splitting methods is harder or whether the new splitting method leads to very simple or perhaps even incomplete training sets, thereby preventing the models from learning the task. To this end, we evaluate the models trained on the training data obtained from

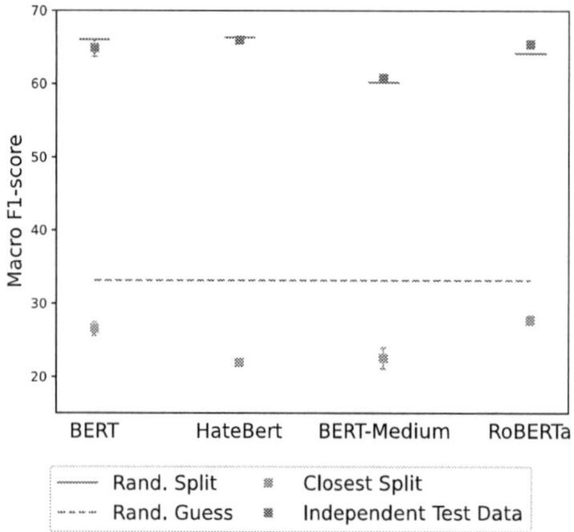

Figure 4: Performance of models trained on training data determined by the CLOSEST-SPLIT and evaluated on the test data of the CLOSEST-SPLIT and on independent test data (HateXplain dataset). Horizontal lines indicate performance for models trained and tested on a random split. Errorbars show the standard error between cluster seeds.

a CLOSEST-SPLIT on the 10% independent test data that was set aside earlier (Section 4.1). The results show that models achieve similar performance on the independent test data as the models trained and tested on random data, strengthening the hypothesis that CLOSEST-SPLIT training data is informative enough to learn the task. Results for these experiments are reported in Fig. 4.[5]

5.3 Cross-Model Generalisation

The previous results have shown that CLOSEST-SPLIT leads to challenging test sets. To show the robustness of these splits, we also examine whether these test sets are generally difficult or only for the model used to develop the split—i.e. we examine cross-model generalisation. The results of the cross-model evaluations can be seen in Fig. 5. They show that data splits developed using one model are indeed also challenging for other models, although the personalised splits are slightly more challenging. These results do not only strengthen the robustness of the challenging data split, but have also practical implications: The data-splitting pipeline only needs to be carried out with one model and multiple models can be assessed and compared with the same split.

[5]The validation accuracy for the models trained on CLOSEST-SPLIT is for most splits around 5 points higher than the accuracy on the validation set of the random data split—i.e. the models perform normally during training as suggested by the validation data.

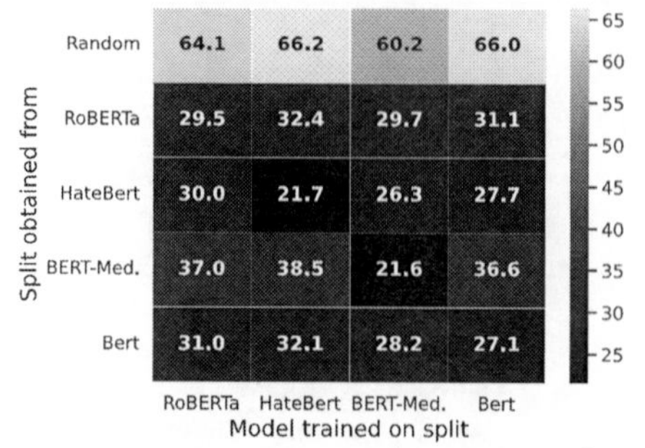

Figure 5: F1-scores for HateXplain on a CLOSEST-SPLIT ($d_B = 50$). Comparison of models trained on the data split obtained with their respective hidden representations (diagonal) and on data splits obtained from representations of other models.

6 Analysis

The performance of models deteriorates heavily when using the proposed splits. This section analyses the generated splits; first examining the surface-level properties of the resulting train and test sets, and then taking a closer look at two specific splits by visualising the datapoints in the train and test sets. Additionally, an analysis of the topics in the train and test sets can be found in Appendix E.2.

6.1 Correlation Analysis: Relating Splits' Features to Performance Drop

For the most challenging split variant, CLOSEST-SPLIT, we investigate the correlation of performance drops compared to the random splits (including three random splits with 0 drop) and surface-level properties of the data split. The properties' implementation is explained in detail in Appendix E.1. We firstly consider *task-agnostic* features: 1) the unigram overlap between the train and test set, 2) the input length in the test set and 3) the number of rare words in the test set.

Secondly, *task-specific* properties are computed: 1) The number of under-represented hate keywords from the lists used by the dataset's creators (see Section 3), 2) the number of under-represented target communities retrieved from the HateXplain annotations, and 3) a quantification of the distributional shift of data sources (Twitter and Gab are present in HateXplain) in the train and test set using the Kullback-Leibler Divergence of token distributions (Kullback and Leibler, 1951).

Table 2 presents the results of this analysis. For the Reddit Dataset, the only significant correlation (bold) is the number of under-represented key-

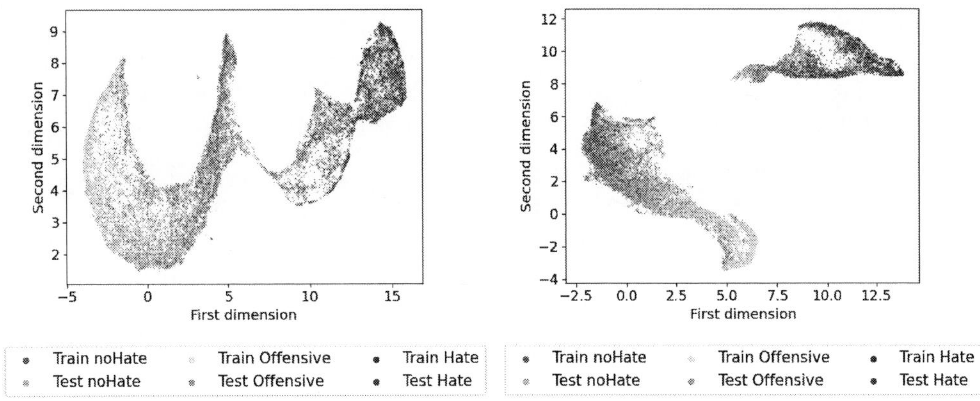

(a) RoBERTa's representations

(b) BERT's representations

Figure 6: Hidden representations for tertiary classification using the CLOSEST-SPLIT for the HateXplain dataset.

	Feature	Reddit	HateXplain
task-agnostic	unigram overlap	0.24	**-0.51***
	sentence length	0.12	0.26
	# Rare words	0.13	0.44*
task-specific	# under-represented keywords	**0.47***	0.32*
	# under-represented targets	—	0.21
	KL-Div. data source	—	0.05

Table 2: Pearson correlation between data split properties and models' F1-score drops in comparison to random splits. Correlations with a p-value < 0.05 are marked with *. Some analysis methods are dataset-specific and cannot be computed for both datasets.

word categories in the training data. Task-agnostic features do not correlate with the decreased performance of models on the CLOSEST-SPLIT for the Reddit data. In contrast, for the HateXplain dataset, task-agnostic features do play a role: The biggest (negative) correlation can be observed for the unigram overlap (bold): The higher the unigram overlap between train and test set, the closer the performance is to the random split F1-score. Another smaller correlation exists concerning the number of rare words in the test set: The more rare words, the more challenging the split. Similar to the Reddit dataset, a significant, albeit weak, correlation exists between the decreased performance and the number of keyword categories that are under-represented in training data.

Taken together, these results suggest that the properties associated with performance drops differ from dataset to dataset. This implies that CLOSEST-SPLIT cannot easily be replicated based on task-specific or task-agnostic features. Using latent representations instead helps uncover weaknesses in models that are otherwise not easily identified.

6.2 Visualisation of Hidden Representations

We now take a closer look at two specific data splits for the HateXplain dataset by visualising their hidden representations. For this analysis, we select the CLOSEST-SPLITS obtained with representations with $d_B = 50$ for BERT and RoBERTa, which are more commonly used than HateBERT or BERT-medium. We make these splits available via the GenBench Collaborative Benchmarking Task.

The CLOSEST-SPLIT assigns clusters of hidden representations that are spatially close to the test set. While the clustering is conducted on high-dimensional representations, a 2-dimensional projection by UMAP (McInnes et al., 2020) can give an intuition about why these data splits are challenging. Fig. 6a shows RoBERTa's representations for the HateXplain dataset. A decision boundary can be observed, with mostly *offensive* examples on the left, *noHate* examples in the middle and *hate* examples on the right. Based on this illustration, the CLOSEST-SPLIT picks a pocket of (mixed) examples between the *noHate* (dark blue) and *hate* (dark green) regions to be the test set. This is mirrored in the F1-scores of the different classes. The *hate* test examples lie closest to the corresponding region, and the F1-score is the highest at 47.0. Similarly, for the *noHate* class, the F1-score is relatively high at 38.28. The offensive class, with test examples farther away, only has an F1-score of 11.88. The same phenomenon can be observed for a BERT-based CLOSEST-SPLIT (Fig. 6b). This suggests that the model overfits its decision boundaries to train set-specific features and, therefore, fails to predict the correct classes in the test set. Developing models using CLOSEST-SPLIT in addition to random splits might thus lead to models that are more robust to such overfitting.

7 Conclusion

Hate speech detection systems are prone to overfitting to specific targets of hate speech and specific keywords in the input, complicating the detection of more implicit hatred and harming the generalisability to unseen demographics. Yet, in addition to those *known* and *interpretable* vulnerabilities, systems may have less obvious weaknesses. The data splitting method we developed aims to highlight those. Our splitting method is based on the clustering of internal representations of finetuned models, thus making the splits task- and dataset-specific. We proposed two variants (SUBSET-SUM-SPLIT and CLOSEST-SPLIT) that differ in how they assign clusters to the train and test set.

The latter variant, in particular, led to consistent catastrophic drops in test set performance, when compared to a random split. Moreover, while each split was developed using the hidden representations from a specific model, we identified that this result generalises when developing the split using one model, and evaluating it using another. The analyses of the resulting data splits showed that the properties of the train and test sets differ from dataset to dataset. Since no property clearly correlates with decreased model performance for both datasets, CLOSEST-SPLIT cannot be easily replicated based on data splits' surface-level properties, and using latent representations is crucial to reveal the weaknesses we observed in the models.

We encourage future work to consider evaluations using the CLOSEST-SPLITS we release for HateXplain, in order to develop more robust systems, but also emphasise that even though our results were specific to hate speech detection, the methodology can be more widely applied. To challenge models beyond i.i.d. evaluation, we do not need costly data annotations. Instead, we can start by relying on systems' latent features to simulate train-test distribution shifts.

8 Limitations

We identify three main limitations of our work:

1. **The scope of our work**: the splitting methodology we developed can be applied to a wide range of tasks, but we only experimented with hate speech detection. Future work is required to confirm the method's wider applicability. Moreover, even though we aim to use the challenging split to improve generalisation, we have not yet made efforts in this direction.
2. **Generality of conclusions**: We experimented with a limited set of model architectures, all of which resemble one another in terms of their structure and the (pre-)training data used. Different models or training techniques could lead to less challenging splits, or splits with significantly different properties. At the same time, we did demonstrate that the split's difficulty is not model-specific (see Section 5.3), and observed that under variation of random seeds CLOSEST-SPLIT consistently leads to performance drops across four models and two datasets.
3. **Naturalness of the experimental setup**: we created an artificially partitioned data split and have no guarantee that the generalisation challenges that language models encounter when deployed in real-world scenarios resemble our splits. However, given that our approach simulated a worst-case scenario, demonstrated by catastrophic failure in performance, we are hopeful that models that are more robust to our train-test shift are also more robust to real-world variations in test data.

9 Ethics Statement

By its very nature, hate speech detection involves working closely with hurtful and offensive content. This can be difficult for researchers. However, considering the severe consequences when hate speech models fail on unseen data and people are confronted with harmful content, it is all the more important to improve the generalisation ability of models and protect others.

While our work intends to contribute to generalisation evaluation in a positive way, we do not recommend using our data splits as representative of generalisation behaviour 'in the wild', but recommend them for academic research instead. While standard and random splits often overestimate real-world performance, our splits are likely to underestimate it, and can in this way reveal real weaknesses. Our splits are designed to improve academic research on the robustness of language models and contribute to improving the generalisation ability for NLP tasks.

Prior to conducting work with potentially harmful hate speech data, this project obtained approval from the Research Ethics committee at the authors' local institution.

Acknowledgments

We thank Agostina Calabrese for helpful suggestions in the early stages of this project. VD is supported by the UKRI Centre for Doctoral Training in Natural Language Processing, funded by the UKRI (grant EP/S022481/1) and the University of Edinburgh, School of Informatics and School of Philosophy, Psychology & Language Sciences. IT is supported by the Dutch National Science Foundation (NWO Vici VI.C.212.053).

References

Charu C. Aggarwal, Alexander Hinneburg, and Daniel A. Keim. 2001. On the surprising behavior of distance metrics in high dimensional space. In *Database Theory — ICDT 2001*, pages 420–434, Berlin, Heidelberg. Springer Berlin Heidelberg.

Aymé Arango, Jorge Pérez, and Barbara Poblete. 2019. Hate speech detection is not as easy as you may think: A closer look at model validation. In *Proceedings of the 42nd International ACM SIGIR Conference on Research and Development in Information Retrieval*, SIGIR'19, page 45–54, New York, NY, USA. Association for Computing Machinery.

Udit Arora, William Huang, and He He. 2021. Types of out-of-distribution texts and how to detect them. In *Proceedings of the 2021 Conference on Empirical Methods in Natural Language Processing*, pages 10687–10701, Online and Punta Cana, Dominican Republic. Association for Computational Linguistics.

Kevin Beyer, Jonathan Goldstein, Raghu Ramakrishnan, and Uri Shaft. 1999. When is "nearest neighbor" meaningful? In *Database Theory — ICDT'99*, pages 217–235, Berlin, Heidelberg. Springer Berlin Heidelberg.

Prajjwal Bhargava, Aleksandr Drozd, and Anna Rogers. 2021. Generalization in NLI: Ways (not) to go beyond simple heuristics.

Tom Bourgeade, Patricia Chiril, Farah Benamara, and Véronique Moriceau. 2023. What did you learn to hate? A topic-oriented analysis of generalization in hate speech detection. In *Proceedings of the 17th Conference of the European Chapter of the Association for Computational Linguistics*, pages 3495–3508, Dubrovnik, Croatia. Association for Computational Linguistics.

Samuel Broscheit, Quynh Do, and Judith Gaspers. 2022. Distributionally robust finetuning BERT for covariate drift in spoken language understanding. In *Proceedings of the 60th Annual Meeting of the Association for Computational Linguistics (Volume 1: Long Papers)*, pages 1970–1985, Dublin, Ireland. Association for Computational Linguistics.

Marc Brysbaert and Boris New. 2009. Moving beyond Kučera and Francis: A critical evaluation of current word frequency norms and the introduction of a new and improved word frequency measure for american english. *Behavior research methods*, 41:977–90.

Tommaso Caselli, Valerio Basile, Jelena Mitrović, and Michael Granitzer. 2021. HateBERT: Retraining BERT for abusive language detection in English. In *Proceedings of the 5th Workshop on Online Abuse and Harms (WOAH 2021)*, pages 17–25, Online. Association for Computational Linguistics.

Michael Chen, Mike D'Arcy, Alisa Liu, Jared Fernandez, and Doug Downey. 2019. CODAH: An adversarially-authored question answering dataset for common sense. In *Proceedings of the 3rd Workshop on Evaluating Vector Space Representations for NLP*, pages 63–69, Minneapolis, USA. Association for Computational Linguistics.

Patricia Chiril, Endang Wahyu Pamungkas, Farah Benamara, Véronique Moriceau, and Viviana Patti. 2022. Emotionally informed hate speech detection: A multi-target perspective. *Cognitive Computation*, 14(1):322–352.

Aakanksha Chowdhery, Sharan Narang, Jacob Devlin, Maarten Bosma, Gaurav Mishra, Adam Roberts, Paul Barham, Hyung Won Chung, Charles Sutton, Sebastian Gehrmann, Parker Schuh, Kensen Shi, Sasha Tsvyashchenko, Joshua Maynez, Abhishek Rao, Parker Barnes, Yi Tay, Noam Shazeer, Vinodkumar Prabhakaran, Emily Reif, Nan Du, Ben Hutchinson, Reiner Pope, James Bradbury, Jacob Austin, Michael Isard, Guy Gur-Ari, Pengcheng Yin, Toju Duke, Anselm Levskaya, Sanjay Ghemawat, Sunipa Dev, Henryk Michalewski, Xavier Garcia, Vedant Misra, Kevin Robinson, Liam Fedus, Denny Zhou, Daphne Ippolito, David Luan, Hyeontaek Lim, Barret Zoph, Alexander Spiridonov, Ryan Sepassi, David Dohan, Shivani Agrawal, Mark Omernick, Andrew M. Dai, Thanumalayan Sankaranarayana Pillai, Marie Pellat, Aitor Lewkowycz, Erica Moreira, Rewon Child, Oleksandr Polozov, Katherine Lee, Zongwei Zhou, Xuezhi Wang, Brennan Saeta, Mark Diaz, Orhan Firat, Michele Catasta, Jason Wei, Kathy Meier-Hellstern, Douglas Eck, Jeff Dean, Slav Petrov, and Noah Fiedel. 2022. Palm: Scaling language modeling with pathways.

Thomas Davidson, Dana Warmsley, Michael Macy, and Ingmar Weber. 2017. Automated hate speech detection and the problem of offensive language. *Proceedings of the International AAAI Conference on Web and Social Media*, 11(1):512–515.

Ona de Gibert, Naiara Pérez, Aitor García Pablos, and Montse Cuadros. 2018. Hate speech dataset from a white supremacy forum. *CoRR*, abs/1809.04444.

Jacob Devlin, Ming-Wei Chang, Kenton Lee, and Kristina Toutanova. 2019. BERT: Pre-training of deep bidirectional transformers for language understanding. In *Proceedings of the 2019 Conference of the North American Chapter of the Association for Computational Linguistics: Human Language Technologies, Volume 1 (Long and Short Papers)*, pages 4171–4186, Minneapolis, Minnesota. Association for Computational Linguistics.

Lucas Dixon, John Li, Jeffrey Sorensen, Nithum Thain, and Lucy Vasserman. 2018. Measuring and mitigating unintended bias in text classification. In *Proceedings of the 2018 AAAI/ACM Conference on AI, Ethics, and Society*, AIES '18, page 67–73, New York, NY, USA. Association for Computing Machinery.

Javid Ebrahimi, Anyi Rao, Daniel Lowd, and Dejing Dou. 2018. HotFlip: White-box adversarial examples for text classification. In *Proceedings of the 56th Annual Meeting of the Association for Computational Linguistics (Volume 2: Short Papers)*, pages 31–36, Melbourne, Australia. Association for Computational Linguistics.

Aparna Elangovan, Jiayuan He, and Karin Verspoor. 2021. Memorization vs. generalization : Quantifying data leakage in NLP performance evaluation. In *Proceedings of the 16th Conference of the European Chapter of the Association for Computational Linguistics: Main Volume*, pages 1325–1335, Online. Association for Computational Linguistics.

Mai ElSherief, Shirin Nilizadeh, Dana Nguyen, Giovanni Vigna, and Elizabeth Belding. 2018. Peer to peer hate: Hate speech instigators and their targets. *Proceedings of the International AAAI Conference on Web and Social Media*, 12(1).

Mai ElSherief, Caleb Ziems, David Muchlinski, Vaishnavi Anupindi, Jordyn Seybolt, Munmun De Choudhury, and Diyi Yang. 2021. Latent hatred: A benchmark for understanding implicit hate speech. In *Proceedings of the 2021 Conference on Empirical Methods in Natural Language Processing*, pages 345–363, Online and Punta Cana, Dominican Republic. Association for Computational Linguistics.

Paula Fortuna, Ilaria Bonavita, and S érgio Nunes. 2018. Merging datasets for hate speech classification in Italian. *EVALITA Evaluation of NLP and Speech Tools for Italian*, 12:218.

Paula Fortuna and Sérgio Nunes. 2018. A survey on automatic detection of hate speech in text. *ACM Comput. Surv.*, 51(4).

Ameya Godbole and Robin Jia. 2022. Benchmarking long-tail generalization with likelihood splits.

Maarten Grootendorst. 2022. BERTopic: Neural topic modeling with a class-based tf-idf procedure.

Suchin Gururangan, Swabha Swayamdipta, Omer Levy, Roy Schwartz, Samuel Bowman, and Noah A. Smith. 2018. Annotation artifacts in natural language inference data. In *Proceedings of the 2018 Conference of the North American Chapter of the Association for Computational Linguistics: Human Language Technologies, Volume 2 (Short Papers)*, pages 107–112, New Orleans, Louisiana. Association for Computational Linguistics.

Xiaolei Huang and Michael J. Paul. 2019. Neural user factor adaptation for text classification: Learning to generalize across author demographics. In *Proceedings of the Eighth Joint Conference on Lexical and Computational Semantics (*SEM 2019)*, pages 136–146, Minneapolis, Minnesota. Association for Computational Linguistics.

Md Saroar Jahan and Mourad Oussalah. 2023. A systematic review of hate speech automatic detection using natural language processing. *Neurocomputing*, 546:126232.

Amita Kamath, Robin Jia, and Percy Liang. 2020. Selective question answering under domain shift. In *Proceedings of the 58th Annual Meeting of the Association for Computational Linguistics*, pages 5684–5696, Online. Association for Computational Linguistics.

Hans Kellerer, Ulrich Pferschy, and David Pisinger. 2004. *The Subset Sum Problem*, pages 73–115. Springer Berlin Heidelberg, Berlin, Heidelberg.

Brendan Kennedy, Xisen Jin, Aida Mostafazadeh Davani, Morteza Dehghani, and Xiang Ren. 2020. Contextualizing hate speech classifiers with post-hoc explanation. In *Proceedings of the 58th Annual Meeting of the Association for Computational Linguistics*, pages 5435–5442, Online. Association for Computational Linguistics.

Daniel Keysers, Nathanael Schärli, Nathan Scales, Hylke Buisman, Daniel Furrer, Sergii Kashubin, Nikola Momchev, Danila Sinopalnikov, Lukasz Stafiniak, Tibor Tihon, Dmitry Tsarkov, Xiao Wang, Marc van Zee, and Olivier Bousquet. 2019. Measuring compositional generalization: A comprehensive method on realistic data. *CoRR*, abs/1912.09713.

Douwe Kiela, Max Bartolo, Yixin Nie, Divyansh Kaushik, Atticus Geiger, Zhengxuan Wu, Bertie Vidgen, Grusha Prasad, Amanpreet Singh, Pratik Ringshia, Zhiyi Ma, Tristan Thrush, Sebastian Riedel, Zeerak Waseem, Pontus Stenetorp, Robin Jia, Mohit Bansal, Christopher Potts, and Adina Williams. 2021. Dynabench: Rethinking benchmarking in NLP. In *Proceedings of the 2021 Conference of the North American Chapter of the Association for Computational Linguistics: Human Language Technologies*, pages 4110–4124, Online. Association for Computational Linguistics.

Najoung Kim and Tal Linzen. 2020. COGS: A compositional generalization challenge based on semantic interpretation. In *Proceedings of the 2020 Conference on Empirical Methods in Natural Language*

Processing (EMNLP), pages 9087–9105, Online. Association for Computational Linguistics.

Solomon Kullback and Richard A Leibler. 1951. On information and sufficiency. *The annals of mathematical statistics*, 22(1):79–86.

Jana Kurrek, Haji Mohammad Saleem, and Derek Ruths. 2020. Towards a comprehensive taxonomy and large-scale annotated corpus for online slur usage. In *Proceedings of the Fourth Workshop on Online Abuse and Harms*, pages 138–149, Online. Association for Computational Linguistics.

Brenden Lake and Marco Baroni. 2018. Generalization without systematicity: On the compositional skills of sequence-to-sequence recurrent networks. In *35th International Conference on Machine Learning, ICML 2018*, pages 4487–4499. International Machine Learning Society (IMLS).

Angeliki Lazaridou, Adhi Kuncoro, Elena Gribovskaya, Devang Agrawal, Adam Liska, Tayfun Terzi, Mai Gimenez, Cyprien de Masson d'Autume, Tomas Kocisky, Sebastian Ruder, Dani Yogatama, Kris Cao, Susannah Young, and Phil Blunsom. 2021. Mind the gap: Assessing temporal generalization in neural language models. In *Advances in Neural Information Processing Systems*, volume 34, pages 29348–29363. Curran Associates, Inc.

Yinhan Liu, Myle Ott, Naman Goyal, Jingfei Du, Mandar Joshi, Danqi Chen, Omer Levy, Mike Lewis, Luke Zettlemoyer, and Veselin Stoyanov. 2019. Roberta: A robustly optimized BERT pretraining approach. *CoRR*, abs/1907.11692.

S. Lloyd. 1982. Least squares quantization in PCM. *IEEE Transactions on Information Theory*, 28(2):129–137.

Binny Mathew, Ritam Dutt, Pawan Goyal, and Animesh Mukherjee. 2019. Spread of hate speech in online social media. In *Proceedings of the 10th ACM Conference on Web Science*, WebSci '19, page 173–182, New York, NY, USA. Association for Computing Machinery.

Binny Mathew, Punyajoy Saha, Seid Muhie Yimam, Chris Biemann, Pawan Goyal, and Animesh Mukherjee. 2020. HateXplain: A benchmark dataset for explainable hate speech detection. *CoRR*, abs/2012.10289.

Chandler May, Alex Wang, Shikha Bordia, Samuel R. Bowman, and Rachel Rudinger. 2019. On measuring social biases in sentence encoders. In *Proceedings of the 2019 Conference of the North American Chapter of the Association for Computational Linguistics: Human Language Technologies, Volume 1 (Long and Short Papers)*, pages 622–628, Minneapolis, Minnesota. Association for Computational Linguistics.

Tom McCoy, Ellie Pavlick, and Tal Linzen. 2019. Right for the wrong reasons: Diagnosing syntactic heuristics in natural language inference. In *Proceedings of the 57th Annual Meeting of the Association for Computational Linguistics*, pages 3428–3448, Florence, Italy. Association for Computational Linguistics.

Leland McInnes, John Healy, and James Melville. 2020. Umap: Uniform manifold approximation and projection for dimension reduction.

Niklas Muennighoff, Nouamane Tazi, Loic Magne, and Nils Reimers. 2023. MTEB: Massive text embedding benchmark. In *Proceedings of the 17th Conference of the European Chapter of the Association for Computational Linguistics*, pages 2014–2037, Dubrovnik, Croatia. Association for Computational Linguistics.

Aakanksha Naik, Abhilasha Ravichander, Norman Sadeh, Carolyn Rose, and Graham Neubig. 2018. Stress test evaluation for natural language inference. In *Proceedings of the 27th International Conference on Computational Linguistics*, pages 2340–2353, Santa Fe, New Mexico, USA. Association for Computational Linguistics.

Isar Nejadgholi and Svetlana Kiritchenko. 2020. On cross-dataset generalization in automatic detection of online abuse. In *Proceedings of the Fourth Workshop on Online Abuse and Harms*, pages 173–183, Online. Association for Computational Linguistics.

Nedjma Ousidhoum, Zizheng Lin, Hongming Zhang, Yangqiu Song, and Dit-Yan Yeung. 2019. Multilingual and multi-aspect hate speech analysis. In *Proceedings of the 2019 Conference on Empirical Methods in Natural Language Processing and the 9th International Joint Conference on Natural Language Processing (EMNLP-IJCNLP)*, pages 4675–4684, Hong Kong, China. Association for Computational Linguistics.

Alexis Palmer, Christine Carr, Melissa Robinson, and Jordan Sanders. 2020. COLD: Annotation scheme and evaluation data set for complex offensive language in english. *Journal for Language Technology and Computational Linguistics*, 34(1):1–28.

Jing Qian, Anna Bethke, Yinyin Liu, Elizabeth Belding, and William Yang Wang. 2019. A benchmark dataset for learning to intervene in online hate speech. In *Proceedings of the 2019 Conference on Empirical Methods in Natural Language Processing and the 9th International Joint Conference on Natural Language Processing (EMNLP-IJCNLP)*, pages 4755–4764, Hong Kong, China. Association for Computational Linguistics.

Yifan Qiao, Chenyan Xiong, Zhenghao Liu, and Zhiyuan Liu. 2019. Understanding the behaviors of BERT in ranking. *CoRR*, abs/1904.07531.

Pranav Rajpurkar, Jian Zhang, Konstantin Lopyrev, and Percy Liang. 2016. SQuAD: 100,000+ questions for machine comprehension of text. In *Proceedings of the 2016 Conference on Empirical Methods in Natural Language Processing*, pages 2383–2392, Austin, Texas. Association for Computational Linguistics.

Yasaman Razeghi, Robert L Logan IV, Matt Gardner, and Sameer Singh. 2022. Impact of pretraining term frequencies on few-shot numerical reasoning. In *Findings of the Association for Computational Linguistics: EMNLP 2022*, pages 840–854, Abu Dhabi, United Arab Emirates. Association for Computational Linguistics.

Joni Salminen, Maximilian Hopf, Shammur A. Chowdhury, Soon-gyo Jung, Hind Almerekhi, and Bernard J. Jansen. 2020. Developing an online hate classifier for multiple social media platforms. *Human-centric Computing and Information Sciences*, 10(1):1.

Joan Serra, Ilias Leontiadis, Dimitris Spathis, Gianluca Stringhini, Jeremy Blackburn, and Athena Vakali. 2017. Class-based prediction errors to detect hate speech with out-of-vocabulary words. In *Proceedings of the first workshop on abusive language online*, pages 36–40.

Koustuv Sinha, Robin Jia, Dieuwke Hupkes, Joelle Pineau, Adina Williams, and Douwe Kiela. 2021. Masked language modeling and the distributional hypothesis: Order word matters pre-training for little. In *Proceedings of the 2021 Conference on Empirical Methods in Natural Language Processing*, pages 2888–2913, Online and Punta Cana, Dominican Republic. Association for Computational Linguistics.

Anders Søgaard. 2020. Some languages seem easier to parse because their treebanks leak. In *Proceedings of the 2020 Conference on Empirical Methods in Natural Language Processing (EMNLP)*, pages 2765–2770, Online. Association for Computational Linguistics.

Anders Søgaard, Sebastian Ebert, Jasmijn Bastings, and Katja Filippova. 2021. We need to talk about random splits. In *Proceedings of the 16th Conference of the European Chapter of the Association for Computational Linguistics: Main Volume*, pages 1823–1832, Online. Association for Computational Linguistics.

Robyn Speer. 2022. rspeer/wordfreq: v3.0.

Zeerak Talat, James Thorne, and Joachim Bingel. 2018. *Bridging the Gaps: Multi Task Learning for Domain Transfer of Hate Speech Detection*, pages 29–55. Springer International Publishing, Cham.

Ming Tan, Yang Yu, Haoyu Wang, Dakuo Wang, Saloni Potdar, Shiyu Chang, and Mo Yu. 2019. Out-of-domain detection for low-resource text classification tasks. In *Proceedings of the 2019 Conference on Empirical Methods in Natural Language Processing and the 9th International Joint Conference on Natural Language Processing (EMNLP-IJCNLP)*, pages 3566–3572, Hong Kong, China. Association for Computational Linguistics.

Laure Thompson and David Mimno. 2020. Topic modeling with contextualized word representation clusters. *CoRR*, abs/2010.12626.

William Timkey and Marten van Schijndel. 2021. All bark and no bite: Rogue dimensions in transformer language models obscure representational quality. In *Proceedings of the 2021 Conference on Empirical Methods in Natural Language Processing*, pages 4527–4546, Online and Punta Cana, Dominican Republic. Association for Computational Linguistics.

Iulia Turc, Ming-Wei Chang, Kenton Lee, and Kristina Toutanova. 2019. Well-read students learn better: The impact of student initialization on knowledge distillation. *CoRR*, abs/1908.08962.

Dusan Varis and Ondřej Bojar. 2021. Sequence length is a domain: Length-based overfitting in transformer models. In *Proceedings of the 2021 Conference on Empirical Methods in Natural Language Processing*, pages 8246–8257, Online and Punta Cana, Dominican Republic. Association for Computational Linguistics.

Bertie Vidgen, Alex Harris, Dong Nguyen, Rebekah Tromble, Scott Hale, and Helen Margetts. 2019. Challenges and frontiers in abusive content detection. In *Proceedings of the Third Workshop on Abusive Language Online*, pages 80–93, Florence, Italy. Association for Computational Linguistics.

Bertie Vidgen, Dong Nguyen, Helen Margetts, Patricia Rossini, and Rebekah Tromble. 2021. Introducing CAD: the contextual abuse dataset. In *Proceedings of the 2021 Conference of the North American Chapter of the Association for Computational Linguistics: Human Language Technologies*, pages 2289–2303, Online. Association for Computational Linguistics.

Alex Wang, Yada Pruksachatkun, Nikita Nangia, Amanpreet Singh, Julian Michael, Felix Hill, Omer Levy, and Samuel R. Bowman. 2019. SuperGLUE: A stickier benchmark for general-purpose language understanding systems. *CoRR*, abs/1905.00537.

Alex Wang, Amanpreet Singh, Julian Michael, Felix Hill, Omer Levy, and Samuel R. Bowman. 2018. GLUE: A multi-task benchmark and analysis platform for natural language understanding. *CoRR*, abs/1804.07461.

Linyi Yang, Shuibai Zhang, Libo Qin, Yafu Li, Yidong Wang, Hanmeng Liu, Jindong Wang, Xing Xie, and Yue Zhang. 2022. GLUE-X: Evaluating natural language understanding models from an out-of-distribution generalization perspective.

Wenjie Yin and Arkaitz Zubiaga. 2021a. Towards generalisable hate speech detection: a review on obstacles and solutions. *PeerJ Computer Science*, 7:e598.

Wenjie Yin and Arkaitz Zubiaga. 2021b. Towards generalisable hate speech detection: a review on obstacles and solutions. *CoRR*, abs/2102.08886.

Wei Emma Zhang, Quan Z. Sheng, Ahoud Alhazmi, and Chenliang Li. 2020. Adversarial attacks on deep-learning models in natural language processing: A survey. *ACM Trans. Intell. Syst. Technol.*, 11(3).

Caleb Ziems, Jiaao Chen, Camille Harris, Jessica Anderson, and Diyi Yang. 2022. VALUE: Understanding dialect disparity in NLU. In *Proceedings of the 60th Annual Meeting of the Association for Computational Linguistics (Volume 1: Long Papers)*, pages 3701–3720, Dublin, Ireland. Association for Computational Linguistics.

A GenBench Eval Card

Motivation					
Practical	*Cognitive*	*Intrinsic* □	*Fairness*		
Generalisation type					
Compo-sitional	*Structural*	*Cross Task*	*Cross Language*	*Cross Domain*	*Robust-ness* □
Shift type					
Covariate □	*Label*	*Full*	*Assumed*		
Shift source					
Naturally occuring	*Partitioned natural* □	*Generated shift*	*Fully generated*		
Shift locus					
Train–test	*Finetune train–test* □	*Pretrain–train*	*Pretrain–test*		

Our work proposes a data split that evaluates the generalisation ability of hate speech detection models. Our motivation is an **intrinsic** one, we aim to understand better what kind of data is most challenging for hate speech detection models.

We focus on testing the **robustness** of such models, especially when it comes to out-of-distribution (o.o.d.) generalisation. However, it is not straightforward to define and detect o.o.d. data (Arora et al., 2021). Moreover, data properties that might seem challenging for humans (Varis and Bojar, 2021; Ebrahimi et al., 2018) might not be equally challenging for models or rely on costly annotations (Arango et al., 2019; Nejadgholi and Kiritchenko, 2020; Bourgeade et al., 2023).

Therefore, we create a train test split by only relying on a model's hidden representations. This **partitioned natural** splitting method yields a **covariate shift**, since we re-split existing data sets. The resulting train test splits indeed challenge hate speech detection models in a **finetune train-test** locus.

B Clustering

Our proposed data split creates a train-test split by assigning whole clusters of latent representations to either the train or the test set. We use k-means clustering (Lloyd, 1982) to perform the clustering. The used hyperparamters can be found below.

Parameter	Value
n clusters	3-50
n initializations with different centroids	10
max. iterations for a run	300
random state	42, 62, 82
algorithm	LLoyd

Table 3: K-Means hyperparameters

C Language Models

We use four transformer language models to obtain and evaluate the data splits: BERT-Base(-Cased) (Devlin et al., 2019), its smaller variant BERT-Medium (Turc et al., 2019; Bhargava et al., 2021), HateBERT (Caselli et al., 2021), a BERT-Base-Uncased model that was further pretrained on abusive Reddit data using the MLM objective, and RoBERTa-Base (Liu et al., 2019). The hyperparamters for finetuning can be found below. They are generally adopted from the finetuned models from Caselli et al. (2021), but due to computational restrictions, the models had to be trained with reduced batch sizes. To compensate for this, models were trained with more epochs with the option of early stopping.

Hyperparameter	Value
batch size	4 (biggest possible)
early stopping	after 5 epochs
maximum epochs	10 (20 for the larger RoBERTa models)
optimizer	AdamW
learning rate	2e-5
adam epsilon	1e-8
scheduling	linear schedule with warmup
warm up steps	0
random seeds	42, 55, 83
max. sequence length	512

Table 4: Hyperparameters for finetuning the language models are adopted from the finetuned models from Caselli et al. (2021).

D Detailed Results

The following section presents detailed results including baselines, hyperparameter selections and further results.

D.1 Baselines

We compare the performance of models trained on our proposed data splits (CLOSEST-SPLIT and SUBSET-SUM-SPLIT) to a random split. We obtain random splits not only from 100% of the data but also from 90% of the data. This is necessary to compare the random split to the CLOSEST-SPLIT and SUBSET-SUM-SPLIT, as these use only 90% of the data. The random split performances are presented below.

model	valid acc.	test acc.	hate f1
SVM*	–	–	75.7
RNN*	–	–	77.5
BERT-base (100%)	94.6 ± 0.21	91.55 ± 0.13	82.24 ± 0.34
BERT-base (90%)	91.69 ± 0.07	91.25 ± 0.11	81.96 ± 0.5
BERT-med. (100%)	94.3 ± 0.23	91.63 ± 0.2	82.27 ± 0.45
BERT-med. (90%)	91.84 ± 0.07	91.2 ± 0.15	81.58 ± 0.66
HateBert (100%)	94.12 ± 0.06	91.87 ± 0.16	82.72 ± 0.38
HateBert (90%)	92.02 ± 0.07	91.51 ± 0.13	82.34 ± 0.59
RoBERTa (100%)	94.4 ± 0.12	91.67 ± 0.2	82.5 ± 0.49
RoBERTa (90%)	91.8 ± 0.09	91.37 ± 0.16	82.15 ± 0.61

Table 5: Results for the Reddit dataset on random splits using 100% and 90% of the data. Random splits are generated using three different seeds and models are trained with three initialisation seeds; mean and standard errors are reported. Results marked with * are taken from Qian et al. (2019).

split	model	valid acc	test acc	Macro f1
stand.	BERT-base *	–	69.0	67.4
stand.	BERT-base	67.45 ± 0.36	68.38 ± 0.35	66.06 ± 0.44
	BERT-med.	63.93 ± 1.2	64.58 ± 0.99	62.32 ± 1.45
	HateBert	68.12 ± 0.16	68.0 ± 0.37	65.97 ± 0.36
	RoBERTa	67.32 ± 0.3	67.83 ± 0.42	65.98 ± 0.26
rand.	BERT-base	67.66 ± 0.31	68.25 ± 0.28	66.0 ± 0.36
	BERT-med.	62.46 ± 0.49	62.85 ± 0.42	60.18 ± 0.42
	HateBert	67.91 ± 0.32	68.51 ± 0.28	66.25 ± 0.35
	RoBERTa	66.45 ± 0.51	66.4 ± 0.56	64.1 ± 0.9

Table 6: Results for the HateXplain dataset on the standard (stand.) split and on random (rand.) splits using 90% of the data. Random splits are generated using three different seeds and models are trained with three initialisation seeds; mean and standard errors are reported. Results marked with * are taken from Mathew et al. (2020).

D.2 Hyperparameter Selection for Proposed Split

We analyse the effects of two hyperparameters. First, we analyse whether task-specific, finetuned representations are needed for challenging data splits or whether task-agnostic, pretrained representations also lead to difficult splits. The results can be found in Fig. 7 and Fig. 8. The second hyperparameter we analyse is the dimensionality of the representations, as displayed in Fig. 9.

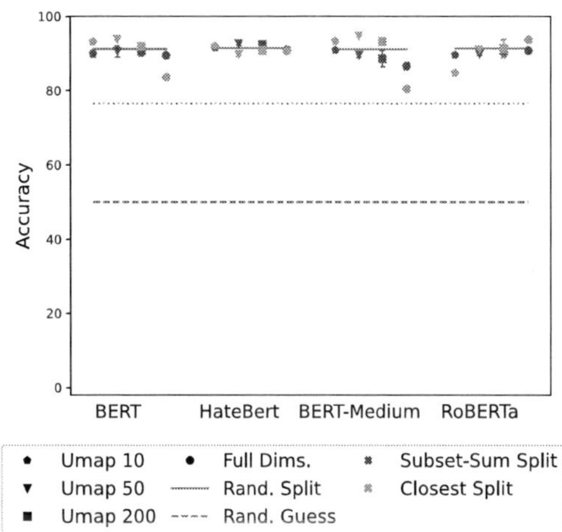

Figure 7: Performance of language models trained on the **pretrained** SUBSET-SUM-SPLIT and pretrained CLOSEST-SPLIT of the Reddit data. The errorbars show the standard error between cluster seeds.

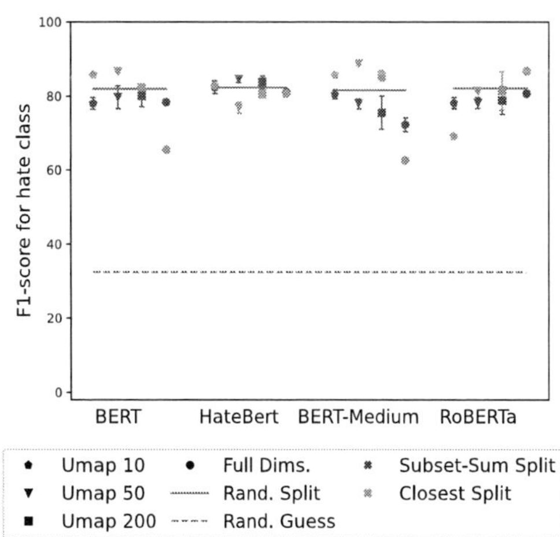

Figure 8: Performance of language models trained on the **pretrained** SUBSET-SUM-SPLIT and pretrained closest split of the Reddit data. The errorbars show the standard error between cluster seeds.

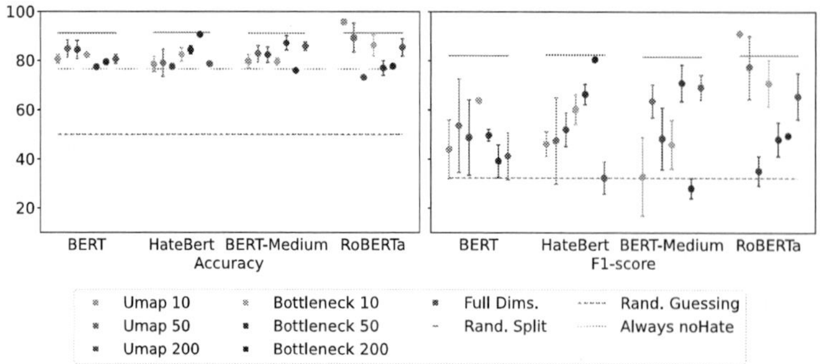

(a) SUBSET-SUM-SPLIT

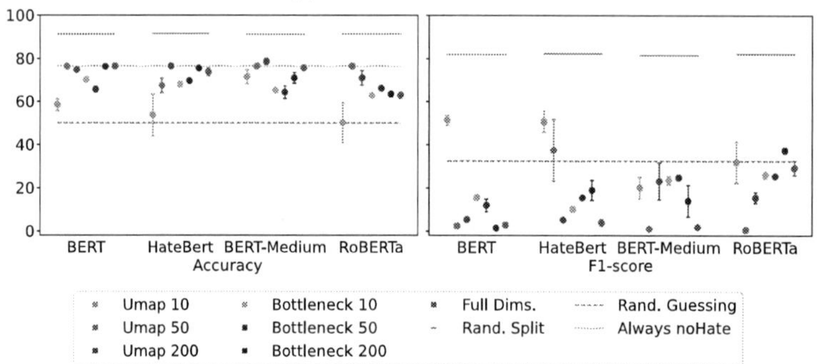

(b) CLOSEST-SPLIT

Figure 9: Performance of language models trained on the SUBSET-SUM-SPLIT and CLOSEST-SPLIT of the Reddit dataset. Random split performance, indicated by the solid horizontal lines, is used as a baseline. The error bars show the standard error between cluster seeds.

D.3 Subset-Sum and Closest Split

SUBSET-SUM-SPLIT and CLOSEST-SPLIT both lead to a decreased performance. The performance on the Reddit dataset in terms of accuracy can be found below in Fig. 10.

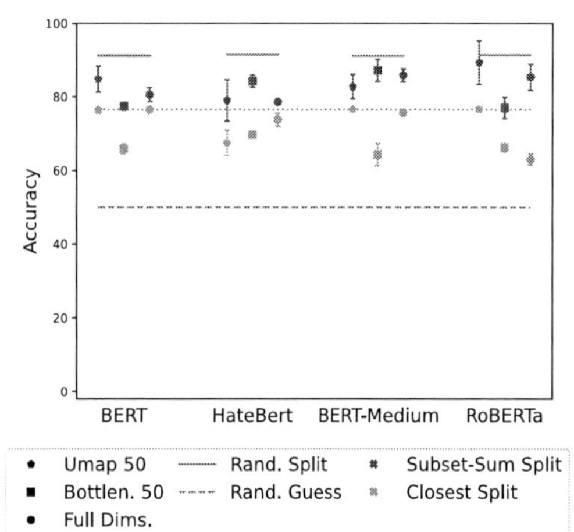

Figure 10: Performance of language models trained on the SUBSET-SUM-SPLIT and CLOSEST-SPLIT of the Reddit data. The errorbars show the standard error between cluster seeds.

The HateXplain accuracy can be found in Fig. 11. For both datasets, models fail to predict some class completely, defaulting instead to one of the other classes. Note that HateXplain is a balanced dataset, while Reddit is highly unbalanced (75% noHate).

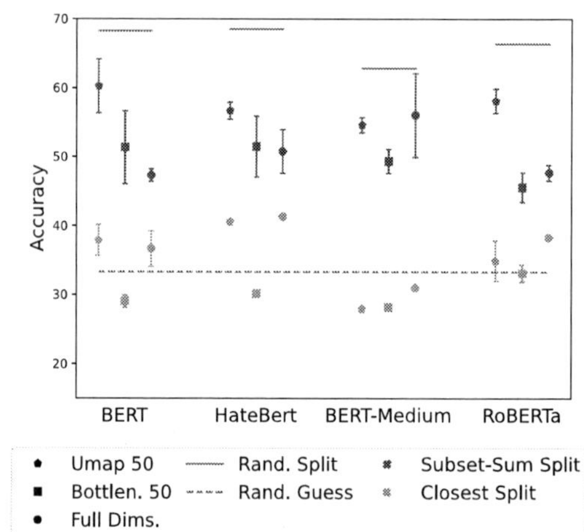

Figure 11: Performance of language models trained on the SUBSET-SUM-SPLIT and CLOSEST-SPLIT of the HateXplain data. The errorbars show the standard error between cluster seeds.

E Analysis

E.1 Data split properties

This section presents a detailed description of the features used for the analysis in Section 6. The following task-agnostic features are included in the analysis:

Unigram Overlap Following the word overlap algorithm in Elangovan et al. (2021), the word overlap o_i for a given test example $test_i$ is the word overlap with the most similar training example $train_k$. The word overlap of the whole test set is then the average over the word overlap of the test examples o_i. For this computation, examples are represented as a vector with unigram counts (ignoring stopwords), and similarity is computed as the cosine similarity.

Sentence Length in the Test Set We use the average length of input examples in the test set in terms of characters.

Number of Rare Words in the Test Set Rare words are defined following the definition of Godbole and Jia (2022): Rare words are words that are not common (i.e. occur at most once per million words) and are not misspelled (i.e. appear in the word list of common words[6]). For word frequency statistics, Godbole and Jia (2022) rely on Brysbaert and New (2009). We use the word frequencies more recently collected by Speer (2022) instead.

Moreover, we compare the dropped performance on the proposed data splits to the following task-specific features:

Number of under-represented keywords in the train set The Reddit and HateXplain dataset have been created by filtering posts based on hate keywords by simply string-matching the posts with the keywords. These keywords can be understood as hate speech categories. We calculate the number of hate speech categories that are under-represented in the train set, i.e. have less than 50% of their occurrences in the train set. Keywords that occur in less than 3% of the data set are excluded.

Number of under-represented targets in the train set This method aims to analyse the different targets of hate speech. For the HateXplain dataset, these targets are annotated as explained in Section 3. We calculate the number of under-represented targets in the train set using the same concept as for the under-represented keywords.

Difference of the data source distribution in the train and test set As described in Section 3, the HateXplain dataset consists of two data sources, Gab (46%) and Twitter (54%). We calculate the distributional shift between the data source distribution in the train and test set. The Kullback-Leibler Divergence (Kullback and Leibler, 1951) is calculated for the two data sources in the dataset and then the average is taken over both classes, weighted by the occurrence of the class in the dataset. Since there is no upper bound for the KL Divergence, it is scaled to be between 0 and 1 by the function

$$f(x) = 1 - e^{-x}. \quad (1)$$

E.2 Topic analysis

Set	Class	Topics RoBERTa
Train	Hate	nigger, kike, white, jews
	Offens.	retarded, bitch, white, ghetto
	noHate	white, people, women, raped
Test	Hate	jews, faggot, muslim, white
	Offens.	faggot, jews, nigger, white
	noHate	white, jews, people, retarded

Table 7: Top 4 topics for different classes in the HateXplain dataset. The topics are obtained from train and test sets of the Closest Split with latent representations from RoBERTA.

We extract topics for each class in the train and test sets using c-TF-IDF (Grootendorst, 2022).

As an example, Table 7 summarises the topics with the highest c-TF-IDF scores. There seems to be a tendency for the offensive and noHate classes to have different topics in the train and test sets, while the hate class is more consistent across the split. A manual analysis of cluster topics for all cluster splits did not lead to conclusive results: Topics are not clearly separated across all classes between the train and test sets. Many of the topics found by c-TF-IDF seem to coincide with the targets that were annotated, and used for the analysis in the previous section. No strong correlation between targets and performance was observed then, which strengthens the result that different targets in the train and test sets are not the reason for the decreased performance.

[6]https://github.com/dwyl/english-words

Syntax-Guided Transformers: Elevating Compositional Generalization and Grounding in Multimodal Environments

Danial Kamali
Michigan State University
kamalida@msu.edu

Parisa Kordjamshidi
Michigan State University
kordjams@msu.edu

Abstract

Compositional generalization, the ability of intelligent models to extrapolate understanding of components to novel compositions, is a fundamental yet challenging facet in AI research, especially within multimodal environments. In this work, we address this challenge by exploiting the syntactic structure of language to boost compositional generalization. This paper elevates the importance of syntactic grounding, particularly through attention masking techniques derived from text input parsing. We introduce and evaluate the merits of using syntactic information in the multimodal grounding problem. Our results on grounded compositional generalization underscore the positive impact of dependency parsing across diverse tasks when utilized with Weight Sharing across the Transformer encoder. The results push the state-of-the-art in multimodal grounding and parameter-efficient modeling and provide insights for future research.

1 Introduction

Compositional Generalization refers to the ability of an intelligent agent to generalize its understanding of the underlying structure of a problem, especially when it is faced with novel compositions of the previously seen building blocks or components (Chomsky, 1957; Montague, 1970). It is fundamental for models to be able to extrapolate from their training environment to novel situations, a common occurrence in real-world applications. Hupkes et al. (2020) categorizes compositional generalization capabilities into five categories, *systematicity*, *substitutivity*, *localism & globalism*, and *overgeneralization*. These abilities are crucial for models to achieve strong performance on tasks that require reasoning and understanding of hierarchical structures, such as natural language understanding, object classification, and robotics.

Humans understand new compositions of previously observed concepts and simpler constructs.

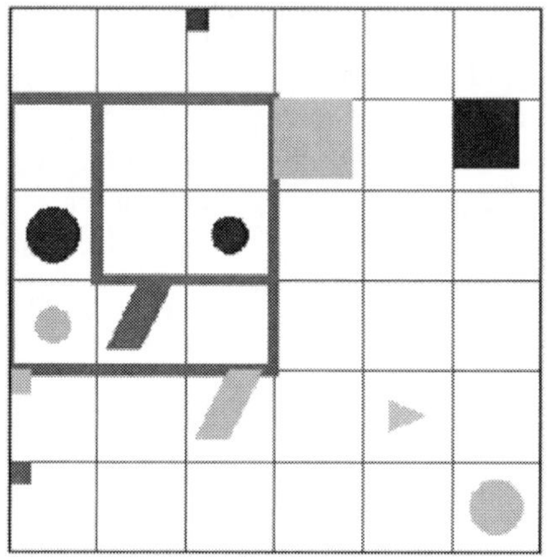

Input Command: pull the small blue object that is inside of the small green box and in the same row as the red circle while zigzagging.
Action sequence: *turn left, turn left, walk, turn right, walk, turn right, walk, pull*

Figure 1: This example is taken from the ReaSCAN dataset. Here, an agent is provided with a command. Its objective is to generate/execute a series of predefined actions to fulfill the task within the given environment.

On the other hand, despite remarkable progress in the field of Artificial Intelligence, even state-of-the-art language models demonstrate limitations in this aspect (Lake and Baroni, 2018; Thomas McCoy et al., 2020; Shaw et al., 2021). Especially, they often fail to effectively generalize in the reasoning depth, which involves handling multi-turn reasoning about entities and their properties in the world or even the co-occurrence of unseen spatial relations (Wu et al., 2021). These limitations indicate a crucial need for innovative approaches to address these issues.

In this research, our objective is to exploit the syntactic structure of language to enhance compositional generalization. Our focus is mainly on the multimodal problem setting that entangles vision and language. In this unique setting, compositional

Proceedings of the 1st GenBench Workshop on (Benchmarking) Generalisation in NLP, pages 130–142
December 6, 2023 ©2023 Association for Computational Linguistics

linguistic descriptions must be accurately grounded in the environment to devise coherent action plans or achieve specific goals. An illustrative example of this scenario is shown in Figure 1.

The motivation behind leveraging syntax in our approach stems from the inherent structure and compositionality of natural language. Syntactic parsing provides crucial structural information about how words in a sentence relate to each other. We hypothesize that syntactic structure can improve intelligent agents' ability to discern the applicable attributes and descriptions for each object in its environment and better apprehend deeper levels of reasoning.

By imposing an understanding of language structure through syntactic parsing, we aim to extend the capabilities of current multimodal language models. This could potentially pave the way for more sophisticated models capable of robustly interacting with dynamic and complex vision and language environments. Apart from using structure, we equipped our end-to-end model with weight sharing that has demonstrated improving the generalization capabilities in single-modality tasks.

As a result, we reach state-of-the-art performance on the ReaSCAN compositional generalization benchmark, showing improvement across all test splits, especially ones requiring sentence structure comprehension. In summary, our contributions include:

- Enhancing grounded compositional generalization by integrating syntactic parsing into our model.
- Using syntax-guided attention masking along with weight sharing, we build a highly parameter-efficient model compared to baselines.
- Our model has shown marked improvement in performance across a variety of tasks that are designed for compositional generalization evaluation while enhancing computational efficacy.

2 Related Work

The machine learning research community primarily focused on understanding the error bounds and the bias-variance trade-off (Hastie et al., 2009) to understand and improve the models' generalizability. Later, techniques like dropout (Srivastava et al., 2014) were introduced to improve neural models' generalization. Recently, studies have examined the generalizability of various neural network architectures using specialized generalization evaluation tasks (Hupkes et al., 2020; Ontanon et al., 2022; Csordás et al., 2021). Additionally, numerous datasets such as SCAN (Lake and Baroni, 2018), CFQ (Keysers et al., 2020), and COGS (Kim and Linzen, 2020) have been developed to assess compositional generalization capabilities. Diverse strategies such as data augmentation (Andreas, 2020; Shaw et al., 2021), innovative architectural designs (Korrel et al., 2019; Gao et al., 2020), and neuro-symbolic methods (Mao et al., 2019), have been proposed to enhance these capabilities. Consequently, these advances in text-based generalization have inspired research in multimodal compositional generalization, with developments including complex benchmarks like gSCAN (Ruis et al., 2020) and ReaSCAN (Wu et al., 2021), and advanced architectures applied to multimodal grounding (Kuo et al., 2021; Jiang and Bansal, 2021; Qiu et al., 2021a; Sikarwar et al., 2022; Shaw et al., 2021).

Furthermore, recent research highlights the significant role of syntactic information in enhancing neural models' compositional generalization capability. Kuo et al. (2021) suggested aligning the compositional structure of networks with the problem domain, resulting in a dynamic compositional neural network. Moreover, Shaw et al. (2021) and Qiu et al. (2022) recommended grammar induction-based data augmentation techniques to improve compositional generalization. Unlike our work that focuses on input command structure, Kim et al. (2021b) introduced the concept of using parse tree node annotations in the target sequence of sequence-to-sequence tasks for enhancing compositional generalization. Meanwhile, Kim et al. (2021a) incorporated parse tree nodes into the ETC (Ainslie et al., 2020) model. They employed attention masking specific for ETC to symbolize the relations of tokens and aid this model in a simplified classification task based on the CFQ dataset.

We are inspired by previous research (Kim et al., 2021a) that employs a similar technique with manually extracted parses for compositional generalization on the single text modality. However, our model utilizes off-the-shelf parsers instead of accurate manually generated parse trees, and it is generally applicable independent of the underlying models.

3 Problem Setting

Various studies on compositional generalization have presented a range of tasks and problem settings (Lake and Baroni, 2018; Keysers et al., 2020; Kim and Linzen, 2020; Wu et al., 2021; Ruis et al., 2020). These datasets are comprised of a training set and several test sets. To ensure rigorous evaluation, the test sets have been deliberately structured to differ from the training set in a way that requires the compositional capability to succeed. Our paper focuses on grounding natural language instructions in the visual modality, where we map words to specific objects or actions in a multimodal environment that provides a framework to evaluate an intelligent agent's compositional structures and spatial reasoning capabilities.

We use the most recent multimodal compositional generalization benchmarks to assess our models comprehensively. In these benchmarks, an agent receives natural language instruction to carry out an action or navigate specific environments. These datasets are inherently synthetic, and they have been carefully crafted to guarantee that the test sets are systematically different from the training sets. By placing commands within a spatial context, these benchmarks bridge the gap between abstract cognitive understanding and practical action execution. Consequently, they stand as both a scholarly tool for studying compositional generalization and a valuable resource for fields like robotics that require comprehension of spatially anchored commands.

Among these benchmarks, our primary focus is ReaSCAN, owing to its heightened complexity and recent introduction to the academic community. An example of this dataset, depicted in Figure 1, consists of three main components: The initial state of the world, the provided input command, and the corresponding target command. Tasked with this information, the agent aims to infer the target command by leveraging both the information from the input command and the initial state. Structurally, the world's representation in ReaSCAN is formulated as a 6×6×17 matrix. Each matrix cell comprises a 17-dimensional vector encapsulating information pertaining to an object's attributes—namely, color, shape, and size—along with indicators of the agent's positioning and orientation. The evaluation metric for this dataset is the percentage of exact matches of the predicted action sequence. The ReaSCAN dataset includes one random test split that mirrors the training's component and compound distribution, in addition to seven compositional generalization test splits. Each of these splits is designed to probe a specific facet of a model's grounding generalization capability, as detailed in Table 1. Category A test splits delve into novel attribute compositions at both the command and object levels, drawing inspiration from gSCAN. Category B test splits assess the model's ability to generalize to unprecedented co-occurrences of concepts and spatial relations. Meanwhile, Category C probes the model's capacity to extrapolate from simple command structures to more intricate structures with higher levels of reasoning (Wu et al., 2021). To illustrate the A1 split, all examples with commands containing variations of "yellow square" (such as "small yellow square" or "big yellow square") are excluded from the training data. This prevents models from associating targets with that phrase. However, the training set does include examples like "yellow cylinder" and "blue square." As a result, during testing, models are expected to accurately interpret the "yellow square" even without prior exposure to the actual composition.

Split	Held-out Examples
Random	Random.
A1	*yellow square* referred with color & shape.
A2	*red square* referred in the command.
A3	*small cylinder* referred with size and shape
B1	co-occur of *small red circle* and *big blue square*.
B2	co-occur of *same size as* and *inside of* relations.
C1	Additional conjunction clause depth added to *2-relative-clause commands*.
C2	*2-relative-clause* command with *that is* instead of *and*.

Table 1: ReaSCAN dataset test splits.

4 Proposed Method

To address the challenge at hand, we implemented a multimodal transformer, as illustrated in Figure 2. In this model, input commands are tokenized and then supplemented with positional encoding before passing to the transformer. Concurrently, the visual environment is segmented into 36 distinct

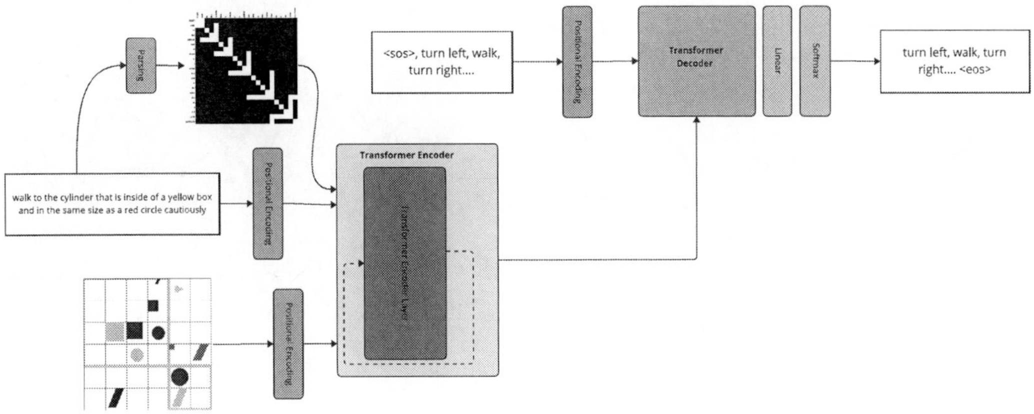

Figure 2: Overall architecture of the proposed model.

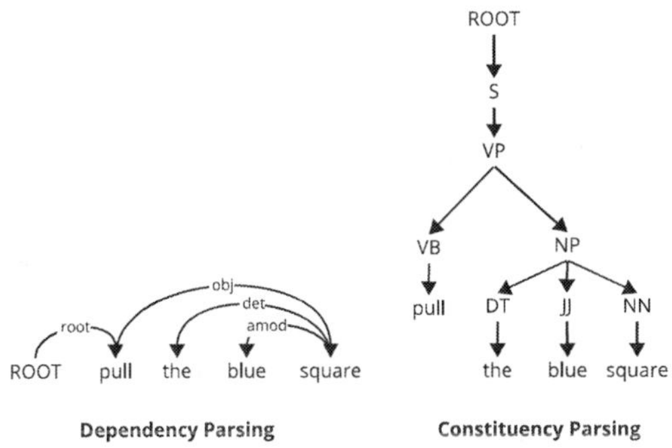

Figure 3: Examples of parse trees.

cells, each serving as a visual token. After passing the visual token to a linear layer, these tokens receive positional encoding and are passed to the transformer.

We've employed a generic parser to seamlessly embed the structure of the textual modality into our model, thereby shaping attention masks for the encoder's textual self-attention. Prioritizing efficiency, parsing each input command is conducted during a preprocessing phase.

Our transformer is based on the GroCoT model (Sikarwar et al., 2022). Each encoder layer employs a cross-attention mechanism between modalities, followed by modality-specific self-attention. Our computed input command masks are utilized in the self-attention modules of the textual modality. Remarkably, encoder layer weights are consistently shared across all layers.

In the end, we concatenate the encoded result of each modality and pass it to the transformer's auto-regressive decoder to generate the action sequence corresponding to the input command given the environment.

4.1 Syntax-guided attention

One main component of our proposed model is exploiting the syntactic structure of the command. For this aim, we investigate using both dependency and constituency parsing. Dependency and constituency trees can be used to analyze the grammatical structure of sentences. Dependency trees focus on the grammatical relationships between individual words, where each word except the root depends on another, and the edges of the tree signify these dependencies. However, constituency trees emphasize the hierarchical organization of words into larger syntactic units or constituents, with internal nodes representing these groupings and leaves representing individual words. While dependency trees are more concerned with identifying grammatical roles and relationships between words, constituency trees aim to show how words group together into larger syntactic units, often carrying syntactic labels like NP (noun phrase) or VP (verb phrase) (Foscarin et al., 2023; Hearne et al., 2008). Examples of these parse trees are shown in Figure 3.

Syntax-guided attention masking. We use the syntactic information to guide the self-attention module of transformer encoder layers as depicted in Figures 2 and 4b. We force each token to only attend to the tokens connected in the syntax tree. In this way, we avoid faulty attention patterns and overfitting irrelevant parts of the sentence. In addition, by imposing the structure with a parse tree, our model can capture the nesting structure of the command's meaning and the relationships between its components. By making the structural information explicit, our model can potentially extrapolate the meaning of novel combinations and nesting linguistic structures encompassing higher reasoning depth.

4.2 Weight Sharing

Parameter sharing is a strategic approach where identical learned parameters are applied across various positions or layers within a model. This technique enables the reuse of the same encoder unit at each phase of the transformer encoder (Dehghani et al., 2019). Such an approach not only streamlines the model but also nurtures the acquisition of more robust and adaptable representations of the input (Ontanon et al., 2022). The findings of Kim et al. (2021a) demonstrate that a transformer employing attention masking requires extended training epochs for convergence, potentially due to masking-induced backpropagation constraints. In light of this, we hypothesize that introducing weight sharing might counterbalance this challenge. Weight sharing reduces the model's complexity by decreasing the number of parameters, which could lead to faster convergence. This method acts as a form of regularization, stabilizing training and facilitating smoother optimization landscapes. In addition, Ontanon et al. (2022) show that a transformer with shared weights across its encoder layers is arguably endowed with a more suitable inductive bias that allows the model to learn the primitive concepts. We hypothesize this will positively affect learning spatial relations or object-property relations, which are frequently used in our model's input. Motivated by these advantages, we incorporated this weight sharing technique into our transformer model to evaluate its efficacy in a multimodal setting. Beyond the enhanced generalizability, weight sharing serves as a computational benefit by reducing the number of learnable parameters during the training phase.

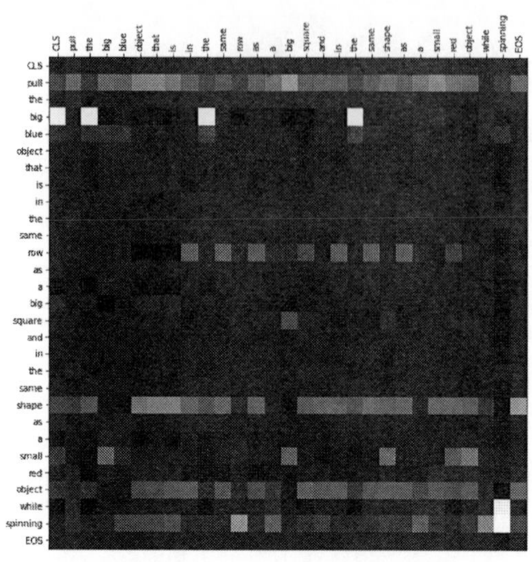

(a) Self-attention w/o masking

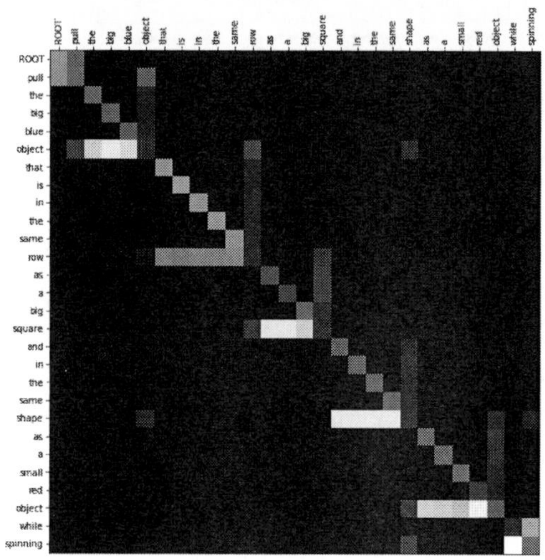

(b) Self-Attention w/ masking

Figure 4: Self-Attention example from the A2 test set of ReaSCAN dataset. Figures (a) and (b) depict the averaged self-attention map from our models' over all encoder layers and heads. Rows and columns correspond to text tokens. Brighter attention cells indicate higher attention weights

5 Experiments

Implementation Details. Our model architecture is founded on the GroCoT framework as detailed by Sikarwar et al. (2022) and is implemented using the PyTorch machine learning library (Paszke et al., 2019). Also, we employed the pre-trained stanza toolkit (Qi et al., 2020) for constituency and dependency parsing. We used 48 GB A6000 GPUs accompanied by 756GB RAM. On average, each experiment took about 52 hours to train the models from scratch, with the Adam optimizer (Kingma and Ba, 2017) parameter updates throughout the training regimen. To ensure a rigorous evaluation, we used the same specialized compositional validation set as Sikarwar et al. (2022), drawing 500 samples from each compositional division of the primary dataset. Model proficiency was assessed against this validation set, with the highest-performing model designated as our optimal choice. Our results are presented as an average derived from three independent runs, each initialized with a random seed. We ran the models for the ReaSCAN benchmark for 120 epochs, and the models for the gSCAN and GSRR benchmarks for 100 epochs. Hyperparameters used for the experiments of each dataset are shown in Appendix A. The code and models proposed in this work are all available in GitHub[1].

Datasets. We used gSCAN (Ruis et al., 2020), GSRR (Qiu et al., 2021b), ReaSCAN (Wu et al., 2021) benchmarks for evaluation. The Grounded SCAN (gSCAN) dataset is a benchmark tailored for examining compositional generalization in machine learning models by translating natural language commands into actions in a grid-world scenario. Its unique splits ensure models move beyond rote memorization to deep compositional understanding of concepts. The Grounded Systematic Relation Reasoning (GSRR) dataset extends gSCAN by aligning natural language instructions intricately with visual elements, emphasizing spatial relationships and object references. ReaSCAN, a further development, brings the challenges of real-world reasoning into this environment by introducing more challenging tasks and concept relations. Together, these datasets offer a high-complexity framework for assessing the compositional and relational understanding of machine learning models in visual environments. A detailed explanation of both the gSCAN and Grounded Systematic Relation Reasoning datasets can be found in Appendix B.

Baselines. We embarked on a series of experiments designed to evaluate our model's effectiveness compared to the most recent state-of-the-art models on the mentioned multimodal compositional generalization datasets. We include the following baselines. **(a)** Ruis et al. (2020) (Multimodal LSTM) is a fusion of sequence-to-sequence (seq2seq) architecture with a visual encoder, employing a recurrent 'command encoder' to process the instructions. **(b)** Gao et al. (2020) (GCN-LSTM) integrates a Graph Convolutional Neural (GCN) network with a multimodal LSTM. The command encoding is achieved via a BiLSTM equipped with multi-step textual attention, while the world is encoded through a GCN layer. **(c)** Qiu et al. (2021b) (Multimodal Transformer) is a multimodal transformer equipped with cross-attention for multimodal compositional generalization. **(d)** Sikarwar et al. (2022) (GroCoT) is another transformer-based model that incorporates interleaved self-attention into the multimodal transformer with cross-attention.

[1]https://github.com/HLR/Syntax-Guided-Transformers

Results. We comprehensively evaluated our approach across all the previously mentioned benchmarks compared to the baselines. Alongside the accuracy and efficacy metrics, we also provide insights into the computational overhead associated with our method. Furthermore, a qualitative analysis is presented, delving deeper into our approach's performance nuances and strengths.

The benchmark results, presented in Tables 2, 3, and 4, demonstrate our model's superior performance over all reported models, with a notable 3% improvement on the average of ReaSCAN benchmark splits. This substantiates our hypothesis that incorporating syntactic parsing significantly boosts the model's generalization derived from grounded compositional training data. Moreover, dependency parsing consistently outperformed constituency or marked a very similar performance across multiple benchmarks, including GSRR and gSCAN. Our model displayed improvements across nearly all ReaSCAN splits except for C2. As per Sikarwar et al. (2022), the C2 split is "unfair," lacking the required information in training data for comprehensive model training. Even including syntactic information could not improve the model's performance on this split and even caused a decrease in the performance. Our methodology also showcased its merit in the object property test cases (A1-3), effectively constraining attention to words pertinent to target object descriptors. For instance, as shown in Figure 4, the attention weights from the properties to the corresponding objects are high.

Notably, our model exhibited considerable strides in the C1 split, indicative of the value added by syntactic information. For a more reliable comparison, we applied a t-test to our C1 test split results. Using a significance level (α) of 0.05, this statistical analysis provided further validation for the observed enhancements in our model's performance, particularly within the context of the C1 test split. Furthermore, our model exhibits enhanced performance on the GSRR dataset. As illustrated in Table 4, both variants of our model demonstrate improvements in the II split. It is worth noting that the II split shares the same challenge as the A2 split from the ReaSCAN dataset but in a less complex

Model	A1	A2	A3	B1	B2	C1	C2	Avg
LSTM*	50.4	14.7	50.9	52.2	39.4	49.7	25.7	40.40
GCN-LSTM	92.3	42.1	87.5	69.7	52.8	57.0	22.1	60.50
Transformer*	96.7	58.9	93.3	79.8	59.3	75.9	25.5	69.90
GroCoT	99.6	93.1	98.9	93.9	86.0	76.3	**27.3**	82.2
Constituency†	**99.75**±0.11	96.70±1.40	**99.68**±0.10	95.19±1.17	88.37±1.50	69.07±0.60	27.00±0.54	82.25±0.63
Dependency†	99.65±0.9	**97.37**±0.48	99.62±0.07	**95.46**±2.01	**90.15**±3.88	**92.55**±1.51	21.77±5.25	**85.22**±0.87

Table 2: The result of our proposed model on the ReaSCAN dataset test splits. The results are an average of three runs. † denotes the models with masking. Models marked with * refer to the multimodal version of their implementation.

Model	A	B	C	E	F	H	Comp. Avg
LSTM*	97.7	54.9	23.5	35.0	92.5	22.7	32.7
GCN-LSTM	98.6	99.1	80.3	87.3	99.3	**33.6**	-
Transformer*	99.9	99.9	99.3	99.0	99.9	22.2	60.0
GroCoT	99.9	99.9	99.9	99.8	99.9	22.9	60.4
Constituency†	**99.95**±0.07	**99.92**±0.06	**99.88**±0.11	99.88±0.09	**100.00**±0.00	22.84±0.93	60.36±0.11
Dependency†	99.92±0.09	99.85±0.18	99.86±0.11	**99.96**±0.06	99.89±0.16	23.89±1.54	**60.49**±0.20

Table 3: The result of our proposed model on the gSCAN dataset test splits. The results are an average of three runs. We did not report the results on D and G splits since we achieved 0.00±0.00 % performance, But take them into account in the averaged result. † denotes the models with masking. Models marked with * refer to the multimodal version of their implementation.

environment.

While our proposed techniques effectively address splits A, B, C, E, and F, mirroring the successes of previous works such as (Sikarwar et al., 2022) and (Qiu et al., 2021b), they struggle with challenges presented by specific gSCAN compositionality splits, notably D, G, and H. These particular splits are designed to assess the model's capacity for systematic generalization when novel patterns should occur on the output sequence rather than in grounding the input instruction (Sikarwar et al., 2022), a facet that is not expected to be captured by our proposed model.

5.1 Ablation

For a granular understanding of the contributions from each alteration to the baseline model, we undertook an ablation study. This involved the sequential removal of each modification to measure its individual impact. As depicted in Table 5, while individual modifications did not significantly change the baseline, their collective integration enhanced the model's generalization. Remarkably, eliminating dependency parsing or weight sharing resulted in a noticeable performance dip. The improvement upon integration posits that weight sharing can potentially offset the masking prolonged convergence challenge by reducing parameter count, thereby mitigating the convergence issues.

5.2 Qualitative Analysis

In our previous discussions, we highlighted the significance of integrating dependency parsing as a fundamental approach to understanding the complex structures inherent in sentences. This integration is not a mere enhancement; it critically enriches the model's grounding capabilities, offering a more robust bridge between raw textual sequences and their semantic structure.

To provide empirical evidence of our technique for guiding attention, we conducted an analysis of the cross-attention module. We aimed to compare its behavior before and after applying attention masking. The results, presented in Figure 5, indicate a clear trend: in 86% of validation samples, the cross-attention module exhibits a pronounced focus on the target object.

Figures 5b and 5c elucidate the impact of self-attention masking on these weights. After using attention masking (see Figure 5b), the attention distribution becomes notably sparser; instead of individual words attending in isolation to every potentially relevant cell, they now form cohesive compositional expressions, each attending to the

Model	I	II	III	IV	V	VI	Comp. Avg
LSTM*	86.5	40.1	86.1	5.5	81.4	81.8	58.9
Transformer*	94.7	64.4	94.9	49.6	59.3	49.5	63.5
GroCoT	99.9	98.6	**99.9**	99.7	**99.5**	96.5	98.8
Constituency†	99.85±0.00	99.90±0.03	99.16±0.26	99.88±0.03	96.73±2.16	**97.85**±0.46	98.58±0.39
Dependency†	**99.91**±0.02	**99.93**±0.01	99.41±0.28	**99.96**±0.01	99.03±0.23	97.38±0.63	**99.07**±0.16

Table 4: The result of our proposed model on the GSRR dataset test splits. The results are an average of three runs. † denotes the models with masking. Models marked with * refer to the multimodal version of their implementation.

W/S	Mask	A1	A2	A3	B1	B2	C1	C2	Avg
-	-	99.29±0.27	91.82±6.50	98.49±1.17	93.50±0.85	83.15±1.41	75.85±1.35	**25.03**±6.82	81.02±0.22
✓	-	99.68±0.22	97.09±1.72	99.64±0.20	94.86±0.77	81.49±4.27	66.30±6.65	21.66±1.83	80.10±1.08
-	Dep.	98.09±0.27	85.21±6.85	97.35±0.75	93.61±2.75	90.62±1.59	75.27±1.77	21.91±1.63	80.29±1.43
✓	Dep.	**99.65**±0.9	**97.37**±0.48	**99.62**±0.07	**95.46**±2.01	**90.15**±3.88	**92.55**±1.51	21.77±5.25	**85.22**±0.87

Table 5: The ablation study result of our modifications on ReaSCAN dataset test splits. Results are reported on an average of three runs. We evaluate every combination of components from our best model. W/S stands for weight sharing, and the ✓shows the presence of the module. *Dep* in this table refers to the Dependency masking. We evaluate the model with or without dependency masking in the masking part.

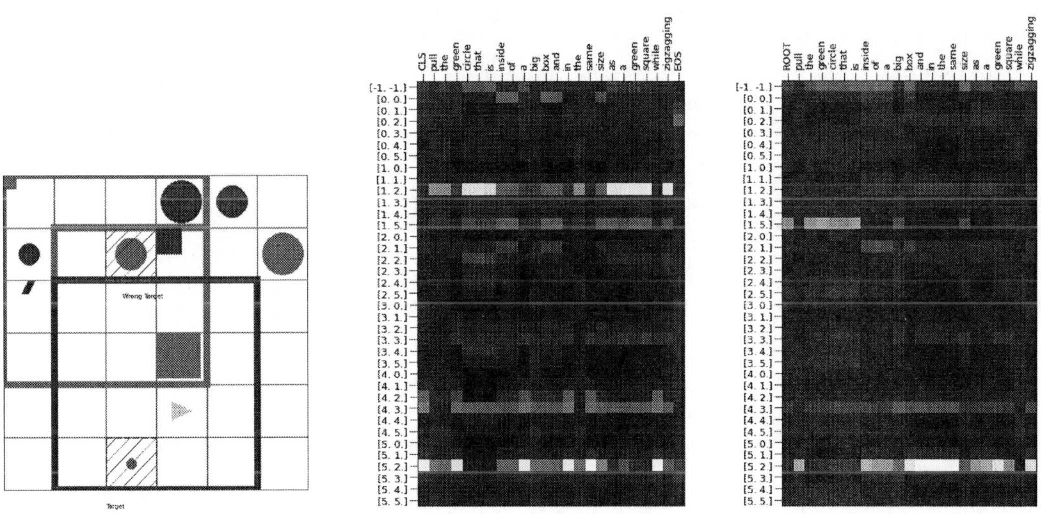

(a) Environment (b) Cross-attention w/o masking (c) Cross-Attention w/ masking

Figure 5: Cross-Attention from Text-to-Image. In Figure (a), the purple zone indicates the model's incorrect object selection, while the red zone highlights the accurate choice. Figures (b) and (c) depict the averaged cross-attention map from our models over encoder layers and attention heads. The rows represent environment cells (the first element shows the row, and the second shows the column index, both starting from 0), and the columns correspond to text tokens. Brighter attention cells signify elevated attention weights.

corresponding cells as a whole. For instance, in Figure 5c, "and in the same," phrase's tokens attend to cells (1,2), (4,3), and (5,2) together with greater attention on the target object in contrast to their attention pattern without masking.

5.3 Efficiency Analysis

In the realm of modern model design, the challenge lies in amplifying capabilities while managing computational overhead. Our methodology adeptly navigates this balance. A cornerstone of our model's efficiency is the strategic adoption of weight sharing within the transformer encoder. By reusing weights across different components, we

Model	#Parameters
Multimodal LSTM	74K
Multimodal Transformer	3M
GroCoT	4.6M
Dependency† (ours)	1.9M

Table 6: Comparing model parameters: our model vs. current state-of-the-art models. Dependency† refers to the model with dependency parsing for attention masking.

significantly reduce the parameter space. This not only streamlines memory utilization and accelerates training but also acts as an implicit regularizer, bolstering the model's generalization capabilities and reducing overfitting. Further enhancing this is our implementation of attention masking, which refines computational efficiency. By enabling the model to selectively bypass attention to certain tokens, we can optimize the model to avoid redundant computational processes, ensuring optimal resource allocation and superior performance.

As illustrated in Table 6, our model stands out in terms of efficiency. Despite having fewer parameters (1.9M) than the models by Qiu et al. (2021a) and Sikarwar et al. (2022), which have 3M and 4.6M parameters respectively, our model consistently outperforms them across all benchmarks.

6 Conclusion

Our research demonstrated that exploiting the syntactic structure of compositional and complex linguistic and spatial expressions improved the grounding ability of the instruction-follower agent in multimodal environments. Our results indicated improvements compared to the previous state-of-the-art models. In particular, we show that our proposed model is effective for generalization on tasks and test splits that require generalization over unobserved reasoning depths, such as the C1 split in the ReaSCAN dataset. By utilizing the syntactic-guided attention masking along with the weight sharing, we achieved not only more accurate but also more parameter-efficient models for grounded compositional generalization.

Limitations

Despite the promising results achieved in our study, several limitations warrant consideration:

Synthetic Data: Our experiments predominantly rely on synthetic datasets. While these datasets provide a controlled environment for assessing model performance, they might not capture the complexities and nuances of real-world data. Evaluating the models on real-world datasets is crucial to ensure their practical applicability.

Error Propagation from the Parser: The model's performance is intrinsically tied to the accuracy of the pre-trained parsers we utilized. Errors or inaccuracies in parsing can lead to suboptimal model outputs. Additionally, our synthetic data, being unambiguous, might not reveal the full extent of potential parser-related issues.

Computational Constraints: Due to computational limitations, the hyperparameter search might not have been exhaustive. A more comprehensive exploration might yield better model configurations.

Acknowledgement

This project is supported by the National Science Foundation (NSF) CAREER award 2028626 and partially supported by the Office of Naval Research (ONR) grant N00014-20-1-2005. Any opinions, findings, and conclusions or recommendations expressed in this material are those of the authors and do not necessarily reflect the views of the National Science Foundation nor the Office of Naval Research. We thank all reviewers for their thoughtful comments and suggestions.

References

Joshua Ainslie, Santiago Ontanon, Chris Alberti, Vaclav Cvicek, Zachary Fisher, Philip Pham, Anirudh Ravula, Sumit Sanghai, Qifan Wang, and Li Yang. 2020. ETC: Encoding long and structured inputs in transformers. In *Proceedings of the 2020 Conference on Empirical Methods in Natural Language Processing (EMNLP)*, pages 268–284, Online. Association for Computational Linguistics.

Jacob Andreas. 2020. Good-enough compositional data augmentation. In *Proceedings of the 58th Annual Meeting of the Association for Computational Linguistics*, pages 7556–7566, Online. Association for Computational Linguistics.

Noam Chomsky. 1957. *Syntactic Structures*. Mouton, The Hague.

Róbert Csordás, Kazuki Irie, and Juergen Schmidhuber. 2021. The devil is in the detail: Simple tricks improve systematic generalization of transformers. In *Proceedings of the 2021 Conference on Empirical*

Methods in Natural Language Processing, pages 619–634, Online and Punta Cana, Dominican Republic. Association for Computational Linguistics.

Mostafa Dehghani, Stephan Gouws, Oriol Vinyals, Jakob Uszkoreit, and Łukasz Kaiser. 2019. Universal transformers.

Francesco Foscarin, Daniel Harasim, and Gerhard Widmer. 2023. Predicting music hierarchies with a graph-based neural decoder.

Tong Gao, Qi Huang, and Raymond Mooney. 2020. Systematic generalization on gSCAN with language conditioned embedding. In *Proceedings of the 1st Conference of the Asia-Pacific Chapter of the Association for Computational Linguistics and the 10th International Joint Conference on Natural Language Processing*, pages 491–503, Suzhou, China. Association for Computational Linguistics.

Trevor Hastie, Robert Tibshirani, and Jerome Friedman. 2009. *The Elements of Statistical Learning*. Springer New York.

Mary Hearne, Sylwia Ozdowska, and John Tinsley. 2008. Comparing constituency and dependency representations for SMT phrase-extraction. In *Actes de la 15ème conférence sur le Traitement Automatique des Langues Naturelles. Articles courts, TALN 2008, Avignon, France, June 2008*, pages 131–140. ATALA.

Dieuwke Hupkes, Verna Dankers, Mathijs Mul, and Elia Bruni. 2020. Compositionality decomposed: How do neural networks generalise? (extended abstract). In *Proceedings of the Twenty-Ninth International Joint Conference on Artificial Intelligence, IJCAI-20*, pages 5065–5069. International Joint Conferences on Artificial Intelligence Organization. Journal track.

Dieuwke Hupkes, Mario Giulianelli, Verna Dankers, Mikel Artetxe, Yanai Elazar, Tiago Pimentel, Christos Christodoulopoulos, Karim Lasri, Naomi Saphra, Arabella Sinclair, Dennis Ulmer, Florian Schottmann, Khuyagbaatar Batsuren, Kaiser Sun, Koustuv Sinha, Leila Khalatbari, Maria Ryskina, Rita Frieske, Ryan Cotterell, and Zhijing Jin. 2023. State-of-the-art generalisation research in nlp: A taxonomy and review.

Yichen Jiang and Mohit Bansal. 2021. Inducing transformer's compositional generalization ability via auxiliary sequence prediction tasks. In *Proceedings of the 2021 Conference on Empirical Methods in Natural Language Processing*, pages 6253–6265, Online and Punta Cana, Dominican Republic. Association for Computational Linguistics.

Daniel Keysers, Nathanael Schärli, Nathan Scales, Hylke Buisman, Daniel Furrer, Sergii Kashubin, Nikola Momchev, Danila Sinopalnikov, Lukasz Stafiniak, Tibor Tihon, Dmitry Tsarkov, Xiao Wang, Marc van Zee, and Olivier Bousquet. 2020. Measuring compositional generalization: A comprehensive method on realistic data. In *8th International Conference on Learning Representations, ICLR 2020, Addis Ababa, Ethiopia, April 26-30, 2020*. OpenReview.net.

Juyong Kim, Pradeep Ravikumar, Joshua Ainslie, and Santiago Ontañón. 2021a. Improving compositional generalization in classification tasks via structure annotations.

Najoung Kim and Tal Linzen. 2020. COGS: A compositional generalization challenge based on semantic interpretation. *CoRR*, abs/2010.05465.

Segwang Kim, Joonyoung Kim, and Kyomin Jung. 2021b. Compositional generalization via parsing tree annotation. *IEEE Access*, 9:24326–24333.

Diederik P. Kingma and Jimmy Ba. 2017. Adam: A method for stochastic optimization.

Kris Korrel, Dieuwke Hupkes, Verna Dankers, and Elia Bruni. 2019. Transcoding compositionally: Using attention to find more generalizable solutions. In *Proceedings of the 2019 ACL Workshop BlackboxNLP: Analyzing and Interpreting Neural Networks for NLP*, pages 1–11, Florence, Italy. Association for Computational Linguistics.

Yen-Ling Kuo, Boris Katz, and Andrei Barbu. 2021. Compositional networks enable systematic generalization for grounded language understanding. In *Findings of the Association for Computational Linguistics: EMNLP 2021*, pages 216–226, Punta Cana, Dominican Republic. Association for Computational Linguistics.

Brenden M. Lake and Marco Baroni. 2018. Generalization without systematicity: On the compositional skills of sequence-to-sequence recurrent networks.

Jiayuan Mao, Chuang Gan, Pushmeet Kohli, Joshua B. Tenenbaum, and Jiajun Wu. 2019. The Neuro-Symbolic Concept Learner: Interpreting Scenes, Words, and Sentences From Natural Supervision. In *International Conference on Learning Representations*.

Richard Montague. 1970. Universal grammar. *Theoria*, 36(3):373–398.

Santiago Ontanon, Joshua Ainslie, Zachary Fisher, and Vaclav Cvicek. 2022. Making transformers solve compositional tasks. In *Proceedings of the 60th Annual Meeting of the Association for Computational Linguistics (Volume 1: Long Papers)*, pages 3591–3607, Dublin, Ireland. Association for Computational Linguistics.

Adam Paszke, Sam Gross, Francisco Massa, Adam Lerer, James Bradbury, Gregory Chanan, Trevor Killeen, Zeming Lin, Natalia Gimelshein, Luca Antiga, Alban Desmaison, Andreas Köpf, Edward Yang, Zach DeVito, Martin Raison, Alykhan Tejani, Sasank Chilamkurthy, Benoit Steiner, Lu Fang, Junjie Bai, and Soumith Chintala. 2019. Pytorch: An imperative style, high-performance deep learning library.

Peng Qi, Yuhao Zhang, Yuhui Zhang, Jason Bolton, and Christopher D. Manning. 2020. Stanza: A Python natural language processing toolkit for many human languages. In *Proceedings of the 58th Annual Meeting of the Association for Computational Linguistics: System Demonstrations*.

Linlu Qiu, Hexiang Hu, Bowen Zhang, Peter Shaw, and Fei Sha. 2021a. Systematic generalization on gSCAN: What is nearly solved and what is next? In *Proceedings of the 2021 Conference on Empirical Methods in Natural Language Processing*, pages 2180–2188, Online and Punta Cana, Dominican Republic. Association for Computational Linguistics.

Linlu Qiu, Peter Shaw, Panupong Pasupat, Pawel Nowak, Tal Linzen, Fei Sha, and Kristina Toutanova. 2022. Improving compositional generalization with latent structure and data augmentation. In *Proceedings of the 2022 Conference of the North American Chapter of the Association for Computational Linguistics: Human Language Technologies*, pages 4341–4362, Seattle, United States. Association for Computational Linguistics.

Yao Qiu, Jinchao Zhang, and Jie Zhou. 2021b. Improving gradient-based adversarial training for text classification by contrastive learning and auto-encoder. In *Findings of the Association for Computational Linguistics: ACL-IJCNLP 2021*, pages 1698–1707, Online. Association for Computational Linguistics.

Laura Ruis, Jacob Andreas, Marco Baroni, Diane Bouchacourt, and Brenden M. Lake. 2020. A benchmark for systematic generalization in grounded language understanding.

Peter Shaw, Ming-Wei Chang, Panupong Pasupat, and Kristina Toutanova. 2021. Compositional generalization and natural language variation: Can a semantic parsing approach handle both? In *Proceedings of the 59th Annual Meeting of the Association for Computational Linguistics and the 11th International Joint Conference on Natural Language Processing (Volume 1: Long Papers)*, pages 922–938, Online. Association for Computational Linguistics.

Ankur Sikarwar, Arkil Patel, and Navin Goyal. 2022. When can transformers ground and compose: Insights from compositional generalization benchmarks. In *Proceedings of the 2022 Conference on Empirical Methods in Natural Language Processing*, pages 648–669, Abu Dhabi, United Arab Emirates. Association for Computational Linguistics.

Nitish Srivastava, Geoffrey Hinton, Alex Krizhevsky, Ilya Sutskever, and Ruslan Salakhutdinov. 2014. Dropout: A simple way to prevent neural networks from overfitting. *Journal of Machine Learning Research*, 15:1929–1958.

R. Thomas McCoy, Ellie Pavlick, and Tal Linzen. 2020. Right for the wrong reasons: Diagnosing syntactic heuristics in natural language inference. In *ACL 2019 - 57th Annual Meeting of the Association for Computational Linguistics, Proceedings of the Conference*, ACL 2019 - 57th Annual Meeting of the Association for Computational Linguistics, Proceedings of the Conference, pages 3428–3448. Association for Computational Linguistics (ACL).

Zhengxuan Wu, Elisa Kreiss, Desmond C. Ong, and Christopher Potts. 2021. ReaSCAN: Compositional reasoning in language grounding. *NeurIPS 2021 Datasets and Benchmarks Track*.

A Hyperparameters

Here, we present the hyperparameters used in the models for every benchmark in Table 7.

B Datasets Description

B.1 Grounded SCAN dataset

The Grounded SCAN (gSCAN) dataset is a pivotal benchmark for assessing compositional generalization in machine learning models. Evolving from the foundational SCAN (Lake and Baroni, 2018) dataset, gSCAN is designed to evaluate a model's proficiency in translating command sequences into actions within a grid world environment, emphasizing on compositional challenges.

This benchmark offers systematic test splits that rigorously examine a model's capability to generalize beyond its training data. These compositional splits include:

- **A (Random)**: Random data with a similar distribution to the training data.
- **B (Color-Shape)**: Novel composition of object properties in the testing. Yellow squares are referred to by color and shape.
- **C (Color Only)**: Red squares as target.
- **D (Novel Direction)**: Challenges a model's spatial comprehension, with targets set in unfamiliar directions, the southwest.
- **E (Novel Contextual References)**: Evaluates a model's understanding of relative sizes, with commands pointing to circles of size 2 described as "small."
- **F (Novel Composition of Actions and Arguments)**: Probes a model's grasp of object classes and their nuances, exemplified by squares of size 3 necessitating two pushes.
- **G (Adverb)**: Commands carrying the adverb "cautiously" test how well the model interprets action modifiers after seeing limited training samples (k=1).

Hyperparameter	gSCAN	GSRR	ReaSCAN
Number of Vision Self-Attention Layers	3	3	6
Number of Text Self-Attention Layers	3	3	6
Number of Cross-Attention Layers	3	3	6
Number of Decoder Layers	3	3	6
Embedding Size	128	128	128
Hidden Layer Size	256	256	256
Number of Attention Heads	8	8	8
Learning Rate	5×10^{-5}	1×10^{-5}	1×10^{-5}
Batch Size	64	64	32
Dropout	0.1	0.1	0.1
Number of Epochs	100	100	120

Table 7: Hypterparameters used in the experiments.

- **H (Adverb-Verb Combination)**: Generalizes to commands pairing actions and their modifiers, like "while spinning" combined with "pull."

The compositional test splits of the gSCAN dataset ensure that models are not indulging in learning statistical shortcuts but are genuinely mastering compositional reasoning. In gSCAN, every command is mapped to an action sequence for an agent in the grid world, whether moving to a particular spot or interacting with a distinct described object.

B.2 Grounded Systematic Relation Reasoning dataset (GSRR)

The Grounded Systematic Relation Reasoning (GSRR) dataset, introduced by (Qiu et al., 2021b), extends the gSCAN benchmark. Their initial analyses of the gSCAN dataset indicated its efficacy; the authors observed that several remaining challenges might not be primarily tied to visual grounding. In light of this, they proposed the GSRR task, characterized by an elevated complexity in aligning natural language instructions with the visual environment.

In this dataset, language expressions specifically delineate target objects and explicitly describe their relationships with a secondary referenced object. They incorporate two types of relations into our dataset: immediate adjacency ("next to") and cardinal directions such as "north" and "west." In addition, they put visual distractors objects within the environment to emphasize the critical role of spatial relations in identifying the target objects.

The dataset is systematically divided into various splits to ensure a comprehensive assessment:

- **I (Random)**: Similar distribution as the training.
- **II (Visual)**: Commands centering on "red squares" either as targets or references.
- **III (Relation)**: Complex instructions involving combinations like "green squares" and "blue circles."
- **IV (Referent)** Emphasizing "yellow squares" as primary targets.
- **V (Relative Position 1)**: Commands where targets are situated to the "north" of their reference points.
- **VI (Relative Position 2)**: Instructions where targets are located "southwest" relative to their references.

C Evaluation Card

Here, we present the evaluation card of our compositional generalization experiments based on (Hupkes et al., 2023) taxonomy.

Motivation			
Practical	*Cognitive*	*Intrinsic*	*Fairness*
□		□	

Generalisation type					
Compositional	*Structural*	*Cross Task*	*Cross Language*	*Cross Domain*	*Robustness*
□	□				

Shift type			
Covariate	*Label*	*Full*	*Assumed*
		□	

Shift source			
Naturally occuring	*Partitioned natural*	*Generated shift*	*Fully generated*
			□

Shift locus			
Train–test	*Finetune train–test*	*Pretrain–train*	*Pretrain–test*
□			

mSCAN: A Dataset for Multilingual Compositional Generalisation Evaluation

Amélie Reymond
University of Washington
attr@uw.edu

Shane Steinert-Threlkeld
University of Washington
shanest@uw.edu

Abstract

Language models achieve remarkable results on a variety of tasks, yet still struggle with compositional generalisation benchmarks. The majority of these benchmarks evaluate performance in English only, leaving us with the question of whether these results generalise to other languages. As an initial step to answering this question, we introduce mSCAN, a multilingual adaptation of the SCAN dataset. It was produced by a rule-based translation, developed in cooperation with native speakers. We then showcase this novel dataset on some in-context learning experiments, with the multilingual large language model `BLOOM` as well as `gpt3.5-turbo`.

1 Introduction

Humans learn quickly by easily recombining previously known concepts in unseen settings. Several benchmarks have been designed to empirically investigate whether neural networks are equipped with similar abilities (Lake and Baroni, 2018; Keysers et al., 2020; Hupkes et al., 2020; Kim and Linzen, 2020). Such benchmarks are composed of tasks in which the training data and the test data have different and carefully chosen distributions. Recent work used these benchmarks to evaluate pretrained large language models (LLMs) and showed that despite their remarkable success on many other tasks they still struggle with compositional generalisation (Qiu et al., 2022).

The majority of the research on compositional generalisation has focussed on English data and models — but do compositional generalisation abilities differ across languages? Indeed, it has been argued that the performance of a model in English is not a guarantee that it will work "equally or even reasonably well" in other languages (Bender, 2011). On top of that, compositional generalisation itself is not guaranteed to work uniformly across human languages (Bittner, 1995).

Furthermore, the exploration of cross- and multilingual compositional generalisation could benefit the expansion of language technology to low-resource languages and settings (Chaabouni et al., 2021), as a potential approach to overcome the need for huge amounts of data that neural models require.

With ever-increased scale, some large language models have shown great performance on downstream tasks while only conditioned on a few examples, and without updating their parameters. This is known as in-context learning, a paradigm in which some very large models such as GPT-3 and PaLM have been shown to manifest reasoning abilities when prompted in specific ways, including in multilingual settings (Shi et al., 2022). Despite these promising perspectives, it does not currently stand as an alternative to fine-tuning. Some recent research has sought to investigate compositional generalisation within the in-context learning paradigm, showing it gets outperformed by smaller fine-tuned models.

As a means to further the study of compositional generalisation in multiple languages, we introduce mSCAN (multilingual SCAN), an adaptation of the SCAN benchmark into French, Hindi, Mandarin Chinese and Russian. We also provide for each language both the original SCAN benchmark splits (`add_jump, add_turn_left, length`) as well as the Maximum Compound Divergence splits (Keysers et al., 2020).

We also present preliminary experimental results using mSCAN in an in-context learning paradigm on `BLOOM` and `gpt3.5-turbo`.

Following the GenBench taxonomy (Hupkes et al., 2023), the primary motivation for this work can be characterised as intrinsic given its primary function to provide a means to evaluate compositional generalisation in multilingual settings. Similarly to the original SCAN benchmark, the source of the distribution shift is fully generated and its

Proceedings of the 1st GenBench Workshop on (Benchmarking) Generalisation in NLP, pages 143–151
December 6, 2023

Motivation			
Practical	*Cognitive*	*Intrinsic*	*Fairness*
		□	

Generalisation type					
Compositional	*Structural*	*Cross Task*	*Cross Language*	*Cross Domain*	*Robustness*
□					

Shift type			
Covariate	*Label*	*Full*	*Assumed*
□			

Shift source			
Naturally occuring	*Partitioned natural*	*Generated shift*	*Fully generated*
			□

Shift locus			
Train–test	*Finetune train–test*	*Pretrain–train*	*Pretrain–test*
			□

Figure 1: GenBench evaluation card

type is covariate. Moreover, the in-context set-up of our experiments places the shift locus between the pre-train and test stages though we note that the data can also be used in a fine-tuning setup in the future.

2 Background

Pre-trained multilingual models seek to address the challenge of low-resource languages, by leveraging the pre-training and the hope that high-resource languages will help lower-resource ones. Large-scale multilingual language models have achieved impressive performance across typologically distinct languages (Ruder et al., 2021). Yet, the cross and within-language performance of downstream tasks on such models remain correlated to their amount of language-specific pertaining data (Lauscher et al., 2020).

However, if scaling up the amount of pre-training data might improve cross-lingual generalisation, it might come at a price when it comes to compositional generalisation. Kim et al. (2022) have questioned the reported benefits of pre-training on compositional generalisation benchmarks and have observed a case of inverse scaling, where the performance degradation on COGS actually increases with the amount of pre-training data.

In a further study on the impact of model scale on compositional generalisation, Qiu et al. (2022) compared fine-tuning, prompt-tuning and in-context learning on multiple compositional generalisation datasets and observed that for in-context learning, the performance is correlated with model size. However, it is worse than for fine-tuned, smaller models. Datasets they used included COGS and the Compositional Freebase Question dataset or CFQ (Keysers et al., 2020), which consists of questions and answers in natural language, as well as accompanying SPARQL queries against a knowledge base. (Qiu et al., 2022)

Hosseini et al. (2022) evaluated four model families for in-context learning on multiple semantic parsing benchmarks. Despite their observation that the larger models tend to do better, they report that the in-context learning performance on SCAN and CFQ is very small for the models tested.

MCWQ (Cui et al., 2022), a multilingual variant of CFQ, is the first adaptation into multiple languages of a compositional generalisation benchmark. It was created with the use of neural machine translation. Wang and Hershocovich (2023) have shown that using neural machine translation to translate already existing benchmarks entails "critical semantic distortion", and favour a rule-based translation of the MCWQ dataset.

The MSGM benchmark (Shi et al., 2022) investigates the mathematical reasoning abilities of LLMs in multilingual settings, by providing data in ten different languages. Even though the decomposition of SCAN commands closely resembles that of arithmetic operations, the MSGM differs in that it does not specifically target the capacity of the model to map forms to a representation of meaning. As such, there has not yet been any investigation specifically targeting the compositional generalisation abilities of multilingual models in an in-context setting.

3 The mSCAN dataset

Our goal was to adapt the Simplified version of the CommAi Navigation dataset or SCAN (Lake and Baroni, 2018) to languages that belong to typologically diverse families and typically are represented in varying proportions in the training data of multilingual models. The languages selected also have different language scripts: Latin, Cyrillic and Devanagari. The original SCAN consists of a set of navigation commands in English such as "jump left", and their corresponding sequence of actions, such as LTURN JUMP. It is a synthetic dataset: the natural language commands are generated by a phrase-structure grammar, and the actions are produced by applying a semantic interpretation function. As such, it is akin to a semantic parsing task.

3.1 Generation methodology: a grammar based-transduction

Following (Wang and Hershcovich, 2023), we translate SCAN in a rule-based manner.

The method we used consists of a set of English grammar rules, their accompanying transduction rules and word mappings.

We used the context-free grammar shown in Figure 2, which is exactly equivalent to the one from (Lake and Baroni, 2018), only differing in notation. We also used the interpretation function as provided in their work. The SCAN grammar does not have recursion and generates an unambiguous and finite set of 20910 natural language commands to action sequence pairs.

Native speakers of French, Mandarin Chinese, Russian and Hindi were asked to provide the corresponding interpretation function in their language. We consequently manually built the transduction functions, which were applied to the English parse trees. The resulting parse trees were then formed into our translated commands by word mappings.

For instance, for French translations, we first parsed the English text using the original SCAN grammar, given in Figure 2, to produce an English parse tree. This parse tree can be transduced into a French parse tree using the transduction rules given in Figure 3. These transduction rules tell us that, for instance, `S AND S` and `S AFTER S` should be translated word-for-word, and the translation of "and" is "et", and "after" is "après". They also tell us that French distinguishes between "turn left" (translated as "tourner à gauche") and "turn around left" (translated as "tourner autour par la gauche").

```
C -> S AND S | S AFTER S | S
S -> V TIMES | V
V -> ACTION VECTOR DIR
     | TURN VECTOR DIR
     | D | ACTION
D -> ACTION DIR | TURN DIR

ACTION -> 'walk' | 'look'
        | 'run' | 'jump'
TURN -> 'turn'
VECTOR -> 'around' | 'opposite'
DIR -> 'left' | 'right'
TIMES -> 'twice' | 'thrice'
AFTER -> 'after'
AND -> 'and'
```

Figure 2: English SCAN grammar

Upon the completion of generation, a sample was manually checked by the native speakers for meaning preservation.

3.2 Splits

We do not introduce a novel way to split our dataset and rather choose to directly reproduce already existing splits on mSCAN.

3.2.1 SCAN splits

The original SCAN dataset contains multiple types of splits, each aimed to test distinct levels of compositional ability: the "simple" split is a random subset of the data, and the "length" one targets commands with corresponding action sequences that are longer than any example seen during training, and finally, the "primitive" split, which tests whether a primitive only encountered in isolation during training can be used adequately novel combinations at test time.

3.2.2 Maximum Compound Divergence Splits

The MCD splits were introduced by (Keysers et al., 2020) with their distribution-based compositionality assessment (DBCA). It consists of a method to measure whether a dataset has been split adequately to test for compositional generalisation, as well as a method to construct such splits. The main principles of the DBCA are that (1) all the atoms or primitive elements existing in the test set should also be present in the training set, and in a distribution as similar as possible, and (2) that

```
# Non-terminals
[S AND S] -> [S] [AND] [S]
[S AFTER S] -> [S] [AFTER] [S]
...
[ACTION VECTOR DIR] -> [ACTION] [VECTOR]
     [DIR]
[ACTION LEFT] -> [ACTION] 'a gauche'
[ACTION RIGHT] -> [ACTION] 'a droite'
...
```

```
# Terminals
'and'    -> 'et'
'after'  -> 'apres'
'turn'   -> 'tourner'
'right'  -> 'par la droite'
'left'   -> 'par la gauche'
...
```

Figure 3: English to French transduction rules

the distribution of compounds (ways of composing the atoms) should be as different as possible between the training and the test set. Intuitively, this method seeks to ensure that what is measured is how the atoms are composed into new compounds and that the compositions are challenging enough so that the model cannot rely on anything else than its capacity to generalise compositionally.

(Keysers et al., 2020) applied MCD to SCAN, and we replicate these splits exactly in mSCAN: each line of the respective test, train and evaluation sets in mSCAN is a direct translation of the corresponding line in the English-language MCD SCAN split.

We make `mSCAN_fra`, `mSCAN_hin`, `mSCAN_rus` and `mSCAN_cmn` and their accompanying splits, available as a public dataset available on the Hugging Face platform[1].

4 Experiment

4.1 Models

The BigScience Large Open-Science Open-access Multilingual Language Model or `BLOOM`, (Workshop et al., 2023) is a Transformer-based language model with 176 billion parameters. As an autoregressive LLM, it is trained to generate text from a prompt. It was trained on 46 languages and 13 programming languages.

We also ran a small experiment on the OpenAI model `gpt3.5-turbo`, accessed via the OpenAI REST API, between 2023/10/23 and 2023/10/26.

4.2 Prompt design

Our approach focussed on the selection methodology of the in-context examples. Our goal was to adapt and mimic the principle underlying the original SCAN benchmark. That is, to test for compositional generalisation, the context examples should not contain the combinations of the test case.

[1] https://huggingface.co/datasets/CLMBR/mSCAN

We therefore randomly select the in-context examples from the training sets of our splits and the test case from the corresponding test sets. For example, a certain number of examples is sampled from the French `add_jump` training set, and its corresponding test case comes from the French `add_jump` test set. This example is cut out to only include the natural language commands and the start of the output sequence token ("OUT:"), therefore prompting the model to generate the adequate sequence of instructions as the output.

An EOS token was added at the end of each example and provided to the model as a stopping criterion parameter.

An example of a prompt is provided in Figure 4.

```
<s>IN: jump right thrice and turn
    opposite left OUT: I_TURN_RIGHT
    I_JUMP I_TURN_RIGHT I_JUMP
    I_TURN_RIGHT I_JUMP I_TURN_LEFT
    I_TURN_LEFT</s

<s>IN: walk after walk opposite left OUT
    : I_TURN_LEFT I_TURN_LEFT I_WALK
    I_WALK</s>

...

<s>IN: turn around left twice and look
    around left thrice OUT:
```

Figure 4: Example of a prompt in English

4.3 Set-up

Due to the context-size restrictions of the `BLOOM` model, we set the number of context examples to 8. In the original `add_primitive` SCAN splits, the primitive is over-represented in the training set by 10%. We imitate this in our set-up by manually adding the primitive to the context examples once, and by having removed the primitive from our train set, which ensures that the sampled remaining 7 in-context examples do not contain it. Therefore, the full prompt consists of 8 examples, of which one contains the primitive and 7 do not, and a test case that includes the primitive. We use greedy decoding for generation to provide a baseline.

5 Results

5.1 BLOOM

Because BLOOM was not trained with an end-of-sequence token, we truncated generated outputs to their expected length. Despite this adjustment, our results get zero exact match accuracies, that is, none of the full output sequences was equal to the correct answer. This is consistent with the results observed by Hosseini et al. (2022).

For a finer-grained measure of model performance than exact match accuracy, we measured the minimum edit distance between the truncated outputs and the target strings.

Table 1 shows the average minimum edit distance compared to the expected output length on 100 runs on the simple, MCD1, length and add_jump splits for each language. There is no result for add_jump on Hindi and Russian due to the encoding being larger than the maximum supported size for these experiments.

It is important to emphasise that there was no exact match, both for the original version of SCAN as well as for our mSCAN multilingual variants, meaning that the model has a 0% accuracy. We can observe however that there is a similar amount of error across languages.

As expected, the simple split achieves the best results, and Russian did not achieve a similar performance as the other languages, which are officially part of the BLOOM training corpus. Surprisingly, there is little difference between English and Hindi, while the model seems to do slightly better on Mandarin and French.

Despite Russian not being an official language part of the training data of BLOOM, we ran the experiments on our mSCAN_rus and we included it with the others.

5.2 GPT 3.5

Unlike with BLOOM, we obtained a few exact sequence matches with gpt-3.5-turbo but they are few, with less than 10% per language over the five languages including English. In this experiment again, Mandarin seems to achieve slightly better results. From these observations, it also appears that the model has the most difficulty with the length split.

The average edit distance results are better than those with BLOOM but display a similar pattern, with the model seeming to struggle the most on the length split and Mandarin achieving slightly better results. As expected, the model seems to be more successful with Russian than BLOOM.

6 Discussion

6.1 Pre-training data contamination

In the in-context set-up, the data from the pre-training corpus cannot be controlled. This means that there is a possibility that the compositional generalisation training set or the whole dataset itself could have been used. Given that BLOOM specifies the content of its training corpus, we are at least guaranteed that it has not learned the English SCAN dataset or that there was some test contamination. As we introduce mSCAN with this paper, it could not have been a part of the training data.

However, there is no guarantee the original SCAN has not been seen during the pre-training of the ChatGPT model. Given that we are not able to check the pre-training data, the data distribution shift is only *assumed* in this case.

6.2 In context-examples selection

It is acknowledged that prompting variations such as the format or order of prompts can have an influence on the in-context learning performance. Our context example selection methodology is rudimentary. A recent study found that the selection of in-context examples affects compositional generalisation performance, by showing that randomly selecting in-context leads to an accuracy gap compared to fine-tuned models (An et al., 2023). They argue that a careful selection of the in-context examples will "fully reveal the potential of in-context learning". They define three requirements for in-context examples: structural similarity, diversity and complexity. They show that this helps compositional generalisation. In the case of SCAN, the structural similarity factor is not as relevant, given the basic nature of the grammar (there are no complex structures such as in COGS). The diversity and complexity factors are not controlled in our experiment, given that we sample from the train set without looking at the number of distinct primitives included. For this reason, our set-up does not follow the principle that the primitives in the test

Model, language \ split		simple (13.55)	mcd1 (18.03)	length (30.04)	add_jump (14.58)
	cmn	5.04	8.28	13.82	7.16
	eng	9.32	11.65	19.15	10.53
BLOOM	fra	7.69	11.85	16.26	7.95
	hin	8.63	11.10	18.72	
	rus	12.04	15.60	27.21	
	cmn	4.52	7.95	14.83	5.81
	eng	5.51	8.75	16.32	6.65
gpt-3.5-turbo	fra	5.63	9.39	17.00	7.26
	hin	6.47	10.17	17.50	8.17
	rus	5.67	9.51	17.70	7.26

Table 1: Average edit distance for each language and split, on BLOOM and gpt-3.5-turbo. The numbers reported in the column headings correspond to the average expected output length. Note that BLOOM produced 0 exact matches.

Language \ split	simple	mcd1	length	add_jump
cmn	10	6	0	6
eng	7	7	0	1
fra	4	4	0	1
hin	0	0	1	2
rus	3	0	0	4

Table 2: Number of exact matches over 100 queries of gpt-3.5-turbo

case should be covered by the in-context examples. Instead, we expect the model to be able to infer the mapping to SCAN instructions from context as the instructions closely match their natural language counterparts (e.g., walk is mapped to I_WALK).

Other research uses a least-to-most prompting strategy: prompts consist of instructions telling explicitly the model to decompose the task into subproblems and showing it how to solve them sequentially (Zhou et al., 2023). The number of in-context examples in our experiment was constrained by the context size of the model in the BLOOM experiment. To work around this, the least-to-most method uses intermediate representations in the form of Python expressions, mapping for example "look twice" to "LOOK*2" instead of "LOOK LOOK". The authors show that the model is able to expand from the Python expression with high accuracy, but further investigation of the potential consequences of these intermediate representations could be pursued.

6.3 Compositional Generalisation and different languages

We observed that there was no large variation between how the different languages performed in our in-context setup, except for Mandarin Chinese, which has slightly better results. Given the limited scope of our experiments, this observation should be confirmed by further investigation. If these results hold then, they would be in contrast with previous findings, where in some NLP tasks, generative models (including BLOOM) perform better on higher-resource languages and languages that are in the Latin script (Ahuja et al., 2023).

6.4 Possibilities for future work

In addition to investigating different strategies for in-context example selection and systematically conducting the experiments on a larger scale than what this work presents, future work could involve adapting more realistic natural language tasks to multiple languages. Indeed, the subset of natural language covered by SCAN is small and its interpretation is more akin to arithmetic expressions than naturally occurring language. As such, it does not make it possible to evaluate for more sophisticated linguistic abstraction (Kim and Linzen, 2020). Adapting COGS to other languages would be an extensive process, requiring the construction of language-specific grammars.

It would also be worth doing experiments with

fine-tuning on multilingual models such as mBART (Liu et al., 2020) or mT5 (Xue et al., 2021).

A systematic study of the interactions between (a) the size of language-specific pretraining data, and (b) both compositional and cross-lingual generalisation, would be an important contribution.

7 Conclusion

The majority of the research on compositional generalisation is focussed on English, leaving open the question as to whether its findings can generalise across languages. As an initial step towards this exploration, we introduce mSCAN, a multilingual adaptation of the SCAN dataset, produced using rule-based translation, with rules developed in cooperation with native speakers. We then showcase this novel dataset on some in-context learning experiments, with the multilingual large language model `BLOOM`.

Limitations

Due to the synthetic nature of the SCAN dataset, the translations in other languages do not aim to capture naturalness or fluency.

This dataset was created with the aim of expanding compositional generalisation evaluation to multiple languages. We evaluate `BLOOM`, a model carefully designed for multilingualism, trained on a meticulously curated corpus. Despite these two points, more typologically diverse and low-resource languages are absent from our dataset and our evaluation.

Finally, the scale of the experiments reported in this paper was limited by different factors, including the cost and time of inference, and the maximum context size of 1000 tokens of `BLOOM`. As such, larger-scale experiments would be needed to form a basis for comparison with other benchmark results.

Acknowledgements

We would like to thank the native speakers for their precious help with this work: Sofia Ahmed, Catalin Gangalic, Qingxia Guo, Sanjana Sharma, Onur Tuna, and Shengqi Zhu.

References

Kabir Ahuja, Harshita Diddee, Rishav Hada, Millicent Ochieng, Krithika Ramesh, Prachi Jain, Akshay Nambi, Tanuja Ganu, Sameer Segal, Maxamed Axmed, Kalika Bali, and Sunayana Sitaram. 2023. MEGA: Multilingual Evaluation of Generative AI. ArXiv:2303.12528 [cs].

Shengnan An, Zeqi Lin, Qiang Fu, Bei Chen, Nanning Zheng, Jian-Guang Lou, and Dongmei Zhang. 2023. How Do In-Context Examples Affect Compositional Generalization? ArXiv:2305.04835 [cs].

Emily M. Bender. 2011. On Achieving and Evaluating Language-Independence in NLP. *Linguistic Issues in Language Technology*, 6.

Maria Bittner. 1995. Quantification in eskimo: A challenge for compositional semantics. In E. Bach, E. Jelinek, A. Kratzer, and B. Partee, editors, *Quantification in Natural Languages*, pages 59–80. Kluwer Academic Publishers.

Rahma Chaabouni, Roberto Dessì, and Eugene Kharitonov. 2021. Can transformers jump around right in natural language? assessing performance transfer from SCAN. In *Proceedings of the Fourth BlackboxNLP Workshop on Analyzing and Interpreting Neural Networks for NLP*, pages 136–148, Punta Cana, Dominican Republic. Association for Computational Linguistics.

Ruixiang Cui, Rahul Aralikatte, Heather Lent, and Daniel Hershcovich. 2022. Compositional Generalization in Multilingual Semantic Parsing over Wikidata. ArXiv:2108.03509 [cs].

Arian Hosseini, Ankit Vani, Dzmitry Bahdanau, Alessandro Sordoni, and Aaron Courville. 2022. On the Compositional Generalization Gap of In-Context Learning. ArXiv:2211.08473 [cs].

Dieuwke Hupkes, Verna Dankers, Mathijs Mul, and Elia Bruni. 2020. Compositionality Decomposed: How do Neural Networks Generalise? *Journal of Artificial Intelligence Research*, 67:757–795.

Dieuwke Hupkes, Mario Giulianelli, Verna Dankers, Mikel Artetxe, Yanai Elazar, Tiago Pimentel, Christos Christodoulopoulos, Karim Lasri, Naomi Saphra, Arabella Sinclair, Dennis Ulmer, Florian Schottmann, Khuyagbaatar Batsuren, Kaiser Sun, Koustuv Sinha, Leila Khalatbari, Maria Ryskina, Rita Frieske, Ryan Cotterell, and Zhijing Jin. 2023. A taxonomy and review of generalization research in NLP. *Nature Machine Intelligence*, 5(10):1161–1174.

Daniel Keysers, Nathanael Schärli, Nathan Scales, Hylke Buisman, Daniel Furrer, Sergii Kashubin, Nikola Momchev, Danila Sinopalnikov, Lukasz Stafiniak, Tibor Tihon, Dmitry Tsarkov, Xiao Wang, Marc van Zee, and Olivier Bousquet. 2020. Measuring Compositional Generalization: A Comprehensive Method on Realistic Data. ArXiv:1912.09713 [cs, stat].

Najoung Kim and Tal Linzen. 2020. COGS: A Compositional Generalization Challenge Based on Semantic Interpretation. ArXiv:2010.05465 [cs].

Najoung Kim, Tal Linzen, and Paul Smolensky. 2022. Uncontrolled Lexical Exposure Leads to Overestimation of Compositional Generalization in Pretrained Models. ArXiv:2212.10769 [cs].

Brenden Lake and Marco Baroni. 2018. Generalization without Systematicity: On the Compositional Skills of Sequence-to-Sequence Recurrent Networks. In *Proceedings of the 35th International Conference on Machine Learning*, pages 2873–2882. PMLR. ISSN: 2640-3498.

Anne Lauscher, Vinit Ravishankar, Ivan Vulić, and Goran Glavaš. 2020. From Zero to Hero: On the Limitations of Zero-Shot Language Transfer with Multilingual Transformers. In *Proceedings of the 2020 Conference on Empirical Methods in Natural Language Processing (EMNLP)*, pages 4483–4499, Online. Association for Computational Linguistics.

Yinhan Liu, Jiatao Gu, Naman Goyal, Xian Li, Sergey Edunov, Marjan Ghazvininejad, Mike Lewis, and Luke Zettlemoyer. 2020. Multilingual denoising pretraining for neural machine translation.

Linlu Qiu, Peter Shaw, Panupong Pasupat, Tianze Shi, Jonathan Herzig, Emily Pitler, Fei Sha, and Kristina Toutanova. 2022. Evaluating the Impact of Model Scale for Compositional Generalization in Semantic Parsing. ArXiv:2205.12253 [cs].

Sebastian Ruder, Noah Constant, Jan Botha, Aditya Siddhant, Orhan Firat, Jinlan Fu, Pengfei Liu, Junjie Hu, Dan Garrette, Graham Neubig, and Melvin Johnson. 2021. XTREME-R: Towards More Challenging and Nuanced Multilingual Evaluation. ArXiv:2104.07412 [cs].

Freda Shi, Mirac Suzgun, Markus Freitag, Xuezhi Wang, Suraj Srivats, Soroush Vosoughi, Hyung Won Chung, Yi Tay, Sebastian Ruder, Denny Zhou, Dipanjan Das, and Jason Wei. 2022. Language models are multilingual chain-of-thought reasoners.

Zi Wang and Daniel Hershcovich. 2023. On Evaluating Multilingual Compositional Generalization with Translated Datasets. ArXiv:2306.11420 [cs].

BigScience Workshop, :, Teven Le Scao, Angela Fan, Christopher Akiki, Ellie Pavlick, Suzana Ilić, Daniel Hesslow, Roman Castagné, Alexandra Sasha Luccioni, François Yvon, Matthias Gallé, Jonathan Tow, Alexander M. Rush, Stella Biderman, Albert Webson, Pawan Sasanka Ammanamanchi, Thomas Wang, Benoît Sagot, Niklas Muennighoff, Albert Villanova del Moral, Olatunji Ruwase, Rachel Bawden, Stas Bekman, Angelina McMillan-Major, Iz Beltagy, Huu Nguyen, Lucile Saulnier, Samson Tan, Pedro Ortiz Suarez, Victor Sanh, Hugo Laurençon, Yacine Jernite, Julien Launay, Margaret Mitchell, Colin Raffel, Aaron Gokaslan, Adi Simhi, Aitor Soroa, Alham Fikri Aji, Amit Alfassy, Anna Rogers, Ariel Kreisberg Nitzav, Canwen Xu, Chenghao Mou, Chris Emezue, Christopher Klamm, Colin Leong, Daniel van Strien, David Ifeoluwa Adelani, Dragomir Radev, Eduardo González Ponferrada, Efrat Levkovizh, Ethan Kim, Eyal Bar Natan, Francesco De Toni, Gérard Dupont, Germán Kruszewski, Giada Pistilli, Hady Elsahar, Hamza Benyamina, Hieu Tran, Ian Yu, Idris Abdulmumin, Isaac Johnson, Itziar Gonzalez-Dios, Javier de la Rosa, Jenny Chim, Jesse Dodge, Jian Zhu, Jonathan Chang, Jörg Frohberg, Joseph Tobing, Joydeep Bhattacharjee, Khalid Almubarak, Kimbo Chen, Kyle Lo, Leandro Von Werra, Leon Weber, Long Phan, Loubna Ben allal, Ludovic Tanguy, Manan Dey, Manuel Romero Muñoz, Maraim Masoud, María Grandury, Mario Šaško, Max Huang, Maximin Coavoux, Mayank Singh, Mike Tian-Jian Jiang, Minh Chien Vu, Mohammad A. Jauhar, Mustafa Ghaleb, Nishant Subramani, Nora Kassner, Nurulaqilla Khamis, Olivier Nguyen, Omar Espejel, Ona de Gibert, Paulo Villegas, Peter Henderson, Pierre Colombo, Priscilla Amuok, Quentin Lhoest, Rheza Harliman, Rishi Bommasani, Roberto Luis López, Rui Ribeiro, Salomey Osei, Sampo Pyysalo, Sebastian Nagel, Shamik Bose, Shamsuddeen Hassan Muhammad, Shanya Sharma, Shayne Longpre, Somaieh Nikpoor, Stanislav Silberberg, Suhas Pai, Sydney Zink, Tiago Timponi Torrent, Timo Schick, Tristan Thrush, Valentin Danchev, Vassilina Nikoulina, Veronika Laippala, Violette Lepercq, Vrinda Prabhu, Zaid Alyafeai, Zeerak Talat, Arun Raja, Benjamin Heinzerling, Chenglei Si, Davut Emre Taşar, Elizabeth Salesky, Sabrina J. Mielke, Wilson Y. Lee, Abheesht Sharma, Andrea Santilli, Antoine Chaffin, Arnaud Stiegler, Debajyoti Datta, Eliza Szczechla, Gunjan Chhablani, Han Wang, Harshit Pandey, Hendrik Strobelt, Jason Alan Fries, Jos Rozen, Leo Gao, Lintang Sutawika, M Saiful Bari, Maged S. Al-shaibani, Matteo Manica, Nihal Nayak, Ryan Teehan, Samuel Albanie, Sheng Shen, Srulik Ben-David, Stephen H. Bach, Taewoon Kim, Tali Bers, Thibault Fevry, Trishala Neeraj, Urmish Thakker, Vikas Raunak, Xiangru Tang, Zheng-Xin Yong, Zhiqing Sun, Shaked Brody, Yallow Uri, Hadar Tojarieh, Adam Roberts, Hyung Won Chung, Jaesung Tae, Jason Phang, Ofir Press, Conglong Li, Deepak Narayanan, Hatim Bourfoune, Jared Casper, Jeff Rasley, Max Ryabinin, Mayank Mishra, Minjia Zhang, Mohammad Shoeybi, Myriam Peyrounette, Nicolas Patry, Nouamane Tazi, Omar Sanseviero, Patrick von Platen, Pierre Cornette, Pierre François Lavallée, Rémi Lacroix, Samyam Rajbhandari, Sanchit Gandhi, Shaden Smith, Stéphane Requena, Suraj Patil, Tim Dettmers, Ahmed Baruwa, Amanpreet Singh, Anastasia Cheveleva, Anne-Laure Ligozat, Arjun Subramonian, Aurélie Névéol, Charles Lovering, Dan Garrette, Deepak Tunuguntla, Ehud Reiter, Ekaterina Taktasheva, Ekaterina Voloshina, Eli Bogdanov, Genta Indra Winata, Hailey Schoelkopf, Jan-Christoph Kalo, Jekaterina Novikova, Jessica Zosa Forde, Jordan Clive, Jungo Kasai, Ken Kawamura, Liam Hazan, Marine Carpuat, Miruna Clinciu, Najoung Kim, Newton Cheng, Oleg Serikov, Omer Antverg, Oskar van der Wal, Rui Zhang, Ruochen Zhang, Sebastian Gehrmann, Shachar Mirkin, Shani Pais, Tatiana Shavrina, Thomas Scialom, Tian Yun, Tomasz Limisiewicz, Verena Rieser, Vitaly Protasov,

Vladislav Mikhailov, Yada Pruksachatkun, Yonatan Belinkov, Zachary Bamberger, Zdeněk Kasner, Alice Rueda, Amanda Pestana, Amir Feizpour, Ammar Khan, Amy Faranak, Ana Santos, Anthony Hevia, Antigona Unldreaj, Arash Aghagol, Arezoo Abdollahi, Aycha Tammour, Azadeh HajiHosseini, Bahareh Behroozi, Benjamin Ajibade, Bharat Saxena, Carlos Muñoz Ferrandis, Daniel McDuff, Danish Contractor, David Lansky, Davis David, Douwe Kiela, Duong A. Nguyen, Edward Tan, Emi Baylor, Ezinwanne Ozoani, Fatima Mirza, Frankline Ononiwu, Habib Rezanejad, Hessie Jones, Indrani Bhattacharya, Irene Solaiman, Irina Sedenko, Isar Nejadgholi, Jesse Passmore, Josh Seltzer, Julio Bonis Sanz, Livia Dutra, Mairon Samagaio, Maraim Elbadri, Margot Mieskes, Marissa Gerchick, Martha Akinlolu, Michael McKenna, Mike Qiu, Muhammed Ghauri, Mykola Burynok, Nafis Abrar, Nazneen Rajani, Nour Elkott, Nour Fahmy, Olanrewaju Samuel, Ran An, Rasmus Kromann, Ryan Hao, Samira Alizadeh, Sarmad Shubber, Silas Wang, Sourav Roy, Sylvain Viguier, Thanh Le, Tobi Oyebade, Trieu Le, Yoyo Yang, Zach Nguyen, Abhinav Ramesh Kashyap, Alfredo Palasciano, Alison Callahan, Anima Shukla, Antonio Miranda-Escalada, Ayush Singh, Benjamin Beilharz, Bo Wang, Caio Brito, Chenxi Zhou, Chirag Jain, Chuxin Xu, Clémentine Fourrier, Daniel León Periñán, Daniel Molano, Dian Yu, Enrique Manjavacas, Fabio Barth, Florian Fuhrimann, Gabriel Altay, Giyaseddin Bayrak, Gully Burns, Helena U. Vrabec, Imane Bello, Ishani Dash, Jihyun Kang, John Giorgi, Jonas Golde, Jose David Posada, Karthik Rangasai Sivaraman, Lokesh Bulchandani, Lu Liu, Luisa Shinzato, Madeleine Hahn de Bykhovetz, Maiko Takeuchi, Marc Pàmies, Maria A Castillo, Marianna Nezhurina, Mario Sänger, Matthias Samwald, Michael Cullan, Michael Weinberg, Michiel De Wolf, Mina Mihaljcic, Minna Liu, Moritz Freidank, Myungsun Kang, Natasha Seelam, Nathan Dahlberg, Nicholas Michio Broad, Nikolaus Muellner, Pascale Fung, Patrick Haller, Ramya Chandrasekhar, Renata Eisenberg, Robert Martin, Rodrigo Canalli, Rosaline Su, Ruisi Su, Samuel Cahyawijaya, Samuele Garda, Shlok S Deshmukh, Shubhanshu Mishra, Sid Kiblawi, Simon Ott, Sinee Sang-aroonsiri, Srishti Kumar, Stefan Schweter, Sushil Bharati, Tanmay Laud, Théo Gigant, Tomoya Kainuma, Wojciech Kusa, Yanis Labrak, Yash Shailesh Bajaj, Yash Venkatraman, Yifan Xu, Yingxin Xu, Yu Xu, Zhe Tan, Zhongli Xie, Zifan Ye, Mathilde Bras, Younes Belkada, and Thomas Wolf. 2023. Bloom: A 176b-parameter open-access multilingual language model.

Linting Xue, Noah Constant, Adam Roberts, Mihir Kale, Rami Al-Rfou, Aditya Siddhant, Aditya Barua, and Colin Raffel. 2021. mt5: A massively multilingual pre-trained text-to-text transformer.

Denny Zhou, Nathanael Scharli, Le Hou, Jason Wei, Nathan Scales, Xuezhi Wang, Dale Schuurmans, Claire Cui, Olivier Bousquet, Quoc Le, and Ed Chi. 2023. LEAST-TO-MOST PROMPTING ENABLES COMPLEX REASONING IN LARGE LANGUAGE MODELS.

Inductive Bias Is in the Eye of the Beholder

Michael Wilson[1] **Robert Frank**[2]
[1] Department of Linguistics & Cognitive Science, University of Delaware
[2] Department of Linguistics, Yale University
mawilson@udel.edu bob.frank@yale.edu

Abstract

Due to the finite nature of any evidence used in learning, systematic generalization is crucially reliant on the presence of inductive bias (Mitchell, 1980). We examine inductive biases in different types of sequence-to-sequence neural network models, including CNNs, LSTMs (with and without attention), and transformers, inspired by Kharitonov and Chaabouni (2021). Crucially, however, we consider a wider range of possible inductive biases than their study did. Investigating preferences for hierarchical generalization compared to other types of generalization, we find that, contrary to their results, transformers display no preference for hierarchical generalization, but instead prefer a counting strategy. We also investigate biases toward different types of compositionality. By controlling for a confound in Kharitonov and Chaabouni (2021)'s test set, we find much less consistent generalization overall, and find that a large number of responses were among types other than the two types of generalization they considered. Nevertheless, we observe consistent compositional generalization to held out combinations of primitives and functions on a SCAN task (Lake and Baroni, 2017) by models of all types, but only when primitives occur with other functions in the training set. The pattern of success indicates generalization in models of these types is highly sensitive to distributional properties of their training data.

1 Introduction

Learners, both human and machine, systematically generalize from finite sets of data, and it is such generalization that makes them such effective agents. Hupkes et al. (2023a,b) review the wealth of work focused on understanding the efficacy of different models for different types of generalization in NLP tasks. As Mitchell (1980) notes, the kind of systematic generalization we hope our models will show is only possible in the presence of *inductive bias*, a preference for some generalization over others. Inductive bias can derive from inherent properties of a model or from previous training. In this paper, we focus on the former. While such inherent inductive bias can be read off to a reasonable degree from the structure of a symbolic model, it is much less easy to understand the biases of a neural network architecture trained with some variant of backpropagation.

Work that documents variation among models in their ability to solve a certain NLP task can be understood as illuminating inductive biases in these models: ones that fare better are more biased toward the correct solution (modulo training differences). Yet because of the complexity of most such tasks, it is typically difficult to identify the specific preferences that lead to a model's generalization behavior. The recent work of Kharitonov and Chaabouni (2021, henceforth KC) aims to avoid this issue by focusing on carefully controlled induction problems, which we can think of as "model induction organisms," where the range of solutions is limited. We aim to build on KC's important groundwork, focusing on two of the tasks that they proposed: Hierarchical-or-Linear and Composition-or-Memorization. We show that the evaluation of model behavior and assessment of inductive bias with even apparently trivial tasks requires great care. In particular, assessing inductive bias requires the consideration of the widest possible range of possible hypotheses, and failing to do so can lead to over- or under-estimating inductive bias for a certain type of hypothesis. In addition, we demonstrate that the process of constructing such model organism tasks must avoid the presence of quirks that lead even appropriately biased models astray.

2 Experiment 1: Hierarchy vs. Counting

In experiment 1, we adapt KC's **hierarchical-or-linear** task to further explore the question of whether any of a range of model architectures displays a bias toward hierarchical generalizations.

Proceedings of the 1st GenBench Workshop on (Benchmarking) Generalisation in NLP, pages 152–162
December 6, 2023

2.1 Materials & methods

In this task, we train sequence-to-sequence models on four example mappings of the form $x^d y x^d \to y$, where $x, y \in \{a, b\}$ and $d = 4$. This describes the following four pairs of inputs and outputs.

1. Input: *aaaaaaaaa*; Output: *a*
2. Input: *aaaabaaaa*; Output: *b*
3. Input: *bbbbbbbbb*; Output: *b*
4. Input: *bbbbabbbb*; Output: *a*

As KC observe, this training set is consistent with multiple rules characterizing the mapping between inputs to outputs. A **hierarchical** rule could assign to the input a center-embedded structure that associates matching symbols in the prefix and suffix, so that the target output is the most deeply embedded element, i.e., the middle symbol. A **linear** rule instead identifies the output through its absolute sequential position in the source, in this case the fifth symbol. A third rule that KC do not consider involves a **counting** strategy, where the output is the symbol that occurs least frequently, but at least once, in the source.

KC's test set went beyond this training set to include inputs of the form $x^m y x^m$ for $m \in [2, 6]$. This set of inputs allows the hierarchical and linear rules to be distinguished: the former would yield output y, while the latter would yield whatever element occurs in fifth position. This set does not, however, allow the counting rule to be distinguished from the hierarchical rule, which would both predict output y. As a result, our testing regime evaluated models on outputs of the form $x^m y x^n$, where $m \geq 0$, $n \geq 0$, and $m + n = d$, for $d \in [2, 6]$, which includes strings like *abbbb*, *babbb*, *bbabb*, etc. To see how this expanded test set distinguishes hierarchical, linear, and counting rules, consider the input *abaaa*. Both hierarchical and linear learners would produce *a* (which occurs both as the middle and the fifth symbol in this string). However, a learner with a bias toward counting would produce *b*, the least frequently occurring symbol in the input. On the other hand, an example like *aabaa* would lead hierarchical- and counting-biased learners to produce *b* (the middle and least frequent symbol), while linear learners would produce *a* (the fifth symbol).

We consider two measures of performance. The first we adopt from KC: "fraction of perfect agreement" (FPA). We train and evaluate 100 models of each architecture we consider with different random initial states. FPA is the proportion of these models for which *all* outputs adhere to a particular rule, whether hierarchical, linear, or counting.

Dataset	Architecture	FPA Counting	FPA Linear	FPA Hierar.	PrAg with counting (100 seeds/row)
KC H-or-L	LSTM (w/o attn.)	0.00	0.00	0.00	
	LSTM (w/ attn.)	0.00	0.00	0.00	
	CNN	0.00	0.84	0.00	
	Transformer	0.79	0.00	0.00	
Mirror CFG	LSTM (w/o attn.)	0.00	–	0.00	
	LSTM (w/ attn.)	0.00	–	0.00	
	CNN	0.00	–	0.00	
	Transformer	1.00	–	0.00	
Mirror CFG (brackets)	LSTM (w/o attn.)	0.00	–	0.00	
	LSTM (w/ attn.)	0.00	–	0.00	
	CNN	0.00	–	0.74	
	Transformer	0.70	–	0.00	
Mirror PCFG	LSTM (w/o attn.)	0.00	–	0.00	
	LSTM (w/ attn.)	0.00	–	0.00	
	CNN	0.00	–	0.00	
	Transformer	0.95	–	0.00	
Mirror PCFG (brackets)	LSTM (w/o attn.)	0.00	–	0.00	
	LSTM (w/ attn.)	0.00	–	0.00	
	CNN	0.00	–	0.55	
	Transformer	0.18	–	0.00	

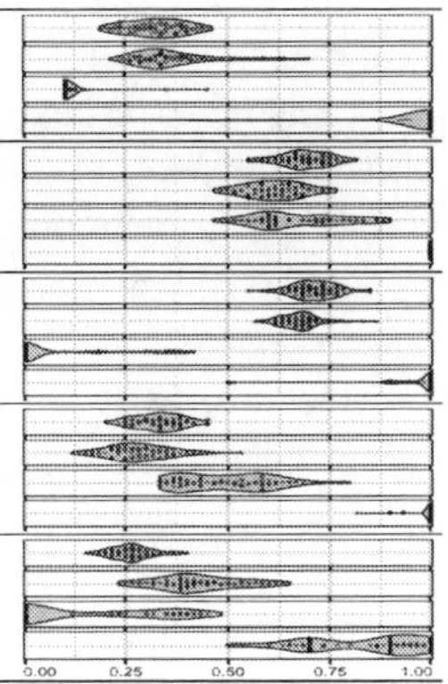

Table 1: Results of experiment 1 and follow-up experiments. Overlapping points are jittered on the *y*-axis.

Our second measure is the proportion of agreement (PrAg) with a particular generalization for individual examples in our test set in a single model. Note that for this task, no example can be entirely unambiguous due to the simplicity of the training language: if one response unambiguously signals the counting generalization (e.g., *baaaa* $\to$ *b*), then the other possible response, *a*, is compatible with both the linear and hierarchical generalizations. For this reason, for this initial task, we provide plots showing only the PrAg with the counting generalization as compared to the hierarchical generalization out of examples where the two would predict different responses.

We train the same types of networks as KC: CNNs, LSTMs (with and without attention), and transformers, using the same hyperparameters; see KC for network architecture and training details.[1]

2.2 Results

Results for experiment 1 are shown in the first set of rows in table 1 (under KC H-or-L). Notably, no model consistently generalizes in accordance with the hierarchical rule on our test set. While we observe, like KC, that CNNs display an inductive bias toward linear generalizations, we find quite different results for transformers: rather than a hierarchical bias, it appears that they actually display a bias toward counting or determination of majority

[1] Our data and code are available at github.com/mawilson1234/FIND.

(Merrill and Sabharwal, 2023), revealed by examining performance on a test set that distinguishes these competing possibilities.

The PrAg results reflect this bias for CNNs and Transformers. LSTMs show a moderate but not overwhelming proportion of counting responses—less than might have been expected from the results of Weiss et al. (2018). However, the plots in the table of necessity only present PrAg with the counting generalization for examples whose possible responses distinguish counting, on the one hand, from hierarchical or linear strategies, on the other. This means these plots alone do not reveal whether LSTMs tend to produce more linear or hierarchical responses in cases that could distinguish those two possibilities. When we consider such examples, we in fact find that LSTMs of both types produce more responses consistent with the hierarchical strategy compared to the linear strategy (50%ile for hierar. responses for LSTMs w/o attn.: 0.875; LSTMs w/ attn.: 0.75), which echoes what KC found using their description length-based measure.

2.3 Attempts to induce hierarchical generalization

The results of experiment 1 indicate that no model architecture exhibits a strong bias toward hierarchical generalizations when we evaluate behavior against a wider space of hypotheses. However, the success of various model architectures, especially transformers, on linguistic data raises the question of whether a richer kind of training data could be sufficient to induce such a bias. In particular, language is replete with rules and constraints that make crucial reference to hierarchical structure. The fact that large pre-trained transformer models have shown general success on tasks probing their sensitivity to such structure clearly shows us that they are able to learn hierarchical generalizations (Mueller et al., 2022). Such large pre-trained models receive input much richer than the four examples given to the models in experiment 1.

Rather than attempting to replicate this full richness, we ask instead whether three changes that begin to approach the ways in which language is richer than the original four-example training set could suffice to induce hierarchical generalizations as opposed to counting generalizations.

Variable length We enrich our training set, so that it is now described by the following recursive phrase structure rules:

- $\mathrm{S} \rightarrow \mathrm{a\ S'\ a} \mid \mathrm{b\ S'\ b}$
- $\mathrm{S'} \rightarrow \mathrm{a\ S'\ a} \mid \mathrm{b\ S'\ b} \mid \mathrm{a} \mid \mathrm{b}$

We refer to this as the "Mirror CFG" set. We cap the maximum length of an example to 11, and randomly generate 2 examples for each length in {3, 5, 7, 9, 11} for each center symbol *a* or *b*.[2] We also include two instances of each of these lengths where all symbols are identical. For examples where symbols were not all identical, we ensured that the center symbol was also the least frequently occurring symbol for each example. This creates a set of 40 sentences. We train models using the same hyperparameters as above, with all 40 examples run as a single batch. Note that including differing example lengths means that a linear hypothesis, in which an element at a fixed position is output, is no longer compatible with the training set.

Our test set consists of all examples of lengths {3, 5, 7, 9, 11} for which the two possible responses distinguish between the counting and hierarchical strategies (i.e., for which the middle symbol and the least frequent symbol are different). For the test set, we ensured that the center symbol was always the *most* frequently occurring symbol, which will allow us to distinguish the hierarchical and linear generalization strategies. Because of this property of our test items, a model with low PrAg score for counting will have a correspondingly high score for the hierarchical hypothesis. Results are shown in the second row of table 1. Both FPA and PrAg measures indicate that all architectures show a bias toward counting, transformers most strongly.

Statistical signature of recursion Next, we consider a dataset generated by a probabilistic version of the grammar above, where the probability of recursion is 0.5, which we call the "Mirror PCFG" set. This provides information not only about examples of different lengths, but also about the relative frequencies of different lengths. The resulting geometric distribution over example lengths is consistent with generation by a recursive process: at each point in generation the structure can either recurse with probability with p or stop with probability $1-p$, resulting in structures with k levels of recursion being generated with probability $p^k(1-p)$. If each step of recursion introduces a fixed amount of material, this will yield a geometric distribution on string lengths. We cap examples to at most length

[2]The 2 examples per length were randomly generated only once, and reused for every architecture/seed.

11, and otherwise randomly generate 10 examples for each center symbol in {a, b}, and 10 examples where all symbols are identical for each symbol in {a, b} (40 total). We train the same way as before, and use the same Mirror CFG test set.

Results are again shown in table 1. Interestingly, the CNNs and LSTMs now show a bias toward hierarchical generalization revealed by the PrAg measure, though none generalized consistently. Nevertheless, transformers remain strongly biased toward the counting generalization.

Explicit Encoding of Structure Finally, we modified the previous two datasets adding left and right brackets to mark constituency (e.g., *babab* becomes [*b*[*a*[*b*]*a*]*b*]). We also added brackets to the test set. As pointed out by an anonymous reviewer, this means there is now a *linear* way of producing a "hierarchical" response—choose the symbol with a preceding "[" and a following "]". Our goal was to see how far we needed to go to produce any kind of generalization consistent with hierarchical structure—even if such a generalization could also be a linear generalization. In other words, if we make the hierarchical generalization "easier," will the models be more likely to take the bait?

Table 1 shows that adding brackets changes the behavior of the CNNs, which show a bias toward the "hierarchical" generalization. We suspect this sharp change is due to the fact that in the bracketed dataset, the "hierarchical" generalization can now be expressed in linear terms (as detailed above). What we find more interesting is that in spite of the availability of this simple strategy, no substantial change in overall bias is seen for LSTMs or transformers—the transformers remain biased toward a counting strategy, and the LSTMs' preferences do not change.[3] For the constant-frequency training set, the LSTMs retain their counting bias; for the PCFG training set, the LSTMs retain their hierarchical bias without much change. The transformers in both cases retain a bias toward the counting generalization, though it is somewhat less pronounced with the addition of brackets.

2.4 Discussion

Experiment 1 showed that despite KC's claims, transformers do not have a bias toward hierarchical generalizations. When we considered a richer set of possible generalizations, we found that transformers favor counting generalizations over hierarchical generalizations when both are compatible with the input. This shows the importance of considering ambiguities in the hypothesis space when discussing inductive biases.

This result led us to see whether we could enrich the training set to induce a hierarchical bias. We considered two simple changes that could make the simple training set more like human language: first, we considered inputs of different lengths described by a CFG. Second, we considered inputs of different lengths generated by a recursive PCFG so that shorter strings were more frequent than longer strings. Finally, we considered both of these manipulations with the addition of brackets in the input that marked the underlying hierarchical structure.

Two manipulations made a difference. First, going from a uniform distribution over example lengths to a geometric distribution of lengths produced by a PCFG reversed the bias of the CNNs and LSTMs from counting to hierarchical, with the change being more noticeable for LSTMs. Second, adding brackets made CNNs strongly biased toward apparently hierarchical responses, but had relatively little effect on other model types.[4] Most interestingly, despite the high success of transformer-based models on linguistic tasks that require reference to hierarchical structure, we found that none of our manipulations sufficed to induce a hierarchical bias in these models—they remained stubbornly in favor of the counting generalization.

3 Experiment 2: Compositionality

In experiment 2, we examine the question of whether different model architectures display a bias toward compositional generalizations of various types. By "compositional," we mean a process whose output is a function of its individual input symbols and their mode of combination (Szabó, 2022). This question has been explored using a variety of tasks and datasets, e.g., SCAN (Lake and Baroni, 2017) and COGS (Kim and Linzen, 2020a), which both explore the problem of assigning structured semantic interpretations to English sentences. While offering useful measures of compositional generalization, the complexity of these datasets makes it difficult to assess the propensity for com-

[3]See also McCoy et al. (2020) for a similar lack of change in LSTM performance in the face of explicit evidence about hierarchical structure.

[4]As noted above, the presence of the brackets gives rise a non-hierarchical alternative, which the CNN may be exploiting.

positional generalization in its simplest guise. Here, we focus on a distilled task probing compositional generalization proposed by KC, which they call **Composition-or-Memorization**. This task targets compositional generalization in a way that is not specific to its role in natural language.

3.1 Materials & methods

In KC's **Composition-or-Memorization** task, models are trained on two types of examples. In one type, input symbols (which we represent as natural numbers) are presented in isolation in the input and are mapped to corresponding output symbols (which we represent as lower case letters) in a one-to-one way. Thus an input symbol a would be mapped to the corresponding output symbol A (which we encode as the corresponding upper case letters). The examples are "non-compositional examples". For a second type of input, there is a modifier, F, which precedes one of these input symbols. Under the intended interpretation of our dataset, F is interpreted like "thrice," so that input $F\ a$ is mapped to a three copies of the corresponding output symbol, namely $A\ A\ A$ ("compositional examples"). For experiment 2, we consider the same model architectures as in experiment 1, and train 100 random seeds/architecture.

KC vary the number of input symbols that are presented in compositional form in the training data, and consider how models perform on held-out compositional examples. They define M as the number of distinct compositional examples in the training set, and N as the number of distinct input (and output) symbols that occur in non-compositional examples in the training set (in all cases, such symbols are a superset of the ones that occur in compositional examples). They consider $N = 40$ with $M \in \{6, 24, 36\}$; that is, they train learners on all 40 non-compositional examples and M compositional examples.[5] Their test set consists of all unobserved compositional examples within the 40 symbol range. For example, when $M = 36$, their test set consists of the four inputs $F\ x_{37}$, $F\ x_{38}$, $F\ x_{39}$, $F\ x_{40}$; when $M = 24$, their test set consists of sixteen inputs, and so on.

A problem with this approach is that it makes it easier for a model to show perfect agreement with a generalization as the number of training examples increases, because this corresponds to the size of the test set decreasing. In other words, a model trained with $M = 36$ need only consistently generalize on 4 examples to be counted as perfectly agreeing with a particular generalization. A model trained with $M = 24$ would instead need to consistently generalize on 16 examples, and so on, making perfect agreement more difficult to achieve.

To address this, we increase N to 100. We still train on $M \in \{6, 24, 36\}$ and all non-compositional examples. However, we test only on compositional examples from $F\ x_i$ for $i \in [50, 100]$, i.e., compositional examples that did not occur for any value of M. This means that the size of the test set remains identical for all M, and eliminates the confound between M and the size of the test set.

3.2 Results

KC evaluate model performance by considering two possible hypotheses. "Composition" for them means that a model generalizes such that $F\ a \rightarrow A\ A\ A$. In contrast, they interpret "memorization" to indicate that a model produces the single symbol output associated with the non-modifier input symbol, i.e., $F\ a \rightarrow A$. However, this is certainly not the full space of possible hypotheses, and narrowly restricts what constitutes compositional behavior. For instance, suppose that the model learns that F means "produce any two identical symbols, followed by the symbol a maps to in non-compositional examples" (i.e, $F\ a = B\ B\ A$, with B an output symbol other than the one associated with input a). This is also a kind of compositional generalization: the output related to the complex input is a function of its individual input symbols and their mode of combination (Szabó, 2022). In this case, $[\![F]\!] = \lambda x.B\ B\ x$ and $[\![a]\!] = A$ with concatenation associated with function application. Following this intuition, we consider as compositional any mapping in which the input a is associated with at least one occurrence of A in the output, and which includes at least two other symbols in output, possibly, but not necessarily identical to A. Many other generalizations are possible under this interpretation of compositionality, even if they don't correspond to the "thrice" interpretation, i.e., $[\![F]\!] = \lambda x.x\ x\ x$. Determining that models fail to generalize according to one compositional interpretation does not preclude the possibility that they

[5] Of course, we have presented this task as mapping lowercase letters to uppercase letters, and English would only provide a maximum of 26 possible input-output pairs for this task—fewer than the 40 described. In practice, we used the natural numbers as input symbols, and the natural numbers prefixed with O as output symbols, to avoid this complication. We use the alphabetic notation for presentational convenience.

have generalized compositionally according to another.

For this reason, we classify responses according to a considerably wider range of possible templates. In particular, we consider all ways in which symbols in the output might be identical or differ for numbers of output symbols from 1–3.[6] We define A as the output symbol corresponding to input symbol a, and B, C, D as symbols other than A that do not correspond to a. For instance, the generalization $F\ a = B\ B\ A$ means the model produced two (identical) non-A symbols, followed by the symbol corresponding to a; while $F\ a = B\ C\ A$ means that the model produced two (distinct) non-A symbols, followed by the symbol corresponding to a. Non-A symbols B, C, and D identify identical output symbols within a response, but may differ across responses from the same model.[7] Both of these responses would, we argue, qualify as compositional in a broader sense, even if they don't instantiate the "thrice" interpretation: the output is a function of both input symbols, with a being mapped to A, and F requiring an output sequence of length 3.

We report the same measures as for experiment 1: the fraction of perfect agreement (Table 2), and the proportion of productions matching a particular generalization (Figure 1). Due to the high number (22) of generalizations we consider, for FPA we only report non-zero results. Only CNNs ever responded completely consistently, and even then, only a very small number of seeds did so (3 of 300 models). Instead, the vast majority of models produced responses consistent with a variety of answer types. Making the size of the test set consistent for all M appears to have made it harder for models to consistently generalize, as expected.

The distribution of response proportions (figure 1) reveals a more nuanced picture of model preferences. Both types of LSTMs have a preference for non-compositional $F\ a = B\ B\ B$ responses for $M = 6$, with KC's memorization $F\ a = A$ responses also among the more common. As M increases, however, the proportion of the (compositional) $F\ a = A\ B\ B$ responses increases, with LSTMs with attention appearing to have equal preference for $F\ a = B\ B\ B$ and the compositional $F\ a = A\ B\ B$ when $M = 36$. CNNs, in contrast, display a wider

Architecture	M	Generalization	FPA
CNN	6	$F\ a = B\ B\ B$	0.02
	24	$F\ a = A\ A\ A$	0.01

Table 2: FPA results from experiment 2. Architectures, M, and generalizations not shown have FPA $= 0.00$.

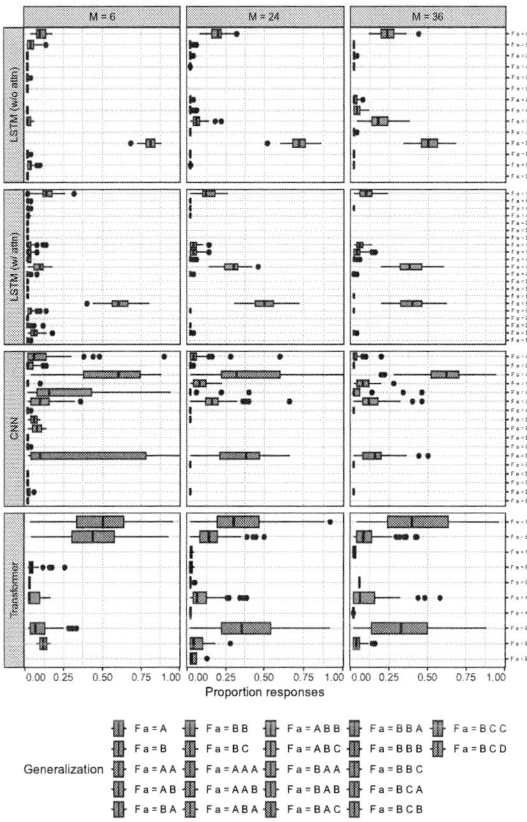

Figure 1: Distributions of PrAg with generalizations of up to 3 symbols in experiment 2. Within each row of plots, generalizations are omitted from the y-axis if no model of that architecture produced any response fitting that template for any M.

[6]Models sometimes produced longer responses (up to the maximum length of 200 symbols). We present results for responses up to at most 3 symbols for perspicuity. In practice, longer responses were entirely absent from CNNs (0% of responses), and almost entirely absent from LSTMs w/o attention ($M = 6$: 0.04%, $M = 24$: 0.16%, $M = 36$: 0%) and LSTMs w/attention ($M = 6$: 0.04%, $M = 24$: 0.08%, $M = 36$: 0.04%). Consequently, our analysis for these networks is essentially exhaustive. For transformers, longer responses were more common, but still a minority, with differences depending on M: longer responses accounted for 29.2% of responses for $M = 6$, 9.2% of responses for $M = 24$, and 2.5% of responses for $M = 36$. Of these, for $M = 6$ the most common lengths were 200 (the maximum length, 20.9% of responses) and 4 (2.86%). For $M = 24$, 1.3% of responses were length-200 and 7.06% were length-4; and for $M = 36$, 0.46% of responses were length-200 and 1.86% were length-4.

[7]In the computation of the FPA measure, we did not require that a model make use of a consistent choice of symbols. That is, in order to count as consistently $F\ a = B\ B\ A$, the model's choice of B in the output could vary by response, but was required to be distinct from A. Since the PrAg measure was calculated at the level of the individual trial, no consistent choice of non-A symbols was required.

range of common response types for smaller M, but as M increases, the compositional "thrice" response $F\ a = A\ A\ A$ becomes the modal response. Finally, transformers with $M = 6$ show equal preference for non-compositional $F\ a = A$ and $F\ a = B$, but with the preference for $F\ a = B$ being replaced with a preference for the similarly non-compositional $F\ a = B\ B\ B$ for $M \in \{24, 36\}$.

Non-A symbols for responses of length > 1 overwhelmingly were drawn from the symbols seen with compositional training examples, with the mean proportion of these symbols in outputs with non-A symbols uniformly being between $[0.976, 0.999]$. However, we did not observe any tendency for particular models to use the same non-A symbols across responses.

In spite of our use of the PrAg measure as opposed to KC's minimal description length-based measure, our results are generally compatible with theirs, especially when we limit our focus to the two hypotheses they considered, namely $F\ a = A$ (their "memorization") and $F\ a = A\ A\ A$ (their "composition"). For LSTMs, KC found a general preference for memorization over composition, except for LSTMs with attention with $M = 36$, where the preference is (barely) reversed. In figure 1, we similarly see that the proportion of $F\ a = A$ responses for LSTMs with and without attention is consistently higher than that of the $F\ a = A\ A\ A$ responses. Our more fine grained analysis reveals however that LSTMs show even stronger preferences for $F\ a = B\ B\ B$ or $F\ a = A\ B\ B$ than either of the hypotheses KC considered. As noted above, this latter rule is plausibly interpreted as compositional, as its output does not include a reflection of the input symbol a. This suggests that LSTMs do not show such a uniform dispreference for compositional generalization. For CNNs, KC report a strong preference for composition over memorization for larger values of M, and our Figure 1 reveals the same preference. We note, however, that many of the responses we observed fell into the $F\ a = B\ B\ B$, $F\ a = A\ B\ B$ and $F\ a = A\ B\ A$ categories, of which the former is plausibly non-compositional. Finally, for transformers, KC report a uniform preference for memorization over composition, which we also see in figure 1. Again, Figure 1 reveals that other preferences are often stronger than either of these. Transformers, for $M = 6$, show a nearly equal preference for $F\ a = B$ as compared to KC's memorization hypothesis, and for larger values of M, $F\ a = B\ B\ B$ is comparably frequent to memorization. Nonetheless, these are both plausibly considered non-compositional responses, once again because the output lacks a symbol corresponding to the input a.

To take stock, we see that expanding the space of hypotheses we consider reveals that learners are less likely to generalize consistently. Further, while CNNs retained a bias for $F\ a = A\ A\ A$ responses with larger Ms, LSTMs and transformers behave considerably differently from what KC reported.

3.3 Inducing compositional generalization

Why are the networks we studied in our previous experiment resistant to systematic compositional generalization? This seems surprising in the face of apparent compositionality in state of the art language models, which are constructed from some of the same architectures we have explored.

One difference between our experiments and such models lies in the training dataset. Our dataset is extremely simple, consisting of single symbol input-output mappings and one compositional operator. It is possible that a model trained on a rich variety of structures, each showing the kind of combinatorics associated with compositionality, could evince more compositional generalization.[8]

To explore this possibility, we conducted an evaluation of the SCAN dataset (Lake and Baroni, 2018). SCAN consists of a finite set of English-like inputs that represent intended movements of a robot, and outputs are step-by-step instructions for achieving these movements. SCAN includes a fair number of different predicates that can combine in different ways. This permits a training set to exhibit broad evidence for compositional combination, and allows us to test for systematic compositional generalization. We experiment with two splits of the SCAN dataset. The first is the `addprim_jump` split of Lake and Baroni (2018). In this split, the training set includes the full range of possible sentences from SCAN, except for those involving compositional uses of the primitive `jump`. The test set consists of all compositional sentences containing this primitive. This split poses the question of whether a model learns to generalize the use of `jump` to all positions in which other simple predicates occur.

Our second split, `addtwicethrice_jump`, comprises a training set that includes all sentences without `jump` as well as sentences in which `jump` is

[8]See Patel et al. (2022) for a related proposal.

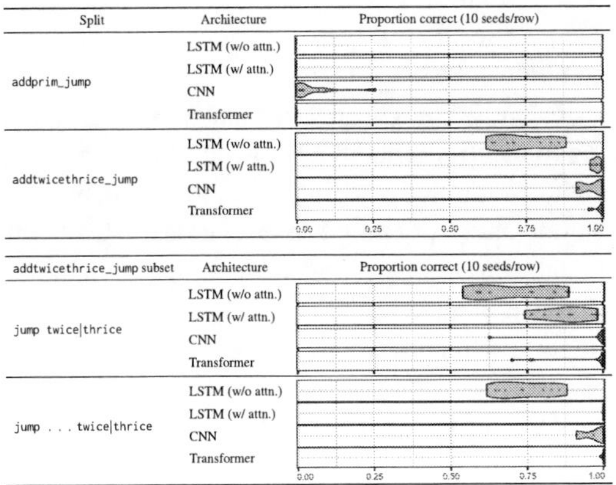

Table 3: Results of SCAN experiments. Overlapping points are jittered on the y-axis.

not under the scope of `twice` or `thrice`, operators whose outputs require repeating the sequence of instructions corresponding to the trajectory to their left 2 or 3 times. The test set contains all inputs where `jump` occurs under the scope of `twice` or `thrice`. This means that, unlike the `addprim_jump` split, `jump` does occurs in the training set in the presence of other compositional operators, just not with `twice` or `thrice`. This avoids the potential problem that a model might learn `jump` has the distinctive property of only appearing by itself.

In their appendix D, KC report results from the `addprim_jump` split. Because we were unable to determine all details of their training regimen from their description, we first repeated their experiment of the `addprim_jump` split. For LSTMs and transformers, we use the architectures they reported. For CNNs, we use models with 5 encoder layers, 1 decoder layer, and a kernel size of 8, the best performing of their CNN models. We trained 10 random initializations per architecture on each split, using 1000 batches sampled with replacement for 500 epochs, for a total of $500,000$ weight updates. Batch sizes matched KC's (LSTMs, CNNs: 16; transformers: 256). We used the same procedure for our `addtwicethrice_jump` split. Accuracy on the training set was uniformly high: the model with the lowest performance achieved 98.2% accuracy on the training set, with most achieving 100%.

Results from these experiments appear in the upper half of table 3. While we did not replicate KC's results on the `addprim_jump` split exactly, we similarly find that on this split, only CNNs show any sort of generalization, though even their performance is quite low. However, the picture is quite different for the `addtwicethrice_jump` split, where all models generalize correctly to most examples. It seems that showing `jump` in a range of compositional contexts helped the models generalize to this predicate's occurrences in other compositional contexts, compared to when we show the models `jump` in only non-compositional contexts.

To investigate this difference further, we consider performance on two subsets of the `addtwicethrice_jump` test set: (1) a subset comprising all examples where `jump` occurs immediately preceding `twice` or `thrice` in the input, and (2) the complement of set (1).[9] On the face of it, test set (1) seems simpler and might yield better performance, as its examples involve less depth of embedding. However, the results (lower half of table 3) reveal the opposite pattern: performance tends to be worse on examples where `jump` occurs immediately adjacent to `twice` and `thrice`.

We hypothesize this is due to models' dependence on (irrelevant) surface properties of the input in the training set: in the `addtwicethrice_jump` split, the bigrams `jump twice` and `jump thrice` never occur—they have a probability of 0. However, all other bigrams permitted in SCAN occur in the training set of this split. So, even though this training set is sufficient to induce compositional generalization, the presence of non-occurring bigrams yields less accurate performance.[10] The data augmentation reported in Andreas (2020), which also reduces non-occurring bigrams in test items, has a similarly salutary impact on generalization. While speculative, this could explain the sharp distinction between the `addprim_jump` and `addtwicethrice_jump` splits, since in the former, no bigram including `jump` occurs in the training set, since it occurs only in isolation. A similar line of reasoning could be behind the poor compositional performance we saw in Section 3.2.

4 Related Work in Architectural Inductive Bias

Here, we briefly discuss work on inductive bias in neural network models that focuses particularly on those aspects of inductive bias that are traceable to

[9]Note that in set (2), `jump` is still under the scope of `twice` or `thrice` in each example, just not adjacent to either, as in `jump opposite right twice`.

[10]We do not consider bigrams privileged in this regard; this is just the simplest way of characterizing the divide given our training datasets. We might expect a more nuanced picture if we take into account n-grams with $n > 2$, though local relationships will need to play a more important role in order to explain the contrasts reported in the lower part of Table 3.

network architecture; see Hupkes et al. (2023a,b) for a more thorough review.

In some cases, inductive biases have been intentionally built in to particular architectures. The parameter sharing and filter structure of CNNs leads directly to a bias for translation invariance and feature locality, which are useful in a variety of tasks (LeCun and Bengio, 1998; Mitchell, 2017). The inclusion of gates with multiplicative interactions in LSTMs (Hochreiter and Schmidhuber, 1997) explicitly addressed deficiencies of RNNs in modeling the long-distance dependencies found in natural language (Elman, 1990). Weiss et al. (2018) discuss the fact that unbounded growth in LSTMs' hidden state vectors leads to a counting bias.

None of these biases relate explicitly to the questions of structural or compositional generalization that we have explored in this paper. Research on language-related biases has explored structural generalization. White and Cotterell (2021) train LSTMs and Transformers on synthetic corpora that exhibit a range of word order patterns, some attested in natural languages, others not. LSTMs, unlike Transformers, showed a preference for certain word order patterns over others, but neither showed a bias toward attested natural language patterns. McCoy et al. (2020) study the ability of different architectures to generalize structurally-defined mappings between sentences. LSTMs, RNNs, and GRUs with different attention mechanisms failed to generalize structurally, preferring linear generalizations. Petty and Frank (2021) find an even more extreme failure for Transformer models. McCoy et al. only find a bias toward structural generalization in models with explicitly hierarchically-structured recurrence (Chen et al., 2017).

To detect bias toward compositionality, researchers have explored tasks requiring the mapping of a natural language input to an interpretation of some sort, including SCAN (Lake and Baroni, 2017), PCFG SET (Hupkes et al., 2020), COGS (Kim and Linzen, 2020b), and SLOG (Li et al., 2023). Success on these datasets is informative about the kinds of generalizations that networks are capable of. Yet their complexity, compared to the tasks we explored, can make it difficult to identify reasons for success or failure. Indeed, modifications to non-crucial properties of a dataset can yield quite different results (Wu et al., 2023). Of course, considering complex cases is important, as we have indeed seen in Section 3.3 above. However, we see the study of simple tasks as providing complementary understanding.

Recently, it has been found that experiments aiming to identify inductive biases must also carefully control for training regimen. For example, training without early stopping can lead to qualitatively different patterns of generalization through "grokking" (Csordás et al., 2021; Power et al., 2022). It will be important to understand the range of applicability of grokking and the like, as well as the challenge such results pose for assessing inductive bias.

5 Conclusion

A finite set of data may be consistent with an infinite number of possible generalizations (Hume, 1739). It is precisely for this reason that studies of inductive bias must proceed with great care to avoid adducing support for the existence of certain kinds of inductive biases prematurely.

Taking this idea to heart, we found that the KC's claim that transformers *tout court* display hierarchical bias to be premature. Instead, we found their behavior to be most consistent with a counting-based strategy.

Similarly, we found that considering a more consistent test set when assessing compositionality led us to find less support for consistent generalization than KC. Though the pattern of results we found was consistent with theirs when limiting our focus to the hypotheses they considered, we found that expanding the range of possible hypotheses revealed a more nuanced picture.

Nevertheless, we found there is hope for inducing compositional generalization: when we ensure that distributional properties of the training set are more like the those in the test set, compositional generalization appears easily achieved.

This suggests low performance on a particular task may be due to irrelevant factors, like surface-level distributional properties of a training dataset. It may not be that a particular model cannot achieve high levels of success on certain tasks due to the inherent complexity of whatever pattern of behavior the task aims to measure, but because it has fixated on some accidental, irrelevant generalization in its training data that impedes its recognizing the correct generalization. Alleviating models' propensity toward fixation on such irrelevancies, perhaps by altering their training data in systematic ways (as in our SCAN experiments), may prove useful in improving their performance in various domains.

Limitations

The small scale of the datasets used here to train the networks represent both an advantage and limitation. While this scale limits information given to the model during training, the unusually small dataset can lead the model to detect and induce unusual distributional properties as relevant to the task at hand. Indeed, we have seen an instance of this problem in experiment 2. Though there is no magic bullet for avoiding this issue we suspect, it is one that future work that seeks to develop "model induction organisms" will need to take into account.

Experiments reported here all made use of the same procedure for parameter optimization, namely Adam (Kingma and Ba, 2014), and therefore differences observed between the models must be due to their structure. However, it is possible that different optimization methods may lead to different inductive biases for the same network architectures.

Acknowledgments

This work was made possible by support from National Science Foundation grant BCS-1919321.

References

Jacob Andreas. 2020. Good-enough compositional data augmentation. In *Proceedings of the 58th Annual Meeting of the Association for Computational Linguistics*, pages 7556–7566. Association for Computational Linguistics.

Huadong Chen, Shujian Huang, David Chiang, and Jiajun Chen. 2017. Improved neural machine translation with a syntax-aware encoder and decoder. In *Proceedings of the 55th Annual Meeting of the Association for Computational Linguistics (Volume 1: Long Papers)*, pages 1936–1945, Vancouver, Canada. Association for Computational Linguistics.

Róbert Csordás, Kazuki Irie, and Juergen Schmidhuber. 2021. The devil is in the detail: Simple tricks improve systematic generalization of transformers. In *Proceedings of the 2021 Conference on Empirical Methods in Natural Language Processing*, pages 619–634, Online and Punta Cana, Dominican Republic. Association for Computational Linguistics.

Jeffrey L Elman. 1990. Finding structure in time. *Cognitive science*, 14(2):179–211.

Sepp Hochreiter and Jürgen Schmidhuber. 1997. Long short-term memory. *Neural Computation*, 9(8):1735–1780.

David Hume. 1739. *A Treatise of Human Nature*. Oxford University Press, Oxford.

Dieuwke Hupkes, Verna Dankers, Mul Mathijs, and Elia Bruni. 2020. Compositionality decomposed: How do neural networks generalise? *Journal of Artificial Intelligence Research*, 67:757–795.

Dieuwke Hupkes, Mario Giulianelli, Verna Dankers, Mikel Artetxe, Yanai Elazar, Tiago Pimentel, Christos Christodoulopoulos, Karim Lasri, Naomi Saphra, Arabella Sinclair, Dennis Ulmer, Florian Schottmann, Khuyagbaatar Batsuren, Kaiser Sun, Koustuv Sinha, Leila Khalatbari, Maria Ryskina, Rita Frieske, Ryan Cotterell, and Zhijing Jin. 2023a. State-of-the-art generalisation research in NLP: A taxonomy and review.

Dieuwke Hupkes, Mario Giulianelli, Verna Dankers, Mikel Artetxe, Yanai Elazar, Tiago Pimentel, Christos Christodoulopoulos, Karim Lasri, Naomi Saphra, Arabella Sinclair, Dennis Ulmer, Florian Schottmann, Khuyagbaatar Batsuren, Kaiser Sun, Koustuv Sinha, Leila Khalatbari, Maria Ryskina, Rita Frieske, Ryan Cotterell, and Zhijing Jin. 2023b. A taxonomy and review of generalization research in NLP. *Nature Machine Intelligence*, 5:1161–1174.

Eugene Kharitonov and Rahma Chaabouni. 2021. What they do when in doubt: a study of inductive biases in seq2seq learners. In *International Conference on Learning Representations*.

Najoung Kim and Tal Linzen. 2020a. COGS: a compositional generalization challenge based on semantic interpretation. In *Proceedings of the 2020 Conference on Empirical Methods in Natural Language Processing (EMNLP)*.

Najoung Kim and Tal Linzen. 2020b. COGS: A compositional generalization challenge based on semantic interpretation. In *Proceedings of the 2020 Conference on Empirical Methods in Natural Language Processing (EMNLP)*, pages 9087–9105, Online. Association for Computational Linguistics.

Diederik P Kingma and Jimmy Ba. 2014. Adam: A method for stochastic optimization. *arXiv preprint arXiv:1412.6980*.

Brenden M. Lake and Marco Baroni. 2017. Still not systematic after all these years: On the compositional skills of sequence-to-sequence recurrent networks. *CoRR*, abs/1711.00350.

Brenden M. Lake and Marco Baroni. 2018. Generalization without systematicity: On the compositional skills of sequence-to-sequence recurrent networks. In *Proceedings of the 35th International Conference on Machine Learning*, Stockholm, Sweden.

Yann LeCun and Yoshua Bengio. 1998. *Convolutional Networks for Images, Speech, and Time Series*, page 255–258. MIT Press, Cambridge, MA, USA.

Bingzhi Li, Lucia Donatelli, Alexander Koller, Tal Linzen, Yuekun Yao, and Najoung Kim. 2023. SLOG: A structural generalization benchmark for semantic parsing.

R. Thomas McCoy, Robert Frank, and Tal Linzen. 2020. Does syntax need to grow on trees? Sources of hierarchical inductive bias in sequence-to-sequence networks. *Transactions of the Association for Computational Linguistics*.

William Merrill and Ashish Sabharwal. 2023. A logic for expressing log-precision transformers.

Benjamin R. Mitchell. 2017. *The Spatial Inductive Bias of Deep Learning*. Ph.D. thesis, Johns Hopkins University.

Tom M. Mitchell. 1980. The need for biases in learning generalizations. Technical Report CBM-TR-117, Rutgers University, Department of Computer Science.

Aaron Mueller, Robert Frank, Tal Linzen, Luheng Wang, and Sebastian Schuster. 2022. Coloring the blank slate: Pre-training imparts a hierarchical inductive bias to sequence-to-sequence models. In *Findings of the Association for Computational Linguistics 2022*.

Arkil Patel, Satwik Bhattamishra, Phil Blunsom, , and Navin Goyal. 2022. Revisiting the compositional generalization abilities of neural sequence models. In *Proceedings of the 60th Annual Meeting of the Association for Computational Linguistics (Volume 2: Short Papers)*, pages 424–434.

Jackson Petty and Robert Frank. 2021. Transformers generalize linearly.

Alethea Power, Yuri Burda, Harrison Edwards, Igor Babuschkin, and Vedant Misra. 2022. Grokking: Generalization beyond overfitting on small algorithmic datasets. *CoRR*, abs/2201.02177.

Zoltán Gendler Szabó. 2022. Compositionality. In Edward N. Zalta and Uri Nodelman, editors, *The Stanford Encyclopedia of Philosophy*. Metaphysics Research Lab, Stanford University.

Gail Weiss, Yoav Goldberg, and Eran Yahav. 2018. On the practical computational power of finite precision RNNs for language recognition. In *Proceedings of the 56th Annual Meeting of the Association for Computational Linguistics*, Melbourne.

Jennifer C. White and Ryan Cotterell. 2021. Examining the inductive bias of neural language models with artificial languages. In *Proceedings of the 59th Annual Meeting of the Association for Computational Linguistics and the 11th International Joint Conference on Natural Language Processing (Volume 1: Long Papers)*, pages 454–463, Online. Association for Computational Linguistics.

Zhengxuan Wu, Christopher D. Manning, and Christopher Potts. 2023. ReCOGS: How incidental details of a logical form overshadow an evaluation of semantic interpretation.

GenBench Evaluation Card

Motivation			
Practical	*Cognitive* □ △	*Intrinsic* □ △	*Fairness*

Generalisation type					
Compositional △	*Structural* □	*Cross Task*	*Cross Language*	*Cross Domain*	*Robustness*

Shift type			
Covariate □ △	*Label*	*Full*	*Assumed*

Shift source			
Naturally occurring	*Partitioned natural*	*Generated shift*	*Fully generated* □ △

Shift locus			
Train–test □ △	*Finetune train–test*	*Pretrain–train*	*Pretrain–test*

Blackbird Language Matrices Tasks for Generalization

Paola Merlo, Chunyang Jiang, Giuseppe Samo, Vivi Nastase
University of Geneva
{Chunyang.Jiang, Paola.Merlo, Giuseppe.Samo}@unige.ch
vivi.a.nastase@gmail.com

Abstract

To develop a system with near-human language capabilities, we need to understand current systems' generalisation and compositional abilities. We approach this by generating compositional, structured data, inspired from visual intelligence tests, that depend on the problem-solvers being able to disentangle objects and their absolute and relative properties in a sequence of images. We design an analogous task and develop the corresponding datasets that capture specific linguistic phenomena and their properties. Solving each problem instance depends on detecting the relevant linguistic objects and generative rules of the problem. We propose two datasets modelling two linguistic phenomena – subject-verb agreement in French, and verb alternations in English. The datasets can be used to investigate how LLMs encode linguistic objects, such as phrases, their grammatical and semantic properties, such as number or semantic role, and how such information is combined to correctly solve each problem. Specifically generated error types help investigate the behaviour of the system, which important information it is able to detect, and which structures mislead it.

1 Motivation

The current reported success of large language models (LLMs) is based on computationally expensive algorithms and large amounts of data that are available for only a few, non-representative languages. Such data may also contain biases and imbalances, and its sheer size prevents curation. To be able to build robust models that can learn better from manageable sized data, we need to understand the current systems' generalisation and compositional abilities.

We argue that a system with high language competence and performance, that is able to learn from small amounts of data, and is cross-linguistically valid, should capture the three fundamental properties of human language: (i) human language is described by several abstract levels of representations (e.g. morphological, phonological, syntactic, semantic), mapped onto each other by complex many-to-many rules; (ii) it is compositional; (iii) it is structured.

For GenBench, we propose several datasets under the same umbrella, as they have the same format, but encode different linguistic phenomena, each in a different language – subject verb agreement in French, verb alternations in English. They can be used separately, or in combination, to explore the properties and the generalisation abilities of a LLM in various ways.

- Test whether sentence representations encode the targeted linguistic information.
- Test generalisation when data has different levels of lexical variation.
- Providing probes into how sentence representations encode the targeted information – by studying different minimal architectures that aim to find patterns in pretrained sentence representations.[1]
- Providing cross-linguistic and multi-task probes for detecting how sentence representations encode different kinds of targeted linguistic information. The fact that our datasets have the same structure allows for a variety of experimental set-ups to probe how sentence embeddings encode different linguistic phenomena across different languages.

Additional datasets are in development, thus expanding the scope of the exploration. With respect to the workshop aims, our motivations are as follows.

[1] By *minimal* we mean the least complex architectures that could be used to discover patterns in the input data.

Proceedings of the 1st GenBench Workshop on (Benchmarking) Generalisation in NLP, pages 163–172
December 6, 2023 ©2023 Association for Computational Linguistics

Cognitive : explore how specific linguistic information is encoded in pretrained sentence representation, and determine whether, or to what degree, we can identify symbolic structures and compositional elements within these representations.

Intrinsic : explore whether pretrained LLMs have learned language representations whose properties can be mapped onto those proposed in linguistics, and whether the tasks we propose are solved through identifiable rules.

While the proposed datasets are presented as a diagnostic tool – to detect patterns that encode linguistic rules and phenomena – we envision that they could also be used to bring such patterns to the fore, through fine-tuning pretrained sentence embeddings, thus pushing continuous distributed representations towards more symbolic, and interpretable, ones.

2 Blackbird Language Matrices

The design of our datasets were inspired by Raven Progressive Matrices (RPMs) (Raven, 1938), an example of which is presented in Figure 1.

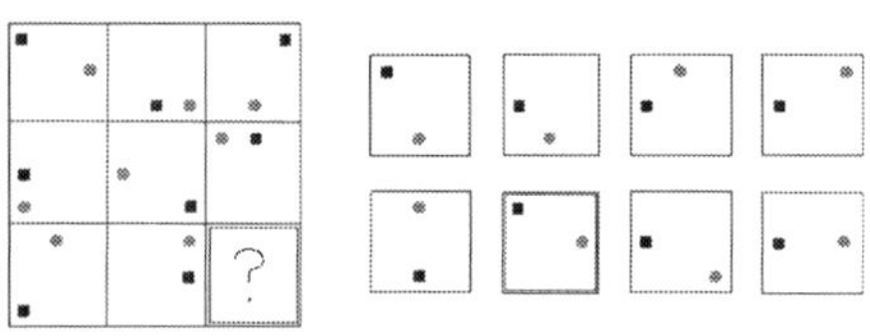

Figure 1: An example Raven's progressive matrix (best seen in colour). The matrix is constructed according to two rules: (i) the red dot moves one place clockwise when traversing the matrix left to right; (ii) the blue square moves one place anticlockwise when traversing the matrix top to bottom. The task consists in finding the tile in the answer set that correctly completes the sequence, indicated with a double border.

RPMs are used in visual IQ tests, as they rely on problem-solvers identifying elements and their attributes such as position, shape, colour and size, and their absolute and relative properties (for instance, how their positions change relative to each other throughout the matrix of images). Analogously, in language, elements correspond to phrase types, attributes correspond to grammatical gender or number, or specific semantic properties, and their connective properties are the relative positions within a syntactic structure or the mapping across levels of representations.

2.1 The Blackbird Language Matrices (BLM) task

Merlo et al. (2022); Merlo (2023) describe the Blackbird Language Matrices (BLM) task. A targeted linguistic phenomenon is presented in the form of a set of sentences that have both syntagmatic and paradigmatic relations. This way, like in the RPM visual version, they give rise to a matrix structure. The language matrices manipulate phrases, dependencies in the syntactic tree, and lexical, grammatical and semantic attributes between connected elements of a sentence and across sentences.

A BLM task comprises a context and an answer set: the context C is a sequence of sentences that share the targeted grammatical phenomenon, but differ in other relevant aspects. BLMs are multiple-choice problems, and each context is paired with a set of candidate answers W. The incorrect answers are built by corrupting the generating rules of the context sequence. This contrastive set up enables targeted error analyses and provides information on structures learned and the type of mistakes a system is prone to. More formally, a BLM task, problem, and matrix can be defined as follows.

BLM TASK: Find $(w_c \in W)$ given C,

given a 4-tuple (LP, C, W, w_c), where LP is the definition of the linguistic grammatical phenomenon, C is the corresponding context matrices, W is the answer set, and w_c is the selected item of W that is correct.

BLM PROBLEM: A *BLM problem* is a tuple(LP, C, W, Aug). It is an instance of a BLM task, where Aug is the augmentation method for the matrices.

BLM MATRIX: A *BLM matrix* is a tuple (S, R, T) s.t. S is the shape of the matrix, R are the relational operators that connect the items of the matrix, T is the set of items of the matrix.

2.2 The BLM Datasets

We propose two datasets encoding two different linguistic phenomena, in different languages: subject-verb agreement in French, and verb alternations in English. We submit to the GenBench task two variations for each dataset: one where each problem in the training data consists of a sequence of sentences with minimal lexical variation (*type I*), and one where the lexical variation is maximal (*type III*). Figure 2 shows the evaluation cards for the two types of datasets (with training with minimal lexical variation, and the training and test data sampled from the same population of automatically generated instances). Table 1 shows the dataset statistics.

type I

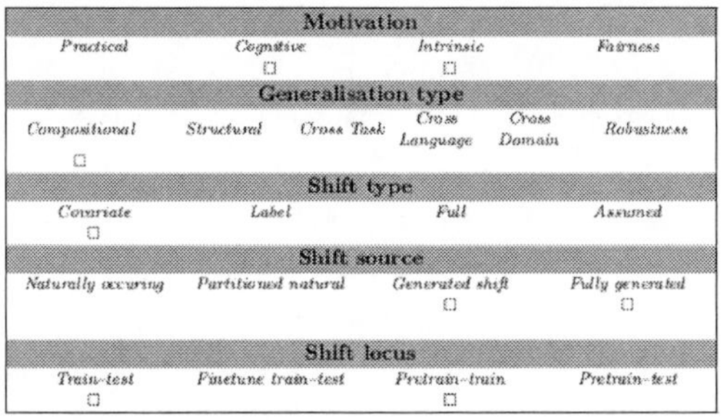

type III

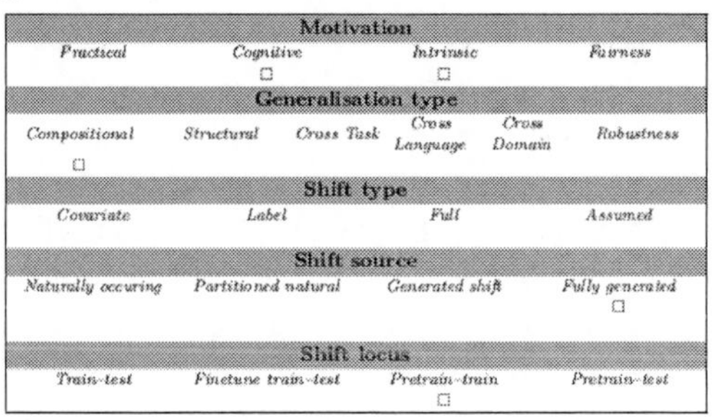

Figure 2: Evaluation cards *type I* (top) and *type III* (bottom).

The shift and generalisation types are as follows.

Shift source : *fully generated* – BLM-AgrF has been automatically generated starting from manually selected seeds and provided templates. + *generated shift*: *type I* variation contains training data sampled from a different distribution than the test data.

Shift type : *covariate*: for *type I* there is a covariate shift between training and testing input data.

Shift locus : *pretrained-trained* – the datasets are designed to make use, as input, of the representations produced by pretrained LLMs, and use them in a novel task. + *train-test* – for the *type I* variations.

Generalisation We aim for *compositional* generalisation, by proposing a dataset that can be used to probe whether different linguistic objects, their properties, and the rules through which they combine are identifiable in pretrained sentence representations.

2.2.1 BLM-AgrF: Subject-verb agreement (in French)

Subject-verb agreement is often used to test the syntactic abilities of deep neural networks (Linzen et al., 2016; Gulordava et al., 2018; Goldberg, 2019; Linzen and Baroni, 2021). While theoretically simple, it can have several complicating factors, such as intervening elements between nouns and the verb, which can interfere with the proper matching of the agreement features.

CONTEXT				
1	Le vase	avec la fleur		est cassé.
2	Les vases	avec la fleur		sont cassés.
3	Le vase	avec les fleurs		est cassé.
4	Les vases	avec les fleurs		sont cassés.
5	Le vase	avec la fleur	du jardin	est cassé.
6	Les vases	avec la fleur	du jardin	sont cassés.
7	Le vase	avec les fleurs	du jardin	est cassé.
8	???			

ANSWER SET		
1	Le vase avec la fleur et le jardin est cassé.	coord
2	**Les vases avec les fleurs du jardin sont cassés.**	correct
3	Le vase avec la fleur est cassé.	WNA
4	Le vase avec la fleur du jardin sont cassés.	AE
5	Les vases avec les fleurs du jardin sont cassés.	WN1
6	Les vases avec les fleurs des jardins sont cassés.	WN2

Figure 3: BLM instances for verb-subject agreement, with two attractors (*fleur* (flower), *jardin* (garden)), with candidate answer set. WNA=wrong number of attractors, AE=agreement error, WN1=wrong nr. for 1st attractor noun (N1), WN2=wrong nr. for 2nd attractor noun (N2)

In BLM-AgrF (An et al., 2023),[2] a BLM problem for subject-verb agreement consists of a context set of seven sentences that share the subject-verb agreement phenomenon, but differ in other aspects – e.g. number of intervening noun phrases between the subject and the verb, called attractors because they can interfere with the agreement, different grammatical numbers for these attractors, and different clause structures. Each context is paired with a set of candidate answers. The answer sets contain minimally contrastive examples built by corrupting some of the generating rules. This helps investigate the kind of information and structure learned, by error analysis. An example is given in Figure 3.

[2]The names of the datasets are composed of a descriptor of the grammatical phenomenon (usually three letters) and the initial of the language (Agr = Agreement; F = French).

EXAMPLE OF CONTEXT	
1	The girl sprayed the wall with paint.
2	Paint was sprayed by the girl
3	Paint was sprayed onto the wall by the girl
4	Paint was sprayed onto the wall
5	The wall was sprayed by the girl
6	The wall was sprayed with the paint by the girl
7	The wall was sprayed with paint
8	???

EXAMPLE OF ANSWERS	
The girl sprayed paint onto the wall	Correct
The girl was sprayed paint onto the wall	AgentAct
The girl sprayed paint the wall	Alt1
The girl sprayed with paint onto the wall	Alt2
The girl sprayed paint for the room	NoEmb
The girl sprayed paint under the wall	LexPrep
Paint sprayed the girl onto the wall	SSM
The wall sprayed the girl with paint	SSM
Paint sprayed the wall with the girl	AASSM

Figure 4: Verb alternations (ALT-ATL): a minimally lexicalised data instance. The labels indicate which (sub)rules are corrupted to create the error. See text for explanation.

EXAMPLE OF CONTEXT	
1	The girl sprayed paint onto the wall.
2	Paint was sprayed by the girl
3	Paint was sprayed onto the wall by the girl
4	Paint was sprayed onto the wall
5	The wall was sprayed by the girl
6	The wall was sprayed with the paint by the girl
7	The wall was sprayed with paint
8	???

EXAMPLE OF ANSWERS	
The girl sprayed the wall with paint	Correct
The girl was sprayed the wall with paint	AgentAct
The girl sprayed the wall the paint	Alt1
The girl sprayed onto the wall with paint	Alt2
The girl sprayed the wall of the room	NoEmb
The girl sprayed the wall under the paint	LexPrep
The wall sprayed the girl with the paint	SSM
Paint sprayed the girl onto the wall	SSM
The wall sprayed the paint with the girl	AASSM

Figure 5: Verb alternation (ATL-ALT), a minimally lexicalised data instance. The labels indicate which (sub)rules are corrupted to create the error. See text for explanation.

2.2.2 BLM-s/lE: verb alternations (in English)

The study of the argument-structure properties of verbs and semantic role assignments is also a testbed for the core syntactic and semantic abilities of neural networks (Kann et al., 2019; Yi et al., 2022). Specifically, Yi et al. (2022) demonstrates that transformers can encode information on the two alternants of the well-studied *spray-load* alternation (Levin, 1993).

The BLM dataset for investigating the encoding of alternation properties is BLM-s/lE (Samo et al., 2023).[3] A naturally occurring example for each verb was extracted from the Spike Amazon subcorpus (Shlain et al., 2020), adopted as seeds for data-augmentation with a fill-mask task. Details are given in (Samo et al., 2023). A BLM s/lE matrix consists of a context set comprising one alternant (e.g. *The girl sprayed the wall with paint*) of the *spray-load* alternation and other sentences that provide the syntactic properties of the arguments of the alternation (e.g. passivization strategies). The target sentence is the other alternant (in our case, *The girl sprayed paint onto the wall*) to be chosen from an answer set of superficially minimally, but, syntactically and semantically, deeply different candidates. An example matrix is shown in Figure 5. We created two templates, one for each of the two alternates. One group has the alternant AGENT-LOCATIVE-THEME (hencefort ALT, e.g. *The girl sprayed the wall with paint)* in the context and the correct answer is the alternant whose configuration is AGENT-THEME-LOCATIVE (henceforth ATL, e.g. *The girl sprayed paint onto the wall*). ALT-ATL data is the data produced from the matrix in Figure 5.[4]

The answer set is contrastive – see caption of Figure 5. The answer labelled as AGENTACT minimally deviates from the correct answer, since the verb is inflected in a passive mood; in ALT errors, the verb of the alternate is followed by two NPs and one PPs; in NOEMB errors, the PP is syntactically embedded in the NP; LEXPREP errors involve a preposition which does not grammatically belong to the alternation. Finally, violations of the syntax-semantic mapping (SSM1 and SSM2) and simultaneous violations of AGENTACT and SSM (AASSM) involve reorderings of the lexical constituents and functional elements (e.g. prepositions).

3 Benchmarking

We used two baselines to benchmark the proposed datasets. They are designed to test whether we can access the relevant information for the targeted phenomena in a given BLM task, in transformer-based sentence representations. Figure 6 shows

[3]The name follows our convention: s/l = spray/load; E = English. The dataset is created on the basis of a class of 30 verbs belonging to the same class of *spray* and *load* in VERBNET (Schuler 2005).

[4]The name of the data subset, ALT-ATL, is transparent towards this logic: ALT is given in the context set, ATL is the correct answer. The second group's template (ATL-ALT) is the converse.

the general process flow. The two baselines are a feed-forward neural network (FFNN) and a convolutional neural network (CNN).

The FFNN baseline is a three-layer feed-forward neural network. It transforms the context C of a BLM instance into a 1D-tensor which is a concatenation of the representation of each sentence. This is passed through three fully-connected layers. The output is a vector that we take to represent the embedding of the answer sentence. This architecture allows the system to find patterns within and across sentences through the nodes in the successive layers.

The CNN baseline consists of three convolutional steps, followed by a linear layer to compress the output to the desired dimensions. The input consists of a stack of context sentence representations. This setup finds localized patterns within sentence representation and across the sequence of sentences.

The output of the two networks is the same – a vector representing the sentence embedding of the correct answer. The learning objective is to maximize the probability of the correct answer from the candidate answer set. Because the incorrect answers in the answer set are specifically designed to be minimally different from the correct answer, we implement the objective through the max-margin loss function. This function combines the distances between the predicted answer and the correct and erroneous ones. We first compute a score for the embedding e_j of each candidate answer a_j in the answer set $\mathcal{A}$ with respect to the predicted sentence embedding e_{pred} as the cosine of the angle between the respective vectors:

$$score(e_j, e_{pred}) = cos(e_j, e_{pred})$$

The loss uses the max-margin between the score for the correct answer e_c and for each of the incorrect answers e_i:

$$loss = \sum_{e_i} [1 - score(e_c, e_{pred}) + score(e_i, e_{pred})]^+$$

At prediction time, we take the answer with the highest $score$ value from a candidate set as the correct answer.

4 Results and Error Analysis

The train/test data splits are presented in Table 1. As the task is set-up as multiple choice, we measure the results in terms of F1 scores for identifying the correct answer. The results below also show the performance on the test set for varying amounts of training data to show their impact, and compares two types of pretrained sentence embeddings – RoBERTa (Liu et al., 2019) and Electra (Clark et al., 2020).

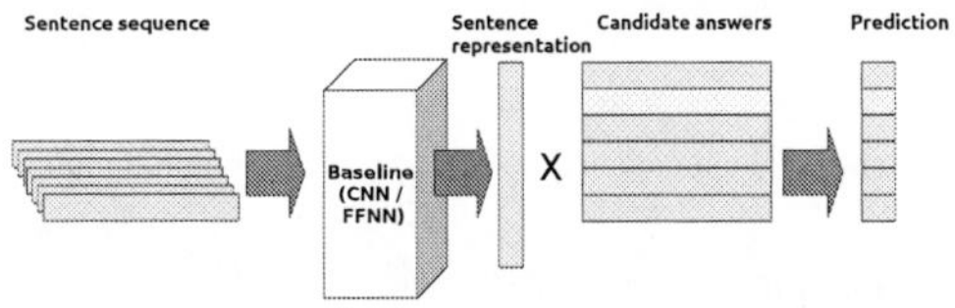

Figure 6: Illustration of the baseline setup experiments.

Datasets		*type I*	*type III*
BLM-AgrF		2073/3840	34650/3840
BLM-s/lE	ALT-ATL	3375/1500	13500/1500
	ATL-ALT	3375/1500	13500/1500

Table 1: Datasets statistics in terms of train/test counts.

4.1 Varying the training data

The results below show the performance on the test set in terms of F1 averages over five runs for each of the two datasets, for RoBERTa and Electra sentence embeddings.[5] The plots in Figure 7 show the results for the *type III* dataset variations (with train and test data sampled from the same population with maximal lexical variation), and the results for the *type I* dataset variations (with training data with minimal lexical variation within an instance). The results obtained with the overall baseline system (FFNN with Electra sentence embeddings) are shown in the tables in the left column.

The results shown in Figure 7 reveal interesting distinguishing properties of the two tasks. For the subject-verb agreement, which is a syntactic task, both types of sentence embeddings lead to similar results when using the FFNN system. Instead, a difference arises across architectures. The fact that the CNN leads to lower performance indicates that it finds more localised patterns and it also indicates that patterns capturing subject-verb agreement are more spread throughout the sentence embeddings. For the verb alternation task, which has a strong semantic component, the embedding type makes more of a difference than the system used to detect patterns. Electra seems to encode verb semantics better for this task, as Yi et al. (2022) also note. Because both the FFNN and the CNN detect successfully these patterns, this indicates that patterns

[5]For all sets of five runs the standard deviation was less than $1e - 10$, so it is not included in the tables.

Results for best baseline (Electra + FFNN) — *type I* — *type III*

tr+dev (80:20)	*type I*	*type III*
50	0.293	0.332
100	0.345	0.374
200	0.451	0.402
500	0.607	0.468
1000	0.661	0.622
1500	0.676	0.711
2000	0.702	0.741

tr+dev (80:20)	*type I*	*type III*
50	0.601	0.795
100	0.676	0.801
200	0.732	0.814
500	0.729	0.882
1000	0.795	0.896
1500	0.795	0.943
2000	0.798	0.938
3000	0.803	0.929

tr+dev (80:20)	*type I*	*type III*
50	0.600	0.731
100	0.665	0.806
200	0.726	0.848
500	0.809	0.876
1000	0.793	0.887
1500	0.800	0.915
2000	0.809	0.903
3000	0.794	0.914

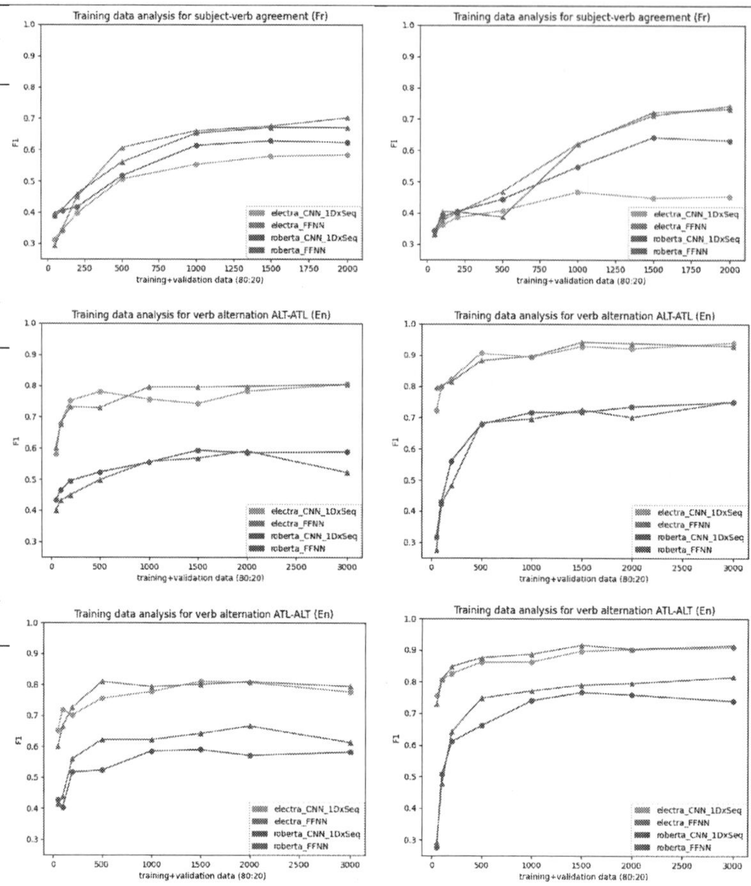

Figure 7: Result plots in terms of F1 averages over five runs, when using the two baselines and RoBERTa and Electra sentence embeddings, and numeric results in the tables for the best combination: Electra with FFNN baseline system

encoding verb alternations are more localised.

Having training data with minimal lexical variation makes the targeted pattern more obvious. On the other hand, it may provide shallow indicators that can confound the system. Comparing the results on *type I* and *type III*, we note that there is a drop of about 0.1 in the F-score for all settings, although for the subject-verb agreement this is lower (0.04). This is probably not surprising and underlines the more structural nature of the subject-verb agreement problem, where lexical variation does not detract from the number agreement pattern. For the verb alternation the drop is higher. This may suggest that since the task is more semantic in nature, variation in the lexical material of the sentence shifts the underlying patterns. Some transformation of the sentence representations may make such patterns more obvious, and separate them from the lexical signal. However, the performance is still high, even with a smaller amount of training data, indicating that the signal that encodes the *spray-load* alternation is strong in the sentence embeddings.

4.2 Error Analysis

Error analysis on the best baseline – RoBERTa sentence embeddings with the CNN system – is given in Figure 8. The upper panel refers to BLM-AgrF, the lower panel provides information about the errors within the ALT-ATL dataset BLM-s/lE.

In both datasets, we observe clear trends. First, more data reduces errors roughly uniformly. Minimal variation is observed in BLM-AgrF, where

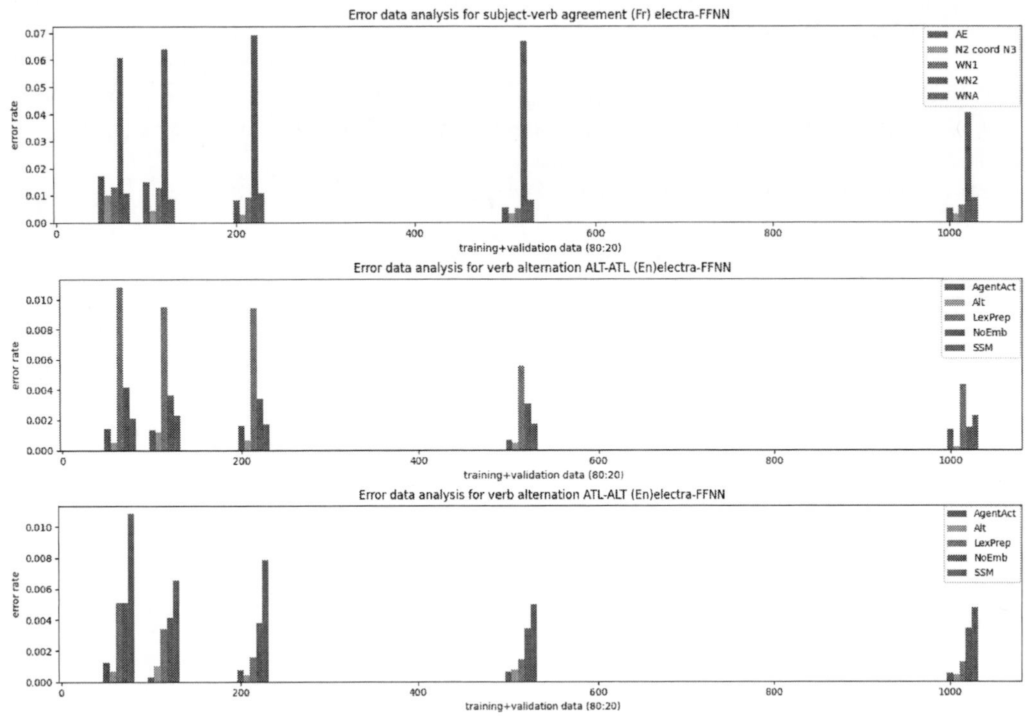

Figure 8: Error analysis (averages over 5 runs) for varying amounts of training data, for the best performing baseline: RoBERTa sentence embeddings with the CNN system.

WN2 (wrong number for 2nd attractor noun) remains the most frequent error across size of the training data. This error has two interesting characteristics: it is the most frequent error also for human speakers, and also it is exhibited by sentences that are grammatical, but do not respect the global pattern of the matrix.

Conversely, a conspicuous trend is distinctly observable within the BLM-s/lE dataset (ALT-ATL). The distribution of mistake types concentrates on lexical mistakes of functional elements (prepositions) with small training sets. However, as the dataset size increases, the SSM error increases proportionally. This error is associated with the semantic properties of the alternation, specifically the semantic roles of the arguments of the verb.

5 Related work

The GenBench taxonomy differs sometimes from the meaning of some existing terms elsewhere referring to generalisation. In situating our work in comparison to other related work, we reason based on the actual nature of the generalisation being sought rather than the terminology.

Our closest related dataset in spirit, in terms of motivation and goals, is the COGS dataset (Kim and Linzen, 2020). It is also different from our dataset in implementation. The COGS dataset aims at providing out-of-distribution test cases to test compositionality of structure and meaning. To this goal, a training set is generated with a CFG and parallel lambda-expressions and a test set with a different CFG, specifically designed to exhibit testing constructions that are previously unseen as such and whose solution requires compositional generalisation of components seen at training.

These unseen constructions comprise both structural and lexical generalisation: the former aiming to test the ability to create new structures from existing parts, the latter to test ability to adapt existing structures to novel content.

While our dataset strives for similar goals, the way to go about it is different in one relevant respect. The COGS dataset determines by design the combinatorics that the network needs to find, imposing therefore preexisting hard independence assumptions generated by a CFG in the test set. These pre-existing discrete rules of combination must be discovered to find a correct parsing solution.

Our approach is more in the spirit of hidden representation learning. We do not require that the network has explicitly learnt new generative ways of combining elements. But we encourage representations that learn soft constraints, in the form of disentangled representations that correspond to the generative underlying factors. Beside testing soft constraints on structural generalisation, we also provide tests of lexical generalisation (through the different types of lexical variability in the matrix).

In this respect, the datasets provided here are related to those used in the literature on disentanglement in computer vision. For example, van Steenkiste et al. (2020) developed a dataset for computer vision similar to RPMs. They evaluate the usefulness of the representations learned for abstract reasoning. They note that learning disentangled representations leads to faster few-shot learning. Also, recently Zheng and Lapata (2022) propose a different method for disentangling relations expressed in a sentence which may share arguments. This is implemented as an extension to sequence-to-sequence (seq2seq) models, where at each decoding step the source input is re-encoded by conditioning the source representations on the newly decoded target context. These specialized representations make it easier for the encoder to exploit relevant-only information for each prediction.

With the appropriate dataset, such approaches can be used to probe the abilities of pretrained LLMs. The datasets we propose in this paper have the necessary properties: they focus on specific linguistic phenomena, they display lexical and structural variation, and include known confounding factors for the targered phenomena. They are, then, close to the work that investigates network representations. For example, Lasri et al. (2022) focus on how BERT encodes grammatical number in English and how this information is used for performing number agreement. The focus is on word embeddings and quantifying how much number information they encode at various layers of the BERT architecture. Using a combination of probing approaches, they discover that subjects and predicates embeddings do encode number information, but at different layers. Further investigations into where and how the number information is shared reveals that number information is not directly shared, but rather passed through intermediate tokens. The study of the argument-structure properties of verbs and semantic role assignments is also a test-bed for the core syntactic and semantic abilities of neural networks (Kann et al., 2019; Yi et al., 2022). In particular, Yi et al. (2022) demonstrates that transformers can encode information on the two alternants of the *spray-load* alternation.

6 Conclusions

In this paper, we describe an approach to generate compositional, structured data, inspired from visual intelligence tests. We presented two datasets, each focused on a different linguistic phenomenon, and in a different language. Solving each problem instance depends on the system detecting the relevant linguistic objects, and their absolute and relative properties. These datasets can be used to investigate whether this type of information can be detected in, and whether it is used by, pretrained LLMs. Because the datasets are formatted in the same way, they can be used separately, or in various combinations, to test cross-task and cross-language model properties. Additional such datasets are under development, thus potentially expanding the scope of the exploration.

Further experiments are also ongoing. One of our goals is to understand how information is encoded in pretrained transformer-based sentence embeddings. We investigate whether there are patterns within sentence representations that reveal specific linguistic phenomena. Towards this end, we have developed architectures designed to discover such patterns that can be applied successfully, without adaptation (in terms of architecture or hyperparameters) to different problems in different languages. This provides insight into how transformers encode sentence-level information.

Limitations

The approach is evaluated on a limited range of syntactic phenomena and models. Expanding the scope could better demonstrate the general utility. In particular, we would like to expand in many directions: (i) the structures that are tried in the different test sets; (ii) the different phenomena under study; (iii) the complexity of the matrices, which can be made progressively harder by combining linguistic phenomena in a single matrix. Finally, we need to tackle the complex problem of how to generate more naturally structured data, while retaining the controllable nature of synthetic, experimental data.

Ethics Statement

To the best of our knowledge, this paper raises no ethics concerns.

Acknowledgements

We gratefully acknowledge the partial support of this work by the Swiss National Science Foundation, through grants #51NF40_180888 (NCCR Evolving Language) and SNF Advanced grant TMAG-1_209426 to PM.

References

Aixiu An, Chunyang Jiang, Maria A. Rodriguez, Vivi Nastase, and Paola Merlo. 2023. BLM-AgrF: A new French benchmark to investigate generalization of agreement in neural networks. In *Proceedings of the 17th Conference of the European Chapter of the Association for Computational Linguistics*, pages 1363–1374, Dubrovnik, Croatia. Association for Computational Linguistics.

Kevin Clark, Minh-Thang Luong, Quoc V. Le, and Christopher D. Manning. 2020. ELECTRA: Pre-training text encoders as discriminators rather than generators. In *ICLR*.

Yoav Goldberg. 2019. Assessing bert's syntactic abilities. *arXiv preprint arXiv:1901.05287*.

Kristina Gulordava, Piotr Bojanowski, Edouard Grave, Tal Linzen, and Marco Baroni. 2018. Colorless green recurrent networks dream hierarchically. In *Proceedings of the 2018 Conference of the North American Chapter of the Association for Computational Linguistics: Human Language Technologies, Volume 1 (Long Papers)*, pages 1195–1205, New Orleans, Louisiana. Association for Computational Linguistics.

Katharina Kann, Alex Warstadt, Adina Williams, and Samuel R. Bowman. 2019. Verb argument structure alternations in word and sentence embeddings. In *Proceedings of the Society for Computation in Linguistics (SCiL) 2019*, pages 287–297.

Najoung Kim and Tal Linzen. 2020. COGS: A compositional generalization challenge based on semantic interpretation. In *Proceedings of the 2020 Conference on Empirical Methods in Natural Language Processing (EMNLP)*, pages 9087–9105, Online. Association for Computational Linguistics.

Karim Lasri, Tiago Pimentel, Alessandro Lenci, Thierry Poibeau, and Ryan Cotterell. 2022. Probing for the usage of grammatical number. In *Proceedings of the 60th Annual Meeting of the Association for Computational Linguistics (Volume 1: Long Papers)*, pages 8818–8831, Dublin, Ireland. Association for Computational Linguistics.

Beth Levin. 1993. *English verb classes and alternations: A preliminary investigation*. University of Chicago Press.

Tal Linzen and Marco Baroni. 2021. Syntactic structure from deep learning. *Annual Review of Linguistics*, 7(1):195–212.

Tal Linzen, Emmanuel Dupoux, and Yoav Goldberg. 2016. Assessing the ability of LSTMs to learn syntax-sensitive dependencies. *Transactions of the Association for Computational Linguistics*, 4:521–535.

Yinhan Liu, Myle Ott, Naman Goyal, Jingfei Du, Mandar Joshi, Danqi Chen, Omer Levy, Mike Lewis, Luke Zettlemoyer, and Veselin Stoyanov. 2019. Roberta: A robustly optimized bert pretraining approach. *arXiv preprint arXiv:1907.11692*.

Paola Merlo. 2023. Blackbird language matrices (BLM), a new task for rule-like generalization in neural networks: Motivations and formal specifications. *ArXiv*, cs.CL 2306.11444.

Paola Merlo, Aixiu An, and Maria A. Rodriguez. 2022. Blackbird's language matrices (BLMs): a new benchmark to investigate disentangled generalisation in neural networks. *ArXiv*, cs.CL 2205.10866.

John C. Raven. 1938. Standardization of progressive matrices. *British Journal of Medical Psychology*, 19:137–150.

Giuseppe Samo, Vivi Nastase, Chunyang Jiang, and Paola Merlo. 2023. BLM-s/lE: A structured dataset of English spray-load verb alternations for testing generalization in LLMs. In *Proceedings of the 2023 Conference on Empirical Methods in Natural Language Processing*, Singapore.

Karin Kipper Schuler. 2005. *VerbNet: A broad-coverage, comprehensive verb lexicon*. University of Pennsylvania.

Micah Shlain, Hillel Taub-Tabib, Shoval Sadde, and Yoav Goldberg. 2020. Syntactic search by example. In *Proceedings of the 58th Annual Meeting of the Association for Computational Linguistics: System Demonstrations*, pages 17–23, Online. Association for Computational Linguistics.

Sjoerd van Steenkiste, Francesco Locatello, Jürgen Schmidhuber, and Olivier Bachem. 2020. Are disentangled representations helpful for abstract visual reasoning? In *NeurIPS 2019*.

David Yi, James Bruno, Jiayu Han, Peter Zukerman, and Shane Steinert-Threlkeld. 2022. Probing for understanding of English verb classes and alternations in large pre-trained language models. In *Proceedings of the Fifth BlackboxNLP Workshop on Analyzing and Interpreting Neural Networks for NLP*, pages 142–152, Abu Dhabi, United Arab Emirates (Hybrid). Association for Computational Linguistics.

Hao Zheng and Mirella Lapata. 2022. Disentangled sequence to sequence learning for compositional generalization. In *Proceedings of the 60th Annual Meeting of the Association for Computational Linguistics (Volume 1: Long Papers)*, pages 4256–4268, Dublin, Ireland. Association for Computational Linguistics.

In-Context Learning for Text Classification with Many Labels

Aristides Milios[1], **Siva Reddy**[1,2,3], **Dzmitry Bahdanau**[1,2]
Mila and McGill University[1], ServiceNOW Research[2], Facebook CIFAR AI Chair[3]
{aristides.milios,siva.reddy,bahdanau}@mila.quebec

Abstract

In-context learning (ICL) using large language models for tasks with many labels is challenging due to the limited context window, which makes it difficult to fit a sufficient number of examples in the prompt. In this paper, we use a pre-trained dense retrieval model to bypass this limitation, giving the model only a partial view of the full label space for each inference call. Testing with recent open-source LLMs (OPT, LLaMA), we set new state of the art performance in few-shot settings for three common intent classification datasets, with no fine-tuning. We also surpass fine-tuned performance on fine-grained sentiment classification in certain cases. We analyze the performance across number of in-context examples and different model scales, showing that larger models are necessary to effectively and consistently make use of larger context lengths for ICL. By running several ablations, we analyze the model's use of: a) the similarity of the in-context examples to the current input, b) the semantic content of the class names, and c) the correct correspondence between examples and labels. We demonstrate that all three are needed to varying degrees depending on the domain, contrary to certain recent works.

1 Introduction

In-context learning (ICL) using large language models (LLMs) has recently exploded in popularity. Models pre-trained on massive amounts of textual data are able to reach reasonable performance on a wide variety of tasks with only a few examples of input and output for a given task provided in the model's input prompt in natural language (Brown et al., 2020; Rae et al., 2021; Chowdhery et al., 2023). In this work, we study whether ICL can handle challenging classification tasks with many possible labels, by augmenting the LM with a secondary pre-trained retrieval model.

The main problem with applying ICL to tasks involving classification with many labels is the limited context window these models have. Ordinarily with ICL, at minimum one example from each class is provided in-context to allow the model to make a choice between all the labels of the task. Because of this limitation, ICL has not been directly applied to these sorts of problems. In this work we relax this requirement, allowing the model to see only a subset of the most relevant labels for the given datapoint we are performing inference on. By testing on intent classification (upwards of 50 classes) and fine-grained sentiment analysis (upwards of 25 classes), we demonstrate that the resulting performance with this method can reach SoTA. By coupling the LLM with an external pre-trained dense retriever model (Reimers and Gurevych, 2019a; Karpukhin et al., 2020), we can dynamically retrieve a set of examples to provide to the LM in-context, that reflects only the most relevant labels to the current example in the label space. Most existing work on augmenting LMs with retrieval models (Ram et al., 2023; Shi et al., 2023) focuses on tuning the retrieval and/or LM. We demonstrate that even without tuning either, when the pre-trained models are strong enough we can still achieve SoTA across various tasks using ICL.

We evaluate LLMs in this setting with three intent classification datasets: BANKING77 (Casanueva et al., 2020), HWU64 (Liu et al., 2019), and CLINC150 (Larson et al., 2019), as well as one fine-grained sentiment classification dataset: GoEmotions (Demszky et al., 2020). Experiments are done using the LLaMA models (Touvron et al., 2023) and the OPT models (Zhang et al., 2022) as LLMs. We compare the performance achieved against adapter-based fine-tuning of MLM models (DeBERTa-v2-XXLarge with the "Pfeiffer" bottleneck-style adapter (Pfeiffer et al., 2020b) implemented with AdapterHub (Pfeiffer et al., 2020a)) and the previous SoTA for intent detection (ConvFit; Vulić et al. 2021), as well as

Proceedings of the 1st GenBench Workshop on (Benchmarking) Generalisation in NLP, pages 173–184
December 6, 2023 ©2023 Association for Computational Linguistics

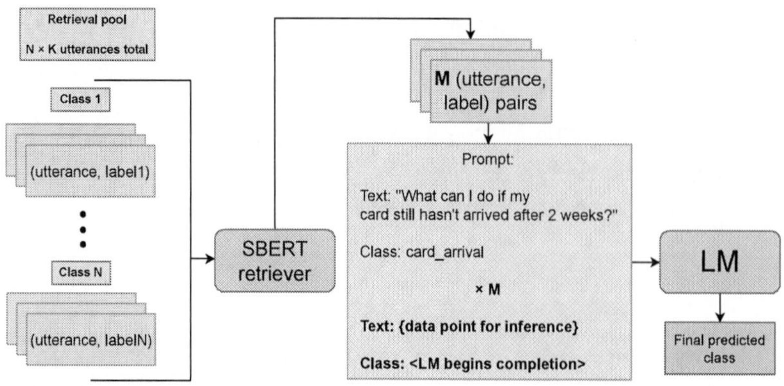

Figure 1: Complete pipeline for intent detection with retrieval-augmented in-context learning

comparing against SetFit (Tunstall et al., 2022), a recent lightweight method involving contrastive training of small MLM models.

The contributions of this work are:

1. We show that retrieval-augmented ICL is an effective way to tackle text classification tasks with many labels without additional tuning of either the retriever or the LM, either matching or outperforming fine-tuned adapter-based and contrastive-pre-training-based methods. Notably, truncating the dataset by showing only a subset to the LM at a time does not prevent us from achieving SoTA performance, and allows us to apply LLMs to problems that they have not been applied to before,

2. We analyze ICL performance over different numbers of examples and demonstrate that larger models better are able to take advantage of more examples in-context than smaller models, which mostly plateau and/or see decreasing performance,

3. We perform several ablation studies to determine what aspects of the inputs and outputs the model is using for ICL. Certain recent works investigating ICL (Min et al., 2022; Razeghi et al., 2022) have recently called into question how much models are actually "learning" with ICL and what they are learning from. We ablate three different elements (semantic label names, correct input-output correspondences, and semantically similar demonstrations to the current input). Contrary to this emerging literature, our experiments demonstrate that they are all used to varying degrees, depending on the dataset and domain.

2 Method

Retrieval-Augmented ICL: Our setup assumes N classes (unique labels) with K examples in each class. Each example is composed of an `(input, label)` tuple. We assume that we have a limited number of examples M to fit in the prompt, based on the model's context length. M can be fixed or based on "saturating" the prompt greedily by selecting examples until we run out of room in the context window. From our total pool of examples of size $N \times K$, we retrieve the M examples using the cosine similarity values given by our retrieval model. Having retrieved our M examples, we then produce the prompt by concatenating the `(input, label)` tuples in a set prompt format (see Figure 1), similar to existing in-context learning setups. The final prediction is then taken from the LM by having it produce a continuation based on our prompt. A full visual description of the retrieval process is visible in Figure 1.

Retrieval model: The retrieval model used is a Sentence-BERT model trained in a Siamese dual-network setup to be able to retrieve text based on cosine similarity of the embedding vectors it produces, described in Reimers and Gurevych (2019b). The model we use is a contrastively trained model which has been pre-trained on a massive generic dataset of text pairs. We use the retrieval model as-is in all experiments. Cosine similarity is used to retrieve examples from the retrieval pool of examples (tested in 5-shot and 10-shot scenarios, signifying the number of examples from each class in the retrieval pool).

3 Experimental Setup

Specific retrieval model: For our sentence encoder/retriever, we use the SentenceTransformers library (Reimers and Gurevych, 2019a), and use the pre-trained "all-mpnet-base-v2" model (a 110M parameter model pre-trained on over 1 billion training pairs). The SetFit results are based on contrastively tuning the same pre-trained model trained by Microsoft through the Setfit library[1].

Prompt saturation: The number of examples that fit in-context when greedily filling the context window depends on the specific dataset. For the intent detection datasets, this number was around 110 examples. For GoEmotions, this number was around 70 (140 using the full 4K context length of the LLaMA-2 models).

Splits: For the intent detection experiments, to allow for direct comparison with previous works, we use the same 5-shot and 10-shot sets as DialoGLUE (Mehri et al., 2020). Experiments are run 3 times and the accuracies are averaged, except the zero-training LLM setups, which are deterministic. For the GoEmotions experiments we average the results across 3 different random 10 and 5-shot splits, as no pre-existing few-shot splits exist. The GoEmotions experiments are composed of the subset of GoEmotions data (84% of training set, 85% of testing set) where the there is only one emotion label, to avoid issues of enforcing an ordering on a linearized version of multiple labels in sequence, as well as to mimic the single-label intent detection datasets setup more closely. Default library parameters were used.

Computing Hardware and model differences: All experiments were performed on a single A100 80GB GPU, except those with OPT 175B, which were performed with 8 A100 GPUs. For LLaMA 65B and 70B 8-bit quantization was used. The main difference between the OPT and LLaMA models is the amount of pre-training data used. The LLaMA models were trained on 1T-1.4T tokens, while the OPT models were only trained on 180B tokens (see (Zhang et al., 2022) and (Touvron et al., 2023) for more details). LLaMA-2 models were trained on 2T tokens.

Restricting model output: To reduce computational load and make inference easier, instead of using the logits of the LLM to rank our many classes (requiring multiple forward passes, as class names consist of multiple tokens), we let the LLM generate freely. Having generated an output text, we then use the retrieval model (SBERT) to retrieve the most similar class label from our set of classes. This allows us to restrict the model output to the set of classes we want without incurring additional inference cost. Instances of generated predictions that do not match our class list are few regardless, and shrink proportionately to the number of examples provided in-context.

Baselines: Several baselines are provided. The baseline "Pre-trained SBERT 1-NN" refers to using the SBERT retrieval model to retrieve the most similar example in the retrieval pool and use its label directly as the prediction (1-nearest-neighbor). The ConvFit baseline is taken from the reported numbers in the ConvFit paper directly. The baseline "DeBERTa (Pfeiffer)" is the DeBERTa-XXL model released by Microsoft, trained via AdapterHub with the Pfeiffer-style bottleneck adapters (Pfeiffer et al., 2020b,a). Preliminary results with other adapter types (LoRA, IA^3, etc.) showed that the Pfeiffer-style adapters were the most effective in this particular use-case. The DeBERTa-XXL model was fine-tuned until performance saturation (early stopping). SetFit (Tunstall et al., 2022) results are also provided, a method involving contrastive fine-tuning of a retriever model with a classification head, as it is also a competitive and lightweight baseline in this setup. The selection of baselines was done based on recent strong progress on few-shot classification using parameter-efficient fine-tuning, in certain cases having been shown to perform better than full fine-tuning (Liu et al., 2022a).

4 Results

Example ordering: We provide a brief study regarding how to order examples in-prompt by similarity, since previous work has been inconclusive on this front, suggesting that the ideal ordering is dataset dependent (Liu et al., 2022b). As seen from Table 3, least-to-most (LTM) similar was the most effective ordering across all datasets. Larger models are significantly less sensitive to ordering.

SoTA performance: Tables 1 and 2 shows the performance comparison of all methods. Performance of the retrieval+ICL pipeline on BANKING, HWU and CLINC is state of the art in both the 5

[1]https://github.com/huggingface/setfit

Table 1: Intent classification accuracy for retrieval+ICL and baseline methods. All retrieval+ICL results are with 20 in-prompt examples unless otherwise specified. The retrieval/training dataset size is given by the second row of the header (10-shot is 10 examples per class, 5-shot is 5).

Model	**BANKING 77**		**HWU 64**		**CLINC 150**	
	5-shot	**10-shot**	**5-shot**	**10-shot**	**5-shot**	**10-shot**
Pre-trained SBERT 1-NN	78.41	85.39	69.89	75.46	82.51	84.84
ConvFit (reported)	-	87.38	-	85.32	-	92.89
SetFit	79.89 $\pm$ 0.14	84.51 $\pm$ 0.60	78.38 $\pm$ 0.73	83.35 $\pm$ 0.57	88.68 $\pm$ 0.20	90.67 $\pm$ 0.29
DeBERTa (Pfeiffer)	81.47 $\pm$ 1.6	88.41 $\pm$ 0.19	79.80 $\pm$ 0.81	86.93 $\pm$ 0.052	91.86 $\pm$ 0.66	95.05 $\pm$ 0.33
OPT 13B	81.23	85.65	78.90	83.64	85.27	89.24
OPT 175B	81.30	86.14	83.74	84.94	90.96	93.09
LLaMA 7B	84.42	87.63	85.87	87.55	88.58	91.73
LLaMA 65B	87.73	90.71	89.03	90.06	91.89	94.47
LLaMA 2 7B	86.40	89.45	87.55	87.82	94.13	95.20
LLaMA 2 7B 4K	85.91	89.48	87.17	90.33	95.35	96.02
LLaMA 2 70B	87.56	90.58	88.20	89.77	96.42	97.13
LLaMA 2 70B 4K	**88.96**	**92.11**	**90.61**	**91.73**	**97.56**	**98.18**

Table 2: Sentiment classification macro F1 score (following prior work) over 3 random splits for retrieval+ICL and baseline methods. All retrieval+ICL results are from saturating the prompt with in-prompt examples (with a 2K prompt length unless otherwise specified). The retrieval/training dataset size is given by the second row of the header (10-shot is 10 examples per class, 5-shot is 5). +Neut refers to the case where the "neutral" class (lack of emotion) is included in the dataset.

Model	**GoEmotions**			
	5-shot	**10-shot**	**5-shot +Neut**	**10-shot +Neut**
Pre-trained SBERT 1-NN	9.48 $\pm$ 0.58	11.02 $\pm$ 1.0	7.55 $\pm$ 0.79	8.38 $\pm$ 0.48
SetFit	25.44 $\pm$ 4.5	34.69 $\pm$ 3.6	21.40 $\pm$ 3.18	27.78 $\pm$ 0.73
DeBERTa (Pfeiffer)	18.43 $\pm$ 2.9	32.33 $\pm$ 0.77	13.86 $\pm$ 1.49	25.42 $\pm$ 1.9
LLaMA 7B	-	-	22.99 $\pm$ 0.64	24.61 $\pm$ 0.47
LLaMA 65B	-	-	24.31 $\pm$ 0.73	25.63 $\pm$ 0.86
LLaMA 2 7B	29.60 $\pm$ 1.5	31.40 $\pm$ 0.83	23.78 $\pm$ 1.1	24.75 $\pm$ 0.43
LLaMA 2 7B 4K	28.01 $\pm$ 1.2	30.33 $\pm$ 1.64	23.79 $\pm$ 1.9	23.57 $\pm$ 0.52
LLaMA 2 70B	**36.14** $\pm$ 1.7	**37.81** $\pm$ 1.3	24.20 $\pm$ 0.13	25.29 $\pm$ 0.42
LLaMA 2 70B 4K	-	37.17 $\pm$ 0.37	**28.26** $\pm$ 0.19	**29.10** $\pm$ 0.68
LLaMA 2 70B 4K Retrieval w/o Neutral	-	-	-	28.95 $\pm$ 0.52

and 10-shot settings. Not only this, but to significantly surpass the previous state of the art for all three intent classification datasets only LLaMA-2 7B is necessary, which with 8-bit quantization can be run on consumer hardware. In the most challenging evaluation setting (the highly-specialized intent classes of the BANKING dataset in the most data-scarce 5-shot setting), the margin between DeBERTa and LLaMA-2 70B is 7.49%. In general the DeBERTa model showed lower performance in the 5-shot scenarios, likely due to the extremely limited data. In the case of GoEmotions (Table 2), when using the neutral category, the Retrieval+ICL pipeline manages to clearly win against the strongest baseline (SetFit) only in the 5-shot case. In the 10-shot case, we can see that Retrieval+ICL performs at least on par, but more likely better than SetFit. Table 4 shows the difficulty of the GoEmotions task, specifically with regards to how granular the classes are.

Performance degredation: We also provide a study of how performance changes given the number of examples provided in-context. Figure 2 shows this variation for the HWU64 dataset. The x-axis value of 110 indicates a fully saturated context window, which is on average this number of examples. In the case of LLaMA-7B, performance somewhat degrades after a certain number of demonstrations. Looking at Tables 1 and 2, comparing

Table 3: Comparison of LLaMA 7B and OPT 13B model prompt orderings on intent detection datasets (20 examples in prompt, 10-shot), random split. MTL is most-to-least similar and LTM is the inverse.

Model	BANKING		HWU		CLINC		GoEmotions		
	MTL	LTM	MTL	LTM	MTL	LTM	MTL	Random	LTM
OPT 13B	73.64	**85.65**	76.39	**83.64**	81.11	**89.24**	-	-	-
LLaMA 7B	83.64	**87.63**	86.99	**87.55**	90.20	**91.73**	15.91	20.89 $\pm$ 0.85	**23.58**
LLaMA 65B	88.08	**90.71**	89.03	**90.06**	93.47	**94.47**	-	-	-

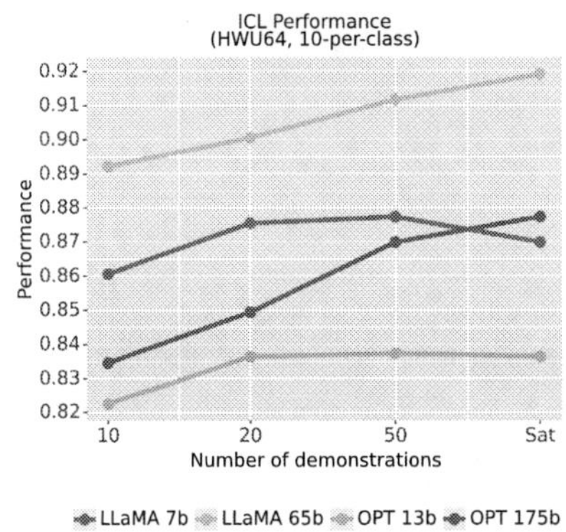

Figure 2: HWU performance as a function of the number of examples in prompt. The x-axis scale is non-linear, meaning that there are diminishing returns with more examples. "Sat" (saturated) indicates filling the prompt greedily until the max length is reached.

LLaMA-2-7B and LLaMA-2-70B in the regular and 4K context window scenarios, we see very clearly that only the 70B model is able to continually improve with the full 4K context. The 7B model instead sees matching (no improvement) or degraded performance in most cases.

Impact of "Neutral" on GoEmotions: From the results in Table 2, by comparing the results with and without the "neutral" category, we see that the difference between the baselines and Retrieval+ICL grows, implying that "neutral" disproportionately hurts the Retrieval+ICL performance. We note that correctly predicting the neural class is challenging for the LM. We demonstrate that removing "neutral" from the retrieval pool does not harm performance ("Retrieval without Neutral" in Table 2). Analyzing the results for one of the runs, we see that out of the 1605 examples of the "neutral" class in the test set, "neutral" only appears in the top 3 classes retrieved by the retriever (by number of examples) only 9% of the time (in the top 5 classes 18%). This suggests that the retriever may be limiting the performance.

5 Ablation Studies

Several ablations studies are done to test what aspects of the retrieved examples the LLM is using to make the predictions. The ablation studies were done on a random split of the HWU dataset and the GoEmotions dataset. Ablation results for HWU are shown visually in Figure 3 and for GoEmotions in Figure 4.

1. **Obfuscated labels:** We change all the class names to randomly set enumerated names ("Class 1", "Class 2", etc.). The intent is to disentangle the model's use of prior (pre-training) knowledge to perform the task (based on the semantic content of the label names) from the input-output provided in the prompt.

2. **Resampled in-context examples:** To test if similarity between the demonstrations provided in the prompt and the current input example is actually necessary for effective performance. By resampling from the classes initially retrieved by the retriever model, we preserve the distribution of labels but change the input demonstrations themselves so that they are no longer the nearest in the embedding space for each class.

3. **Shuffled labels:** Similarly to Min et al. (2022), after the retrieval step we shuffle the correspondence between the inputs and labels of the retrieved examples, such that inputs are matched randomly from the set of labels the inputs originally belonged to. The intent of this ablation is to examine if the model requires correct input-label correspondences (something that Min et al. (2022) calls into question), or if the model is simply using structural (e.g. prompt format) and distributional (e.g. the distribution of labels in the prompt) elements to produce a prediction.

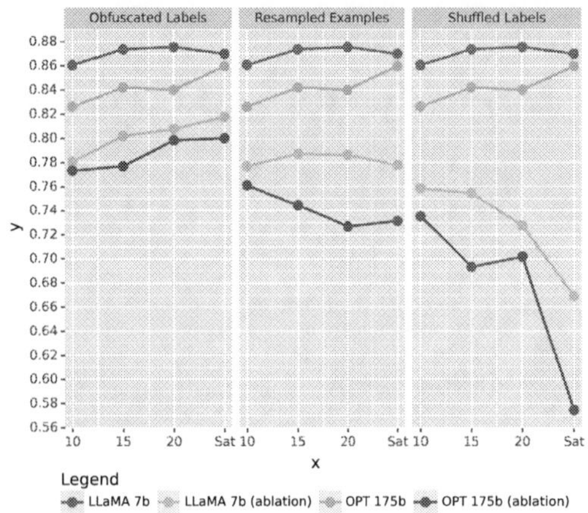

Figure 3: Classification accuracy for three ablations for HWU64: obfuscated labels (left), resampled in-context examples (center), shuffled labels (right).

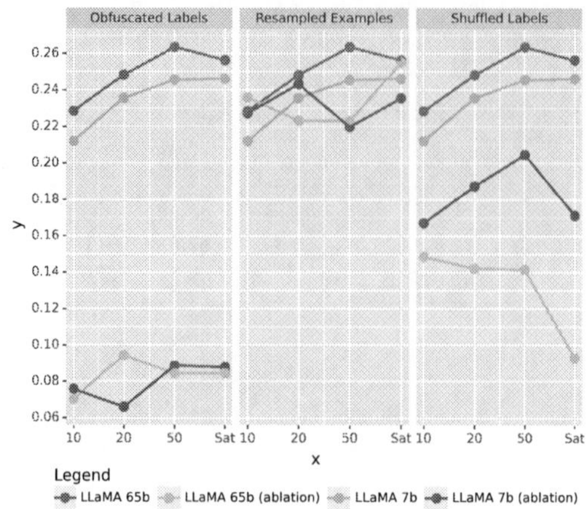

Figure 4: Classification accuracy for three ablations for GoEmotions: obfuscated labels (left), resampled in-context examples (center), shuffled labels (right).

6 Discussion

6.1 Small models cannot use long contexts as effectively as large models

One trend noticeable from the performance graph as a function of the number of examples for HWU (see Figure 2) is that small models seem to be unable to use more examples as effectively as large models. The smaller OPT model is unable to effectively make use of the entire context window when it is filled and remains at relatively low performance. In contrast, OPT 175B shows continual improvement when more examples are added. A similar trend is visible for the LLaMA models, where the performance of the 7B model does not change significantly (see 2), but the 65B model is able to continuously improve. The smaller models either level off (OPT-13B) or lose performance (LLaMA-7B). In the 4K full context window settings for LLaMA-2, the difference between model scales is even more apparent (Tables 1 and 2). We see the small model showing inconsistent use of the longer contexts; sometimes improving, but mostly staying the same or worsening performance. Meanwhile, the large model consistently improves with the full context in almost all cases.

6.2 Similarity to current datapoint matters for intent classification

In the resampling ablation for HWU (see Figure 3) we see that resampling from the initial class distribution provided by the retriever model damages the performance across both OPT 175B and LLaMA 7B. This supports the strong performance numbers of the LLMs, showing that the similarity between in-context demonstrations and the current input matters. This implies that the LM is doing more than just selecting the most common class or just using the shortlist of class labels from the full set of classes to select in a more zero-shot fashion. One interesting difference to note is that OPT 175B, the larger model, shows a larger drop from the resampling as the number of in-context demonstrations increases, compared to LLaMA-7B, whose performance stays roughly constant (but lower than non-resampled). This may indicate that the LLaMA models with their additional training data are more robust to the resampling process, due to stronger pre-training knowledge and/or more robust performance overall. In the case of GoEmotions, we see almost no variation with resampling, showing that similarity to the input example is less influential, though the ordering of the examples relative to each other does seem to make a difference for the 7B model (Table 3).

6.3 Semantically significant label names matter greatly for sentiment classification

In the obfuscation ablation (see Figure 3), we see that all models are hurt by obfuscating label names. We see however that models are still able to learn to perform the task effectively, and in fact show similar improvement curves with increasing number of examples, just with a lower starting performance. This demonstrates that the semantic content of the

Table 4: Sample datapoints from GoEmotions

Text	Prediction LLaMA-2-70B	Gold label
Lmao the brigading is real	amusement	amusement
Enjoy the void	neutral	neutral
I really relate to this.	realization	approval
This is the only viable way out of Brexit.	optimism	approval
want* a source on that, sorry.	desire	remorse
I didn't know that, thank you for teaching me something today!	gratitude	gratitude
Well it obviously helps you rationalize your total unwillingness to take action to make the world a better place. I hope that you grow past that.	sadness	admiration
Damn, we need healthy PGs.	sadness	annoyance
Welcome to The Church of Jesus Christ of Latter Day Saints, where families can be SEPARATED forever	sadness	gratitude

labels is significantly useful to the models but simultaneously it is not integral to performing the task, which can also be done without semantically significant labels. In the case of GoEmotions, we see that the obfuscated labels particularly hurt the model, bringing it down significantly.It seems to be the case that the class names are integral to performance, but at the same time more examples are still helpful to the model, as in the 4K context window it still sees improved performance.

6.4 Input-label correspondence matters for all datasets

Shuffling the input-label correspondence is the ablation in which we see the performance of all the models decrease the most in the intent detection case (see Figure 3). Specifically, we see that the performance drop is proportional to the number of examples (more shuffled examples brings a larger drop). That being said, it is noteworthy that the performance of both models in this shuffled regime is still significantly above random chance for every number of demonstrations shown, implying perhaps that the LM's prior knowledge based on the label names is still contributing significantly to performance. In all 4 datasets (intent classification and GoEmotions), shuffling the labels hurts the large model more in particular. This aligns with the results of Wei et al. (2023), whose authors show that larger models are more able to learn perturbed input correspondences than smaller models, which manifests in this experiment as lower performance. In other words, the larger model is trying to learn the perturbed input correspondence, and thus losing more and more performance with more examples, while the smaller model is able to more effectively ignore the perturbation.

7 Retriever and LM Generalization

One interesting result from our experiments is the fact that generic retrievers seem to be able to quite effectively generalize across domains and tasks. Using the same exact retriever model across 3 different intent detection datasets (which according to the taxonomy of Hupkes et al. (2022) constitutes cross-task generalization) as well as a sentiment classification dataset (according to the previous taxonomy, a cross-domain generalization) demonstrates SoTA or better performance in almost all cases. The distribution shift locus, for both the retriever and the language model generating the final prediction, is from pretraining to testing time. This is because they are both pre-trained on massive generic data before being tested in a zero-shot setting.

8 Related Work

Nearest neighbor selection of in-context examples: One of the earliest studies of the role of example selection in ICL is "KATE" (Liu et al., 2022b). In this paper, the authors probe the performance of GPT-3 on NLP tasks using KNN retrieval (RoBERTa) for example selection. They compare this method against random selection and using the retrieval model directly (plain KNN). They also examine the effect of example ordering on performance and conclude that the most performant ordering (least-to-most and most-to-least similar orderings are tested) depends on the dataset. In our work, we also experiment with example ordering, and conclude that least-to-most ordering is the most effective across all datasets tested.

Works demonstrating order instability: Several recent works have demonstrated that the order of in-context examples makes a larger difference in performance, including Lu et al. (2022); Zhao et al. (2021). These works demonstrate such order instability that certain permutations bring near SoTA performance on tasks while others perform at near random guessing.

Fine-tuned retrieval: Several works employ the use of fine-tuned retrievers, re-rankers, and/or LMs, including Rubin et al. (2022); Ram et al. (2023); Shi et al. (2023). Some, like REPLUG (Shi et al., 2023), use LM feedback in the form of using the LM to score documents to train the retriever. The goal of both Ram et al. (2023) and Shi et al. (2023) is to improve language modeling and not ICL ability. Rubin et al. (2022) uses a similar LM-score-based feedback to train a retriever (like REPLUG) but for ICL. The difference between all of these works and this work is that we demonstrate that an off-the-shelf retriever is sufficient out-of-the-box for SoTA performance with no additional tuning.

Works calling into question efficacy of ICL: Certain recent works have called into question the efficacy of ICL and models' ability to learn tasks they were not exposed to during pre-training (Min et al., 2022; Razeghi et al., 2022). In Min et al. (2022) authors show that randomly perturbing input-label pairings for some tasks can still lead to reasonably good performance, calling into question whether any "learning" is happening at all with ICL. The work in Razeghi et al. (2022) demonstrates that models perform better on data instances they have seen frequently during pre-training, implying that models are primarily memorizing and that their generalization capabilities in terms of ICL remain limited. Xie et al. (2022) suggests that ICL ability emerges due to the specific structure of the training data, specifically long-range dependencies.

Use of long contexts: Several works have demonstrated that long contexts are difficult for LMs to handle and show certain peculiarities. Kazemnejad et al. (2023) investigates the relationship between length generalization and positional embedding types, showing that in certain cases no positional embeddings can perform better. This work is closely related to use of long contexts for ICL, as it demonstrates the difficulty involved in generalizing to long context lengths, as well as providing an explanation for LMs' sensitivity to ordering (positional embeddings). In Liu et al. (2023), the authors investigate the impact of long contexts on document question answering, finding that the positions of the answers within the context matter greatly for performance, and generally demonstrating that longer contexts cause lower performance. In this work we show that larger models are needed to effectively take advantage of long contexts for ICL.

Few-shot intent detection: The current state of the art in few-shot intent detection is the ConvFit method (Vulić et al., 2021). ConvFit uses a pre-trained LM in a dual-encoder configuration (e.g. BERT or RoBERTa) with two training stages. The first stage is a conversational fine-tuning stage using a generic conversational corpus with a retrieval task (using tuples of (context, response) retrieve the correct response for each context). The second stage is fine-tuning on the specific intent classification dataset with a contrastive loss, allowing the resulting LM to be used in a KNN fashion.

9 Conclusion

In this work, we show that ICL with off-the-shelf frozen pre-trained retriever models can provide strong performance for text classification tasks with many labels. We show state of the art performance across three different intent classification datasets, and competitive performance with fine-grained sentiment classification. We also show that larger models are necessary to make use of more in-context examples, whereas small models mostly plateau or even show decreasing performance after a point. Through several ablation experiments, we demonstrate that LMs make use of all aspects of the input examples: semantically significant label names, correct input-label correspondences, as well as the similarity between the in-context demonstrations and the current input point, however to varying degrees depending on the dataset and domain.

10 Acknowledgement

SR is supported by the Canada CIFAR AI Chairs program and the NSERC Discovery Grant program. AM is supported by an IVADO Excellence Scholarship.

11 Limitations

One limitation of the research in this paper is that the experiments of this paper use the pre-existing DialoGLUE few-shot splits for each dataset, following the example of prior works and to remain comparable to them (with the exception of the ablation study, which uses a separate split). However, since experiments were done only on this split, it is not necessarily the case that the results/model rankings are transferable to other splits as well (although it is worth noting from Figure 3 that performance on the random ablation split is very similar to the DialoGLUE split, and the model ranking remains the same). This limitation is not the case with GoEmotions, whose results are given as averages across three random splits. Another limitation is the relatively small number of runs/seeds (only 3) due to limitations on compute.

One further limitation is that the experiments are all performed on English-language data.

References

Tom B. Brown, Benjamin Mann, Nick Ryder, Melanie Subbiah, Jared Kaplan, Prafulla Dhariwal, Arvind Neelakantan, Pranav Shyam, Girish Sastry, Amanda Askell, Sandhini Agarwal, Ariel Herbert-Voss, Gretchen Krueger, Tom Henighan, Rewon Child, Aditya Ramesh, Daniel M. Ziegler, Jeffrey Wu, Clemens Winter, Christopher Hesse, Mark Chen, Eric Sigler, Mateusz Litwin, Scott Gray, Benjamin Chess, Jack Clark, Christopher Berner, Sam McCandlish, Alec Radford, Ilya Sutskever, and Dario Amodei. 2020. Language Models are Few-shot Learners. In *Advances in Neural Information Processing Systems 33: Annual Conference on Neural Information Processing Systems 2020, NeurIPS 2020, December 6-12, 2020, virtual.*

Iñigo Casanueva, Tadas Temcinas, Daniela Gerz, Matthew Henderson, and Ivan Vulic. 2020. Efficient Intent Detection with Dual Sentence Encoders. In *Proceedings of the 2nd Workshop on NLP for ConvAI - ACL 2020*. Data available at https://github.com/PolyAI-LDN/task-specific-datasets.

Aakanksha Chowdhery, Sharan Narang, Jacob Devlin, Maarten Bosma, Gaurav Mishra, Adam Roberts, Paul Barham, Hyung Won Chung, Charles Sutton, Sebastian Gehrmann, Parker Schuh, Kensen Shi, Sasha Tsvyashchenko, Joshua Maynez, Abhishek Rao, Parker Barnes, Yi Tay, Noam Shazeer, Vinodkumar Prabhakaran, Emily Reif, Nan Du, Ben Hutchinson, Reiner Pope, James Bradbury, Jacob Austin, Michael Isard, Guy Gur-Ari, Pengcheng Yin, Toju Duke, Anselm Levskaya, Sanjay Ghemawat, Sunipa Dev, Henryk Michalewski, Xavier Garcia, Vedant Misra, Kevin Robinson, Liam Fedus, Denny Zhou, Daphne Ippolito, David Luan, Hyeontaek Lim, Barret Zoph, Alexander Spiridonov, Ryan Sepassi, David Dohan, Shivani Agrawal, Mark Omernick, Andrew M. Dai, Thanumalayan Sankaranarayana Pillai, Marie Pellat, Aitor Lewkowycz, Erica Moreira, Rewon Child, Oleksandr Polozov, Katherine Lee, Zongwei Zhou, Xuezhi Wang, Brennan Saeta, Mark Diaz, Orhan Firat, Michele Catasta, Jason Wei, Kathy Meier-Hellstern, Douglas Eck, Jeff Dean, Slav Petrov, and Noah Fiedel. 2023. PaLM: Scaling Language Modeling with Pathways. *J. Mach. Learn. Res.*, 24:240:1–240:113.

Dorottya Demszky, Dana Movshovitz-Attias, Jeongwoo Ko, Alan Cowen, Gaurav Nemade, and Sujith Ravi. 2020. GoEmotions: A Dataset of Fine-grained Emotions. In *Proceedings of the 58th Annual Meeting of the Association for Computational Linguistics*, pages 4040–4054, Online. Association for Computational Linguistics.

Dieuwke Hupkes, Mario Giulianelli, Verna Dankers, Mikel Artetxe, Yanai Elazar, Tiago Pimentel, Christos Christodoulopoulos, Karim Lasri, Naomi Saphra, Arabella Sinclair, Dennis Ulmer, Florian Schottmann, Khuyagbaatar Batsuren, Kaiser Sun, Koustuv Sinha, Leila Khalatbari, Maria Ryskina, Rita Frieske, Ryan Cotterell, and Zhijing Jin. 2022. State-of-the-art generalisation research in NLP: a taxonomy and review. *CoRR*, abs/2210.03050.

Vladimir Karpukhin, Barlas Oguz, Sewon Min, Patrick S. H. Lewis, Ledell Wu, Sergey Edunov, Danqi Chen, and Wen-tau Yih. 2020. Dense Passage Retrieval for Open-domain Question Answering. In *Proceedings of the 2020 Conference on Empirical Methods in Natural Language Processing, EMNLP 2020, Online, November 16-20, 2020*, pages 6769–6781. Association for Computational Linguistics.

Amirhossein Kazemnejad, Inkit Padhi, Karthikeyan Natesan Ramamurthy, Payel Das, and Siva Reddy. 2023. The Impact of Positional Encoding on Length Generalization in Transformers. *CoRR*, abs/2305.19466.

Stefan Larson, Anish Mahendran, Joseph J. Peper, Christopher Clarke, Andrew Lee, Parker Hill, Jonathan K. Kummerfeld, Kevin Leach, Michael A. Laurenzano, Lingjia Tang, and Jason Mars. 2019. An Evaluation Dataset for Intent Classification and Out-of-scope Prediction. In *Proceedings of the 2019 Conference on Empirical Methods in Natural Language Processing and the 9th International Joint Conference on Natural Language Processing, EMNLP-IJCNLP 2019, Hong Kong, China, November 3-7, 2019*, pages 1311–1316. Association for Computational Linguistics.

Haokun Liu, Derek Tam, Mohammed Muqeeth, Jay Mohta, Tenghao Huang, Mohit Bansal, and Colin Raffel. 2022a. Few-shot Parameter-efficient Fine-tuning is Better and Cheaper than In-context Learning. In *NeurIPS*.

Jiachang Liu, Dinghan Shen, Yizhe Zhang, Bill Dolan, Lawrence Carin, and Weizhu Chen. 2022b. What Makes Good In-context Examples for GPT-3? In *Proceedings of Deep Learning Inside Out: The 3rd Workshop on Knowledge Extraction and Integration for Deep Learning Architectures, DeeLIO at ACL 2022, Dublin, Ireland and Online, May 27, 2022*, pages 100–114. Association for Computational Linguistics.

Nelson F. Liu, Kevin Lin, John Hewitt, Ashwin Paranjape, Michele Bevilacqua, Fabio Petroni, and Percy Liang. 2023. Lost in the Middle: How Language Models Use Long Contexts. *CoRR*, abs/2307.03172.

Xingkun Liu, Arash Eshghi, Pawel Swietojanski, and Verena Rieser. 2019. Benchmarking Natural Language Understanding Services for Building Conversational Agents. In *Increasing Naturalness and Flexibility in Spoken Dialogue Interaction - 10th International Workshop on Spoken Dialogue Systems, IWSDS 2019, Syracuse, Sicily, Italy, 24-26 April 2019*, volume 714 of *Lecture Notes in Electrical Engineering*, pages 165–183. Springer.

Yao Lu, Max Bartolo, Alastair Moore, Sebastian Riedel, and Pontus Stenetorp. 2022. Fantastically Ordered Prompts and Where to Find Them: Overcoming Few-shot Prompt Order Sensitivity. In *Proceedings of the 60th Annual Meeting of the Association for Computational Linguistics (Volume 1: Long Papers), ACL 2022, Dublin, Ireland, May 22-27, 2022*, pages 8086–8098. Association for Computational Linguistics.

Shikib Mehri, Mihail Eric, and Dilek Hakkani-Tür. 2020. DialoGLUE: A Natural Language Understanding Benchmark for Task-oriented Dialogue. *CoRR*, abs/2009.13570.

Sewon Min, Xinxi Lyu, Ari Holtzman, Mikel Artetxe, Mike Lewis, Hannaneh Hajishirzi, and Luke Zettlemoyer. 2022. Rethinking the Role of Demonstrations: What Makes In-context Learning Work? In *Proceedings of the 2022 Conference on Empirical Methods in Natural Language Processing, EMNLP 2022, Abu Dhabi, United Arab Emirates, December 7-11, 2022*, pages 11048–11064. Association for Computational Linguistics.

Jonas Pfeiffer, Andreas Rücklé, Clifton Poth, Aishwarya Kamath, Ivan Vulic, Sebastian Ruder, Kyunghyun Cho, and Iryna Gurevych. 2020a. AdapterHub: A Framework for Adapting Transformers. In *Proceedings of the 2020 Conference on Empirical Methods in Natural Language Processing: System Demonstrations, EMNLP 2020 - Demos, Online, November 16-20, 2020*, pages 46–54. Association for Computational Linguistics.

Jonas Pfeiffer, Ivan Vulić, Iryna Gurevych, and Sebastian Ruder. 2020b. MAD-X: An Adapter-Based Framework for Multi-Task Cross-Lingual Transfer. In *Proceedings of the 2020 Conference on Empirical Methods in Natural Language Processing (EMNLP)*, pages 7654–7673, Online. Association for Computational Linguistics.

Jack W. Rae, Sebastian Borgeaud, Trevor Cai, Katie Millican, Jordan Hoffmann, H. Francis Song, John Aslanides, Sarah Henderson, Roman Ring, Susannah Young, Eliza Rutherford, Tom Hennigan, Jacob Menick, Albin Cassirer, Richard Powell, George van den Driessche, Lisa Anne Hendricks, Maribeth Rauh, Po-Sen Huang, Amelia Glaese, Johannes Welbl, Sumanth Dathathri, Saffron Huang, Jonathan Uesato, John Mellor, Irina Higgins, Antonia Creswell, Nat McAleese, Amy Wu, Erich Elsen, Siddhant M. Jayakumar, Elena Buchatskaya, David Budden, Esme Sutherland, Karen Simonyan, Michela Paganini, Laurent Sifre, Lena Martens, Xiang Lorraine Li, Adhiguna Kuncoro, Aida Nematzadeh, Elena Gribovskaya, Domenic Donato, Angeliki Lazaridou, Arthur Mensch, Jean-Baptiste Lespiau, Maria Tsimpoukelli, Nikolai Grigorev, Doug Fritz, Thibault Sottiaux, Mantas Pajarskas, Toby Pohlen, Zhitao Gong, Daniel Toyama, Cyprien de Masson d'Autume, Yujia Li, Tayfun Terzi, Vladimir Mikulik, Igor Babuschkin, Aidan Clark, Diego de Las Casas, Aurelia Guy, Chris Jones, James Bradbury, Matthew J. Johnson, Blake A. Hechtman, Laura Weidinger, Iason Gabriel, William Isaac, Edward Lockhart, Simon Osindero, Laura Rimell, Chris Dyer, Oriol Vinyals, Kareem Ayoub, Jeff Stanway, Lorrayne Bennett, Demis Hassabis, Koray Kavukcuoglu, and Geoffrey Irving. 2021. Scaling Language Models: Methods, Analysis & Insights from Training Gopher. *CoRR*, abs/2112.11446.

Ori Ram, Yoav Levine, Itay Dalmedigos, Dor Muhlgay, Amnon Shashua, Kevin Leyton-Brown, and Yoav Shoham. 2023. In-context Retrieval-augmented Language Models. *CoRR*, abs/2302.00083.

Yasaman Razeghi, Robert L. Logan IV, Matt Gardner, and Sameer Singh. 2022. Impact of Pretraining Term Frequencies on Few-shot Reasoning. *CoRR*, abs/2202.07206.

Nils Reimers and Iryna Gurevych. 2019a. Sentence-BERT: Sentence Embeddings using Siamese BERT-networks. In *Proceedings of the 2019 Conference on Empirical Methods in Natural Language Processing and the 9th International Joint Conference on Natural Language Processing (EMNLP-IJCNLP)*, pages 3982–3992, Hong Kong, China. Association for Computational Linguistics.

Nils Reimers and Iryna Gurevych. 2019b. Sentence-BERT: Sentence Embeddings using Siamese BERT-networks. In *Proceedings of the 2019 Conference on Empirical Methods in Natural Language Processing and the 9th International Joint Conference on Natural Language Processing (EMNLP-IJCNLP)*, pages 3982–3992, Hong Kong, China. Association for Computational Linguistics.

Ohad Rubin, Jonathan Herzig, and Jonathan Berant. 2022. Learning To Retrieve Prompts for In-context Learning. In *Proceedings of the 2022 Conference of the North American Chapter of the Association for Computational Linguistics: Human Language Technologies, NAACL 2022, Seattle, WA, United States,*

July 10-15, 2022, pages 2655–2671. Association for Computational Linguistics.

Weijia Shi, Sewon Min, Michihiro Yasunaga, Minjoon Seo, Rich James, Mike Lewis, Luke Zettlemoyer, and Wen-tau Yih. 2023. REPLUG: Retrieval-augmented Black-box Language Models. *CoRR*, abs/2301.12652.

Hugo Touvron, Thibaut Lavril, Gautier Izacard, Xavier Martinet, Marie-Anne Lachaux, Timothée Lacroix, Baptiste Rozière, Naman Goyal, Eric Hambro, Faisal Azhar, Aurélien Rodriguez, Armand Joulin, Edouard Grave, and Guillaume Lample. 2023. LLaMA: Open and Efficient Foundation Language Models. *CoRR*, abs/2302.13971.

Lewis Tunstall, Nils Reimers, Unso Eun Seo Jo, Luke Bates, Daniel Korat, Moshe Wasserblat, and Oren Pereg. 2022. Efficient Few-shot Learning Without Prompts. *CoRR*, abs/2209.11055.

Ivan Vulić, Pei-Hao Su, Samuel Coope, Daniela Gerz, Paweł Budzianowski, Iñigo Casanueva, Nikola Mrkšić, and Tsung-Hsien Wen. 2021. ConvFiT: Conversational Fine-tuning of Pretrained Language Models. In *Proceedings of the 2021 Conference on Empirical Methods in Natural Language Processing*, pages 1151–1168, Online and Punta Cana, Dominican Republic. Association for Computational Linguistics.

Jerry W. Wei, Jason Wei, Yi Tay, Dustin Tran, Albert Webson, Yifeng Lu, Xinyun Chen, Hanxiao Liu, Da Huang, Denny Zhou, and Tengyu Ma. 2023. Larger language models do in-context learning differently. *CoRR*, abs/2303.03846.

Sang Michael Xie, Aditi Raghunathan, Percy Liang, and Tengyu Ma. 2022. An Explanation of In-context Learning as Implicit Bayesian Inference. In *The Tenth International Conference on Learning Representations, ICLR 2022, Virtual Event, April 25-29, 2022*. OpenReview.net.

Susan Zhang, Stephen Roller, Naman Goyal, Mikel Artetxe, Moya Chen, Shuohui Chen, Christopher Dewan, Mona T. Diab, Xian Li, Xi Victoria Lin, Todor Mihaylov, Myle Ott, Sam Shleifer, Kurt Shuster, Daniel Simig, Punit Singh Koura, Anjali Sridhar, Tianlu Wang, and Luke Zettlemoyer. 2022. OPT: Open Pre-trained Transformer Language Models. *CoRR*, abs/2205.01068.

Tony Z. Zhao, Eric Wallace, Shi Feng, Dan Klein, and Sameer Singh. 2021. Calibrate Before Use: Improving Few-shot Performance of Language Models. *CoRR*, abs/2102.09690.

A GenBench Evaluation Card

Motivation			
Practical	*Cognitive*	*Intrinsic*	*Fairness*
□			

Generalisation type					
Composit.	*Structural*	*Cross Task*	*Cross Language*	*Cross Domain*	*Robustness*
		□		□	

Shift type			
Covariate	*Label*	*Full*	*Assumed*
		□	

Shift source			
Naturally occuring	*Partitioned natural*	*Generated shift*	*Fully generated*
□			

Shift locus			
Train–test	*Finetune train–test*	*Pretrain–train*	*Pretrain–test*
			□

Taxonomy taken from Hupkes et al. (2022).

B Classical vs. Neural Retriever

In this section we compare the SentenceTransformers neural BERT-based retriever against a classic Okapi-BM25 retriever on the HWU64 and BANKING77 datasets. The setup used is the same as in the main paper, which is 20 examples in-context with regular nearest neighbor retrieval. In Table 5 we can see that the classical BM25 retriever performs measurably worse than the neural SentenceTransformer retriever, indicating that semantically-aware neural retrieval provides a significant boost in performance.

Table 5: Comparison vs. Classical (BM25) Retriever

Model	**BANKING**	**HWU**
	10-shot	**10-shot**
LLaMA-2-7B (mpnet)	89.45	87.82
LLaMA-2-7B (BM25-Okapi)	84.90	84.76

C Fine-tuned Retriever

The contrastively fine-tuned retriever was trained for one epoch to avoid overfitting, using three times as many negative pairs as positive pairs (roughly 5-10 mins depending on the dataset).

C.1 Discussion

We note large improvements in the pure 1-NN mode accuracy, as expected, as we are optimizing

Table 6: Comparison of Models with Fine-tuned Retriever (20 examples in prompt), compared against non-fine-tuned performance

Model	BANKING	HWU	CLINC
	10-shot	10-shot	10-shot
SBERT KNN	87.40 ± 0.21	83.05 ± 0.47	91.48 ± 0.13
vs. frozen	+ 2.0%	+ 7.6%	+ 6.64%
OPT 13B	87.71 ± 0.18	83.83 ± 0.83	91.83 ± 0.22
vs. frozen	+ 2.06%	+ 0.19%	+ 2.59%
LLaMA 7B	87.39 ± 0.08	87.98 ± 0.75	94.17 ± 0.32
vs. frozen	- 0.24%	+ 0.43%	+ 2.44%
LLaMA 65B	88.93 ± 0.056	**90.12** ± 0.51	**95.62** ± 0.17
vs. frozen	- 1.79%	+ 0.062%	+ 1.16%

a metric that is directly correlated with 1-NN performance. With fine-tuning, the pure 1-NN setup becomes near-competitive with ConvFit, the previous SoTA. In terms of retrieval+ICL performance, we see mixed results. In general the performance delta is quite small, suggesting that there is no significant retrieval quality bottleneck. In general, the fine-tuned CLINC retriever provides the most boost, which is also the least data-scarce scenario (it is reasonable to expect the retriever fine-tuning to be more effective with more data).

D Overview of Negative Results

In this section the experiments we performed that gave negative results are enumerated. Specifically, we tried several retrieval strategies with the intention of improving performance above naive nearest-neighbor retrieval.

1. We tried "balancing" the classes in the prompt, i.e. giving a fixed N examples from each of the nearest M classes, where "nearest M classes" is defined by each class's nearest example to the input instance.

2. With CLINC150, which has a hierarchical label structure (labels are grouped into higher-level domain categories), we tried a two-step prediction process, where the LM would first predict the domain, then the individual label. The accuracy of predicting the domain was too poor.

3. We tried clustering the datapoints and providing N examples from each of the nearest clusters, again as defined by their nearest example to the input instance.

4. We tried a "deduplicative" approach to try a more diverse prompt, where an example would not be added to the prompt demonstration pool if it was too similar to an existing example in the pool.

5. We tried doing the pure nearest example approach (what is presented in the paper), but with a restriction to a fixed M number of classes represented in the prompt (i.e. as we are adding examples, if we reach a certain M number of classes represented in the prompt, we stop adding examples of other classes, and just fill the prompt with examples of the first M classes, in order of similarity). This was to see if the LM potentially was having issues handling examples of too many classes in the prompt.

GQG: Generalized Quantifier Generalization
A Dataset for Evaluating Quantifier Semantics in Language Models

Leroy Z. Wang
University of Washington
lryw@uw.edu

Shane Steinert-Threlkeld
University of Washington
shanest@uw.edu

Abstract

We present a new dataset consisting of various quantifier expressions to evaluate the generalization abilities of language models. The dataset contains 18,360 prompts encompassing diverse quantifiers, forming the basis of a new framework for assessing semantic understanding in this domain. We test the effectiveness of our dataset using Pythia models, ranging from 410 million to 6.9 billion parameters, showing that quantifier-based tasks can be challenging for current language models. We make our code and data publicly available[1], such that the dataset can be easily extended or updated based on different evaluation needs.

1 Introduction

In recent years, the Natural Language Processing (NLP) community has witnessed the rise of increasingly larger and more sophisticated language models (LMs) capable of generating coherent texts over extended passages. However, the ability of these models to understand and generate human language that aligns with the underlying semantics remains a topic of debate (Yogatama et al., 2019). Neural language models may rely on heuristics learned from the training data to generate seemingly coherent texts, but fail to generalize to scenarios that are more complex and cannot be solved by simple heuristics (McCoy et al., 2019). Whether language models can acquire *meaning* when trained only on text is also a topic of ongoing debate. Bender and Koller (2020) have argued, through thought experiments, that LMs cannot learn semantics through texts since they lack access to explicit representations of the external world. We hope to contribute to this ongoing dicussion by releasing this dataset on quantifiers, which will enable more research on this direction.

In this paper, we introduce a new framework that uses formal semantics to test the generalization capabilities of language models, by developing a dataset that assesses LMs' understanding of quantifier semantics. We ask the question – to what extent do language models capture the semantics of quantifiers?

Quantifiers are well-suited for evaluating language model generalization because compared to other linguistics objects, their meanings are more abstract, and can be fully specified in theoretical terms that do not require grounding. Common examples of quantifiers include *some*, *all*, *a few*, *many*, etc. To construct the dataset, we use a deterministic algorithm to generate prompts and gold labels automatically, covering 15 different quantifiers in the English language. In each prompt, we ask the LM to give a truth value judgment (true or false) to a statement about a given quantifier in a constructed scenario.

This dataset does not exhaust common quantifiers in English, but is designed to enable more research on evaluating LMs' understanding of semantic objects. More specifically, the dataset will allow further investigation into different axes of generalization in this domain, i.e. for the same quantifier, does using different nouns in the prompts affect LM's acquisition of the semantics of the quantifier? And how do different number ranges or different word orders affect LM's understanding of the same quantifier? The dataset presented in this paper provides a valuable framework for researchers to study these types of questions, grounded by rich formal semantics literature on quantifiers. As demonstrated in section 3, the data generation pipeline can be easily extended to study new quantifiers, nouns, and number ranges. Given initial native speaker annotated prompts and quantifiers, the data can also be easily extended to different languages.

This paper is structured as follows. In section 2, we discuss the literature on quantifiers in formal semantics and demonstrate how they can be useful for evaluating LMs. In section 3, we discuss how

[1] https://github.com/lerow/llm-quantifier

Proceedings of the 1st GenBench Workshop on (Benchmarking) Generalisation in NLP, pages 185–192
December 6, 2023 ©2023 Association for Computational Linguistics

the dataset is constructed and how LMs are evaluated. We discuss future work directions in section 4 and remark on limitations at the end.

2 Background

2.1 Quantifiers

Quantifiers are semantic objects expressed by determiners. In formal semantics, determiners can be considered as *generalized quantifiers* that describe the relations between two subsets in a discourse (Barwise and Cooper, 1981). Examples of quantifiers include *some*, *a few*, *all*, *most*, etc. They are useful for evaluating language models' generalization ability because their semantics is well-defined. Unlike content words, such as common nouns, quantifiers' semantics is fully abstract and can be specified in set-theoretic terms. Therefore, when measuring the alignment between language models and quantifier semantics, the evaluation can be completed fully unsupervised without human annotations while achieving high accuracy.

Based on literature in formal semantics (Barwise and Cooper, 1981; Peters and Westerstl, 2006; Szymanik, 2016; Steinert-Threlkeld and Szymanik, 2019), we define a quantifier to be a relation between two subsets A and B of a given discourse domain M. For example:

$$[\![\text{at least } n]\!] = \{\langle M, A, B\rangle : |A \cap B| \geq n\}$$
$$[\![\text{all}]\!] = \{\langle M, A, B\rangle : |A \cap B| = |A \cup B|\}$$
$$[\![\text{more than half}]\!] = \{\langle M, A, B\rangle : |A \cap B| > |A \backslash B|\}$$
$$[\![\text{a few}]\!] = \{\langle M, A, B\rangle : |A \cap B| > 1\}$$

We use $[\![Q]\!]$ to denote the semantic meaning of quantifier Q. For the quantifier "at least n", $[\![\text{at least } n]\!]$ describes sentences that satisfy $|A \cap B| \geq n$ when interpreted in model M.[2] For example, let set A denote the flowers, and set B denote the red objects in a discourse. Suppose $|A| = 5, |B| = 5, |A \cap B| = 5$, then the sentence "at least 5 flowers are red" would be true, because the situation $\langle M, A, B\rangle$ would belong to to $[\![\text{at least } 5]\!]$ since it satisfies $|A \cap B| \geq 5$.

Given a prompt as a way of representing a situation M, A, B in natural language, we can define the meaning of a quantifier according to a language model as:

$$[\![Q]\!]^{\text{LM}}_{\text{prompt}} = \{\langle M, A, B\rangle : \text{LM}(\text{prompt}(Q, M, A, B)) = T\},$$

We can then measure how similar $[\![Q]\!]^{\text{LM}}_{\text{prompt}}$ is to the true underlying $[\![Q]\!]$. The LM and the prompt are considered as parameters that need to be specified by the researcher.

2.2 Related Work

Benchmarks and Datasets There have been many benchmarks and datasets developed to evaluate the language understanding abilities of NLP models. Benchmarks such as SuperGLUE (Wang et al., 2019) and WinoGrande (Sakaguchi et al., 2021) test commonsense and logical reasoning abilities of LMs. In NLI datasets such as SNLI (Bowman et al., 2015) and LAMBADA (Paperno et al., 2016), designed to measure LMs' reasoning abilities through quantifiers. In AMBIENT, Liu et al. (2023) have curated a linguist-annotated dataset with various kinds of linguistic ambiguities, including quantifier scope ambiguity, to measure the disambiguation abilities of LMs. Understanding the relationships between quantifiers is important for LMs to perform well in these NLI datasets [3], but whether LMs can correctly acquire the semantics of quantifiers has not been systematically tested.

LMs and Semantics Bender and Koller (2020) have argued that LMs cannot acquire full meanings from text data alone, since they have no access to the explicit representations of entities in the world. In response, Li et al. (2021) demonstrate that language models can use contextual word representations to model changes of entities in a discourse, which presents preliminary empirical evidence suggesting that neural language models are capable of encoding partial representations of meaning when trained only on text data. Patel and Pavlick (2022) show that language models can learn to map a conceptual domain (such as color or direction) onto a grounded world representation. Utilizing psycholinguistic tests, Ettinger (2020) have shown that the BERT model has difficulty acquiring generalizable meanings of negation quantifiers.

[2] See Peters and Westerstl (2006) for a more detailed discussion.

[3] e.g. "A soccer game with multiple males playing" entails "Some men are playing a sport." (Bowman et al., 2015), but not vice versa

3 Methodology

3.1 Dataset Creation

We use a deterministic algorithm to generate the prompts in the dataset. Demonstrated in algorithm 1, we iterate through all available object and quantifier combinations, and generate a prompt for each combination. n is the number of objects in total and i is the number of objects modified by the first predicate (i.e. "are large" in the first example in Table 4), or by the second predicate (i.e. "are small") in the current iteration.

The GENERATE_PROMPT function can be fully customized by the user. In this work, we use the prompt template "There are 50 items. n of the items are large. m of the items are small. Are Q of the items small / large? Answer with only one word, true or false." for all 18,360 prompts in the dataset.

For the vanilla GQG dataset, we set $n = 50$, and the two predicates to be “are large” and “are small”. Researchers can use the framework to easily generate more prompts with different number ranges, predicates, and noun objects, to test various kinds of LM generalization.

Label Generation The gold labels in the dataset are generated using lambda functions that represent the exact semantics of the quantifiers – e.g. for quantifier "at least 3", its function would be

$$\lambda\ n, a, b : a >= 3,$$

where n is the total number of objects, a is the number of objects modified by the first predicate, and b is the number of objects modified by the second predicate. Using the notation presented in section 2.1, we have $n = |M|$, $a = |A \cap B|$, and $b = |M| - |A \cap B|$.

The lambda functions are manually coded by human experimenters, and it is the only place that requires human labeling in this evaluation framework (besides creating the prompt template).

Number of prompts The number 18,360 comes from $18360 = 12 \times 15 \times 51 \times 2$, where

- 12: number of objects
- 15: number of quantifers
- 51: (0 to 50) number of objects modified by the predicate
- 2: we have 2 predicates, so for the same quantifier, number of objects, and nouns, we prompt for both the first predicate and for the second predicate. For example, if $n = 50$, $q = \{\text{at least half}\}$, $o = \{\text{apples}\}$, $i = 5$, there will be two prompts generated, one asking "are at least half of the apples large?" with gold label *false*, and the other one asking "are at least half of the apples small?" with gold label *true*.

Algorithm 1 Data Generation

Inputs: set of quantifiers Q, set of objects O, function GENERATE_PROMPT, number range m, n $(m \leq n)$

```
for o in O do
    for q in Q do
        for i := m to n do
            append
            GENERATE_PROMPT (o, q, i, n)
            to prompts
        end for
    end for
end for

return prompts
```

3.2 Data Statistics

We present some statistics of the vanilla GQG dataset in this section. The dataset is consisted of prompts describing different scenarios using various quantifiers and noun objects shown in Table 2 and Table 3. The GQG framework is highly modular, allowing researchers to easily extend the vanilla dataset beyond the scope of the lexical items presented in this paper.

Number of prompts	18360
Average # of tokens per prompt	31.9
# of prompts with true label	8592 (46.8 %)
# of prompts with false label	9768 (53.2 %)

Table 1: Data Statistics

List of Quantifiers:

No.	Quantifier
1	at least 3
2	at least 4
3	at most 5
4	at most 6
5	more than 1
6	more than 5
7	more than 10
8	all
9	none
10	between 4 and 6
11	between 2 and 10
12	at most half
13	more than half
14	less than half
15	at least half

Table 2: Quantifiers in the dataset

List of objects:

No.	Object
1	tables
2	chairs
3	circles
4	squares
5	apples
6	bikes
7	pans
8	shelves
9	trees
10	birds
11	penguins
12	mountains

Table 3: Objects in the dataset

Prompt	Label
There are 50 tables. 50 of the tables are large. 0 of the tables are small Are **at least 3** of the tables small? Answer with only one word, true or false.	false
There are 50 circles. 7 of the circles are large. 43 of the circles are small. Are **at least 4** of the circles small? Answer with only one word, true or false.	true
There are 50 apples. 49 of the apples are large. 1 of the apples is small. Are **less than half** of the apples large? Answer with only one word, true or false.	false
There are 50 mountains. 24 of the mountains are large. 26 of the mountains are small. Are **at most half** of the mountains large? Answer with only one word, true or false.	true

Table 4: Examples of prompts in the dataset

3.3 Evaluation

We use both accuracy and F_1 scores to measure the alignment between quantifier semantics and LMs' understanding. Since the data is not perfectly balanced ($> 53\%$ of prompts have *false* gold labels), a language model can easily perform better than random by always answering "false".

During evaluation, a parser is used to process the output from the LM. When the parser encounters a token that matches with the string "true"[4], it will consider the LM as giving a positive response. Otherwise, the parser considers the LM as giving a negative response to the prompt. Constrained decoding is used during evaluation – the LM's response must contain either the token "true" or the token "false".

This approach has its limitations, since how good the language models are at following instructions can affect the performance. Language models may also leak their training data when being prompted in this manner – we have observed that instead of answering the question, the LM will output texts resembling multiple choice questions when given the prompt, which may be part of its training data. We discuss the potential issues of our evaluation

[4]when converted to lowercase, with punctuations and whitespace removed

method in Limitations.

3.4 Generalization Testing

The GQG dataset enables researchers to test LM generalization in quantifier understanding across different lexical items. For example, given a quantifier q, does changing the noun objects o in the prompts affect LMs' understanding of $[\![q]\!]$? In other words, we can use the GQG framework to test whether LMs' understanding of the semantics of a quantifier is consistent with respect to different nouns used in the prompt.

Testing generalization with respect to different axes is also possible, by fixing different elements in the dataset. For instance, one can test whether LMs have the same level of understanding across different quantifiers by fixing the noun o and only alternating q in the prompts. It should be noted that the vanilla GQG dataset does not support testing generalization in arbitrary axes; however, such data can be easily constructed using the code framework released in the paper.

3.5 Experimental Results

Model size	Accuracy	F1	Precision	Recall
410M	0.464	0.418	0.412	0.425
1B	0.503	0.289	0.216	0.437
1.4B	**0.519**	0.355	0.283	**0.476**
2.8B	0.515	0.626	0.283	**0.476**
6.9B	0.484	**0.639**	**0.976**	0.475

Table 5: Performance of Pythia models on vanilla GQG

Highlighted by low accuracies and F_1 scores[5], the GQG dataset can be quite challenging for the Pythia language models. It's intriguing to observe that the test accuracy does not increase significantly as the model size increases – the test accuracy for the 6.9B model is even lower than the 1B model.

We also perform a small pilot study on LM generalization across lexical items with different frequencies in the corpus, using Mistral-7B (Jiang et al., 2023) language model. As seen in Figure 1, the test accuracy of Mistral-7B drops as the nouns used in the prompts become less common.

For each word group, we use 10 different words with similar frequencies to generate prompts, using $q = \{\text{at least half}\}, m = 0, n = 50$.

[5] F_1 scores are included during evaluation since the dataset does not have a perfectly balanced True/False label ratio.

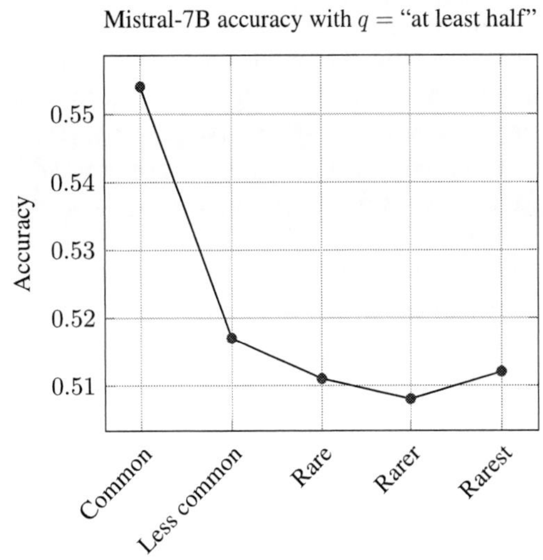

Figure 1: Mistral-7B accuracy with respect to word frequencies

Since The Pile dataset (Gao et al., 2020) that was used by Pythia LMs is not publicly available at the time of publication, we used the Leipzig Corpora (Richter et al., 2006; Goldhahn et al., 2012) to approximate the frequencies of tokens in Pythia training data. In each word group, the authors randomly select 10 different words with similar [6] frequencies in the Leipzig Corpora. Words that are in a less frequent group are guaranteed to have lower frequencies[7] than those in high-frequency groups. Examples of *common* words include "books", "doors", and "reports"; examples of *rarest* words include "lidars", "medullas", and "ornamentals". See Appendix A for the full list of words in each group.

The result of this small-scale experiment shows that large language models can be sensitive to the frequency of lexical items used in the prompt in certain scenarios. It also showcases the diverse kinds of research and generalization testing the GQG framework can enable.

4 Conclusion

This paper presents a new dataset to evaluate language models' understanding of quantifier semantics. The dataset can be easily extended to different languages and quantifiers, enabling more research on assessing language models' understanding of semantic objects and investigation into different axes of generalization. The poor performance of

[6] the difference between frequencies is less than 3

[7] in the Leipzig Corpora

the Pythia models during evaluation shows the dataset can be challenging for neural language models, but more research is required to understand how instruction-tuned LMs (and more sophisticated prompt-engineering) will perform on this dataset. We also note the limitations of our study, particularly on evaluation methods, and hope that this dataset will be a basis well-grounded in theoretical literature for more research on LMs and semantics.

Future work includes developing datasets in more diverse prompt formats, analyzing how LMs' performance can differ based on different types of quantifiers or linguistic objects, and investigating how finetuning can affect model performance.

Limitations

Monolingual Dataset We note that our dataset is curated only in English. How LMs may perform in low-resource languages has not been tested. What kind of impact will languages with more complex morphology/syntax have on benchmark performance also has not been investigated.

Prompt Format Our data is generated using one type of prompt format. Other types of prompt templates, including those designed in an adversarial manner, have not been evaluated in this paper. How the prompt is structured can also be an interesting axis of generalization to investigate – i.e. for the same quantifier and nouns, does different wordings of the prompt change how the LM acquire the semantics?

Finetuning The LMs tested have not been finetuned on the dataset. Whether finetuning can improve LMs' performance on understanding the semantics of quantifiers is a promising direction of future research.

Evaluation on LLMs The dataset has only been tested on Pythia models (Biderman et al., 2023). Larger and more recent language models such as GPT-4 (OpenAI, 2023), Llama-2 (Touvron et al., 2023), etc. have not been evaluated.

Ethics Statement

The data in this paper is artificially generated using a deterministic algorithm and does not violate any copyright laws. The dataset does not contain any content that is explicitly triggering, offensive, or toxic.

References

John Barwise and Robin Cooper. 1981. Generalized quantifiers and natural language. *Linguistics and Philosophy*, 4(2):159–219.

Emily M. Bender and Alexander Koller. 2020. Climbing towards NLU: On meaning, form, and understanding in the age of data. In *Proceedings of the 58th Annual Meeting of the Association for Computational Linguistics*, pages 5185–5198, Online. Association for Computational Linguistics.

Stella Biderman, Hailey Schoelkopf, Quentin Anthony, Herbie Bradley, Kyle O'Brien, Eric Hallahan, Mohammad Aflah Khan, Shivanshu Purohit, USVSN Sai Prashanth, Edward Raff, Aviya Skowron, Lintang Sutawika, and Oskar van der Wal. 2023. Pythia: A suite for analyzing large language models across training and scaling.

Samuel R. Bowman, Gabor Angeli, Christopher Potts, and Christopher D. Manning. 2015. A large annotated corpus for learning natural language inference. In *Proceedings of the 2015 Conference on Empirical Methods in Natural Language Processing*, pages 632–642, Lisbon, Portugal. Association for Computational Linguistics.

Allyson Ettinger. 2020. What BERT is not: Lessons from a new suite of psycholinguistic diagnostics for language models. *Transactions of the Association for Computational Linguistics*, 8:34–48.

Leo Gao, Stella Rose Biderman, Sid Black, Laurence Golding, Travis Hoppe, Charles Foster, Jason Phang, Horace He, Anish Thite, Noa Nabeshima, Shawn Presser, and Connor Leahy. 2020. The pile: An 800gb dataset of diverse text for language modeling. *ArXiv*, abs/2101.00027.

Dirk Goldhahn, Thomas Eckart, and Uwe Quasthoff. 2012. Building large monolingual dictionaries at the Leipzig corpora collection: From 100 to 200 languages. In *Proceedings of the Eighth International Conference on Language Resources and Evaluation (LREC'12)*, pages 759–765, Istanbul, Turkey. European Language Resources Association (ELRA).

Dieuwke Hupkes, Mario Giulianelli, Verna Dankers, Mikel Artetxe, Yanai Elazar, Tiago Pimentel, Christos Christodoulopoulos, Karim Lasri, Naomi Saphra, Arabella Sinclair, Dennis Ulmer, Florian Schottmann, Khuyagbaatar Batsuren, Kaiser Sun, Koustuv Sinha, Leila Khalatbari, Maria Ryskina, Rita Frieske, Ryan Cotterell, and Zhijing Jin. 2023. A taxonomy and review of generalization research in nlp. *Nature Machine Intelligence*, 5, 1161–1174.

Albert Qiaochu Jiang, Alexandre Sablayrolles, Arthur Mensch, Chris Bamford, Devendra Singh Chaplot, Diego de Las Casas, Florian Bressand, Gianna Lengyel, Guillaume Lample, Lucile Saulnier, L'elio Renard Lavaud, Marie-Anne Lachaux, Pierre Stock, Teven Le Scao, Thibaut Lavril, Thomas Wang,

Timothée Lacroix, and William El Sayed. 2023. Mistral 7b. *ArXiv*, abs/2310.06825.

Belinda Z. Li, Maxwell Nye, and Jacob Andreas. 2021. Implicit representations of meaning in neural language models. In *Proceedings of the 59th Annual Meeting of the Association for Computational Linguistics and the 11th International Joint Conference on Natural Language Processing (Volume 1: Long Papers)*, pages 1813–1827, Online. Association for Computational Linguistics.

Alisa Liu, Zhaofeng Wu, Julian Michael, Alane Suhr, Peter West, Alexander Koller, Swabha Swayamdipta, Noah A. Smith, and Yejin Choi. 2023. We're afraid language models aren't modeling ambiguity.

Tom McCoy, Ellie Pavlick, and Tal Linzen. 2019. Right for the wrong reasons: Diagnosing syntactic heuristics in natural language inference. In *Proceedings of the 57th Annual Meeting of the Association for Computational Linguistics*, pages 3428–3448, Florence, Italy. Association for Computational Linguistics.

OpenAI. 2023. Gpt-4 technical report.

Denis Paperno, Germán Kruszewski, Angeliki Lazaridou, Ngoc Quan Pham, Raffaella Bernardi, Sandro Pezzelle, Marco Baroni, Gemma Boleda, and Raquel Fernández. 2016. The LAMBADA dataset: Word prediction requiring a broad discourse context. In *Proceedings of the 54th Annual Meeting of the Association for Computational Linguistics (Volume 1: Long Papers)*, pages 1525–1534, Berlin, Germany. Association for Computational Linguistics.

Roma Patel and Ellie Pavlick. 2022. Mapping language models to grounded conceptual spaces. In *International Conference on Learning Representations*.

Stanley Peters and Dag Westersthl. 2006. *Quantifiers in Language and Logic*. Oxford University Press UK, Oxford, England.

Matthias Richter, Uwe Quasthoff, Erla Hallsteinsdóttir, and Chris Biemann. 2006. Exploiting the leipzig corpora collection.

Keisuke Sakaguchi, Ronan Le Bras, Chandra Bhagavatula, and Yejin Choi. 2021. Winogrande: An adversarial winograd schema challenge at scale. *Commun. ACM*, 64(9):99–106.

Shane Steinert-Threlkeld and Jakub Szymanik. 2019. Learnability and semantic universals. *Semantics and Pragmatics*.

Jakub Szymanik. 2016. *Quantifiers and Cognition: Logical and Computational Perspectives*. Springer.

Hugo Touvron, Louis Martin, Kevin Stone, Peter Albert, Amjad Almahairi, Yasmine Babaei, Nikolay Bashlykov, Soumya Batra, Prajjwal Bhargava, Shruti Bhosale, Dan Bikel, Lukas Blecher, Cristian Canton Ferrer, Moya Chen, Guillem Cucurull, David Esiobu, Jude Fernandes, Jeremy Fu, Wenyin Fu, Brian Fuller, Cynthia Gao, Vedanuj Goswami, Naman Goyal, Anthony Hartshorn, Saghar Hosseini, Rui Hou, Hakan Inan, Marcin Kardas, Viktor Kerkez, Madian Khabsa, Isabel Kloumann, Artem Korenev, Punit Singh Koura, Marie-Anne Lachaux, Thibaut Lavril, Jenya Lee, Diana Liskovich, Yinghai Lu, Yuning Mao, Xavier Martinet, Todor Mihaylov, Pushkar Mishra, Igor Molybog, Yixin Nie, Andrew Poulton, Jeremy Reizenstein, Rashi Rungta, Kalyan Saladi, Alan Schelten, Ruan Silva, Eric Michael Smith, Ranjan Subramanian, Xiaoqing Ellen Tan, Binh Tang, Ross Taylor, Adina Williams, Jian Xiang Kuan, Puxin Xu, Zheng Yan, Iliyan Zarov, Yuchen Zhang, Angela Fan, Melanie Kambadur, Sharan Narang, Aurelien Rodriguez, Robert Stojnic, Sergey Edunov, and Thomas Scialom. 2023. Llama 2: Open foundation and fine-tuned chat models.

Alex Wang, Yada Pruksachatkun, Nikita Nangia, Amanpreet Singh, Julian Michael, Felix Hill, Omer Levy, and Samuel R. Bowman. 2019. *SuperGLUE: A Stickier Benchmark for General-Purpose Language Understanding Systems*. Curran Associates Inc., Red Hook, NY, USA.

Dani Yogatama, Cyprien de Masson d'Autume, Jerome T. Connor, Tomás Kociský, Mike Chrzanowski, Lingpeng Kong, Angeliki Lazaridou, Wang Ling, Lei Yu, Chris Dyer, and Phil Blunsom. 2019. Learning and evaluating general linguistic intelligence. *CoRR*, abs/1901.11373.

A Appendix

Examples of LM Leaking Training Data When given the prompt: "There are 50 tables. 28 of the tables are large. 22 of the tables are small. Are all of the tables small? Answer with only one word, true or false.", Pythia LMs will sometimes generate

```
A. True

B. False

C. It is not possible to determine
```

as its response.[8]

Experiment Infrastructure All experiments were run on a single NVIDIA RTX 3090 GPU. For all Pythia models, step 143000 (the last model checkpoint) and temperature 1.0 were used during inference.

Constrained Decoding The constrained decoding used during evaluation is implemented using

[8]listed example is a generated text from Pythia-2.8B given the prompt

Huggingface `force_words_ids` during `generate`; beam search is used during generation with `num_beams=4`.

Words in Different Frequency Group

- common = ["books", "chairs", "doors", "participants", "activities", "systems", "wars", "blocks", "words", "reports"]
- less common = ["crowds", "negotiations", "cup holders", "arteries", "identifiers", "payrolls", "hostages", "coupons", "remedies", "butterflies"]
- rare = ["jaws", "turbines", "rooftops", "hikers", "purses", "empires", "insurers", "camels", "entitlements", "coils"]
- rarer = ["auroras", "borrowers", "fasteners", "headscarves", "hickories", "geneticists", "catapults", "blurbs", "glaciers", "eyewitnesses"]
- rarest = ["ocean basins", "jests", "lidars", "inequalities", "microchips", "humanoids", "philanthropies", "medullas", "ornamentals", "jabs"]

An example prompt using a word from the *rare* group:

```
There are 50 empires. 10 of the empires are large. 40 of the empires are small. Are at least half of the empires large? Answer with only one word, true or false.
```

GenBench 2023 Evaluation Card The GenBench evaluation card (Hupkes et al., 2023) is attached.
Shift locus: Pretrain-test.

Motivation					
Practical	*Cognitive*	*Intrinsic*	*Fairness*		
	□	□			
Generalisation type					
Compositional	*Structural*	*Cross Task*	*Cross Language*	*Cross Domain*	*Robustness*
□					□
Shift type					
Covariate	*Label*	*Full*	*Assumed*		
□					
Shift source					
Naturally occuring	*Partitioned natural*	*Generated shift*	*Fully generated*		
		□			
Shift locus					
Train–test	*Finetune train–test*	*Pretrain–train*	*Pretrain–test*		
			□		

Cross-Lingual Data Augmentation For Thai Question-Answering

Parinthapat Pengpun[‡], Can Udomcharoenchaikit[†],
Weerayut Buaphet[†], Peerat Limkonchotiwat[†]
[‡]Bangkok Christian International School, Thailand
[†]School of Information Science and Technology, VISTEC, Thailand
parinzee@protonmail.com
{canu_pro,weerayut.b_s20,peerat.l_s19}@vistec.ac.th

Abstract

This paper presents an innovative data augmentation framework with data quality control designed to enhance the robustness of Question Answering (QA) models in low-resource languages, particularly Thai. Recognizing the challenges posed by the scarcity and quality of training data, we leverage data augmentation techniques in both monolingual and cross-lingual settings. Our approach augments and enriches the original dataset, thereby increasing its linguistic diversity and robustness. We evaluate the robustness of our framework on Machine Reading Comprehension and the experimental results illustrate the potential of data augmentation to effectively increase training data and improve model generalization in low-resource language settings, offering a promising direction for the data augmentation manner.

1 Introduction

Question Answering (QA) systems are algorithms developed to answer questions posed in a natural language format accurately. A primary task in QA is Machine Reading Comprehension (MRC), which aims to extract answers from text passages given a question. Previous works demonstrate that improving the performance of MRC increases the accuracy in real-world applications, i.e., conversational chatbots (Yang et al., 2023; Jin and Lee, 2022; Hardalov et al., 2019).

While the performance of QA systems in English is largely considered to be a solved problem, it is still an open problem in low-resource languages, i.e., Thai. Recent works in QA demonstrate that the performance gap in QA systems for Thai and English is wide. For example, the baseline performance of English on the XQuAD (Artetxe et al., 2019) dataset has an F1 score of 83.5, while only 42.7 on Thai. Moreover, only five of the research works (Noraset et al., 2021; Decha and Patanukhom, 2017; Hochreiter and Schmidhuber, 1997; Wongpraomas et al., 2022; Limkonchotiwat et al., 2022b) has been published on QA for the Thai language within the last five years. Such disparity has led to a significant gap in the capabilities of NLP systems between high-resource languages and low-resource ones (Artetxe et al., 2019; Lewis et al., 2019; Wongpraomas et al., 2022). The robustness of NLP applications in low-resource languages leaves much to be desired due to the lack of extensive and diverse language data that covers all aspects of the language.

Existing literature offers several methods to mitigate the problem of robustness specifically for low data in QA, such as transfer learning (Pandya et al., 2021), back translation (Riabi et al., 2021), and the use of multilingual language models (Kumar et al., 2022). However, these techniques present drawbacks, e.g., transfer learning's success hinges largely on the relatedness of the source and target languages. In addition, multi-lingual models are impacted by the imbalanced data distribution and often do not perform as well as monolingual models (Artetxe et al., 2019; Lewis et al., 2019). For example, WangchanBERTa (Lowphansirikul et al., 2021), a monolingual RoBERTa-based (Liu et al., 2019) model trained explicitly on the Thai Language, outperforms multilingual models (XLM-R (Lample and Conneau, 2019) and mBERT (Devlin et al., 2018)). Additionally, there is a noticeable lack of studies focusing on these methods in the context of the Thai language, rendering the extension of such strategies unclear. The issue of robustness and generalization also remains largely unaddressed in recent literature, thereby leaving a significant gap in the field.

To improve performance in a low-resource setting, we propose an automatic framework for improving out-of-distribution robustness in QA. Our framework integrates back translation, word replacement, large language model (LLM) automated paraphrase generation, and LLM automated gram-

Proceedings of the 1st GenBench Workshop on (Benchmarking) Generalisation in NLP, pages 193–203
December 6, 2023

mar correction to construct a 10-way parallel corpus. This corpus features multiple varied sentence formulations to encourage robustness and generalization. While our framework heavily leverages machine translation (MT), which allows our augmentations to leverage the vast library of English augmentations thereby improving the robustness of Thai QA, it is our quality control system that sets our work apart. By rigorously removing noisy samples from the data—filtering the distances between the semantic representations of the augmented and the original data—the system ensures that the dataset obtained contains an optimal signal-to-noise ratio.

As shown in Figure 1, the proposed framework works as follows. Firstly, we aggregate, clean and normalize our datasets: TyDiQA (Clark et al., 2020), XQuAD (Artetxe et al., 2019), Iapp Wiki QA (Viriyayudhakorn and Polpanumas, 2021), and Thai QA (Trakultaweekoon et al., 2019). Then, we translate all questions into English and back-translate to Thai using Google Translate. Next, the gpt-3.5-turbo-0301 model is used in the third stage for grammar correction and paraphrasing of these translated questions. In the fourth stage, the Quality Controlled Paraphrase Generation (QCPG) (Bandel et al., 2022) model generates additional paraphrases for the translated questions, which are then translated back to Thai. In addition, we leverage WordNet, Thai2Fit, Thai2Transformers, and Large Thai Word2Vec (LTW2Vec) for word-replacement on the Thai questions without back-translation. Lastly, we utilize our quality control mechanism to filter noisy augmented samples from our corpora. The end corpora is a versatile, 10-way parallel corpus, ready for use in the MRC task.

We evaluate the effectiveness of our framework compared to common augmentations without any cross-lingual augmentations on standard QA datasets for the MRC task. Specifically we test for out-of-distribution by using completely different MRC Datasets for evaluation. For more information please refer to our evaluation card in the Appendix. The experimental results demonstrate that our framework significantly enhances the robustness and generalization of Thai QA systems. For example, we improve the performance (Exact Match/F1) of WangchanBERTa on TyDiQA and XQuAD datasets from 39.46/54.87 and 34.92/48.80, to 42.76/56.51 and 35.25/49.43, respectively. Our design analysis of the quality control mechanism demonstrates that our mechanism

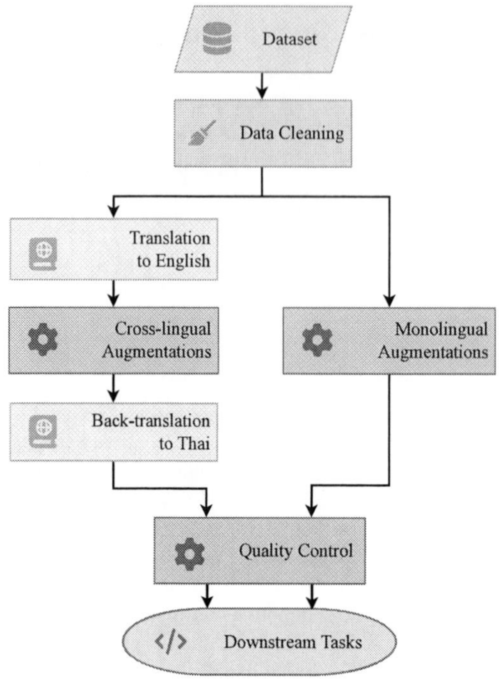

Figure 1: Our proposed automatic framework for improving the robustness of Thai QA systems.

removes noisy data from augmentation schemes and decreases the training time of MRC from 80 to 50 minutes ($\sim$38.25% faster).

We summarize the contribution of our work as follows:

- We propose a unified framework leveraging cross-lingual augmentations to improve Thai QA performance. The framework consists of 10 augmentations, including monolingual and cross-lingual settings.
- We release the first extensively cleaned, 10-way parallel QA corpus which unifies all publicly available QA datasets for the Thai language.
- We conduct an extensive study on large-scale experiments: 10 augmentation schemes, two benchmark datasets, and two ablation studies.
- We release all the datasets, code, and trained models at this GitHub Repo.

2 Related Work

2.1 Thai Question Answering

Numerous studies have attempted to address Thai QA systems in monolingual and multilingual settings. Noraset et al. (2021) introduced Wabi QA, a Wikipedia-based QA system that integrated both a retrieval model and an MRC model. Their method used a bidirectional Long Short-Term

Memory (LSTM) (Hochreiter and Schmidhuber, 1997) model as the MRC model and surpassed several extant methodologies in Thai QA. Similarly, Decha and Patanukhom (2017) proposed an open-domain Thai QA system that employed a keyword extraction system in combination with rule-based word segmentation and neural network-based sentence segmentation. Furthermore, an alternative QA system was put forward by Wongpraomas et al. (2022), which used a rule-based pattern-matching method relying on regular expressions and cosine similarity with a SQL database. Although these methods exhibited strong performance within their respective benchmarks, they fall short in providing results on any standardized or widely-recognized datasets, thereby rendering an accurate performance evaluation challenging. Furthermore, it is apparent that there is a lack of integration of Transformer-based models (Vaswani et al., 2017), and the concerns pertaining to system generalization and robustness are not addressed.

There are also multilingual approaches to tackling Thai QA. A common technique is to train a transformer model on multilingual QA datasets, such as XQuAD (Artetxe et al., 2019) and TyDiQA (Clark et al., 2020). Recently, there have been multilingual QA works focused on improving multilingual performance. Asai et al. (2021) proposed CORA, a unified multilingual many-to-many QA model. This work consisted of two QA models: (i) a multilingual dense passage retriever (mDPR); and (ii) an autoregressive answer generation model (mGEN) trained on multilingual Wikpedia. Notably, it did not use translation and can generalize to languages without annotated data sources but with large-scale training data. Limkonchotiwat et al. (2022b) proposed CL-ReLKT, a cross-lingual ReQA learning approach using knowledge transfer. In particular, this work distilled the performance of high-resource to low-resource languages, resulting in increased performance in a wide range of low-resource languages, including Thai.

Despite these advances, it becomes apparent that there are still significant gaps in the literature concerning implementing multilingual models in Thai QA. Specifically, these works do not address the robustness aspect of the model nor the specifics of the Thai language. Our research recognizes and addresses these gaps within the literature. Our approach employs a Transformer-based model, introduces a novel data augmentation technique to enhance robustness and generalization, and benchmarks results on well-established datasets.

2.2 Improving Robustness in QA

Robustness plays a crucial role in QA systems to perform efficiently on unseen data with varying distributions (Hupkes et al., 2023). There are numerous aspects to robustness in QA such as resistance to adversarial questions, ability to generalize to unseen domains, and capability to understand different phrasings or expressions of the same sentence. Various strategies have been proposed to improve this aspect of QA models, applicable across languages.

Bartolo et al. (2021) proposed an adversarial QA data generation pipeline that automatically generates question-answer pairs to bolster the QA model's robustness against adversarial questions. This pipeline improved both F1 and exact match (EM) scores of the models trained on adversarial synthetic data. Khashabi et al. (2020) proposed using natural human-driven perturbations on a small dataset to improve model performance instead of constructing new large-scale datasets. Each perturbation is independently verified to ensure minimal yet meaningful changes and that the questions are answerable. The experimental results demonstrated that the proposed model is more generalized and robust when dealing with small variations in a question.

The aforementioned studies have introduced remarkable advancements in the field of QA robustness. However, there are notable gaps in the literature regarding the application of these techniques in low-resource languages, specifically Thai. Despite the proven effectiveness of these strategies in languages with abundant resources, their applicability to Thai remains under-explored. This is particularly significant given the unique challenges presented by the Thai language, such as word and sentence boundary issues and scarcity of resources. Moreover, these works do not provide an established best practice for adapting these techniques to Thai or similar languages, presenting an additional obstacle to their application.

Despite this, we observe that many of the main ideas in the literature apply to the Thai language. Thus, our research aims to bridge these gaps by creating a framework that applies robustness-improvement techniques to Thai QA. We aim to develop and implement an efficient cross-lingual data augmentation system that can help overcome the specific challenges associated with the Thai language. Although our framework was designed for Thai specifically, it can easily be modified for usage in other languages by adjusting the translation part and the monolingual embedding-based augmentations.

3 Methodology

3.1 Overview

To increase the out-of-distribution robustness of QA models, we introduce a data augmentation framework (Figure 1), which employs back translation, word replacement, and the application of Large Language Models (LLMs) for automated paraphrase generation and grammar correction. This also includes cross-lingual data augmentation strategies that allow us to use high-performance NLP tools that only perform well in high-resource languages, such as paraphrase generation models. Moreover, our framework also incorporates a quality control step that can remove noisy samples to ensure the quality of the generated data.

Our framework enhances the quality of training data by synthetically adding linguistic diversity. This allows QA models to handle a diverse array of queries more effectively and improve their generalization. We detail how we formulate and augment our training data for enhanced robustness as follows.

3.2 Data Selection and Preprocessing

We select two standard multilingual QA datasets, such as TyDiQA (Clark et al., 2020) and XQuAD (Artetxe et al., 2019) since both datasets had Thai in their datasets. However, we found that there is no Thai training data for XQuAD. Thus, we add standard Thai QA datasets: Iapp Wiki QA (Viriyayudhakorn and Polpanumas, 2021) and Thai QA (Trakultaweekoon et al., 2019) into our framework. Then, we perform data cleaning by first stripping out HTML, XML, and other markup syntaxes inside the questions, answers, and contexts. We also drop rows that contain invalid answers and markup syntax that could not be removed automatically. Such invalid answers include incomplete answers and answers that start with a Thai tone mark or syllable. Then, we dropped all the duplicated questions and context sets to prevent data leakage into the test set. We then format all the questions to have a question mark at the end for extra clarity. Lastly, we realign all answer start positions (labels) to match the cleaned context with the cleaned answers.

3.3 Data Augmentation

As discussed in Section 2.1, Thai QA systems lack the generalization ability to handle unseen questions. The studies from previous work demonstrated promising results to improve the generalization by applying data augmentation schemes. However, previous augmentation schemes do not apply to Thai, it is unclear how to extend those beyond a monolingual setting. Thus, we apply these augmentation schemes using the back-translation (TH$\rightarrow$EN and EN$\rightarrow$TH) method [1] on questions of the training data.

We present 10 data augmentation schemes to enhance linguistic diversity and improve the generalization of our model. We split the data augmentation into two groups: *cross-lingual data augmentation* and *monolingual data augmentation*. The first group used the back-translation process (TH$\rightarrow$EN$\rightarrow$TH) with English augmentation schemes. The second group used monolingual data augmentation without the back-translation process.

Cross-lingual data augmentation. We employ four off-the-shelf data augmentation schemes from English QA to improve the robustness of Thai QA as follows:

- *Back-translation*: We utilize Google Translate to translate our Thai questions to English, then translate those questions back to Thai again. The Thai texts before and after the translation will be changed, which helps enhance the model's robustness, as it is trained to understand and respond to a broader set of phrasings. Moreover, it boosts the model's generalization capacity by enabling it to recognize and respond appropriately to imperfect translations and improper grammar (Zhang et al., 2021; Limkonchotiwat et al., 2022a).
- *LLM Grammar Error Correction (GEC)*: We utilized the gpt-3.5-turbo-0301 model [2] to perform GEC on English-translated data from the previous step, then used Google Translate to translate the corrected dataset back to Thai. This approach not only allows the model to understand

[1] We employ Google NMT as the back-translation method where the version date is 19 May 2023

[2] We use the version of 03.01.23. If an updated version is used, exact results may be hard to replicate. However, results obtained should be similar or better.

the core meaning of questions amidst grammatical inaccuracies but also enhances the model's robustness by expanding its exposure to a variety of corrected syntax. Furthermore, it improves the model's capacity to handle diverse and complex grammatical structures, thereby fostering better generalization.

- *LLM Paraphrase*: We also utilized the gpt-3.5-turbo-0301 model to generate a paraphrase of each question on the English translation of our questions, then used Google Translate to translate the paraphrased questions back to Thai. Prompting was done to allow GPT to assume the meaning of ambigious grammatically incorrect translations. For example, "You are a highly skilled language model AI that returns only one line of grammatically perfect text. Your task is to evaluate the text below and correct its grammar. Even if the text is incomplete or unintelligible, YOU MUST make a grammatical correction, you can make assumptions about the intended meaning. If the text is grammatically correct, do not change it. Your output should be presented WITH ONLY the corrected text IN ONE LINE and without any extra dialogue from you." This strategy improves the QA model's robustness by exposing it to a wider range of expressions and phrasing.
- *QCPG Paraphrase*: We utilize QCPG (Bandel et al., 2022), specifically the qcpg-questions model, to generate a paraphrase of each question on the English translation and the LLM GEC set of our questions, then used Google Translate to translate the paraphrased questions back to Thai. In total, three distinct paraphrase sets were generated by experimenting with three different values of settings applied to each dataset. These variations result from adjusting three QCPG settings, namely lexical, syntactic, and semantic, across the range of 0 to 1. Specifically, the chosen values for these settings were 0.2, 0.5, and 0.8, leading to the creation of three separate datasets. We select the best-performing dataset to be included in our main corpora (the 0.8 setting).
- *LLM GEC + QCPG Paraphrase*: We apply the QCPG Paraphrase atop the LLM GEC augmentation. This decision was driven by the hypothesis that the noisy translation might influence the QCPG model's performance and that rectifying this issue would yield an improved performance in paraphrasing. By employing this method, the model's robustness is enhanced, as it is exposed to modified yet semantically congruent expressions. Furthermore, this dataset variation promotes the model's generalization capabilities, facilitating its comprehension of the diverse manners in which a question might be framed.

Monolingual data augmentation. All the methods below are based on synonym replacement using pre-trained word embeddings. This method enriches the dataset and trains the model to recognize and understand equivalent words, resulting in improving the model's generalization ability and semantic understanding. These augmentations were selected since they represent monolingual methods commonly found in text augmentation and have been widely used. One such commonly used method is word or token replacement.

We leverage five monolingual pre-trained models as follows: (i) the **Thai WordNet** (Thoongsup et al., 2009) is employed for embedding-based word replacement; (ii) **Thai2Fit** (Polpanumas and Phatthiyaphaibun, 2021), a Thai adaptation of ULMFit (Howard and Ruder, 2018), which we used in the same manner as Thai WordNet; (iii) **Thai2Transformers** (Lowphansirikul et al., 2021) which utilizes the embeddings from the WangchanBERTa model to perform word-replacement; (iv) **LTW2Vec** (Phatthiyaphaibun, 2022), a comprehensive Thai Word2Vec model; and (v) **FastText** (Bojanowski et al., 2017) is also utilized for embedding-based word substitution.

3.4 Quality Control of Data Augmentation

As discussed in the data augmentation schemes, we use back-translation as the backbone of the cross-lingual augmentation. As the translation process is imperfect, this will lead to a variation of sentences with a similar meaning being produced. Despite this, the produced translation can be nearly perfect to almost unintelligible. Thus, we need to control the quality of our augmentation training data to not let low-quality paraphrases into our dataset.

One such consideration is that a good paraphrase should have a similar meaning between the original and augmented texts (Bandel et al., 2022). Thus, we chose to control the quality by evaluating the semantic score of augmentation datasets and selecting the best semantic score threshold (calculated on the development dataset) to find high-quality data for training QA models. We calculate the semantic score using the cosine distance between the embedding of augment and original questions obtained from Multilingual Universal Sentence Encoder (mUSE) (Yang et al., 2020). For monolingual augmentations, we can simply use the cosine distance between it and the original questions. In contrast, for cross-lingual augmentations, we use the harmonic distance (HD) between two measures: (i) the distance between the original questions and the English augmentation and (ii) the between the original questions and the translated English augmentation. We calculate the HD score as follows:

$$\text{HD} = \frac{2(1-\cos(t_{\text{org}}, t_{\text{en}}))(1-\cos(t_{\text{org}}, t_{\text{th}}))}{(1-\cos(t_{\text{org}}, t_{\text{en}})) + (1-\cos(t_{\text{org}}, t_{\text{th}}))} \quad (1)$$

where $\cos(\cdot)$ is cosine similarity, t_{org} is the original text before back-translation, t_{en} is the English text obtain from back-translation, t_{th} is the Thai text obtain from back-translation. While the arithmetic mean could oversimplify and skew results by providing equal weight to both measures, we opted for the harmonic mean, which is less sensitive to large discrepancies and offers a more balanced representation of the data. This approach ensures that neither the translation nor back-translation distances dominate the final score, yielding a more representative score that appreciates the intricacies of the multi-faceted nature of translation tasks. For more information and examples about how we calculate and select the augmentation ratio with the HD score, please see Appendix A.1.

4 Experimental Setting

4.1 Downstream tasks: MRC

We train the MRC model based on WangchanBERTa model (Lowphansirikul et al., 2021) on iAPP QA and ThaiQA datasets with a single V100 GPU for 140 hours with hyperparameters, as shown in Table 1. In addition, we report F1 and extract match (EM) scores for this task. For the hypothesis test, due to resource constraints, we were only able to test our results with one seed. Thus, we chose McNeMar due to its ability to work using one seed.

To incorporate our data augmentation schemes, we supplement the original training set with the augmented set of questions while maintaining the original context. To perform quality control, we benchmark each top-k% sample of the augmented data, systematically examining increments of 10% using harmonic distance. We select the best ratio on the validation set and show only the best score.

Hyperparameter	Value
Learning rate	$2e^{-5}$
Per-device train batch size	32
Per-device evaluation batch size	128
Gradient accumulation steps	2
Number of training epochs	20
Warmup ratio	0.2
Weight decay	0.01
Seed	42
Use fp16 precision	True

Table 1: Hyperparameters for the MRC task.

4.2 Datasets

- XQuAD (Artetxe et al., 2019). A cross-lingual QA dataset consists of 240 paragraphs and 1190 question-answer pairs from the development set of SQuAD v1.1, translated by professionals into 11 different languages, including Thai.
- iAPP QA (Viriyayudhakorn and Polpanumas, 2021). A Thai QA dataset from Thai Wikipedia consists of 9,170 question-answer pairs across 1,961 documents.
- ThaiQA (Trakultaweekoon et al., 2019). A Thai QA dataset from various domains of Wikipedia consists of 4051 question-answer pairs.
- TyDiQA (Clark et al., 2020). A multilingual QA dataset includes around 4500 questions in the Thai language.

For the evaluation setting, we use iAPP and ThaiQA as the training data for the MRC task while testing our model on XQuAD and TyDiQA datasets. Note that we use only Thai questions and context for multilingual datasets.

5 Experimental Results

We demonstrate the experimental results of the machine reading comprehension task in out-of-domain settings in Section 5.1. Section 5.2 demonstrates the analysis of the harmonic distance method on the performance and training speed efficiency. In addition, we present error analysis by comparing various augmentation texts with the original text in Section 5.3.

5.1 Machine Reading Comprehension

To identify the most efficacious augmentation strategy, we evaluate our MRC models with various

Augmentation	Ratio	Val EM/F1	TyDiQA EM/F1	XQuAD EM/F1
Original	N/A	50.75 / 62.40	39.46 / 54.87	34.92 / 48.80
Cross-lingual Augmentations				
Back translation	0.4	⬆ 0.05 / 0.27	⬆ 2.55 / 1.56 †	⬇ -1.02 / -0.76 †
LLM GEC	0.4	⬆ 0.31 / ⬇ -0.16	⬆ 2.66 / 1.23 †	⬆ 0.33 / 0.63 †
LLM Paraphrase	0.7	⬇ -0.88 / -0.47	⬆ 3.28 / 1.62 †	⬇ -2.55 / -1.37 †
QCPG	1.0	⬆ 0.36 / 0.22	⬆ 2.86 / 0.92 †	⬆ 0.16 / 0.21 †
LLM GEC + QCPG	0.7	⬆ 0.23 / 0.22	⬆ 3.30 / 1.64 †	⬇ -0.60 / ⬆ 0.16 †
Monolingual Augmentations				
WordNet	0.4	⬆ 1.60 / 1.32	⬆ 2.86 / 1.34 †	⬇ -1.28 / ⬆ 0.17 †
Thai2Fit	0.7	⬇ -0.48 / ⬆ 0.06	⬆ 2.26 / 1.13 †	⬇ -0.77† / -0.05
Thai2Transformers	0.4	⬆ 0.58 / 0.44	⬆ 2.70 / 1.39 †	⬇ -0.51 / ⬆ 1.40 †
LTW2Vec	1.0	⬆ 1.38 / 1.43	⬆ 1.84 / 1.75 †	⬇ -0.09 / ⬆ 1.23†
FastText	0.9	⬆ 0.27 / 0.33	⬆ 1.93 / 1.29 †	⬇ -2.21 / -1.13 †

Table 2: Optimal ratio for best performance in each augmentation— selected from validation scores. The ratio is obtained by performing the quality control method. † represents a significant result calculated from McNeMar's test.

ratios in out-of-domain settings. We discussed the experiment setup in Section 4.1.

Results. Table 2 exhibits the performance of the most effective models for each augmentation strategy, presenting both F1 and EM scores. The table also elucidates the optimal ratio of augmented to real data (calculated from the harmonic distance method). The experimental results demonstrate that using cross-lingual augmentations improves the performance of the original model in all test datasets except for Back translation and LLM Paraphrase. Moreover, we found that the performance of cross-lingual augmentations is higher than monolingual augmentations in the XQuAD dataset. For example, the QCPG method outperforms the FastText method by 0.93 EM score and 1.34 F1 score. While cross-lingual augmentations somewhat show reduced performance here, the overall results still surpass those of monolingual augmentations.

Discussion. The results in Table 2 substantiate the nuanced benefits of data augmentation techniques in MRC. While monolingual augmentations show promise of improvement in validation and TyDiQA datasets, their impact on the performance of the XQuAD dataset. For example, WordNet and Thai2Transformers increase the performance of validation and TyDiQA datasets while decreasing the performance on XQuAD compared to the original model. It is possible that these augmentations are too noisy, perhaps performing word replacement on a crucial section of the question, thus changing the semantic meaning altogether. In contrast, "LLM GEC" and "QCPG" are the most effective, delivering statistically significant improvements. This also implies that cross-lingual augmentations can improve the MRC's generalization better than the monolingual strategy.

5.2 Harmonic Distance (HD)

As stated in Section 3.4, we benchmark the performance of each dataset performing top-k% sampling in increments of 10% (see more information about top-k% in Appendix A.1). To investigate the efficacy of sampling using HD score, we choose to examine the best-performing augmentations: "LLM GEC" and "QCPG" on the TyDiQA test set.

Results. As shown in Figures 3 and 4, employing the quality control mechanism to filter noise data improves the MRC performance compared to the original model. We found that the best threshold of LLM GEC is 0.9, which improves the F1 score from the original model by 1.41 points. In addition, at the best ratio of QCPG, we observe the performance improvement of 1.69 points by the F1 score. Moreover, when comparing the whole dataset and only the 0.3 dataset, the performance remains identical with the training time decrease from $\sim$80 to $\sim$50 minutes ($\sim$38.25% reduction).

Discussion. The HD score demonstrates its effectiveness by the compelling performance gains with lower data ratios—in this scenario, ratios of 0.2 and 0.3 outperform even a full dataset. Generally, using a lower ratio than 0.1 still results in equal or better performance, however, the ratio has to be searched

Original	LLM GEC	FastText	Ratio
โปแลนด์บอล เป็นการ์ตูนที่สร้างขึ้นโดยใคร? (Poland Ball is a cartoon created by who?	ใครเป็นผู้สร้างการ์ตูนโปลันด์บอล? (Who created Poland Ball?)	โปแลนด์โลก2026 เป็นการ์ตูน 4ช่องที่สร้างมากกว่าโดยแล้ว? (Poland World2026 is a cartoon 4 channel which created more than?)	0.20
แม่น้ำไนล์ตั้งอยู่ในทวีปใด? (In which continent is the Nile River located in?)	แม่น้ำไนล์ตั้งอยู่ที่ไหน? (Where is the Nile River located?)	บริเวฯกีปตั้งอยู่นำทวีปใด? (Boriwaekip is located in front of which continent?)	0.40
ประเทศเลบานอนอยู่ในภูมิภาคใด? (The country of Lebanon is located in which area?)	เลบานอนอยู่ที่ไหน? (Where is Lebanon?)	ประเทศ Lebanonข้อ อยู่ในแอฟริกาหรือ? (The country of Lebanon number is in Africa?)	0.60
ประพันธ์โดยใคร? (Composed by who?)	แต่งโดยใคร? (Produced by who?)	ป.ชื่นเช่นใคร? P. Cheen such who?	0.80

Figure 2: Dataset examples from the robustness augmentation (LLM GEC) compared to the original texts and poor augmentation (FastText) with varying ratios.

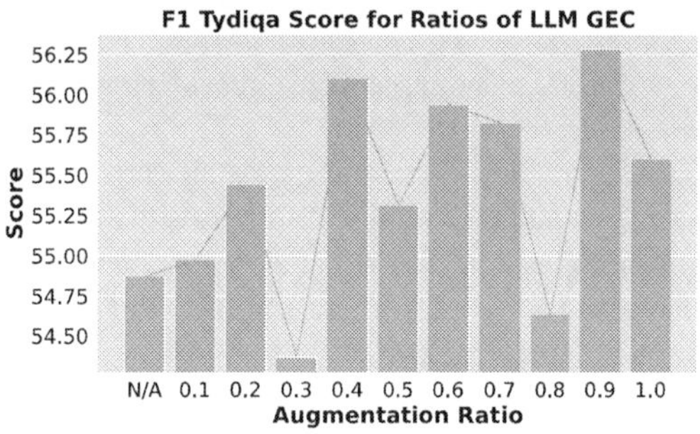

Figure 3: F1 Score of the LLM GEC dataset when finetuned with different augmentation ratios on TyDiQA.

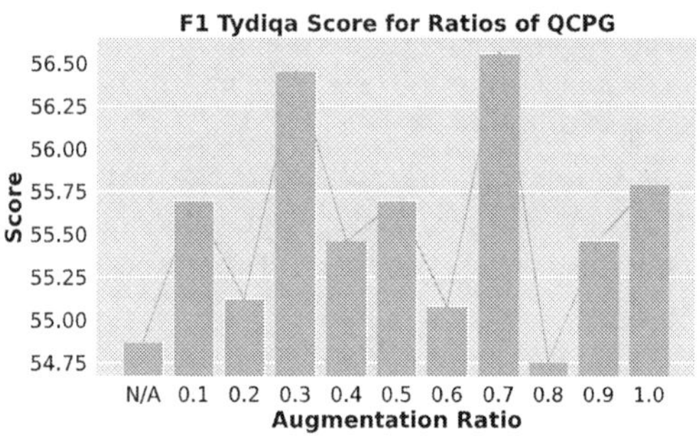

Figure 4: F1 Score of the QCPG dataset when finetuned with different augmentation ratios on the TyDiQA.

(see Appendix A.2). This underlines HD's value in reducing computational load while optimizing performance, signifying its potential as a cornerstone in future data augmentation strategies.

5.3 Error Analysis

In this study, we demonstrate error analysis from different datasets and augmentation ratios to decipher why certain augmentations and ratios perform better and to identify the characteristics of augmentations at these specific ratios. In addition, we use the augmented datasets from the LLM GEC and FastText augmentation schemes.

Figure 2 presents sentences from varying ratios from the best and worst performing augmentation. The LLM GEC augment scheme maintains better semantic meaning than the FastText augmentation. Sentences at around 0.1-0.2 ratios tend to produce more conservative paraphrases, preserving the semantic integrity of the original text. For the ratio between 0.4 and 0.6, sentences lean toward more liberal paraphrasing strategies, often omitting some keywords and introducing higher noise levels into the data. In addition, we observe that sentences at 0.8 replace key-specific words with more ambiguous synonyms. However, the augmentation results from FastText demonstrate that it fails to produce robust augmentation in all cases, resulting in performance degradation (Table 2). Additionally, the results from Figures 3 and 4 also support our findings, indicating that top-performing scores can be achieved without utilizing the entire dataset.

6 Conclusion and Future Work

We present an automatic framework for improving robustness in QA tasks. The experimental results demonstrate that our cross-lingual augmentation improved the performance of Thai QA more consistently than monolingual augmentations. Moreover, we present the quality control for data augmentations, which decrease the training time and maintain the performance with only 20% of total augmented data. For future work, we would like to explore the application and task of our augmentation and quality control approaches to improve the generalization, such as conversational chatbots (Yang et al., 2023; Jin and Lee, 2022; Hardalov et al., 2019) and retrieval QA (Asai et al., 2021; Limkonchotiwat et al., 2022b).

References

Mikel Artetxe, Sebastian Ruder, and Dani Yogatama. 2019. On the cross-lingual transferability of monolingual representations. *CoRR*, abs/1910.11856.

Akari Asai, Xinyan Yu, Jungo Kasai, and Hanna Hajishirzi. 2021. One question answering model for many languages with cross-lingual dense passage retrieval. In *Advances in Neural Information Processing Systems*, volume 34, pages 7547–7560. Curran Associates, Inc.

Elron Bandel, Ranit Aharonov, Michal Shmueli-Scheuer, Ilya Shnayderman, Noam Slonim, and Liat Ein-Dor. 2022. Quality controlled paraphrase generation. In *Proceedings of the 60th Annual Meeting of the Association for Computational Linguistics (Volume 1: Long Papers)*, pages 596–609, Dublin, Ireland. Association for Computational Linguistics.

Max Bartolo, Tristan Thrush, Robin Jia, Sebastian Riedel, Pontus Stenetorp, and Douwe Kiela. 2021. Improving question answering model robustness with synthetic adversarial data generation. In *Proceedings of the 2021 Conference on Empirical Methods in Natural Language Processing*, pages 8830–8848, Online and Punta Cana, Dominican Republic. Association for Computational Linguistics.

Piotr Bojanowski, Edouard Grave, Armand Joulin, and Tomas Mikolov. 2017. Enriching word vectors with subword information. *Transactions of the Association for Computational Linguistics*, 5:135–146.

Jonathan H. Clark, Eunsol Choi, Michael Collins, Dan Garrette, Tom Kwiatkowski, Vitaly Nikolaev, and Jennimaria Palomaki. 2020. Tydi qa: A benchmark for information-seeking question answering in typologically diverse languages. *Transactions of the Association for Computational Linguistics*.

Hatsanai Decha and Karn Patanukhom. 2017. Development of thai question answering system. In *Proceedings of the 3rd International Conference on Communication and Information Processing, ICCIP 2017, Tokyo, Japan, November 24-26, 2017*, pages 124–128. ACM.

Jacob Devlin, Ming-Wei Chang, Kenton Lee, and Kristina Toutanova. 2018. BERT: pre-training of deep bidirectional transformers for language understanding. *CoRR*, abs/1810.04805.

Momchil Hardalov, Ivan Koychev, and Preslav Nakov. 2019. Machine reading comprehension for answer reranking in customer support chatbots. *Information*, 10(3).

Sepp Hochreiter and Jürgen Schmidhuber. 1997. Long short-term memory. *Neural Comput.*, 9(8):1735–1780.

Jeremy Howard and Sebastian Ruder. 2018. Universal language model fine-tuning for text classification. In *Proceedings of the 56th Annual Meeting of the Association for Computational Linguistics (Volume 1: Long Papers)*, pages 328–339, Melbourne, Australia. Association for Computational Linguistics.

Dieuwke Hupkes, Mario Giulianelli, Verna Dankers, Mikel Artetxe, Yanai Elazar, Tiago Pimentel, Christos Christodoulopoulos, Karim Lasri, Naomi Saphra, Arabella Sinclair, Dennis Ulmer, Florian Schottmann, Khuyagbaatar Batsuren, Kaiser Sun, Koustuv Sinha, Leila Khalatbari, Maria Ryskina, Rita Frieske, Ryan Cotterell, and Zhijing Jin. 2023. State-of-the-art generalisation research in nlp: A taxonomy and review.

Nayoung Jin and Hana Lee. 2022. StuBot: Learning by teaching a conversational agent through machine reading comprehension. In *Findings of the Association for Computational Linguistics: EMNLP 2022*, pages 3008–3020, Abu Dhabi, United Arab Emirates. Association for Computational Linguistics.

Daniel Khashabi, Tushar Khot, and Ashish Sabharwal. 2020. More bang for your buck: Natural perturbation for robust question answering. In *Proceedings of the 2020 Conference on Empirical Methods in Natural Language Processing (EMNLP)*, pages 163–170, Online. Association for Computational Linguistics.

Gokul Karthik Kumar, Abhishek Gehlot, Sahal Shaji Mullappilly, and Karthik Nandakumar. 2022. MuCoT: Multilingual contrastive training for question-answering in low-resource languages. In *Proceedings of the Second Workshop on Speech and Language Technologies for Dravidian Languages*, pages 15–24, Dublin, Ireland. Association for Computational Linguistics.

Guillaume Lample and Alexis Conneau. 2019. Cross-lingual language model pretraining. *CoRR*, abs/1901.07291.

Patrick S. H. Lewis, Barlas Oguz, Ruty Rinott, Sebastian Riedel, and Holger Schwenk. 2019. MLQA: evaluating cross-lingual extractive question answering. *CoRR*, abs/1910.07475.

Peerat Limkonchotiwat, Wuttikorn Ponwitayarat, Lalita Lowphansirikul, Can Udomcharoenchaikit, Ekapol Chuangsuwanich, and Sarana Nutanong. 2022a. ConGen: Unsupervised control and generalization distillation for sentence representation. In *Findings of the Association for Computational Linguistics: EMNLP 2022*, pages 6467–6480, Abu Dhabi, United Arab Emirates. Association for Computational Linguistics.

Peerat Limkonchotiwat, Wuttikorn Ponwitayarat, Can Udomcharoenchaikit, Ekapol Chuangsuwanich, and Sarana Nutanong. 2022b. CL-ReLKT: Cross-lingual language knowledge transfer for multilingual retrieval question answering. In *Findings of the Association for Computational Linguistics: NAACL 2022*, pages 2141–2155, Seattle, United States. Association for Computational Linguistics.

Yinhan Liu, Myle Ott, Naman Goyal, Jingfei Du, Mandar Joshi, Danqi Chen, Omer Levy, Mike Lewis,

Luke Zettlemoyer, and Veselin Stoyanov. 2019. Roberta: A robustly optimized BERT pretraining approach. *CoRR*, abs/1907.11692.

Lalita Lowphansirikul, Charin Polpanumas, Nawat Jantrakulchai, and Sarana Nutanong. 2021. Wangchanberta: Pretraining transformer-based thai language models. *CoRR*, abs/2101.09635.

Thanapon Noraset, Lalita Lowphansirikul, and Suppawong Tuarob. 2021. Wabiqa: A wikipedia-based thai question-answering system. *Information processing & management*, 58(1):102431.

Hariom Pandya, Bhavik Ardeshna, and Brijesh Bhatt. 2021. Cascading adaptors to leverage English data to improve performance of question answering for low-resource languages. In *Proceedings of the 18th International Conference on Natural Language Processing (ICON)*, pages 544–549, National Institute of Technology Silchar, Silchar, India. NLP Association of India (NLPAI).

Wannaphong Phatthiyaphaibun. 2022. Ltw2v: The large thai word2vec.

Charin Polpanumas and Wannaphong Phatthiyaphaibun. 2021. thai2fit: Thai language implementation of ulmfit.

Arij Riabi, Thomas Scialom, Rachel Keraron, Benoît Sagot, Djamé Seddah, and Jacopo Staiano. 2021. Synthetic data augmentation for zero-shot cross-lingual question answering. In *Proceedings of the 2021 Conference on Empirical Methods in Natural Language Processing*, pages 7016–7030, Online and Punta Cana, Dominican Republic. Association for Computational Linguistics.

Sareewan Thoongsup, Thatsanee Charoenporn, Kergrit Robkop, Tan Sinthurahat, Chumpol Mokarat, Virach Sornlertlamvanich, and Hitoshi Isahara. 2009. Thai WordNet construction. In *Proceedings of the 7th Workshop on Asian Language Resources (ALR7)*, pages 139–144, Suntec, Singapore. Association for Computational Linguistics.

Kanokorn Trakultaweekoon, Santipong Thaiprayoon, Pornpimon Palingoon, and Anocha Rugchatjaroen. 2019. The first wikipedia questions and factoid answers corpus in the thai language. In *2019 14th International Joint Symposium on Artificial Intelligence and Natural Language Processing (iSAI-NLP)*, pages 1–4.

Ashish Vaswani, Noam Shazeer, Niki Parmar, Jakob Uszkoreit, Llion Jones, Aidan N. Gomez, Lukasz Kaiser, and Illia Polosukhin. 2017. Attention is all you need.

Kobkrit Viriyayudhakorn and Charin Polpanumas. 2021. iapp_wiki_qa_squad.

Pongsathorn Wongpraomas, Chitsutha Soomlek, Wanna Sirisangtragul, and Pusadee Seresangtakul. 2022. Thai question-answering system using pattern-matching approach. In *2022 1st International Conference on Technology Innovation and Its Applications (ICTIIA)*, pages 1–5.

Changlin Yang, Siye Liu, Sen Hu, Wangshu Zhang, Teng Xu, and Jing Zheng. 2023. Improving knowledge production efficiency with question answering on conversation. In *Proceedings of the 61st Annual Meeting of the Association for Computational Linguistics (Volume 5: Industry Track)*, pages 225–234, Toronto, Canada. Association for Computational Linguistics.

Yinfei Yang, Daniel Cer, Amin Ahmad, Mandy Guo, Jax Law, Noah Constant, Gustavo Hernandez Abrego, Steve Yuan, Chris Tar, Yun-hsuan Sung, Brian Strope, and Ray Kurzweil. 2020. Multilingual universal sentence encoder for semantic retrieval. In *Proceedings of the 58th Annual Meeting of the Association for Computational Linguistics: System Demonstrations*, pages 87–94, Online. Association for Computational Linguistics.

Yan Zhang, Ruidan He, Zuozhu Liu, Lidong Bing, and Haizhou Li. 2021. Bootstrapped unsupervised sentence representation learning. In *Proceedings of the 59th Annual Meeting of the Association for Computational Linguistics and the 11th International Joint Conference on Natural Language Processing (Volume 1: Long Papers)*, pages 5168–5180, Online. Association for Computational Linguistics.

A Appendix

A.1 How Ratio Was Selected

As shown in Figure 5, we demonstrate how the ratio was selected. We calculate the HD from the LLM GEC method and arrange the semantic distance from lowest to highest to formulate the distance distribution. We then select the top-k% of the distribution as the training data, the k value can be between 0.0 (using only the original training data) to 1.0 (using entirely augmentation and training corpora). This technique can control the quality of the final dataset by maintaining a good signal-to-noise ratio of the dataset, maintaining a similar meaning between the original and augmented texts.

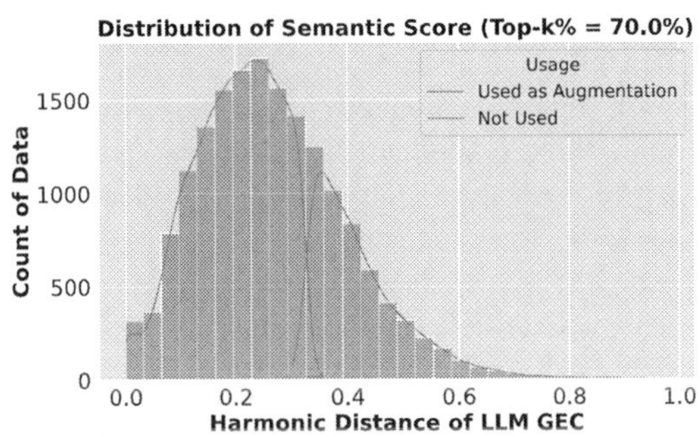

Figure 5: Example distribution of semantic score on the LLM GEC augmentation. With top-k% = 0.7, we will select the top 70% of the dataset that has the closest semantic similarity to the original data. The blue distribution indicates that data was selected for augmentation, while the red line indicates unselected data for this top-k% value.

Motivation					
Practical □	*Cognitive*	*Intrinsic*	*Fairness*		
Generalisation type					
Compositional	*Structural*	*Cross Task*	*Cross Language*	*Cross Domain*	*Robustness* □
Shift type					
Covariate □	*Label*	*Full*	*Assumed*		
Shift source					
Naturally occuring □	*Partitioned natural*	*Generated shift*	*Fully generated*		
Shift locus					
Train–test	*Finetune train–test* □	*Pretrain–train*	*Pretrain–test*		

A.2 Effectiveness of Harmonic Distance Scores in Reducing Augmentation Ratio While Maintaining Performance

As shown in Figure 6, for all of our augmentation sets, an higher or similar score can be obtained by using a smaller ratio when compared to using the whole augmentation dataset. While there may be no clear pattern in what the best ratio might be for each augmentation, it is evident that for the large majority of the augmentations, using less than a 1.0 ratio leads to a better if not equal score— while reducing the computational resources needed.

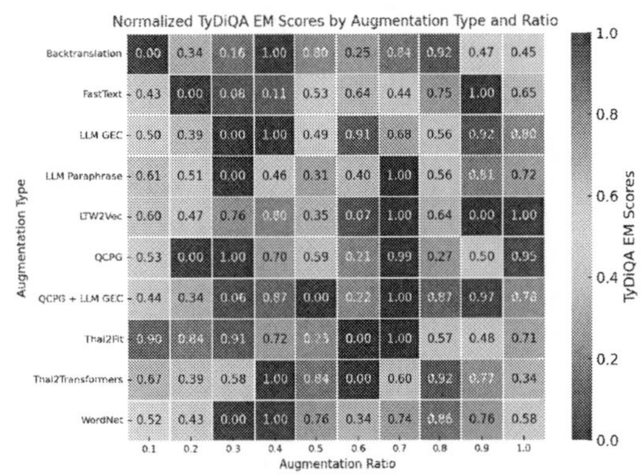

Figure 6: Heatmap illustrating the normalized TyDiQA Exact Match (EM) scores across various data augmentation techniques and ratios. The color scale represents the normalized EM score, with blue indicating lower performance and red indicating higher performance. Each cell displays the average normalized EM score for a specific combination of augmentation type and ratio.

On Using Distribution-Based Compositionality Assessment to Evaluate Compositional Generalisation in Machine Translation

Anssi Moisio[1,2], **Mathias Creutz**[2], and **Mikko Kurimo**[1]
[1]Department of Information and Communications Engineering, Aalto University, Finland
[2]Department of Digital Humanities, University of Helsinki, Finland
anssi.moisio@aalto.fi, mathias.creutz@helsinki.fi, mikko.kurimo@aalto.fi

Abstract

Compositional generalisation (CG), in NLP and in machine learning more generally, has been assessed mostly using artificial datasets. It is important to develop benchmarks to assess CG also in real-world natural language tasks in order to understand the abilities and limitations of systems deployed in the wild. To this end, our GenBench Collaborative Benchmarking Task submission utilises the *distribution-based compositionality assessment* (DBCA) framework to split the Europarl translation corpus into a training and a test set in such a way that the test set requires compositional generalisation capacity. Specifically, the training and test sets have divergent distributions of dependency relations, testing NMT systems' capability of translating dependencies that they have not been trained on. This is a fully-automated procedure to create natural language compositionality benchmarks, making it simple and inexpensive to apply it further to other datasets and languages. The code and data for the experiments is available at https://github.com/aalto-speech/dbca.

1 Introduction

An often-used definition, by Partee (1995), of the concept of *compositionality* of language is that the "meaning of a whole is a function of the meanings of the parts and of the way they are syntactically combined". A more stringent definition adds that the composition of meaning is *systematic*: each part's meaning is the same in all the different sequences it appears in, the syntactical rules work the same way for different parts, and the same function determines meaning for different wholes (Fodor and Pylyshyn, 1988; Pavlick, 2022, 2023). Compositionality enables generalising to new meanings by combining familiar parts, and to understand each other language users need to employ common systematic rules.

A number of benchmarks have been developed to assess systematic generalisation from different perspectives and in different NLP tasks. Many of these consist of artificial data, such as the popular SCAN (Lake and Baroni, 2018) and COGS (Kim and Linzen, 2020) benchmarks. These artificial datasets are typically constructed to be highly systematic, to include straightforward syntactical rules. Natural languages, however, have varied irregularities, idiomatic expressions, and other exceptions to the rules, which make composition of meaning much more complicated than in the case of the highly-regular artificial datasets. It's therefore important to assess whether NLP systems are able to generalise systematically also in the case of natural language, where systematic rules are obscured by exceptions (Dankers et al., 2022).

Works that aim to assess systematic generalisation in natural language tasks often still synthesise some part of the dataset in order to create test examples where systematic generalisation is needed (for example Li et al. (2021) and Dankers et al. (2022)). This enables precise testing of specific systematic rules, but comprehensive test suites that would assess the use of, for example, numerous syntactical rules can be arduous to synthesise. To sidestep the need to synthesise examples, a natural language dataset can be partitioned into training and test sets in such a way that the test set includes examples whose processing requires some systematic generalisation ability. A framework for partitioning data in this way was developed by Keysers et al. (2020), called *distribution-based compositionality assessment*, or DBCA for short. The main idea of DBCA is to control the distributions of *atoms* (primitive elements) and *compounds* (combinations of the atoms) to get approximately the same atom distributions but divergent compound distributions in the training and test sets.

We utilise the DBCA framework in our GenBench Collaborative Benchmarking Task submission, which consists of train-test splits of the Europarl parallel corpus with divergent distributions

Proceedings of the 1st GenBench Workshop on (Benchmarking) Generalisation in NLP, pages 204–213
December 6, 2023 ©2023 Association for Computational Linguistics

Sentence	Atoms	Compounds
"Our vigilance is not partisan."	nsubj, poss, our, vigilance, partisan	(vigilance, poss, our), (partisan, nsubj, vigilance)
"We shall now hear Mr Wurtz speaking against this request."	hear, aux, shall, speak, nsubj, wurtz, hear, ccomp, speak	(hear, aux, shall), (speak, nsubj, wurtz), (hear, ccomp, speak)
"This seems to me to be a workable solution."	solution, amod, workable, seem, xcomp, solution	(solution, amod, workable), (seem, xcomp, solution)

Table 1: Examples of what we call "atoms" and "compounds". Atoms are the lemmas and dependency relations, and compounds the three-element tuples of the head lemma, the relation, and the dependant lemma.

of dependency relations. These data splits can be used to assess the ability of NMT systems to translate novel dependency relations. In the terminology of the DBCA framework, we define the atoms as lemmas and dependency relations, and the compounds as the three-element tuples of the head lemma, the dependant lemma, and the relation between them (see Table 1 for examples). This method to create compositional generalisation benchmarks does not require manual test suite construction, making it easy to extend it to other datasets and other languages.

2 Related work

2.1 Compositional generalisation in machine translation

Compositional generalisation has been assessed in machine translation in a few works in recent years. Raunak et al. (2019) partitioned a dataset into short training sentences and longer test sentences in order to assess generalisation from short sentences to longer ones, a subtype of compositional generalisation sometimes called *productivity* (Hupkes et al., 2020). Li et al. (2021) synthesised sentences for the test set with novel constituents, such as noun and verb phrases to create the CoGnition benchmark. Dankers et al. (2022) assessed three aspects of compositionality in NMT, which they called systematicity, the ability to combine familiar parts into novel combinations; substitutivity, the consistency of translations when a word is replaced with its synonym; and over-generalisation, the tendency to follow a compositional rule even when the case is actually an exception to the rule.

Perhaps the most similar benchmark to ours is ReaCT by Zheng and Lapata (2023). In ReaCT, the IWSLT 2014 German-English corpus is used as the training set, and a test set is created by selecting sentences that have a high *compositionality degree* from the WMT 2014 corpus. The compositionality degree of a test set sentence is defined as the number of training set n-grams needed to create the sentence, divided by the length of the sentence. The reasoning is that a test set sentence that includes long n-grams from the training set can be composed of fewer n-grams, having a low compositionality degree, whereas if we need to back off to shorter n-grams to create a sentence, the compositionality degree is high. This train-test data split has similar general characteristics as our data splits: it is completely natural data (no synthetic sentences) partitioned so that the test set has novel combinations of familiar primitives. In contrast to our work, the primitives in this scheme can be sequences of multiple words, whereas we assess the ability to translate novel combinations of just two words and their dependency relation. We also pay attention to the relative frequency distributions of the primitives and the combinations, following the DBCA framework, whereas in ReaCT the compositionality score is a function of the unique n-gram types.

In addition to word-based compositionality, *morphological* compositional generalisation in translation has been assessed by Meyer and Buys (2023) and Moisio et al. (2023). In these works, the atoms are defined as the morphemes (or surface-level morphs), and compounds as the inflected word forms that consist of multiple morphemes. The test set therefore includes novel combinations of familiar morphemes, assessing NMT systems' capacity for morphological generalisation.

2.2 Other related work

Aside from NMT tasks, Shaw et al. (2021) utilised the DBCA framework to assess compositional generalisation in a natural language semantic parsing task. Søgaard et al. (2021) provide a more general discussion and review of non-random training-test

Motivation			
Practical	*Cognitive*	*Intrinsic* □	*Fairness*

Generalisation type					
Compositional □	*Structural*	*Cross Task*	*Cross Language*	*Cross Domain*	*Robustness*

Shift type			
Covariate □	*Label*	*Full*	*Assumed*

Shift source			
Naturally occuring	*Partitioned natural* □	*Generated shift*	*Fully generated*

Shift locus			
Train–test □	*Finetune train–test*	*Pretrain–train*	*Pretrain–test*

Figure 1: The categorisation of our benchmark in the taxonomy by Hupkes et al. (2023).

data splitting.

Besides creating artificial train-test splits, another option to test systematic generalisation in NLP systems, without the need for manual test suite design, is to leverage the fact that systematicity can be seen as an inherent symmetry in the data (Manino et al., 2022), which has also been utilised to generate new training examples (Akyurek and Andreas, 2023).

A study not on compositional generalisation, but in other ways related to our work, is that by McCoy et al. (2023), who evaluated the degree of novelty of the text generated by language models, using both n-grams and dependency relations. They found that language-model-generated text tends to be less novel than the baseline of human-generated text in local structure (small n-grams), but more novel than the human baseline in more global structure (large n-grams). This finding provides a good backdrop for our research question of how NMT models handle a test set that includes novel *local* structure, such as dependency relations.

2.3 The taxonomy

The eval card in Figure 1 shows how our benchmark can be categorised in the taxonomy of Hupkes et al. (2023). The motivation is primarily intrinsic: it is important to assess if translation models learn the systematic rules that characterise natural language, in order to get some understanding how the models work. Another motivation is practical; testing compositional generalisation is important for the practical reason of knowing how robustly the models generalise to novel dependency relations. The type of the generalisation is compositional, and the shift type is covariate, since the input data distribution changes but the task remains otherwise the same. Shift source is partitioned natural data, since we do not use any artificial data, but the train-test split is artificial. Lastly, the shift locus in our experiments is train-test, but the method and benchmark could also possibly be used as a finetune train-test benchmark, by finetuning a pretrained model on the training set.

3 Europarl data splits

3.1 Data partitioning process

We use the Europarl corpus (Koehn, 2005) of transcribed European parliament proceedings, with the multilingual sentence alignments from the OPUS corpus (Tiedemann, 2012). We chose the Europarl corpus because of the good quality of the translations and because it includes parallel sentences for multiple languages. For our benchmark submission, we select English as the source language, and as the target languages we use four languages that represent different (branches of) language families: German, French, Greek, and Finnish.

As pre-processing, duplicate sentences are removed and maximum sentence length is restricted to 30 words before tokenisation. We take a random subsample of 300k sentences from which we extract the data splits. This relatively small size was chosen for convenient use as well as to allow comparison with previously published similar benchmarks: CoGnition Li et al. (2021) and ReaCT Zheng and Lapata (2023), which are similar in size.

The dependency parsing for the English source corpus is done using the LAL-parser (Mrini et al.,

2020). To calculate the divergences in data splitting, we only consider the English side. Therefore, the benchmark primarily assesses the encoder's capacity to represent novel syntactic relations. However, presumably a high compound divergence of the source side sentences means that the target side sentences also include an increased number of novel syntactical, or possibly morphological, structures, assessing at the same time the decoder's capacity to generate these. We define the atoms as the lemmas and dependency relations and compounds as the three-element-tuples of the dependant lemma, the head lemma and their relation. To make the number of atoms manageable, we exclude from the distribution calculations lemmas that appear either very frequently (the 200 most frequent lemmas, which each appear from 387k times (most frequent word "the") to 3576 times (200th most frequent word "then")), or fewer than 10 times in total in the corpus. After this filtering, about 8000 lemmas remain in the atom set, which includes also the dependency relation tags.

Following Keysers et al. (2020), we calculate a weight for each compound so that those subcompounds that appear predominantly only in one super-compound get lower weight than those appearing in many different super-compounds. In our case, this means that if a (dependant lemma, relation type) pair occurs for example 8/10 times with just one head lemma, this pair gets a score of $1 - (8/10) = 0.2$. The idea is somewhat similar to that behind the Kneser-Ney smoothing (Kneser and Ney, 1995), where the number of different bigrams a word appears in correlates with the unigram backoff probability. We filter out compounds that get a weight less than 0.5, after which there are about 8000 atom types and 400k compound types whose distributions are controlled in the data splits.

Atom and compound divergences are calculated similarly to Keysers et al. (2020): divergence $\mathcal{D}$ between distributions P and Q is calculated using the Chernoff coefficient $C_\alpha(P\|Q) = \sum_k p_k^\alpha q_k^{1-\alpha} \in [0, 1]$ (Chung et al., 1989), with $\alpha = 0.5$ for the atom divergence and $\alpha = 0.1$ for the compound divergence. Keysers et al. (2020) notes about the α values that $\alpha = 0.5$ for atom divergence "reflects the desire of making the atom distributions in train and test as similar as possible", and $\alpha = 0.1$ for compound divergence "reflects the intuition that it is more important whether a certain compound occurs in P (train) than whether the probabilities in P (train) and Q (test) match exactly". The divergence is the complement of the Chernoff coefficient, since the Chernoff coefficient measures similarity between two vectors. The atom and compound divergences for training set V and test set W are:

$$\mathcal{D}_A(V\|W) = 1 - C_{0.5}(\mathcal{F}_A(V) \,\|\, \mathcal{F}_A(W))$$
$$\mathcal{D}_C(V\|W) = 1 - C_{0.1}(\mathcal{F}_C(V) \,\|\, \mathcal{F}_C(W)).$$

where $\mathcal{F}_A$ is the atom distribution and $\mathcal{F}_C$ is the compound distribution of a data set.

Splitting the data is done using a greedy algorithm similar to that by Moisio et al. (2023). This algorithm places one sentence at each iteration into either the training or test set, such that the atom and compound divergences are as close to the respective desired values as possible. Specifically, at each iteration we try to maximise a score that is the negated linear combination of the differences between the desired and actual divergence values:

$$\text{score}(V, W) = -|c - \mathcal{D}_C(V\|W)| - \mathcal{D}_A(V\|W),$$

where c is the desired compound divergence, and the desired atom divergence is 0 (minimum).

3.2 Comparison to random splits and previous benchmarks

Table 2 lists the sizes, and atom and compound divergences ($\mathcal{D}_A$ and $\mathcal{D}_C$) for the Europarl data splits, as well as for random splits, and for the CoGnition and ReaCT benchmarks for comparison. All the divergences are calculated after similar filtering of the atoms and compounds as described for the Europarl splits above. From the divergences of the random train-test splits we can notice that the size of the test set correlates inversely with both atom and compound distributions; when the training and test sets are closer in size, the distributions are also naturally closer to each other.

From the table, we can also see that CoGnition includes relatively short sentences and, importantly, a relatively small number of unique lemmas. Creating CoGnition, Li et al. (2021) removed some of the complexity of natural language, such as polysemous words, and deliberately kept the vocabulary small and excluded all low-frequency words. This follows the design choices made by Keysers et al. (2020) of aiming to have only few meaningful atoms from which a large number of compounds can be created, which was motivated by practical concerns: this way it is easier to have a large range

	# sentences		# words		# unique lemmas	$\mathcal{D}_A$	$\mathcal{D}_C$
	train	test	train	test			
Europarl random split 3k	200k	3k	3.6M	54k	29k	0.28	0.60
Europarl random split 10k	200k	10k	3.6M	180k	30k	0.18	0.55
Europarl random split 30k	200k	30k	3.6M	540k	31k	0.13	0.52
CoGnition (Li et al., 2021)	196k	10k	1.9M	96k	1.7k	0.13	0.47
ReaCT (Zheng and Lapata, 2023)	160k	3k	3.3M	45k	53k	0.32	0.90
Europarl min$\mathcal{D}_C$ split #1	203k	37k	3.9M	650k	34k	0.01	0.10
Europarl min$\mathcal{D}_C$ split #2	194k	36k	3.7M	625k	34k	0.01	0.10
Europarl min$\mathcal{D}_C$ split #3	195k	35k	3.7M	625k	34k	0.01	0.10
Europarl max$\mathcal{D}_C$ split #1	197k	23k	3.8M	390k	34k	0.001	1.0
Europarl max$\mathcal{D}_C$ split #2	198k	22k	3.8M	390k	34k	0.002	1.0
Europarl max$\mathcal{D}_C$ split #3	198k	22k	3.8M	390k	34k	0.001	1.0

Table 2: Comparison of the Europarl splits to other translation benchmarks that aim at assessing compositional generalisation. The number of unique lemmas includes both training and test set lemmas.

of compound divergences while keeping the atom divergences same. However, this contrasts with the distribution of primitives in natural language, an issue we discuss more in Section 5. ReaCT, on the other hand, has similarly sized vocabulary as natural language data; in fact the vocabulary is significantly larger than the Europarl random sample vocabulary, possibly because the WMT and IWSLT corpora are lexically more diverse than Europarl.

Table 2 also lists, for reference, the atom and compound divergences, calculated for the dependency relations as described in Section 3, for CoGnition and ReaCT, even though neither of these data splits are designed to minimise or maximise these values. In both of these data sets, the test set is designed to contain novel combinations of familiar parts, as is our test sets, but in these works the parts are normally sequences of multiple words. In spite of this, the ReaCT data split has a relatively high dependency relation compound divergence.

The last rows of Table 2 show the sizes and divergences of the minimum- and maximum-compound-divergence Europarl data splits. The atom divergences are significantly lower for these splits than they are for the random splits. As noted above, the low atom divergence follows the principles of the DBCA framework: the compositional generalisation test set should be difficult not because of novel primitive elements (in our case mostly lemmas) but because of *novel combinations* of the known elements. The maximum-compound-divergence splits get a $\mathcal{D}_C$ of exactly 1, but here we note that, as described in Section 3, the most frequent and most infrequent lemmas are left out from the divergence calculations, which means that only a subset of the dependency relation compounds are novel in the test set, even though $\mathcal{D}_C = 1.0$.

4 Experiments

4.1 Transformer NMT system results

We train Transformer (Vaswani et al., 2017) models on the Europarl data splits using the OpenNMT python library (Klein et al., 2017) and the same hyperparameters as in the example OpenNMT-py Transformer configuration[1], including the standard 6 transformer layers with 8 heads, a hidden layer size of 512 and feed-forward layer size of 2048. The configuration includes around 60M parameters. We create a BPE (Sennrich et al., 2016) vocabulary for each language with 10k token types. We didn't tune any of the hyperparameters for these datasets, and didn't use a validation set. We trained the models for 6000 training steps, evaluated the test set translations at intervals of 1000 steps, and report the best of these 6 results for each model. For more details on training the models, see the Github repository linked on the first page.

Figure 2 displays the chrF2++ (Popović, 2017) scores for the minimum- and maximum-compound-divergence splits and the four target languages: German, French, Greek, and Finnish. We run the data split algorithm three times using different random

[1] https://github.com/OpenNMT/OpenNMT-py/blob/9d617b8b/config/config-transformer-base-1GPU.yml

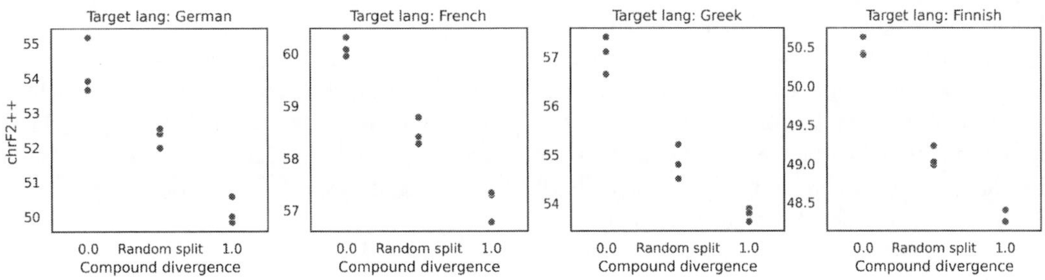

Figure 2: The chrF2++ scores for the Transformer NMT systems trained on the minimum and maximum compound divergence splits. Source language is English and target languages are German, French, Greek, and Finnish. The middle scores are for the random data splits, which happen to have a compound divergence of about 0.5. Each data split setup (min$\mathcal{D}_C$, max$\mathcal{D}_C$, and random) is run 3 times with different random seeds, creating 9 different data splits for which NMT models are trained.

seeds. Between the min$\mathcal{D}_C$ and max$\mathcal{D}_C$ split results are the results for the random splits, of which there are also 3 random runs (with 200k sentences in training and 30k sentences in test set). As shown in Table 2 the random splits with 30k-sentence test set happen to have a compound divergence of about 0.5.

Figure 2 shows a modest but statistically significant and consistent decrease in performance from the random data split to the max$\mathcal{D}_C$ split, for all four target languages. This is expected, as the max$\mathcal{D}_C$ split includes more novel dependency relations than the random split. However, as shown in Table 2, the max$\mathcal{D}_C$ split has a significantly lower *atom* divergence than the random split, as this is deliberately minimised in the artificial data splits, which follows the principle of the DBCA framework of having the same atom distribution in training and test sets. This means that the max$\mathcal{D}_C$ split should be easier than the random split in this regard, but it still gets worse results because of the high compound divergence.

The min$\mathcal{D}_C$ split, on the other hand, has a similar atom divergence as the max$\mathcal{D}_C$ split, so comparison between these two results is in that sense fairer. There is a larger difference in the results between these two data splits; depending on the target language the chrF2++ drops from about 4% to 8%. Since we use relatively large test corpora (from about 20k to 40k sentences), even small differences in chrF2++ are statistically significant.

4.2 Generalisation score

To assess whether one NMT system is more capable in (this dependency-relation-related type of) compositional generalisation than some other system, one option is simply to compare their translation performances on the max$\mathcal{D}_C$ split. However, to get a sense of the generalisation capacity as a part of the system's translation capacity in general, it may be more meaningful to assess how the performance deteriorates between the min$\mathcal{D}_C$ and max$\mathcal{D}_C$ splits. To get a *generalisation score*, we propose to take the ratio of the results on these two data splits. This way the generalisation scores, using the average of the three chrF2++ scores for each experiment setup listed in Figure 2, are: $50.12/54.23 = 0.92$ for the German-target Transformer system, $57.13/60.11 = 0.95$ for French, $53.77/57.05 = 0.94$ for Greek, and $48.30/50.48 = 0.96$ for Finnish. Since this a relative score, the absolute chrF2++ results should be reported in addition to this generalisation score.

5 Discussion: handling the long tail

The core of each natural language is a set of words (a lexicon), and a set of grammar rules that define how to combine the words into meaningful sequences. The lexicon is divided into content words, which possess semantic content, and function words, which denote the grammatical relationships between content words. The function words belong to closed classes, for example prepositions, that normally do not accept new words, while content words belong to open classes; new nouns, for example, are coined regularly. The long tail of the Zipfian distribution of word frequencies consists of content words while the grammar-enforcing function words are mostly in the head of the distribution.

Recent studies suggest that the distinction between content and function words as well as the

Zipfian distribution are important for (compositional) generalisation to arise: Steinert-Threlkeld (2020) provides empirical evidence that function words enable robust forms of non-trivial compositional communication, and Chan et al. (2022) found that the Zipfian distribution helps language models strike a balance between memorisation and (in context) generalisation. As shown also by Feldman (2020), memorising some of the long tail is not in conflict with generalisation; on the contrary, it *enables* optimal generalisation.

At the same time, some studies have shown that neural NLP system have some difficulties with handling the long tail, or at least handling the tail in a way that we as users of the models would expect and want. Wei et al. (2021) and Czarnowska et al. (2019) found that NLP systems' performance is heavily influenced by word frequency in training. LeBrun et al. (2022) compared language-model-generated text to a reference and found that the models underestimate the long tail of well-formed sequences; furthermore, this probability mass didn't go to the head of the distribution but rather the models overestimate the probability of ill-formed sequences.

As noted in previous sections, the desired distribution of atoms in the DBCA framework contrasts with the Zipfian distribution found in natural language. As Keysers et al. (2020) explain, they design their CFQ benchmark "so as to have few and meaningful atoms" which means there is no long tail of infrequent primitives. This is related to having a close-to-zero atom divergence: if the atom distribution had a long tail, it would not be easy to have the same relative atom distributions in training and test sets since at least those atoms that appear only once would make the distributions diverge. This harks back to the question of how compositional generalisation could be assessed in purely natural tasks, where every rule has an exception, and where idioms and irregularities muddle the systematicity (as discussed by Dankers et al. (2022)).

Our benchmark provides one answer to this question. Although we use the principles of the DBCA framework regarding distribution divergence, we don't make the corpus less natural by artificially shrinking the vocabulary size of the corpus. Instead, to make the divergence calculations manageable in practice, we leave some of the vocabulary out of the calculations. A downside of this choice is that the test sentences in the max$\mathcal{D}_C$ splits don't contain exclusively novel dependencies. The advantage is that the vocabulary is similar to that in the original real-world natural language dataset, while the test set includes an increased number of novel dependencies to test generalisation.

6 Conclusion

Our GenBench Collaborative Benchmarking Task submission consists of train-test splits of the Europarl parallel corpus with divergent distributions of dependency relations. These data splits can be used to assess the ability of NMT systems to translate novel dependency relations in a purely natural language translation task. We derive the data partitioning method from the distribution-based compositionality assessment framework, which provides generalisable principles of how to assess compositionality. Our application of the DBCA framework is straightforward to extend further to new datasets and languages, and to any other NLP task where the training and test sets consist of sentences, such as paraphrase detection. The DBCA framework is useful for real-world natural language tasks too, even though it was originally designed for a more artificial data setting. It should be kept in mind, however, how the principles of the DBCA framework diverge from the reality of natural language data.

7 Limitations

7.1 Applicability of the method

Nowadays, the state-of-the-art methods in many NLP tasks are based on pretrained language models. However, our data partitioning method, as used in this work, requires controlling the training data, as well as the test data, to have partitions with specific atom and compound divergence values. Therefore, the method is not directly applicable to a pretrain-finetune training scheme, if the pretraining dataset is not modifiable. However, there are no limitations, in principle, on having a fixed training corpus and compiling only a new test set to have specific divergence values, although the divergence values might not be so easy to minimise and maximise in this case.

7.2 Validity of the method

We have not conclusively assessed whether the benchmark actually tests what we assume it tests, that is, compositional generalisation ability. To rule out the most obvious potential confounding variable, we checked the sentence lengths to see if the max$\mathcal{D}_C$ test sets for some reason included longer sentences, making the test set more difficult this way. We did not find large differences: in the min$\mathcal{D}_C$ splits the average sentence lengths in train/test sets are 19.3/17.6 words, and in the max$\mathcal{D}_C$ splits 19.1/17.3 words. Although there is a difference (of unknown origin) between train and test set sentence lengths, there is no significant difference between min$\mathcal{D}_C$ and max$\mathcal{D}_C$ splits that could confound the results. From Table 2 we can also see that the training sets are similar in size.

7.3 Limitations of the experiments

There are multiple levels of compositionality in language, from morphemes to words to phrases to clauses. Our experiments focus on just one intermediate level of compositionality, since we define compounds as dependencies between two words. This choice was based primarily on convenience: we could define compounds as constructions of more than just two words, but the large number of these constructions would make the data partitioning heavier computationally. Focusing on just one level of compositional constructions means that our experiments are not exhaustive in this regard, and we hope to assess other levels of compositionality in future work.

Our goal was to create a benchmark that tests generalisation to novel dependency relations in as comprehensively as possible, not selecting some specific types of dependency relations and leaving out other types. However, memory requirements of the data splitting algorithm do not permit us to use all of the atoms and compounds in the distribution divergence calculations, so we opted to leave out the most frequent and the most infrequent lemmas, and the dependency relations that include them. This means that our set of atoms represents a middle section of the distribution, where the head turns into a tail. Therefore, the controlled dependency relations include lemmas both from the head of the distribution and the tail, although neither of the extremes. We have not been able to assess how this particular choice affects the results.

8 Acknowledgements

We thank the anonymous reviewers for their insightful comments and feedback, which significantly improved this paper. The work was supported by the Academy of Finland grant 337073. The computational resources were provided by Aalto ScienceIT.

References

Ekin Akyurek and Jacob Andreas. 2023. LexSym: Compositionality as lexical symmetry. In *Proceedings of the 61st Annual Meeting of the Association for Computational Linguistics (Volume 1: Long Papers)*, pages 639–657, Toronto, Canada. Association for Computational Linguistics.

Stephanie Chan, Adam Santoro, Andrew Lampinen, Jane Wang, Aaditya Singh, Pierre Richemond, James McClelland, and Felix Hill. 2022. Data distributional properties drive emergent in-context learning in transformers. In *Advances in Neural Information Processing Systems*, volume 35, pages 18878–18891. Curran Associates, Inc.

JK Chung, PL Kannappan, CT Ng, and PK Sahoo. 1989. Measures of distance between probability distributions. *Journal of mathematical analysis and applications*, 138(1):280–292.

Paula Czarnowska, Sebastian Ruder, Edouard Grave, Ryan Cotterell, and Ann Copestake. 2019. Don't forget the long tail! A comprehensive analysis of morphological generalization in bilingual lexicon induction. In *Proceedings of the 2019 Conference on Empirical Methods in Natural Language Processing and the 9th International Joint Conference on Natural Language Processing (EMNLP-IJCNLP)*, pages 974–983, Hong Kong, China. Association for Computational Linguistics.

Verna Dankers, Elia Bruni, and Dieuwke Hupkes. 2022. The paradox of the compositionality of natural language: A neural machine translation case study. In *Proceedings of the 60th Annual Meeting of the Association for Computational Linguistics (Volume 1: Long Papers)*, pages 4154–4175, Dublin, Ireland. Association for Computational Linguistics.

Vitaly Feldman. 2020. Does learning require memorization? A short tale about a long tail. In *Proceedings of the 52nd Annual ACM SIGACT Symposium on Theory of Computing*, pages 954–959.

Jerry A Fodor and Zenon W Pylyshyn. 1988. Connectionism and cognitive architecture: A critical analysis. *Cognition*, 28(1-2):3–71.

Dieuwke Hupkes, Verna Dankers, Mathijs Mul, and Elia Bruni. 2020. Compositionality decomposed: How do neural networks generalise? *Journal of Artificial Intelligence Research*, 67:757–795.

Dieuwke Hupkes, Mario Giulianelli, Verna Dankers, Mikel Artetxe, Yanai Elazar, Tiago Pimentel, Christos Christodoulopoulos, Karim Lasri, Naomi Saphra, Arabella Sinclair, Dennis Ulmer, Florian Schottmann, Khuyagbaatar Batsuren, Kaiser Sun, Koustuv Sinha, Leila Khalatbari, Maria Ryskina, Rita Frieske, Ryan

Cotterell, and Zhijing Jin. 2023. A taxonomy and review of generalization research in NLP. *Nature Machine Intelligence*, 5(10):1161–1174.

Daniel Keysers, Nathanael Schärli, Nathan Scales, Hylke Buisman, Daniel Furrer, Sergii Kashubin, Nikola Momchev, Danila Sinopalnikov, Lukasz Stafiniak, Tibor Tihon, Dmitry Tsarkov, Xiao Wang, Marc van Zee, and Olivier Bousquet. 2020. Measuring compositional generalization: A comprehensive method on realistic data. In *International Conference on Learning Representations*.

Najoung Kim and Tal Linzen. 2020. COGS: A compositional generalization challenge based on semantic interpretation. In *Proceedings of the 2020 Conference on Empirical Methods in Natural Language Processing (EMNLP)*, pages 9087–9105, Online. Association for Computational Linguistics.

Guillaume Klein, Yoon Kim, Yuntian Deng, Jean Senellart, and Alexander Rush. 2017. OpenNMT: Open-source toolkit for neural machine translation. In *Proceedings of ACL 2017, System Demonstrations*, pages 67–72, Vancouver, Canada. Association for Computational Linguistics.

R Kneser and H Ney. 1995. Improved backing-off for m-gram language modeling. In *Acoustics, Speech, and Signal Processing, IEEE International Conference on*, volume 1, pages 181–184. IEEE Computer Society.

Philipp Koehn. 2005. Europarl: A parallel corpus for statistical machine translation. In *Proceedings of Machine Translation Summit X: Papers*, pages 79–86, Phuket, Thailand.

Brenden Lake and Marco Baroni. 2018. Generalization without systematicity: On the compositional skills of sequence-to-sequence recurrent networks. In *International Conference on Machine Learning*, pages 2873–2882. PMLR.

Benjamin LeBrun, Alessandro Sordoni, and Timothy J O'Donnell. 2022. Evaluating distributional distortion in neural language modeling. In *International Conference on Learning Representations*.

Yafu Li, Yongjing Yin, Yulong Chen, and Yue Zhang. 2021. On compositional generalization of neural machine translation. In *Proceedings of the 59th Annual Meeting of the Association for Computational Linguistics and the 11th International Joint Conference on Natural Language Processing (Volume 1: Long Papers)*, pages 4767–4780, Online. Association for Computational Linguistics.

Edoardo Manino, Julia Rozanova, Danilo Carvalho, Andre Freitas, and Lucas Cordeiro. 2022. Systematicity, compositionality and transitivity of deep NLP models: a metamorphic testing perspective. In *Findings of the Association for Computational Linguistics: ACL 2022*, pages 2355–2366, Dublin, Ireland. Association for Computational Linguistics.

R. Thomas McCoy, Paul Smolensky, Tal Linzen, Jianfeng Gao, and Asli Celikyilmaz. 2023. How much do language models copy from their training data? evaluating linguistic novelty in text generation using RAVEN. *Transactions of the Association for Computational Linguistics*, 11:652–670.

Francois Meyer and Jan Buys. 2023. Subword segmental machine translation: Unifying segmentation and target sentence generation. In *Findings of the Association for Computational Linguistics: ACL 2023*, pages 2795–2809, Toronto, Canada. Association for Computational Linguistics.

Anssi Moisio, Mathias Creutz, and Mikko Kurimo. 2023. Evaluating morphological generalisation in machine translation by distribution-based compositionality assessment. In *Proceedings of the 24th Nordic Conference on Computational Linguistics (NoDaLiDa)*, pages 738–751, Tórshavn, Faroe Islands. University of Tartu Library.

Khalil Mrini, Franck Dernoncourt, Quan Hung Tran, Trung Bui, Walter Chang, and Ndapa Nakashole. 2020. Rethinking self-attention: Towards interpretability in neural parsing. In *Findings of the Association for Computational Linguistics: EMNLP 2020*, pages 731–742, Online. Association for Computational Linguistics.

Barbara Partee. 1995. Lexical semantics and compositionality. *An invitation to cognitive science*, 1:311–360.

Ellie Pavlick. 2022. No one metric is enough! combining evaluation techniques to uncover latent structure. In *Workshop on The Challenge of Compositionality for AI*.

Ellie Pavlick. 2023. Symbols and grounding in large language models. *Philosophical Transactions of the Royal Society A*, 381(2251):20220041.

Maja Popović. 2017. chrF++: words helping character n-grams. In *Proceedings of the Second Conference on Machine Translation*, pages 612–618, Copenhagen, Denmark. Association for Computational Linguistics.

Vikas Raunak, Vaibhav Kumar, and Florian Metze. 2019. On compositionality in neural machine translation. In *NeurIPS Workshop on Context and Compositionality in Biological and Artificial Neural Systems*.

Rico Sennrich, Barry Haddow, and Alexandra Birch. 2016. Neural machine translation of rare words with subword units. In *Proceedings of the 54th Annual Meeting of the Association for Computational Linguistics (Volume 1: Long Papers)*, pages 1715–1725, Berlin, Germany. Association for Computational Linguistics.

Peter Shaw, Ming-Wei Chang, Panupong Pasupat, and Kristina Toutanova. 2021. Compositional generalization and natural language variation: Can a semantic parsing approach handle both? In *Proceedings of the*

59th Annual Meeting of the Association for Computational Linguistics and the 11th International Joint Conference on Natural Language Processing (Volume 1: Long Papers), pages 922–938, Online. Association for Computational Linguistics.

Anders Søgaard, Sebastian Ebert, Jasmijn Bastings, and Katja Filippova. 2021. We need to talk about random splits. In *Proceedings of the 16th Conference of the European Chapter of the Association for Computational Linguistics: Main Volume*, pages 1823–1832, Online. Association for Computational Linguistics.

Shane Steinert-Threlkeld. 2020. Toward the emergence of nontrivial compositionality. *Philosophy of Science*, 87(5):897–909.

Jörg Tiedemann. 2012. Parallel data, tools and interfaces in OPUS. In *Proceedings of the Eighth International Conference on Language Resources and Evaluation (LREC'12)*, pages 2214–2218, Istanbul, Turkey. European Language Resources Association (ELRA).

Ashish Vaswani, Noam Shazeer, Niki Parmar, Jakob Uszkoreit, Llion Jones, Aidan N Gomez, Ł ukasz Kaiser, and Illia Polosukhin. 2017. Attention is all you need. In *Advances in Neural Information Processing Systems*, volume 30. Curran Associates, Inc.

Jason Wei, Dan Garrette, Tal Linzen, and Ellie Pavlick. 2021. Frequency effects on syntactic rule learning in transformers. In *Proceedings of the 2021 Conference on Empirical Methods in Natural Language Processing*, pages 932–948, Online and Punta Cana, Dominican Republic. Association for Computational Linguistics.

Hao Zheng and Mirella Lapata. 2023. Real-world compositional generalization with disentangled sequence-to-sequence learning. In *Findings of the Association for Computational Linguistics: ACL 2023*, pages 1711–1725, Toronto, Canada. Association for Computational Linguistics.

Shifted PAUQ ⋇: Distribution shift in text-to-SQL

Oleg Somov[1], Elena Tutubalina[1,2,3]

[1]AIRI, [2]Kazan Federal University, [3]HSE University
Correspondence: somov@airi.net

Abstract

Semantic parsing plays a pivotal role in advancing the accessibility of human-computer interaction on a large scale. Spider, a widely recognized dataset for text-to-SQL, contains a wide range of natural language (NL) questions in English and corresponding SQL queries. Original splits of Spider and its adapted to Russian language and improved version, PAUQ, assume independence and identical distribution of training and testing data (i.i.d split). In this work, we propose a target length split and multilingual i.i.d split to measure compositionality and cross-language generalization. We present experimental results of popular text-to-SQL models on original, multilingual, and target length splits. We also construct a context-free grammar for the evaluation of compositionality in text-to-SQL in an out-of-distribution setting. We make the splits publicly available on HuggingFace hub via `https://huggingface.co/datasets/composite/pauq`.

1 Introduction

In this paper, we focus on a subtask of semantic parsing called text-to-SQL, which involves mapping natural language (NL) questions to Structured Query Language (SQL). Sequence-to-sequence (seq-to-seq) models such as RAT-SQL (Wang et al., 2020), BRIDGE (Lin et al., 2020), and RESDSQL (Li et al., 2023) have been widely employed for the text-to-SQL task. However, recent studies have highlighted the limitations of seq-to-seq models in out-of-distribution settings (Shaw et al., 2021; Gu et al., 2021; Chang et al., 2023).

The evaluation process for text-to-SQL models is currently a topic of active research. Yu et al. (2018a) determined the difficulty of requests based on the number of SQL components, resulting in four distinct categories: "Easy", "Medium", "Hard", and "Extra Hard". Finegan-Dollak et al. (2018) demonstrated that the division of the popular text-to-SQL dataset into training and test sets is

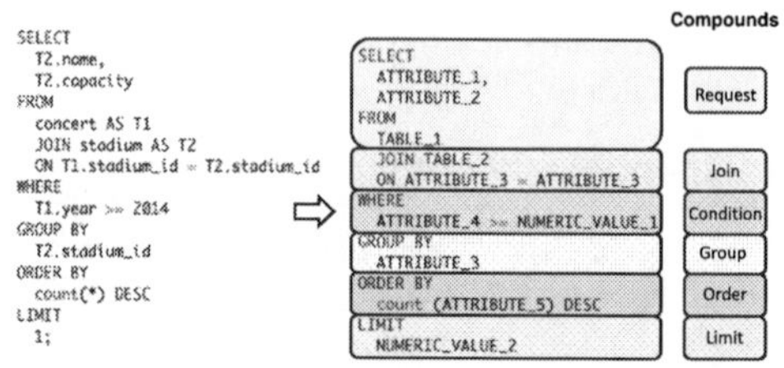

Figure 1: SQL is transformed into an SQL template via masking technique for subsequent compositional evaluation. Token compositions, referred to as compounds, are extracted via context-free grammar and then compared against the predicted query.

inadequate for assessing the model's generalization abilities. Ribeiro et al. (2020) highlighted that it is important to access performance on functional test sets and out-of-distribution examples, as random train and test splits can overestimate real-world performance and miss important error cases. Chang et al. (2023) proposed a text-to-SQL specific perturbation benchmark . This benchmark encompasses 17 categories for evaluation on text-to-SQL models robustness. Shaw et al. (2021) proposed new train and test splits of non-synthetic datasets for modeling out-of-distribution (OOD) setting in order to measure compositionality in semantic parsing.

In this work, we propose three splits of the existing PAUQ dataset (Bakshandaeva et al., 2022), an improved version of Spider (Yu et al., 2018b), for measuring across-language generalization and compositional generalization. The first split evaluates how models benefit from training in multiple languages of the same task. The split is constructed by joining original splits of Russian and English versions of PAUQ (MPAUQ). The original i.i.d splits of Russian and English will be referred to as **RuPAUQ OS** and **EnPAUQ OS**, respectively. The second two splits, target length, evaluate how the models perform if the text-to-SQL data is split by target length characteristic. The first split is

Proceedings of the 1st GenBench Workshop on (Benchmarking) Generalisation in NLP, pages 214–220
December 6, 2023 ©2023 Association for Computational Linguistics

	RuPAUQ OS		EnPAUQ OS		EnPAUQ TRL		EnPAUQ TSL	
	Train	Test	Train	Test	Train	Test	Train	Test
Split size	8800	1076	8800	1076	7890	1975	7900	1975
Avg. template length	21.04	16.79	21.1	16.8	23.74	8.27	15.28	42.06
Avg. question length	8.95	9.05	12.01	12.31	12.57	9.92	11.68	13.46

Table 1: Statistics for PAUQ original split (OS) for both Russian (RuPAUQ), English (EnPAUQ), and target length splits (TRL and TSL). The length is calculated as the length of sequences in tokens.

when samples in the train set are longer than samples in the test set named **TRL**. The second split is when samples in the test are longer than samples in the train named **TSL**. TRL examines the ability of the model to generalize to simpler SQL without directly learning to construct them. As stated in (Hupkes et al., 2020), TRL evaluates model systematicity, while TSL assesses its productivity.

2 Spider and PAUQ

Spider (Yu et al., 2018b) comprises a substantial collection of 10,181 English questions and 5,693 unique complex SQL queries, spanning 200 databases with multiple tables that encompass 138 distinct domains. Spider was randomly split into train, dev, and test sets. In the case of PAUQ, the Russian version of Spider, all three components - questions, SQL queries, and database content, have been modified and localized. PAUQ improved the original Spider by inserting the missing values, correcting errors, and adding new samples of poorly represented types. As the Spider test set is not publicly available, PAUQ uses the dev set for testing. PAUQ contains 8,800 and 1,076 NL samples for training and testing, respectively. In PAUQ, the total numbers of different elements of databases are: (i) **Databases:** 166 entities (88.0% – train set, 12.0% – dev set); (ii) **Tables:** 876 entities (90.8% – train set, 9.2% – dev set); **Columns:** 4503 entities (90.2% – train set, 9.8% – dev set); **Values:** 531,164 and 533,751 unique values respectively (88.4% – train set, 11.6% – dev set). We adopt three components (NL questions, SQL queries, database) from GitHub via `https://github.com/ai-spiderweb/pauq`, where each query corresponds to Russian and English texts.

3 Proposed Split

We propose a target length-based split to mimic full shift (Hupkes et al., 2020) in the text-to-SQL task for measuring the compositional generalization ability of NLP models. We design split in the following way:

1. Normalize SQL by masking tables, attributes, textual and numeric values with corresponding mask token (see Figure 1) - this way, we get an SQL template by which the target length split will be done. Text-to-SQL solutions are expected to infer attributes, tables, and values from a given question and schema. The ability to handle it correctly is called substitutivity (Hupkes et al., 2020). Since our split is purely for compositional generalization evaluation, we use that template for splitting instead of the original query. During an evaluation, we also use that masking technique and true SQL template to estimate compositional ability of the models.

2. For both splits, we sort SQL templates in ascending or descending order based on template token size. Then, we iterate by the sorted template list in order to fill train and test splits. We require the test size of both splits to be 20% of the original dataset.

3. Since we want to check how the model recombines known tokens to form novel structures, we clear the test set from such queries where there is no full token intersection with train tokens.

We make sure that there is no template intersection in train/test for both TRL and TSL splits. TSL is the most complicated split because the model has to recombine known tokens to form new complex and long queries. TRL split requires the model to also recombine new tokens but to generate queries of shorter length.

For measuring cross-language generalization, we merge English and Russian train sets and evaluate English and Russian test sets separately. Our motivation for the multilingual split is whether training in two languages on the same task can benefit one model. Table 1 shows statistics for OS and target length English and Russian splits.

4 Baselines and Experiments

We focus our dataset on two types for generalization evaluation - compositional generalization and generalization across languages (see Appendix B for the GenBench card (Hupkes et al., 2022)).

We utilized four popular Spider models:

- T5-base (Raffel et al. 2020);
- RESDSQL (Li et al. 2023);
- RAT-SQL (Wang et al. 2020);
- BRIDGE (Lin et al. 2020);

T5-base is a pre-trained encoder-decoder transformer with a language modeling head.

RESDSQL decouples schema linking and query generation tasks into two stages. The first stage selects the most relevant schema items for the question. During the second stage, the model learns to decode the SQL template of the actual query concatenated with the original actual query. That way, the model can condition generating SQL skeleton before the full original query. RESDSQL uses ROBERTA-large (Zhuang et al., 2021) large for the schema linking and T5-base for query generation. For RuPAUQ and MPAUQ, we replace T5-base model with MT0-base (Muennighoff et al., 2022).

RAT-SQL is an encoder-decoder model that uses a relation-aware transformer within the encoder to model alignments between database schema and content and question tokens. The decoder of the model is tree-structured and generates an abstract syntax tree in the context-free SQL grammar.

BRIDGE, in turn, utilizes database schema and content as input to the model. It has an encoder-decoder architecture with the pointer-generator network using beam-search. The model generates queries in execution-guided order. Both RAT-SQL and BRIDGE use the BERT-base (Devlin et al., 2019) language model as an encoder. The details on hyperparameters are presented in the Appx. A.

5 Overall results

We evaluate 4 models on our splits - T5-base, RESDSQL (with T5-base or MT0-base), RAT-SQL, and BRIDGE. We trained each model on a split train set and evaluated it on a test set with 3 random seeds and averaged predictions. Our evaluation metrics are Exact Matching and Execution Accuracy. Results are presented in Tab. 2, 3, 4.

EnPAUQ	Exact Match		Exec Match	
split	T5	RESDSQL	T5	RESDSQL
OS	0.46	0.69	0.45	0.74
TRL	0.56	0.72	0.55	0.80
TSL	0.10	0.19	0.08	0.30

Table 2: Compositional generalization exact match and exec match metrics for T5-base and RESDSQL. Each model is evaluated on a corresponding test split.

Train	Test	T5-base	RESDSQL	RAT-SQL	BRIDGE
En	En	0.46	0.69	0.66	0.60
M	En	0.48	0.66	0.66	0.68
Ru	Ru	0.42	0.39	0.51	0.52
M	Ru	0.43	0.39	0.57	0.55

Table 3: Exact match metrics for across language generalization. En is EnPAUQ, Ru is RuPAUQ, and M is for MPAUQ.

Train	Test	T5-base	RESDSQL	RAT-SQL	BRIDGE
En	En	0.45	0.74	0.63	0.60
M	En	0.45	0.68	0.65	0.65
Ru	Ru	0.39	0.43	0.49	0.48
M	Ru	0.40	0.42	0.53	0.53

Table 4: Execution match metrics for across language generalization. En is EnPAUQ, Ru is RuPAUQ, and M is MPAUQ.

Target length split is our evaluation towards compositional generalization measurements (Table 5). We evaluate T5-base and RESDSQL on this split. The predictions for both models are stable across different seed runs with standard deviation for less than 1% for both T5-base and RESDSQL. Since RESDSQL is a more advanced model with multiple query generation stages, it tends to over-fit less on TSL and generate novel queries - its execution match is much higher than its exact match. On TRL compared to the OS split, the metrics are higher. It is not surprising because our test set for TRL consists mostly of PAUQ question pairs from **easy** category. Such evaluation shows that the model is able to generalize from complex queries to simple ones without overcrowding the training dataset with simple queries for text-to-SQL. In Tab. 3 and 4, we see that training simultaneously on two languages with multilingual models can give a slight boost to some models. In our experiments, we see an increase in execution match metric for T5-base (Russian +1%), RAT-SQL (English +2%, Russian +4%), and BRIDGE (English +5%, Russian +2%). However, RESDSQL had a drop in English (-6%) when trained in such a setting.

EnPAUQ	Syntax accuracy		Compound accuracy		OOD Compound accuracy	
Split	T5	RESDSQL	T5	RESDSQL	T5	RESDSQL
OS	0.75	0.81	0.81	0.82	0.54	0.48
TRL	0.75	0.91	0.93	0.94	0.65	0.66
TSL	0.73	0.57	0.71	0.68	0.47	0.42

Table 5: Compositional generalization in-depth evaluation of two models.

6 In-depth compound analysis

We wanted to explore the ability of compositional generalization for proposed target length splits. We have developed context-free grammar (CFG) in order to parse queries. In order to analyze, we utilize the concept of compound. For example, we have dataset tokens `SELECT`, `COUNT`, `SUM`, `Goals`, `Teams` (`Goals` and `Teams` are table attributes). Composition of these tokens such `SELECT COUNT Goals` is called *compounds*. CFG covers compounds for `REQUEST`, `JOIN`, `CONDITION`, `GROUP`, `ORDER`, `LIMIT`. For evaluation, we apply the same masking technique used for split generation for generated SQL. Then we parse it with CFG to extract compounds (see Figure 1). For in-depth compound analysis, we propose and evaluate three accuracy metrics derived from our compounds:

- **Syntax accuracy** - this accuracy metric estimates whether all expected true SQL compounds are present in predicted SQL. For example, if the true SQL has `REQUEST` compound and `CONDITION` compounds `SELECT count(ATTRIBUTE_1) FROM TABLE_1 WHERE ATTR_2 = TEXT_VAL_1 OR ATTR_3 = TEXT_VAL_2;` and predicted SQL has only `REQUEST` compound in `SELECT count(ATTRIBUTE_1) FROM TABLE_1` - the syntax accuracy for such query will be 0.5;

- **Compound accuracy** - this accuracy metric estimates the proportion of predicted compounds to expected ones in the query. For example, if true query has 1 `REQUEST` compound and 2 `CONDITION` compounds `SELECT count(ATTRIBUTE_1) FROM TABLE_1 WHERE ATTRIBUTE_2 = TEXT_VALUE_1 OR ATTRIBUTE_3 = TEXT_VALUE_2;` while the predicted query has 1 `REQUEST` compound and 1 `CONDITION` compounds in `SELECT count(ATTRIBUTE_1) FROM TABLE_1 WHERE ATTRIBUTE_2 = TEXT_VALUE_1` the compound accuracy will be 0.33.

- **OOD Compound accuracy** - compound accuracy, which is only calculated on compounds that were not seen during training.

We calculate the proposed metrics independently for each sample and then average over all test set predictions. In Tab. 5, we see that a more advanced RESDSQL overall model increases only syntax accuracy metric compared to the T5-base on OS and TRL splits, while other two metrics are relatively close to each other for all splits. OOD Compound Accuracy is significantly lower then Compound Accuracy (e.g., 0.66 vs 0.94 for RESDSQL on the TRL split, respectively). The TRL split compound metrics show that both models are able to generate unseen compounds in approximately 1.5 times better than in the TSL split.

7 Discussion and Conclusion

In this work, we have explored two types of generalization - compositional generalization (TRL and TSL splits) and across language generalization (MPAUQ). We have evaluated 4 text-to-SQL models on these splits. For an in-depth analysis on compositional generalization, we have developed CFG and proposed two metrics for compound evaluation. Our results show that TSL split is the most challenging split for the model. TRL split shows that the models are able to generalize to unseen short SQL. Multilingual split shows that some models can benefit from learning on the translated task to gain performance on individual language.

In future work, we plan to perform more experiments to make more compositional generalization splits (e.g., template or target maximum compound divergence splits (Shaw et al., 2021)). We also plan to explore different neural architectures and training strategies to enhance the model's ability to handle complex queries and measure compositional generalization and generalization across languages. We hope to prepare the PAUQ leaderboard and encourage further research in this area.

Acknowledgments

This research was supported in part through computational resources of HPC facilities at HSE University. The work of E.T. has been supported by the Russian Science Foundation grant # 23-11-00358. We would also like to thank the anonymous reviewers for their comments on this paper.

Limitations and Ethics

We note that large language models such as Codex, a 175B GPT model further fine-tuned on code, are out of the scope of this work.

PAUQ and Spider's limitations First of all, the data is still 'artificial', which means that it was created by a limited number of people specifically for training and evaluating text-to-SQL models; thus, it lacks the diversity and complexity of natural data formed by questions that people formulate in order to get the desired information from the database. For instance, the real-world data contain NL queries that require common sense knowledge that cannot be extracted directly from the database, ambiguous questions allowing various ways of interpretation that are quite frequent, and queries with window functions that make the process easier and more convenient, – all of these are not included in the Spider dataset, as well as in PAUQ.

Train and test tokens Our research explores full shift by splitting the dataset based on target template length. Specifically, we examine the scenario where test template tokens are present in the training set and do not explore the more challenging case of modeling unseen tokens.

References

Daria Bakshandaeva, Oleg Somov, Ekaterina Dmitrieva, Vera Davydova, and Elena Tutubalina. 2022. PAUQ: Text-to-SQL in Russian. In *Findings of the Association for Computational Linguistics: EMNLP 2022*, pages 2355–2376, Abu Dhabi, United Arab Emirates. Association for Computational Linguistics.

Shuaichen Chang, Jun Wang, Mingwen Dong, Lin Pan, Henghui Zhu, Alexander Hanbo Li, Wuwei Lan, Sheng Zhang, Jiarong Jiang, Joseph Lilien, Steve Ash, William Yang Wang, Zhiguo Wang, Vittorio Castelli, Patrick Ng, and Bing Xiang. 2023. Dr.spider: A diagnostic evaluation benchmark towards text-to-sql robustness.

Jacob Devlin, Ming-Wei Chang, Kenton Lee, and Kristina Toutanova. 2019. BERT: Pre-training of deep bidirectional transformers for language understanding. In *Proceedings of the 2019 Conference of the North American Chapter of the Association for Computational Linguistics: Human Language Technologies, Volume 1 (Long and Short Papers)*, pages 4171–4186, Minneapolis, Minnesota. Association for Computational Linguistics.

Catherine Finegan-Dollak, Jonathan K Kummerfeld, Li Zhang, Karthik Ramanathan, Sesh Sadasivam, Rui Zhang, and Dragomir Radev. 2018. Improving text-to-sql evaluation methodology. In *Proceedings of the 56th Annual Meeting of the Association for Computational Linguistics (Volume 1: Long Papers)*, pages 351–360.

Yu Gu, Sue Kase, Michelle Vanni, Brian Sadler, Percy Liang, Xifeng Yan, and Yu Su. 2021. Beyond i.i.d.: Three levels of generalization for question answering on knowledge bases. In *Proceedings of the Web Conference 2021*. ACM.

Dieuwke Hupkes, Verna Dankers, Mathijs Mul, and Elia Bruni. 2020. Compositionality decomposed: How do neural networks generalise? *Journal of Artificial Intelligence Research*, 67:757–795.

Dieuwke Hupkes, Mario Giulianelli, Verna Dankers, Mikel Artetxe, Yanai Elazar, Tiago Pimentel, Christos Christodoulopoulos, Karim Lasri, Naomi Saphra, Arabella Sinclair, Dennis Ulmer, Florian Schottmann, Khuyagbaatar Batsuren, Kaiser Sun, Koustuv Sinha, Leila Khalatbari, Maria Ryskina, Rita Frieske, Ryan Cotterell, and Zhijing Jin. 2022. State-of-the-art generalisation research in NLP: a taxonomy and review. *CoRR*.

Haoyang Li, Jing Zhang, Cuiping Li, and Hong Chen. 2023. Resdsql: Decoupling schema linking and skeleton parsing for text-to-sql. In *Proceedings of the AAAI Conference on Artificial Intelligence*, volume 37, pages 13067–13075.

Xi Victoria Lin, Richard Socher, and Caiming Xiong. 2020. Bridging textual and tabular data for cross-domain text-to-sql semantic parsing. In *Findings of the Association for Computational Linguistics: EMNLP 2020*, pages 4870–4888.

Niklas Muennighoff, Thomas Wang, Lintang Sutawika, Adam Roberts, Stella Biderman, Teven Le Scao, M Saiful Bari, Sheng Shen, Zheng-Xin Yong, Hailey Schoelkopf, et al. 2022. Crosslingual generalization through multitask finetuning. *arXiv preprint arXiv:2211.01786*.

Colin Raffel, Noam Shazeer, Adam Roberts, Katherine Lee, Sharan Narang, Michael Matena, Yanqi Zhou, Wei Li, and Peter J Liu. 2020. Exploring the limits of transfer learning with a unified text-to-text transformer. *The Journal of Machine Learning Research*, 21(1):5485–5551.

Marco Tulio Ribeiro, Tongshuang Wu, Carlos Guestrin, and Sameer Singh. 2020. Beyond accuracy: Behavioral testing of NLP models with CheckList. In

Proceedings of the 58th Annual Meeting of the Association for Computational Linguistics, pages 4902–4912, Online. Association for Computational Linguistics.

Peter Shaw, Ming-Wei Chang, Panupong Pasupat, and Kristina Toutanova. 2021. Compositional generalization and natural language variation: Can a semantic parsing approach handle both? In *Proceedings of the 59th Annual Meeting of the Association for Computational Linguistics and the 11th International Joint Conference on Natural Language Processing (Volume 1: Long Papers)*, pages 922–938, Online. Association for Computational Linguistics.

Kaiser Sun, Adina Williams, and Dieuwke Hupkes. 2023. A replication study of compositional generalization works on semantic parsing. In *ML Reproducibility Challenge 2022*.

Bailin Wang, Mirella Lapata, and Ivan Titov. 2021. Meta-learning for domain generalization in semantic parsing. In *Proceedings of the 2021 Conference of the North American Chapter of the Association for Computational Linguistics: Human Language Technologies*, pages 366–379, Online. Association for Computational Linguistics.

Bailin Wang, Richard Shin, Xiaodong Liu, Oleksandr Polozov, and Matthew Richardson. 2020. Rat-sql: Relation-aware schema encoding and linking for text-to-sql parsers. In *Proceedings of the 58th Annual Meeting of the Association for Computational Linguistics*, pages 7567–7578.

Tao Yu, Rui Zhang, Kai Yang, Michihiro Yasunaga, Dongxu Wang, Zifan Li, James Ma, Irene Li, Qingning Yao, Shanelle Roman, Zilin Zhang, and Dragomir Radev. 2018a. Spider: A large-scale human-labeled dataset for complex and cross-domain semantic parsing and text-to-SQL task. In *Proceedings of the 2018 Conference on Empirical Methods in Natural Language Processing*, pages 3911–3921, Brussels, Belgium. Association for Computational Linguistics.

Tao Yu, Rui Zhang, Kai Yang, Michihiro Yasunaga, Dongxu Wang, Zifan Li, James Ma, Irene Li, Qingning Yao, Shanelle Roman, et al. 2018b. Spider: A large-scale human-labeled dataset for complex and cross-domain semantic parsing and text-to-sql task. In *Proceedings of the 2018 Conference on Empirical Methods in Natural Language Processing*, pages 3911–3921.

Liu Zhuang, Lin Wayne, Shi Ya, and Zhao Jun. 2021. A robustly optimized BERT pre-training approach with post-training. In *Proceedings of the 20th Chinese National Conference on Computational Linguistics*, pages 1218–1227, Huhhot, China. Chinese Information Processing Society of China.

A Experimental Setup

For English OS, TRL, TSL splits we train T5-base from HF checkpoint provided at `https://huggingface.co/t5-base`. We trained model for 10k iterations with a batch size of 256 and learning rate 10^{-4} as in Sun et al. 2023. As optimizer we have used Adafactor.

For training RESDSQL, we used the original implementation of RESDSQL provided at `https://github.com/RUCKBReasoning/RESDSQL`.

For training RuPAUQ OS, MPAUQ for the first stage of schema linking in RESDSQL we used `https://huggingface.co/DeepPavlov/xlm-roberta-large-en-ru-mnli` and for query generation in both T5-base and RESDSQL we used `https://huggingface.co/bigscience/mt0-base`

We used Tensor2Struct package (Wang et al., 2021) to train RAT-SQL. The hyperparameters are taken from the original implementation of RAT-SQL provided at `https://github.com/berlino/tensor2struct-public`. In monolingual setup, RAT-SQL models are trained for a maximum of 25k iterations, then the best checkpoint on the corresponding dev set in terms of exact match was picked (in all cases it is a checkpoint obtained after training in the range of 20k to 25k iterations). In multilingual setup, when training data is double-sized, the maximum number of iterations is increased to 40k.

As for BRIDGE, in all cases it was trained for a maximum of 20k iterations. Then the best checkpoint according to exact-match top-1 metric on the corresponding dev set was selected. During training, we used default hyperparameters from the original implementation of BRIDGE provided at `https://github.com/salesforce/TabularSemanticParsing`.

To develop the context-free grammar, we use a Yargy library provided at `https://github.com/natasha/yargy`.

For training RuPAUQ OS, MPAUQ RAT-SQL and BRIDGE encoders we have used `https://huggingface.co/bert-base-multilingual-cased`

All models were trained on one Tesla V100 32 GB.

For evaluation we have used original Spider evaluation script `https://github.com/taoyds/test-suite-sql-eval`.

B GenBench Card

Motivation

Practical	*Cognitive*	*Intrinsic*	*Fairness*
□			

Generalisation type

Compositional	*Struct-l*	*Cross Task*	*Cross Language*	*Cross Domain*	*Robustness*
□			□		

Shift type

Covariate	*Label*	*Full*	*Assumed*
		□	

Shift source

Naturally occuring	*Partitioned natural*	*Generated shift*	*Fully generated*
	□		

Shift locus

Train–test	*Finetune train–test*	*Pretrain–train*	*Pretrain–test*
	□		

Author Index

Association for Computational Linguistics
209 N. Eighth Street
Stroudsburg, Pennsylvania 18360

ISBN 978-1-7138-8600-6
9 781713 886006